D1225224

BEYOND THE URALS

Beyond the Urals

ECONOMIC DEVELOPMENTS
IN SOVIET ASIA

VIOLET CONOLLY

LONDON
OXFORD UNIVERSITY PRESS
NEW YORK   TORONTO
1967

Library
I.U.P.
Indiana P.

330.957 C763b
C. 1

Oxford University Press, Ely House, London W.1

GLASGOW NEW YORK TORONTO MELBOURNE WELLINGTON
CAPE TOWN SALISBURY IBADAN NAIROBI LUSAKA ADDIS ABABA
BOMBAY CALCUTTA MADRAS KARACHI LAHORE DACCA
KUALA LUMPUR HONG KONG TOKYO

© Oxford University Press 1967

*Printed in Great Britain
by The Alden Press, Oxford*

Contents

PART ONE

The Russian Empire in Asia

I. Historical Introduction

II. The Economic Development of the Eastern Regions under Tsardom

PART TWO

The Economic Development of Central Asia and Kazakhstan under the Soviets (1917–45)

III. The Soviet Approach to the Development of the Eastern Regions (1917–45)

PART THREE
Economic Development (1945–66)

IV. Soviet Central Asia and Kazakhstan

V. Siberia (East and West)

VI. Soviet Far East

Conclusion

Appendixes

MAPS

List of Illustrations

Plates 4a and 4b are reproduced by permission of the British Broadcasting Corporation; Plates 3 and 5–11 by permission of the Society for Cultural Relations with the USSR.

Foreword

Several factors have hitherto tended to obscure the truth about the economic potential of Soviet Asia and the extent of Soviet success in exploiting it. Chief among these are Soviet exaggeration and the ingrained habit of concealment, and the Western inclination either to accept Soviet claims at their face value, or to discount them as nothing but propaganda.

Of recent years the situation has improved somewhat in both these respects. Soviet propaganda organizations continue to publish—primarily for the benefit of foreigners—laudatory accounts of various economic and engineering achievements, accounts which contain no hint of faulty planning, muddle, waste, and the ever-increasing labour difficulties. But there is now greater realization of the need to face the facts in dealing with pressing economic and political problems, and since those most closely acquainted with the facts are often non-Party specialists, the unvarnished truth now gets considerable prominence not only in the Press but also in specialized literature not intended for foreign consumption.

In the West, too, the view—quite widely held until the 1950s—that Soviet ability to exploit the manifold resources of Siberia, Central Asia, and the Far East had been wildly overstated and that most of the Asian agricultural and industrial projects were doomed to ultimate failure for political as well as economic reasons, has been to a large extent abandoned. But there have been few, and certainly no successful, attempts to get the whole matter of the Soviet Asian economy into proper perspective. Several useful volumes have been published on the geography of the Soviet Union which deal fully with the natural resources lying to the east of the Urals, but which give little or no indication of how far Soviet attempts to exploit these resources have succeeded. There have also been a few competent studies of particular regions, of which Terence Armstrong's

Russian Settlement in the North is an outstanding example. Certain works purporting to describe economic and other conditions in Soviet Asia as a whole have appeared in the West since the Revolution, but none since the emergence of the more realistic point of view just referred to. No work has so far been published in the USSR on the lines of *Aziatskaya Rossiya* (Asiatic Russia) produced by the Russian Resettlement Directorate in 1914, now out of date in many respects but none the less a mine of geographical, demographic, and other information.

Miss Conolly's *Beyond the Urals* is the product of a lifetime of research into Soviet affairs of every description with a special emphasis on those of Soviet Asia. She has kept abreast of Soviet writing in books, periodicals, and newspapers for over thirty years; and for the express purpose of the present study she has concentrated on the vast mass of specialized Soviet writing on Asia of which the ordinary Sovietologist dealing with more general economic and political problems has but the barest inkling. The result is a book which not only contains a great deal of carefully analysed statistical information derived from Soviet sources, but also presents a shrewd assessment of the economic possibilities of this vast region and of the real extent of Russian success in exploiting them. The difficulties which confronted the Tsarist conquerors of the region, some of which still confront their Soviet successors, were many and various. Russian dynamism, toughness, and ruthlessness have helped to overcome many of them to a degree not always understood in the West. But certain other well-known Russian characteristics combined with the present régime's rigidity in political matters and its clumsy inefficiency in dealing with labour problems have exacerbated some existing difficulties as well as creating new ones.

It is still uncertain how the great Soviet experiment in Asia will develop in the future. That it will be abandoned or that present efforts will be relaxed is improbable: but its nature and its tempo may well be affected by internal as well as external factors. Among the latter is the somewhat similar experiment now being embarked upon in Communist China, which was originally informed by the same ideology as the USSR but which now shows signs of a divergence amounting to permanent hostility. The uncertainty which China's emergence brings to the future of Soviet, as well as of the

rest of Asia, underlines the importance of a dispassionate and pene-
trating appreciation of the economic and political realities of Soviet
Asia, which is what the present study is intended to provide.

GEOFFREY WHEELER

Director
Central Asian Research Centre

Introduction

Asiatic Russia, now the scene of vast and complex economic activities, is historically and economically a relatively recent extension of the old European Russian motherland. Pre-Mongol Russia knew little and cared less about its Asian hinterland. But once started, Russia's expansion across the Urals splayed out in all directions and now seems as inevitable as it was believed to be God-ordained by the satraps of these new dominions of the Tsars. The propinquity of the new and the old lands and the lack of natural barriers between them made colonization and economic integration with the metropolis much easier than in the case of the Western European powers and their overseas colonies. This advantage has, of course, been retained by Soviet Russia and has helped to obscure the issues in Soviet anti-colonial propaganda against the Western powers.

The story of Russia's advance through the uncharted forests and tundra of Siberia and the Far North to the Pacific outpost of Okhotsk in little more than sixty years (1581–1647) and her more systematic military conquest some centuries later of the Kazakh-Kirgiz nomads and of the great deserts and oases of Turkestan has many facets of interest. It is in the first place one of the world's great sagas of exploration involving dire hazards and feats of endurance certainly on a par with those faced by Columbus. Yet the names of the Russian standard-bearers who put Siberia on the map, Poyarkov, Khabarov, Atlasov, Dezhnev, Nevel'skoy, are scarcely known outside Russia.

Politically and economically, the advance to the east through Siberia and Central Asia had major consequences for Russia. Economically, it gave her access to a vast treasure house of mineral and agricultural wealth ranging from gold, platinum, and diamonds, oil, hydro-power, and coal, to cotton, natural gas, oil, and non-ferrous metals in Central Asia. After years of neglect following the sale of the Russian-American colony (now known as Alaska) to the United States in 1867, the exciting economic prospects originally opened up by Russia's acquisition of an open door to the Pacific are once again being actively developed. Politically it brought her into direct contact with China. In time, the Sino-Russian frontiers extended for some 4,500 km. from the Amur to Sinkiang and the Pamirs (providing many points of friction and dispute), with a break of 1,500 km. from the Altay to Transbaykalia formed by the Russo-Mongolian frontier.

Tsarist Russia always took careful stock of Chinese reactions to her policies in eastern Siberia and in Turkestan. In recent years, Soviet Russia has had good reason to look apprehensively towards a hostile militant China at her back door to which the under-populated territories of Siberia and the Far East with their rich natural resources, and the possibilities of trouble-making among the Turkic-Muslim peoples of Central Asia might prove irresistible temptations.

Russia's advance to the Pacific also opened up relations with Japan, economical and political. But as a result of bitter memories of disastrous wars and shifting alliances in the last hundred years both tend to be suspicious of the other, though in the most recent period they recognize how much they both stand to gain from peace and economic co-operation in the Far East. Relative new-comers though the Russians are in the Pacific, Soviet spokesmen seem to regard the Japanese as interlopers who threaten their interests in Far Eastern waters; even Japanese efforts to regain some of the islands seized by the Russians after the last war are often dismissed as 'imperialistic'.

Soviet treatment of Tsarist economic policy in Siberia and Central Asia is in many respects so misleading and distorted that it seemed to me essential to lead into the study of Soviet planned development of these areas with a brief background survey of the position under Tsardom.

My aim in this work has been to provide an assessment of the economic resources of Asiatic Russia, their role in the Soviet economy, and the nature and results of Soviet development plans for Siberia, the Far East, and the Central Asian republics. Apart from statistical details of targets and results, there is a surprising amount of information in the Soviet metropolitan and regional Press, especially the journals of the republican parties and the works of the academies of the four Central Asian republics and Kazakhstan, about the operation of these plans at ground level. These accounts, as nothing else, help to convey the authentic feel and atmosphere of Soviet construction. Many Soviet experts and other commentators bluntly describe the discrepancies between planned targets and achievements in mines and plants throughout the area and the almost incredible conditions of muddle, waste, and general incompetence prevailing even in major development schemes like the Tyumen' oilfields of west Siberia or the important hydro-electric station now being constructed at Nurek in Tadzhikistan.

Little of this regional material finds its way into the more general works in English on the Soviet economy. There is, therefore, I think, a growing need for a layman's conspectus of economic developments in Asiatic Russia where interested readers can find information on such disparate questions as the progress of industrialization in the Soviet Central Asian republics and Siberia; population and migration questions; the value of the new discoveries in the eastern areas of oil and gas, gold, diamonds, copper, and other minerals; the Central Asian cotton industry; labour problems on Asian construction sites; Soviet-Japanese economic co-operation in the Far East and Siberia; or the now ice-cold but very interesting joint Sino-Soviet Amur development plans and other aspects of the Sino-Soviet Amur frontier dispute. This is the gap I have tried to fill; and the treatment of the subject is admittedly more selective than in an exhaustive textbook.

I have thus been mainly concerned with agricultural and industrial development and only incidentally with the social services and education. Moreover, I have not ventured to tackle the very pertinent question of 'Who paid for what?' or to what extent the Central Asian republics themselves financed their industrialization and modernization (including a great expansion of education and the social services) or were financed by central Soviet funds. The question, of course, is of the greatest importance but I do not believe it can be satisfactorily answered on the basis of the incomplete Soviet statistics now available. There is, nevertheless, no doubt that large investments of central Soviet funds have promoted industrialization, education, and other social services in these republics.

In developing the natural resources of Asiatic Russia the Soviet

Government is confronted with formidable problems. Many valuable raw materials are located in inaccessible, inhospitable areas of extreme cold or heat where living conditions are wretched and there are few amenities. As a result there is a huge labour turnover in Siberia and there are also labour difficulties in the Mangyshlak oilfield and other desert sites of Central Asia. In spite of these problems, a great new industrial region is rapidly taking shape. New towns and mining settlements are mushrooming in the Siberian taiga and the Central Asian deserts in uninhabited places often not yet marked on any Soviet map, where only yesterday the mere existence of oil or ore was totally unsuspected. It is a fascinating exercise to trace the fortunes of some of these enterprises from their inception in the wild to growing maturity.

It is also interesting to note that the pattern of economic relations between the Central Asian republics seems to be undergoing change. Whereas Moscow's decisions were formerly implemented without demur by the republican governments, criticism of defects in projects of Gosplan and other central authorities is now frequently voiced in Tashkent, Dushanbe, and Frunze (less frequently in Ashkhabad), and also at the sessions of the Supreme Soviet in Moscow by republican representatives. If this trend continues, economic co-operation between the Centre and the periphery could become more genuine and the absurdities of some of the Moscow armchair planning (which I discuss later) become a thing of the past. It is impossible at the moment to foresee how this trend will develop, though it opens up new and intriguing perspectives in a previously static situation.

The impact of Tsarist and Soviet economic policies on the native peoples of Asia (and the Far North) are only discussed here in a strictly economic context. The effect of these policies on the traditional cultures and ways of life of these people lies outside the scope of this book.[1]

I have used the now conventional term Central Asia to denote

[1] The following works may be recommended to those interested in this subject:

Richard A. Pierce, *Russian Central Asia 1867–1917* (University of California Press, California, 1960).

Alexander Park, *Bolshevism in Turkestan 1917—1927* (Columbia Press, New York, 1957).

Terence Armstrong, *Russian Settlement in the North* (Cambridge University Press, Cambridge, 1965).

the Russian *Srednyaya A{iya* (literally, Middle Asia) which includes
the four Soviet Central Asian republics of Uzbekistan, Turkmenistan, Tadzhikistan, and Kirgizia, but *not* Kazakhstan. There may
seem a lack of balance in my more detailed treatment of Central Asia
and Kazakhstan than of Siberia. This is entirely due to the much
greater volume of material available to me on the five Soviet Asian
republics and the fact that each of them has to be discussed separately.
No newspapers and only a few periodicals published east of the Urals
are obtainable in this country whereas the Russian daily Press from
each of the republican capitals and the most interesting journals of
their respective academies and Communist parties can be procured
without much difficulty. This Central Asian material contains a
mine of valuable detail for which there is no counterpart (at least in
our libraries) in regard to Siberia and the Far East. My study closes
in March 1966, culminating in the important discussions and decisions of the Twenty-Third CPSU Party Congress on the fulfilment
of the Seven Year Plan and the targets of the new Five Year Plan
in Soviet Asia; subsequent items of marginal interest are added in
footnotes.

For the convenience of readers I have decided to divide my work
into three broad, natural geographical regions: Central Asia and
Kazakhstan, Siberia, and the Far East, without bothering much
about the confusing shifts in the internal divisions of these regions.
The administrative-territorial structure of the USSR, it has been
well said, is characterized by an instability seldom encountered in
the organization of other countries[1] and I have not tried to keep
exact track of these constant changes. Thus the Tyumen' *oblast*, the
site of the new west Siberian oil and gas industry, is now included in
the Urals region. As, geographically, it fills a large proportion of the
west Siberian plain, which is not subject to these administrative-
territorial changes, it is treated as such here.

I find it impossible to thank individually all those to whom I am
deeply indebted for technical advice in many fields where I was out
of my depth. But a special word of gratitude is due to the following:
The London School of Slavonic and East European Studies, whose
award of a senior Hayter Research Fellowship in Soviet Studies
enabled me to devote two years to writing this book, and in particular

[1] T. Shabad, *Geography of the USSR* (Columbia University Press, New York, 1951), p. 42.

B

to its Director, Dr. George Bolsover, for his encouraging interest in the progress of my work; Colonel Geoffrey Wheeler for his sagacious counsel and the help which I have deeply appreciated from the staff of the Central Asian Research Centre and the use of its specialized library; Dr. E. J. Lindgren for generous loans of valuable material and much spontaneous help; Mr. Quintin Bach, whose tireless efforts to underpin my research were invaluable, and Mrs. Moody who so competently and indefatigably typed my erratic manuscript; Miss Blayney and the staff of the Foreign Office Printed Library who have always responded to my queries with equal goodwill and efficiency.

VIOLET CONOLLY

List of Abbreviations

ASSR	Avtonomnaya Sovetskaya Sotsialisticheskaya Respublika
BAM	Baykal-Amur-Magistral'
CPSU	Communist Party of the Soviet Union
GES (HES)	Gidroelektricheskaya Stantsiya (Hydro-electric Station)
GRES	Gosdudarstvennaya rayonnaya elektro-stantsiya (State regional electric station)
Iz.	Izdatel'stvo (Publishing House)
MTS	Mashinno-Traktornaya Stantsiya
NEP	Novaya Ekonomicheskaya Politika
RSFSR	Rossiyskaya Sovetskaya Federativnaya Sotsialisticheskaya Respublika
SOPS	Sovet Po Izucheniyu Proizvoditel'nykh Sil (Council for the Study of Productive Forces)
SSSR	Soyuz Sovetskikh Sotsialisticheskikh Respublik
USSR	Union of Soviet Socialist Republics
TETs	Termo-Elektricheskaya Tsentr
AN SSSR	Akademiya Nauk (Academy of Sciences) USSR
AN Kaz. SSR	Akademiya Nauk (Academy of Sciences) Kazakh SSR
AN Kirg. SSR	Akademiya Nauk (Academy of Sciences) Kirgiz SSR
AN Tad. SSR	Akademiya Nauk (Academy of Sciences) Tadzhik SSR
AN Turk. SSR	Akademiya Nauk (Academy of Sciences) Turkmen SSR
AN Uzbek SSR	Akademiya Nauk (Academy of Sciences) Uzbek SSR
Ekon. i Zhizn'	Ekonomika i Zhizn'

Ekon. G.	Ekonomicheskaya Gazeta
Nar. Khoz. S.A.	Narodnoye Khozyaystvo Sredney Azii
KP	Kazakhstanskaya Pravda
KT	Kommunist Tadzhikistana
Lit. Gaz.	Literaturnaya Gazeta
Ob. Nauk. v Uzbekistane	Obshchestvennyye Nauki v Uzbekistane
PV	Pravda Vostoka
SK	Sovetskaya Kirgizia
SU	Soviet Union
TI	Turkmenskaya Iskra

Desiatine: a measure of land (2.7 acres)
Pood: 36 lb. avoirdupois
Verst: 3,500 ft.

PART ONE

The Russian Empire in Asia

I

Historical Introduction

Asiatic Russia, forming in territorial and administrative relations one indivisible whole with European Russia, in the economic sense, is a typical colony (*Aziatskaya Rossiya*, vol. II, p. 413).

THE RUSSIAN CONQUEST OF SIBERIA

The Soviet State has inherited the great land mass of Asiatic Russia sporadically yet inexorably annexed by the Cossacks and armies of the Tsars from the sixteenth to the nineteenth centuries. 'Throughout Central Asia and far to the East, three thousand miles away, the red star followed where the imperial eagle had gone.'[1] As with Tsardom, the Soviet title-deeds to these vast possessions are rooted in *force majeure*, the triumph of a stronger people over smaller, weaker units. In spite of Lenin's genuine abhorrence of the policies and ideas of the Tsarist Empire and the radically new social-economic policies he inspired, Asiatic Russia still in many ways bears the imprint of this Tsarist past. Today, as yesterday, official policy in this multi-national state is devised and implemented mainly by Russians in Moscow. Soviet bureaucracy can be obtuse, arbitrary, often corrupt as in the past, while, owing to massive Soviet colonization, Asiatic Russia has become increasingly Russian in character. The brilliance and the brutality of the Russian psyche, the best and much of the worst of old Russia, is still very much alive. Soviet Russia breeds dedicated scholars and explorer scientists like the great nineteenth-century figure, Semënov-Tyan Shanskiy, side by side with intrepid frontier pioneers foreshadowed by adventurous figures like Khabarov who blaze new trails in untrodden places and discover gold and diamonds in the Yakutian wilderness, gas and oil in the

---

[1] B. H. Sumner, *Survey of Russian History* (Duckworth, London, 1944), p. 298.

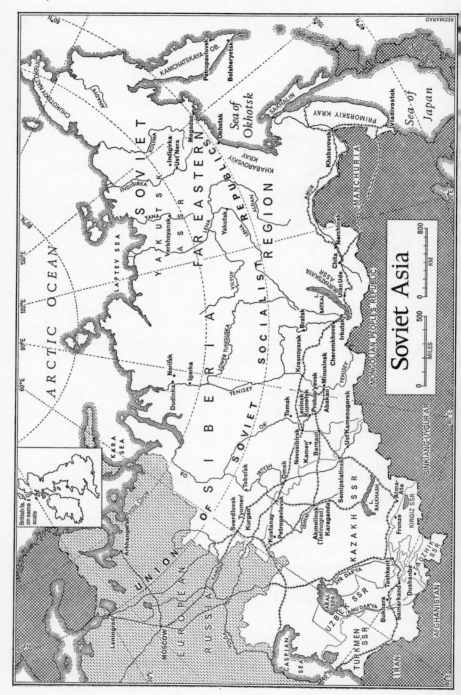

Soviet Asia

remote depths of the Siberian taiga and tundra, gas, oil, and gold beneath the sands of the Central Asian deserts.

The story of how Tsarist Russia acquired and developed this empire in which China and Western Europe would comfortably fit must therefore be briefly recalled. It is the jumping-off ground for the Soviet development of Asiatic Russia with which this study is mainly concerned.

Russian traders and fur trappers first entered Siberia using the northern routes over the Urals and the lower Ob' River from early in the fourteenth century. Some of these Russian pioneers settled in the Arctic but had no thought of territorial conquest. Later, Yermak and a small force of Don Cossacks crossed the Urals, defeated the Tatar khan, Kuchum Khan, and seized his head-quarters, Isker on the Irtysh, in 1582. Yermak's territorial conquest was insignificant but the defeat of the Khan was politically very important as a symbol of Russian power among the local tribes. The Vogul and Ostyak peoples submitted and paid homage and tribute to the Tsar. Here as elsewhere on their march through Siberia, the Russians had the advantage of 'the thunder and lightning' of fire power, while in resisting them, the native people had only bows and arrows. After Yermak's success in 'the land of the sable', and his death in 1584, a pattern of Russian domination of this great and unknown land of Siberia quickly developed under the patronage of the Tsars.

Fortified stockades or *ostrogs* were built and manned by the Cossacks as a defence against attack from hostile natives, and the fur tribute or *yasak* exacted as a symbol of submission to the Russian Government. At this time the Russians had only the haziest notion of the enormous territory through which they advanced with the greatest tenacity and endurance to reach the Pacific in 1641. This great saga of exploration in the face of most difficult country, enormous distances, and a rigorous northern climate cannot be described in detail here. It has inspired a considerable and fascinating Russian literature. There are also rich contemporary archives, and a few first-class works in English. On their way east, the Cossacks built a trail of stockaded posts mostly on the sites of native settle-ments which in time became the now familiar Russian towns of Tyumen' (1586), Tobol'sk (1587), Surgut (1593), Tomsk (1604),

Turukhansk (1638), Kuznetsk (1608), Yeniseysk (1618), Krasnoyarsk (1627), Yakutsk (1632), Okhotsk (1647), Nizhneudinsk (1647), Barguzin (1648), Irkutsk (1651), Chita (1655), and Omsk (1716).[1] Russia's north-eastern expansion reached its limits with the exploits of the Cossack Semën Dezhnev and his companions in being 'the first to navigate to the end of the Eurasian land mass' in 1647–9[2] and Atlasov's rapacious annexation of Kamchatka about 1697. By an unkind quirk of history, the straits separating the Eurasian mainland from Alaska and the American continent were named not after Dezhnev who actually discovered them but after Vitus Bering's expedition eighty years later.

When the Russians reached the lands of the Buryat-Mongol tribes round Lake Baykal, they met fierce opposition to their advance. To avoid often costly contests, they diverted their route to the more difficult terrain through north-east Siberia and the Lena River where the natives were more scattered or more primitive than the hostile Buryats and Kirgiz. Okhotsk on the Pacific was settled in 1647 (after bloody encounters with the local Tungus) while Irkutsk farther south and Chita in eastern Siberia were only established in 1651 and 1655 respectively.

By the end of the seventeenth century the Russians had swept across the entire expanse of north Asia to the Pacific, lured ever farther east by the seemingly inexhaustible stocks of fur-bearing animals and rumours of rich gold and silver treasure. The conquest of Siberia was indeed inspired by lust for fur, the exploitation of the gold and silver mines coming much later. Furs were the most important single item in Russia's home and foreign trade in the sixteenth and seventeenth centuries and a main source of revenue for the Russian treasury. Tribute in the form of furs was collected from the natives by government agents and the entire administrative expenses of Siberia were covered by the fur trade, leaving a large surplus. The Government retained a monopoly of the lucrative trade in sables and black foxes sold to China to adorn the garments of the mandarins and the court. One reason for the rapid Russian advance from the Urals to the Pacific was that the Russians did not have to

---

[1] *Aziatskaya Rossiya* (St. Petersburg, 1914), vol. I, pp. 345–6. Robert Kerner, *The Urge to the Sea* (University of California Press, Berkeley and Los Angeles, 1946).

[2] Armstrong, op. cit. pp. 23–24.

adapt themselves to any extent to new physical conditions. The Russian European north was very similar in climate and they were accustomed to using water routes and porterages.

Throughout their advance to the Pacific the Russians had only isolated groups of primitive native peoples to contend with: Nentsy (or Samoyed), Khanty (Ostyak) and Mansi (Vogul), Tungus, Yakut, Chukchi. There was no organized foreign power to oppose them. The situation was different when the Yakutsk Cossacks moved south from the Lena to the Amur River into nominally Manchu-Chinese territory. Poyarkov's small expedition was resisted by local forces when he succeeded, after a hazardous journey from Yakutsk through the wild Argun country, in sailing down the Amur to its mouth in 1643–5. Poyarkov's tales of treasure, fur, and grain drew another expedition from Yakutsk, under the Ataman Khabarov, back to the Amur. He was also resisted by the Daurs (as the Russians called the native Dagurs) and Chinese who, unlike the Siberian natives, were well armed with cannon and muskets. The struggle for the control of the Amur continued for forty years with swaying fortunes. But the Russian forces were too small and too remote from their base to defeat the Chinese decisively and annex the Amur at this time. The China trade through Mongolia was a matter of considerable importance to Russia and she did not want to jeopardize it by open war with China. On the other hand, the continuing Russian raids into north Manchuria from the Amur disturbed the Chinese about Russia's intentions in this wild, undelimited frontier area. It therefore suited both sides to parley when the Chinese announced that they wanted to settle the frontier question.

The Russian and Chinese envoys met near Nerchinsk in Transbaykalia in 1689 and after much argumentation signed the Treaty of Nerchinsk (1689).[1] The Russian advance along the Amur was halted for nearly two centuries by this treaty, the first to be signed by China with any foreign power. It fixed the Sino-Russian frontier along the Gorbiza and Argun rivers in the west of the area and along the River Uda in the east. Vague though these territorial clauses were,

[1] The Russian text of the Treaty of Nerchinsk is given in *Russko-Kitayskiye Otnosheniya, 1689–1916* (AN Moscow, 1958). Russian was one of the three original languages of this treaty, the others being Latin and Manchurian. The Russian texts of the Treaties of Bura and Kyakhta are also contained in this volume.

the treaty made it clear that Russia must get out of the Amur basin and that no Russian colonists would be permitted to settle there. The Russian town of Albazin, the scene of many bloody encounters between Russians, Daurs, and Chinese, was to be destroyed. In return, China opened her frontiers to Russian citizens and to traders for trade purposes. The circumstances in which this treaty was signed strongly suggest that the Russians signed under pressure. They were face to face with a Chinese embassy escorted by some thousands of armed men. Behind them were the lands of politically unreliable Mongol–Tatar peoples. No Russian military help could be expected in remote Nerchinsk, an unfortified town which the Chinese threatened to storm if the Russians did not sign. When the Chinese quietly dropped their original claim for a Lena frontier the Russian envoy Golovin accepted the Gorbiza line. It later transpired that both sides were equally vague about the topography of the Gorbiza area and that there were two rivers of this name, one familiar to the Russians, the other to the Chinese. Misunderstandings about the lie of the frontier inevitably arose from this confusion. Both the Russians and the Chinese frankly admitted in the treaty that owing to their mutual ignorance of the country between the Uda and Amur rivers, it was impossible to define this boundary more precisely. And so the frontier fixed at Nerchinsk remained unchanged officially for a century and a half. But in spite of the recognition of Chinese claims in this treaty, China made no attempt subsequently to colonize the Amur lands nor to expand farther north into the great, virtually uninhabited wilderness stretching out to the Pacific and Arctic shores. 'The Chinese kept well to the south of the Amur except for a few outposts.' According to Owen Lattimore's expert analysis of the frontier position at this time, the maintenance of a huge, trackless, forested waste between the Manchus and the Russians minimized frontier incidents and tied in with Peking's traditional policy in such regions.[1]

The Treaty of Nerchinsk fixed the Far Eastern frontier with China but did not discuss the 1,200-mile-long stretch of Sino-Russian frontier west of the Argun River between Transbaykalia and Mongolia where the Chinese were apprehensive of Russian moves

[1] I. O. Lattimore, *Manchuria: Cradle of Conflict* (The Macmillan Co., New York, 1932), pp. 10–16.

in support of the Mongols and were anxious for a frontier agreement. The treaties of Bura and Kyakhta signed in 1727 demarcated this frontier from Kyakhta to the Argun River and westwards to Shabina Dabag, a pass in the Sayan Mountains. Detailed arrangements were also included in the Kyakhta Treaty regulating the important Russo-Chinese caravan trade in which Kyakhta remained the focal point until the caravan was replaced by the sea-borne trade in the mid-twentieth century.

An effective drive for Russian control of the Amur began in the middle of the nineteenth century when the dynamic Governor-General of east Siberia, Count Murav'yëv-Amurskiy, took the matter more or less into his own hands. Once more the Amur frontier overshadowed Sino-Russian relations. Murav'yëv passionately believed in Siberia's future prospects for colonization and economic development. He was also convinced that its rear and access to the Pacific must be secured against attack from the British (who had been permitted to trade in China's maritime ports since 1842) by establishing Russian control over the Amur, Sakhalin, and Kamchatka.

Murav'yëv was enthusiastically backed by the prosperous Siberian merchant class who were in favour of direct action on the Amur to give Russia free access to the Pacific. The Chinese position was felt to be intolerably legalistic. Treaty rights or no, the Chinese presence on the Amur was known to be extremely tenuous, frontier posts or pickets very thin on the ground, and Chinese sovereignty over the native peoples of the area amounted to little more than the occasional symbolic collection of tribute. Virtually nothing was done by them to administer or develop the area. Various foreigners visiting the Amur in the '40s and '50s also supported Russia's pragmatic stand, stressing that the Chinese for the last one hundred and fifty years had kept the Russians from the use of the 'natural channel for commerce so essential to them' and that there were few Chinese living in the country, while the natives were friendly to Russian rule. The last point is open to question failing decisive or impartial evidence about the reactions of the native peoples of the Amur to the Russians or the Chinese at this time. P. McDonough Collins, the U.S. commercial agent who sailed the entire length of the Amur on the eve of the Russian annexation, recorded his impression as follows: 'Whether subjects of Russia or the Celestial Empire, I do not know but they [the indigenous Tungus] evidently wanted a master.'[1] The scholarly Dr. Leopold Shrenk, who headed the first Expedition of the Imperial Academy of Sciences to the Amur kray in 1855–6, recalled the situation there at that time, some twenty years later:

From the time of the unification of this Amur kray to Russia, its ethnographical features quickly changed. With the exception of a relatively small belt along the Amur between the mouth of the Zeya and Bureya rivers with Chinese towns and Manchu-Chinese villages and 2–3 recently established Russian military posts, the entire Amur kray in the '50s when I knew it had the appearance of a still untouched country where indigenous fishermen and hunters quietly occupied themselves with their own pursuits. Now, along the entire Amur and Ussuri river banks you can meet post stations and villages of Cossacks or free colonists every 20–30 versts. . . . The indigenous peoples of the Amur are at present in the same process of degeneration as the Siberian natives and it may proceed still more rapidly with them as a result of the fact that colonization in the Amur kray is being tackled more energetically than anywhere in Siberia. . . . Already the distinctiveness of their manners and customs is difficult to trace under the influence of foreigners. The only cultural nations for them before we Russians appeared were the Chinese and Japanese, but these contacts were, for the most remote of them, limited almost to trade. Moreover, these Eastern-Asian people, Chinese and Japanese, at least up to the present did not make any special efforts to spread their culture and thus their influence on the native was less strong.[2]

The first move in Murav'yëv's Amur plans was taken by his astute sailor friend, Captain (later Admiral) G. N. Nevel'skoy. Nevel'skoy 'instinctively felt' that the Amur delta could not be impassable and shared Murav'yëv's zeal for the acquisition of a Pacific port for Russia. He set sail from St. Petersburg in August 1848 with military supplies for Kamchatka and equipment for an expedition to investigate the Amur delta, thanks to the personal support of the Emperor. Within fourteen months, he was able to inform Murav'yëv that Sakhalin was an island and that the Amur delta was accessible for sea-going ships from the north and the

---

[1] P. McDonough Collins, *A Voyage Down the Amur*, (Appelton, New York, 1860), p. 184.
[2] L. Shrenk, *Ob Inorodtsakh Amurskogo Kraya* (Izd. Imperatorskoy Akademii Nauk, St. Petersburg, 1883), pp. 1–3.

south. Emboldened by this success and contrary to orders, Nevel'-skoy sailed up the Amur in 1850 and planted the Russian flag thirty-five versts up-stream at a post which he named Nikolayevsk—having convinced himself from a very casual reconnaissance that 'the local natives were independent and that the Manchurian traders did not regard this region as theirs'.[1] He was saved from the severe punishment his high-handed action incurred in St. Petersburg by the Emperor Nicholas himself whose imperial dictum was: 'Where once the Russian flag has been raised it must never be lowered.'[2] In subsequent expeditions over five years, Nevel'skoy set up several Russian military posts along the coast of the new maritime province and in southern Sakhalin, and surveyed the entire coast of the Gulf of Tartary to the borders of Korea.

Meanwhile Murav'yëv had been busy preparing for the occupation of the Amur, collecting men and supplies and building boats on the River Shilka. He was officially authorized to deal directly with the Chinese about the Amur frontier questions. At last in 1854 he sailed down the Amur leading an impressive flotilla with reinforcements for the Kamchatka garrison. These troops soon proved their worth by repulsing the Anglo-French fleet at Petropavlovsk-Kamchatka in 1855. Despite many Chinese protests, Murav'yëv continued to sail up and down the Amur in a lordly manner, settling Cossack forces and Russian colonists in the lower Amur and behaving as if he were already on Russian territory (1855–7). Before the frontier negotiations had even begun with the Chinese, the Russians had included the lower Amur in the imperial administration and Nikolayevsk-na-Amure became the provincial centre of the new Russian Primorskiy (Maritime) province. The Russian position was thus well established when at last Murav'yëv met the Chinese plenipotentiaries at Aigun in 1858, to discuss the frontier.

The Chinese had as far as possible avoided armed clashes with the Russians during their advance on the Amur, not because they had any doubts about it being Chinese/Manchu territory but because they feared defeat and humiliation at the hands of a stronger, better organized Russia.

The situation during the Aigun negotiations was very different from what it had been when the Treaty of Nerchinsk was signed in

---

[1] *Aziatskaya Rossiya*, vol. I, p. 517. 　　[2] Ibid. p. 517.

1689. Russia was now a great power with well-organized armed forces at her command while China was rent by internal dissensions. Murav'yëv profited by this advantage virtually to dictate the terms of the Treaty of Aigun[1] to the badly briefed, vacillating Chinese, and cowed them with a display of personal pomp and power in his barge. These were the circumstances under which China ceded to Russia the left bank of the Amur to the Ussuri River and both banks from thence to the sea and permitted Russian merchants and seamen to travel on the Sungari and Ussuri rivers. Two years later, in 1860, the Treaty of Peking completed Russia's triumph in the Far East by the cession to her by China of the whole of the Maritime Province of Manchuria down to the Korean boundary. On the splendid site of Peter the Great Bay Murav'yëv founded the city of Vladivostok in 1860, later Russia's naval base on the Pacific and the capital of the Russian Far East. An official Tsarist Russian comment conveyed the prevailing sentiment about these treaties in the Empire: 'The energy and tenacity of Murav'yëv-Amurskiy rectified the errors of the 1689 Treaty of Nerchinsk.' A century later, however, Mao's China would regard Nerchinsk as the only frontier treaty concluded with the Russians which was not 'unequal'. The acquisition of the Amur-Ussuri basin and control of the long north Pacific coast was potentially a valuable asset to Russia, even though a hundred years later Murav'yëv's dreams of wealth and colonization had not yet been realized.

By the conquest of Siberia, a territory twice as large as European Russia was added to the Empire. The many native tribes scattered sparsely throughout the vast spaces of Siberia were shamelessly exploited and degraded by rapacious officials and traders in the fur business. Official regulations to protect these peoples from their machinations and especially those forbidding the sale of vodka to the northern tribes were all too easily ignored. Often the sole result of this prohibition was to raise the price of vodka and encourage illicit sales. Drunkenness and syphilis introduced by the Russians undermined the stamina of the natives. Before the nineteenth century, little or nothing had been done for the northern peoples of

---

[1] The Russian texts of the treaties of Aigun (p. 29) and Peking (p. 34) are given in *Russko-Kitayskiye Otnosheniya 1689–1916*. It is pointed out in the preface to this work that in all previous Russian texts of the Aigun Treaty the words 'for protection from foreigners' in the opening clause of the Treaty were omitted.

1. *The Conquest of Siberia*, V. I. Surikov, 1895

2a. Tomsk University, est. 1878

2b. Tomsk Technological Institute

Siberia either in the field of education or medical care. The first school for natives in the Yakut province was a missionary school (1801). By 1911 there were in all 114 schools in the north. In Siberia one doctor had to look after an area of 19,365 square versts.[1] In spite of this official neglect of the Siberian natives' welfare, Tsarist officials and historians blandly described them as 'perfidious' and 'treacherous' when they attempted to resist Russian exactions or to get their own back on the Russians; loyalty was apparently automatically expected by the Russians from them as from an inferior to a superior being. Tsarist Russia did not, however, actively interfere with the tribal pattern of life or the traditional beliefs and customs of the primitive people of Siberia. This disruption came later with the imposition of collectivization and the attempted settlement of the nomadic fisher-folk and reindeer-breeders of Siberia, after the Revolution.

TSARIST POPULATION AND COLONIZATION POLICIES IN SIBERIA[2]

The history of Russia is the history of a country which is being colonized. Its region of colonization expanded together with its state territory. Now rising, now falling, this age-old movement has continued to our times.[3]

The vast spaces through which the Cossacks advanced from the Urals to the Pacific Ocean from the sixteenth to the nineteenth centuries were at first very sparsely populated. There were small groups of different native tribes living in the woods and along the rivers of Siberia and often separated by great distances. As they pushed east the Cossacks left behind them a trail of armed and manned *ostrogs* (stockaded posts). After them came Russian traders and trappers to reinforce the long-established, small Russian trading-posts on the Ob', and other northern Siberian rivers which in earlier centuries had been reached through the Kara Sea and over the northern Urals. Settlement of this great land was at first slow and erratic and

---

[1] *Aziatskaya Rossiya*, vol. I, p. 271.

[2] In this narrative I have largely relied for detailed information on Siberian migration on Donald W. Treadgold's excellent work *The Great Siberian Migration* (Princeton University, New Jersey, 1957).

[3] V. O. Klyuchevskiy, *Kurs Russkoy Istorii* (Moscow, 1911). Quoted in preface to *Aziatskaya Rossiya*, vol. I, p. 5.

C

largely confined to forced labour in the Urals mines, fugitive rebels, runaway serfs from European Russia, and dissenters fleeing from religious persecution. The northern Arctic coast was too remote and climatically too inhospitable to attract settlers in any number. The more favourable climate and good black earth of western Siberia was a much more attractive proposition for free settlers, peasants, and ordinary Russians, who came in considerable numbers in search of a better, freer life than at home. They thus escaped the bondage of serfdom and the gentry, neither of which ever found a footing in Siberia.

From the seventeenth century Siberia was used as a place of hard labour for criminal and political prisoners, mostly in the mines, but they never formed a major element in the population in spite of the notorious reputation they gave the country (a reputation much resented by the free settlers). A more interesting group were the political exiles banished for their liberal opinions and who included many highly educated scholars and scientists and not a few politically advanced aristocrats. These people often chose to remain in Siberia after their period of exile was over, or were obliged to do so by law. They left their mark on the social life of the towns they lived in, like Irkutsk, where liberal aristocrats such as Prince Volkonskiy and Prince Trubetskoy settled when released from the mines, pursued their studies, founded learned institutions, and investigated the ethnology, flora, and fauna of the country.[1] Later Lenin, Stalin, and Trotsky were exiled to Siberia. Stalin and Trotsky made dramatic escapes but Lenin's period of exile in Shushenskoye on the Yenisey, where he had leisure for writing and shot wild fowl, was far from disagreeable. Stalin's deportees were less fortunate in their miserable concentration camps stretching from the Urals to the gold mines of Kolyma. Between 1825 and 1862 it is estimated on the basis of published official Russian data that about 56,000 people were sent into forced labour in Siberia. (No similar official figures of the much larger Soviet deportations have ever been published.)

Free peasant colonization from European Russia did not get going in earnest until the turn of the century when it moved ahead rapidly owing to the facilities offered by the construction of the

[1] F. A. Kudryavtsev and G. A. Vendrikh, *Ocherki po Istorii Goroda* (Irkutskoe Knizhnoye Izdatel'stvo, Irkutsk, 1958), p. 104.

Trans-Siberian railway. The Trans-Siberian railway (over 6,000 miles long) is one of the greatest feats of railway engineering in the world.[1] It was started from both ends, from Vladivostok in the east in 1891 and Chelyabinsk in the Urals in 1892, and was completed by the stretch round Lake Baykal in 1904, just in time to rush soldiers to the Japanese–Manchurian front in 1904–5. The original Amur line was abandoned for the Chinese eastern route through Manchuria when the railway concession was granted by China to Russia in 1896. But the idea was revived in 1908 and the Amur line, 1,200 miles long from Kuenga to Khabarovsk, was opened to traffic in 1916 with the completion of the bridge nearly one and a half miles long over the Amur at Khabarovsk. The Trans-Siberian railway was an event of major importance for the colonization and development of Siberia and eliminated the rough hazards for man, beast, and freight of the old post roads. It cost over £150 million but its value to the economic development of the area served can scarcely be reckoned in such terms. Unfortunately, it also took a heavy toll of the lives of the workmen of many nationalities who built it under appalling conditions in the severe Siberian climate.

Until the railway was built, only the hardiest of settlers and their families braved the primitive state of communications and the enormous distances between the settlements. The Government, which had shown little or no interest in the irregular spontaneous movement of population over the Urals, at last realized the importance of colonization as a means of developing the richest agricultural lands of west Siberia. Intelligent Tsarist officials like Stolypin and Krivosheyn took a personal interest in promoting it. Several influential bodies were set up to improve the chaotic migration conditions, for example, the Special Resettlement Administration of the Interior (1896) and the Chief Administration of Land Settlement and Agriculture (1905). The Siberian Railway Committee also took a hand in this work eventually and reduced tariffs on the railways. The Government assisted migrants by grants in money and kind. As a result of these measures peasant migration to Siberia climbed rapidly in the peak years of 1908–9. Professor Treadgold's expert

[1] The Trans-Siberian railway has found an enthusiastic biographer in H. Tupper, author of *To a Great Ocean* (Secker & Warburg, London, 1965). There is also important material in V. F. Borzunov, *Arkhivniye Materialy po Istorii Stroitelstva Sibirskoy Zheleznoy Dorogi (1880–1905), Istoricheskiy Arkhiv*, 5 (Iz. AN SSSR, 1960).

estimate (based on official statistics) of the total number of settlers who crossed the Urals from 1801 to 1914 is 7 million.[1] The Siberian population rose massively in less than a century from 2.9 million in 1815 to 9.4 million in 1911. These figures were nevertheless small in relation to the need for millions more settlers in the vast Siberian territory. The greater part of these colonists settled in the most fertile lands of west and central Siberia.

By 1914 these lands were mostly settled and colonization was pressing southwards into the steppes of the Kazakh nomads, where Russian peasant-colonists blazed the trail for Khrushchev's 'Virgin Lands' settlement of 1954–5. In spite of various government inducements including assisted land and sea passages (via the long sea route from the Black Sea ports to the Russian Pacific coast), migration to the areas east of Lake Baykal remained unsatisfactory and settlers had to rely on food and other supplies from west Siberia and abroad.

Owing to the great increase in exports of grain, meat, and butter since the beginning of the century, central Siberia was extremely prosperous. There were no restrictions on foreigners visiting Siberia and the Far East, and many of them reported enthusiastically on Siberia's promising future as an exporter of dairy produce, meat, grain, flax, hides, hemp, bristles, timber, and as a source of valuable raw materials, primarily gold. The annual value of the butter exports totalled £7 million before 1914. The business was in the hands of the Danes who exported Siberian butter in bulk and had their own creameries throughout central-western Siberia.[2] A great new market was opening up in Siberia. Many foreign firms and businessmen were actively interested in getting their wares into Siberian towns and trading-posts on the rivers. Danish cement was imported for the Trans-Siberian railway, British mining machinery and tool steel were highly appreciated as well as Peterhead herrings and other British consumer goods. Two fervent supporters of Siberian trade via the Kara Sea route were Mr. Alfred Derry (of the Kensington emporium Derry & Toms) and the Norwegian Jonas Lied, who established a Norwegian consulate at Krasnoyarsk, travelled freely all over Siberia in search of business, and informs

[1] Treadgold, op. cit. pp. 34–35.

[2] Jonas Lied, *Return to Happiness* (Macmillan & Co. Ltd., London, 1943). Mr. Lied was active in promoting Siberian trade before World War I. His book gives many interesting details of Siberian life and prospects of development.

readers of his fascinating autobiography that in Siberia at least 100 per cent. was the norm for trade profits.[1] The Siberians themselves welcomed this trade but Russian sugar refiners and cotton printers effectively guarded their monopoly from European competition by opposing any lowering of duties on their products. The agricultural prosperity of the country was also reflected in the fact that the Siberian farms were better supplied with agricultural machinery and tools in 1914 than central Russia or the Ukraine, and the numbers of stock per hundred of the population greatly exceeded that in European Russia.[2]

Agricultural machinery worth 20 million roubles was imported by Siberia in 1910–11.[3] Creamery and credit co-operatives played an important part in promoting butter manufacture. Some English firms importing butter from Siberia also aided the co-operatives with credit, separators, and refrigeration for the export of butter.[4]

The Soviet economic historian Lyashchenko points out that most of the sown area belonged to Russian settlers old and new, while the aboriginal peoples had a very small amount of tillage and only a primitive type of agriculture.[5] He compares the situation in Siberia and Turkestan where almost half of the sown areas were in the hands of the native population. The Siberian settlers from central Russia tenaciously clung to their Russian customs and mode of life. The public buildings, churches, schools, and the whole aspect of Siberian towns such as Omsk, Tomsk, or Irkutsk immediately recalled the motherland and might have been transplanted ready made from there. This imitative attitude has survived the Revolution, and the ugly, badly proportioned buildings favoured by Stalin (now on the way out, judging by press photographs) can be found all over Russia from Noril'sk to Magadan and Central Asia wherever Russians have settled.

In spite of its ominous repute, pre-Soviet Siberia was relatively easy of access for foreign visitors, and many scholars, scientists, journalists, businessmen, and ordinary travellers all made their own way there. There were no *Intourist* organizations with their handicaps to private travel. These travellers were almost without exception

---

[1] Lied, op. cit. p. 165.   [2] *Aziatskaya Rossiya*, vol. II, pp. 406–7.
[3] P. I. Lyashchenko, *Istoriya Narodnogo Khozyaystva SSSR* (Moscow, 1956), vol. II, p. 526.
[4] Ibid. pp. 526–7.   [5] Ibid. p. 525.

captivated by the country and many wrote about it and its future with enthusiasm. Some of these books about a way of life that has vanished and places now banned to foreign visitors for half a century are worth recalling. It was thanks to the willing courtesies of the Russian Government that the young Polish anthropologist, Miss M. A. Czaplicka, fresh from her studies in Oxford, spent over a year during World War I with a scientific expedition on the lower Yenisey within the Arctic Circle studying the life of the indigenous tribes. Her book, *My Siberian Year*, is packed with closely observed notes about the Tungus and other tribes among whom she lived in the native *chums*. That was her professional job. She also has much to say about Siberian life in various strata of the Russian population. Among these people there were the owners of mining claims 'who had made rich strikes, lived on their claims or in the towns nearest to the mines in a kind of barbaric luxury';[1] and the Sibiryak *starozhily* (the old Siberian settlers) who practised more modern farming methods than the Russian peasants. She also discusses the effect of the government policy of handing over the communal farms to individual owners in order to encourage colonization. 'The elementary truth being at last recognized that a man will take a greater interest in trying to get out of the land as much as it will yield, if he knows that the fruits of his labour will go to himself and his family and need not be shared equally with the shiftless and indolent among his neighbours.' Little did she guess that this policy would soon be jettisoned and her views confirmed by the results of Bolshevik nationalization-collectivization policies on agricultural production in Siberia and elsewhere in the Soviet Union.

John Foster Fraser went to Siberia in 1901 'on a mission of curiosity with the average Briton's prejudice against things Russian'.[2] 'I saw', he reported, 'that the popular idea about Siberia is altogether wrong. I saw a land capable of immense agricultural possibilities, great stretches of prairie waiting for the plough, huge forests, magnificent waterways and big towns with fine stores, with great hotels with electric light gleaming everywhere; in a word, instead of a gaunt lone land, inhabited only by convicts, I saw a country that reminded me from the first day to the last of Canada and the best

[1] M. A. Czaplicka, *My Siberian Year* (Mills & Boon Ltd., London, 1916), pp. 290-2.
[2] John Foster Fraser, *The Real Siberia* (Cassell & Co., London, 1902), p. 7.

parts of America.' Fraser had a poor impression of the Russian peasant as a farmer: 'The fact is, the Russian is one of the worst farmers on the face of the earth. It is probably the strong strain of the Tartar in him that makes him indolent. He is certainly no born agriculturalist. . . . The Russian Government with all its faults is acting benevolently to the Siberian settlers, buying agricultural machinery and selling it on easy instalment terms. . . . That impetus which has done so much to spur the American is non-existent.'[1]

The experiences of the young Mr. Philips Price making 'a journey to West and Central Siberia and the adjacent parts of Mongolia'[2] are perhaps most enviable of all these free-ranging pre-Soviet travellers. His keen eye for detail makes him an excellent reporter on the economic conditions of the day and the prospects of Siberia which were his main interest. He was free to inquire exactly into prices and living conditions everywhere he went and anticipated a very bright future for Siberian agriculture, livestock, and general industrial development on more modern but still capitalistic lines. The idea of a revolution which would radically change the picture did not occur to him. Nobody interfered with him in his rambles, even in the 'neutral zone along the frontier where Siberia and Mongolia meet'. 'In this no-man's-land which is not administered directly by any political authority the scum of human society seemed to have drifted . . . a cosmopolitan crowd of every conceivable race that the adjacent parts of Siberia and Mongolia seem capable of producing.' Siberian traders in wool and hides stood out in this motley crowd. 'The Eastern Slav is born to conquer and assimilate the Asiatic races, because in character and habits he is so Asiatic himself that he can in fact absorb his neighbours without either absorber or absorbed being aware of the process', affirms Mr. Price. Even if, like most generalizations, this is only a half truth there is a good deal to it. When Mr. Price accompanied a Siberian wool and skins trader to an alpine summer encampment of the Altay 'Tartars', he developed this line of thought further: 'Alexieff showed me how easily the Russians get on with the native Tartars. They win the respect of Asiatic races as no one else can do. They talk with them in their own tongue at their own firesides, they sleep in their tents by night, they personally conduct business with them, exchanging their

[1] Ibid. pp. 48–49. [2] M. Philips Price, *Siberia* (Methuen, London, 1912), ch. VI.

wool for tea. . . . How different from the overbearing tone of a
British colonist or a British soldier in an Eastern colony.'[1] The young
Mr. Price had obviously fallen under Alexieff's Slav charm. Siberia,
he learned, had various rankling grievances against European Russia.
This vast, rich, developing country was deliberately under-represented
in the Duma—with only nine members—to prevent her becoming
too powerful. The great commercial interests in old Russia opposed
the growing feeling for Siberian autonomy fearing that if the Siberians had their way, they might carry out various fiscal reforms which
would affect the big manufacturing trusts in Moscow, for example,
free ports at the mouths of the Yenisey and the Ob' to admit cheap
foreign manufactured goods instead of the highly priced and often
inferior Russian goods. He also felt that the industrial development
of Siberia was being retarded by the high prices of machinery and
other commodities essential for agricultural and industrial development.

According to Mr. Price's observations these rich lands yielded an
average of thirty bushels of cereals to the acre in spite of primitive
methods of cultivation and the fact that no manure was used in the
best soils of western and central Siberia.

TSARIST CONQUEST OF TURKESTAN AND THE KAZAKH STEPPES[2]

Having gained a Far Eastern Pacific frontier after three centuries
of struggle in the vast Siberian continent and a decisive victory over
the Chinese at Aigun in 1858, the Russian Empire expanded rapidly
in another direction in the mid-nineteenth century. The intermittent
advance south of Siberia continued deep into the heart of Central
Asia till Russia's frontiers marched with those of Persia, Afghanistan,
and Chinese Sinkiang in the east. This advance differed radically
from the Siberian conquest, its main objective being the search
for a firm frontier and security for Russian trade, not in the first

---

[1] Price, op. cit.

[2] The Russian conquest of Kazakhstan and the Central Asian khanates is discussed in fuller
detail in *The Modern History of Soviet Central Asia* by Geoffrey Wheeler (Asia–Africa
Series, Weidenfeld & Nicolson, London, 1964), and *Turkestan in the Nineteenth Century*
by Mrs. Mary Holdsworth (Central Asian Research Centre, London, 1959). In the preparation of this section I have leaned heavily on both works.

place a hunt for fur or treasure as in Siberia. There was no firm frontier between Siberia and the Kazakh steppes and Russia's trade with the settled peoples of the Central Asian khanates of Bukhara, Khiva, and Kokand was constantly harassed by attack from the nomadic peoples of the deserts and steppes through which this caravan trade had to pass.

In their march south-south-east the Russians met much stronger resistance from better organized and more developed peoples than in the hopelessly unequal struggle with the primitive Siberian tribes. The rich agricultural settlements of southern Siberia merged into and often encroached on the traditional grazing lands of the Kazakh nomads. 'The steppe fields, which are partly very rich black soil, did not belong to an agricultural people, a Christian people, but remained in the possession of wild nomads, the majority of whom professed Islam.'[1] This official statement clearly reflects the Russian attitude towards the nomads, namely, that as the nomads were a nuisance they must be subjugated. And subjugated they were. It has been well said that the Russian advance into the Steppe Region from western Siberia was for the most part such a gradual process that it is difficult to say exactly when it began. The submission of the Lesser Kazakh Horde to the Russians in 1730 is usually regarded as a landmark in the gradual incorporation of the Kazakh steppe in the Russian Empire. But the dates of Russian settlements such as Yaitsk, now Ural'sk (1520), Ust'-Kamenogorsk (1720), and several other towns in the area show that Russian penetration of the vast, undefined Kazakh steppe lands and the Altay had begun much earlier. It was nevertheless only at the beginning of the nineteenth century that definite plans of annexation began to emerge. By this time the Russians realized that the formal submission of this or that khan meant little or nothing in terms of 'peace and security for the Russian caravans through the Khan's territory to the trading marts of Turkestan' or change in their brigandish way of life. They also had good reason to know that the Kazakhs resented their presence.

The series of Kazakh risings against Russian power in the early nineteenth century expressed these peoples' bitter resistance to attempts to control 'their wild and independent existence'. *L'appétit vient en mangeant.* Having formally pacified the Kazakhs—in fact

---

[1] *Aziatskaya Rossiya*, vol. I, p. 24.

they remained constantly restless—and incorporated their lands in
the Russian Empire, the Russians now found themselves spread out
along a fortified line facing 'the khanates hostile to Russia: Bukhara,
Khiva, and Kokand. Only by subduing these could the Kirgiz
[Kazakh] country become Russian not only in name but in fact',
frankly explains an official Russian commentator on these operations
in *Aziatskaya Rossiya*.[1] In still blunter terms, he continues: 'Pacifica-
tion of the Steppe was only possible by terrorizing or subduing these
khanates, which adopted an insolent attitude towards Russia, and
because they considered themselves unassailable, incited others to
do likewise. . . . It was therefore necessary to strike a decisive blow
against the khanates. By the 1850s the Russian Government had
adopted this course.'

In their military movements south against the fertile oases of the
ancient khanates of Central Asia, Bukhara, Khorezm (or Khiva as it
was called in nineteenth-century Russia), and Kokand the Russians
encountered a very different type of country, peoples, and problems
from those faced earlier in Siberia. These khanates had relatively
stable governments and organized if despotic administrations compared to the primitive native organization in Siberia. They were also
the heirs, however degenerate, of a great Islamic civilization. But
they had neither stable boundaries with each other nor with the
limitrophe areas of Persia, Afghanistan, and China.

The Russian military operations against the khanates, the
Turkmen nomads in the Transcaspian deserts in the west of the
region and the Kirgiz nomads in the Semirech'ye eastern borderland
of China, are only of marginal interest to this study and will not be
discussed in detail. The main fact to note here is that Russian power
was established by military force (and this remains the basis of Soviet
power there today).

The important cultural and commercial centre of Tashkent fell to
the Russians in 1865. 'With the seizure of Tashkent we have acquired
a position in Central Asia in conformity with the interests of the
Empire and the might of the Russian people', announced Major-
General M. G. Chernyayev on the capture of the city.[2] The khanates
of Bukhara and Khiva became vassal states of the Russian Empire by

---

[1] *Aziatskaya Rossiya*, vol. I, p. 32.
[2] Quoted in *Central Asia Review*, no. 2 (1965), p. 104.

treaties and agreements which gave Russia control of their foreign relations, slices of their territory, and valuable transport rights on the Amu Dar'ya River, while the historic khanate of Kokand lost its independent existence and was swallowed up in the new Russian *oblast* of Fergana in 1876. Finally, the resistance of the bitterly hostile Turkmen tribes was broken at the battle of Geok Tepe in 1881. The whole area (excluding the much-reduced khanates of Bukhara and Khiva) was then formed into new administrative units of the Tsarist Empire: the Governate-General of Turkestan, the Governate-General of the Steppe Region (Stepnoy Kray), and the two separate west Kazakh *oblasts* of Turgay and Ural'sk. This administrative system lasted until the break-up of the Tsarist régime in 1917.

The attitude of St. Petersburg to the extension of Russian power in Central Asia which had given rise to considerable alarm abroad (especially in England) was very frankly stated in a Circular Note in 1864 addressed to the powers by the then Foreign Minister Prince Gorchakoff. Uninhibited by latter-day scruples about imperialism and the rights of native peoples or 'savages', he put his country's case with persuasive consistency. This statement is therefore worth recalling as the official apologia for this phase of Tsarist colonial policy:

The position of Russia in Central Asia is that of all civilised states which are brought into contact with half-savage nomad populations possessing no fixed social organisation.

In such cases, the more civilised state is forced in the interest of the security of its frontier, and its commercial relations, to exercise a certain ascendancy over its turbulent and undesirable neighbours. Raids and acts of pillage must be put down. To do this, the tribes on the frontier must be reduced to a state of submission. . . . It is a peculiarity of Asiatics to respect nothing but visible and palpable force. . . . The State is thus forced to choose between two alternatives—either to give up this endless labour . . . or to plunge deeper and deeper into barbarous countries. . . .

Such has been the fate of every country which has found itself in a similar position. The United States in America, France in Algeria, Holland in her Colonies, England in India; all have been forced by imperious necessity into this onward march, where the greatest difficulty is to know where to stop. . . .

It is needless for me to lay stress on the interest which Russia evidently has not to increase her territory, and above all to avoid raising complications on her frontiers which can but delay and paralyse her domestic development. Very frequently of late years the civilisation of these countries which are her neighbours on the Continent of Asia has been assigned to Russia as her special mission.[1]

Prince Gorchakoff's unvarnished, hard-headed analysis of the relations between the imperial power and the indigenous people of Central Asia is a refreshing contrast to the twists and turns of Soviet historiography in regard to the facts of native resistance to Tsarist rule. Thus the long struggle of the Kazakhs against the Russians is either overlooked or attributed for the most part to 'feudal elements' since the official history of Kazakhstan (1943) was condemned for historical 'errors' in giving a nationalist rather than a class origin to Kazakh resistance to Tsardom. Many Tsarist commentators, however, freely admitted that relations were embittered between officialdom and the native peoples of Central Asia 'who had no desire to reconcile themselves to the new situation and to see around them separate Russian garrison towns'[2] such as were gradually built alongside all the old native cities and settlements of, for example, Tashkent, Samarkand, Pishpek (Frunze), Vernyy (Alma-Ata).

The general pattern of domestic life in the khanates was not disrupted to any extent by the Russian conquest of Turkestan: 'The picturesque and colourful past lingered on at the cost of disease, squalor, ignorance and despotism.'[3] Russian slaves were no longer sold in the Khiva market but domestic slavery continued.

By these conquests, Russia acquired a new strategic and economic dominance in Central Asia. Firm frontiers were established for the first time in the south of the region by treaties between imperial Russia, and Persia and Afghanistan. The situation on the long eastern frontier with China was more fluid, as throughout the century Russia 'nibbled away large tracts of at least nominally Chinese territory'. In 1895 Russia seized the Chinese sector of the great Pamir plateau (now part of Soviet Tadzhikistan) which abutted on Chinese Turkestan. Unlike the other parts of the new Sino-Russian frontier

[1] Alexis Krausse, *Russia in Asia* (London, 1900), pp. 224–5.
[2] *Aziatskaya Rossiya*, vol. I, pp. 36–37. [3] Pierce, op. cit. p. 58.

Library
I.U.P.
ndiana, Pa.

330.957 C763b
C. 1

in Central Asia, this sector was never confirmed by treaty and is
marked 'undelimited' on Chinese maps today.[1]

THE ECONOMIC RESULTS OF THE RUSSIAN CONQUEST OF TURKESTAN

The economic advantages of Russia's control of the rich oases of
Turkestan and the wide steppe lands of the Kazakh and Kirgiz
nomads were considerable for trade, a cheap domestic source of
cotton (and some other tropical products), and for the expansion
of Russian settlement from the overcrowded depressed areas of
central Russia and the Ukraine. In the course of centuries the peoples
of Turkestan had become famous for their production of tropical
products, especially silk, cotton, and fruit on irrigated ground,
and were highly skilled in a wide range of handicrafts: carpets,
jewellery, metal, and woodwork. The developing market for
manufactured goods in Bukhara and the other khanates was an object of jealous competition between Russia and the Asian purveyors
of British and other foreign goods, in the first place textiles. Both
internal and foreign trade was well developed in all the khanates
which exchanged goods not only with Russia but also with Persia,
Afghanistan, Kashgar, and India. Their main exports to Russia
were karakul skins, cotton, silk, wool, and hides. Bukharan merchants
were astute traders and handled most of this trade; they were
regular visitors to the great Russian fair of Nizhniy-Novgorod, on
the Volga.

Russia took full advantage of her newly won power over the
oases and the steppe lands to further her economic and commercial
interests and as far as possible eliminate trade competitors in the area.
Russian forces now controlled and improved the primitive lines of
communications with Turkestan, formerly harassed by hostile
nomadic tribes, and made them relatively safe for merchants and
trade. A number of post-roads were constructed and manned with
horse-relay stations while regular postal communications between
Tashkent and Orenburg existed by 1868, that is, before the main

[1] Francis Watson, 'The Central Asian Area', *The Frontiers of China* (Chatto & Windus,
London, 1966), p. 34. Owen Lattimore, 'International Boundaries on the Pamirs',
Pivot of Asia (Little, Brown & Company, Boston, 1950), p. 259.

railway system was started, in 1881. Russian trade with Central
Asia was relatively small in the first half of the nineteenth century.
It had, however, great potential significance in the eyes of the Russian
merchants and manufacturers engaged in it. They realized that
Central Asia was one of the only markets for the expansion of
Russian manufactured goods which were not of a type or quality at
this time to find sale in the more sophisticated markets of Western
Europe. As long as the khanates, especially Bukhara, were free to do
so, they imposed restrictions and disabilities on Russian trade and
Russian merchants trading in their markets. Non-Muslims like
British or Russian merchants were forbidden to trade directly in
Bukhara and had to use often unreliable Muslims who might make
off with their capital or otherwise cheat them with impunity. Non-
Muslim merchants paid higher taxes on goods than Muslims.

The hesitation often shown in the early years of the nineteenth
century in the highest military and political circles of Russia about
the wisdom of annexing Turkestan was therefore not shared by the
Russian merchant and banking circles.[1] Both were solidly behind
the annexation policy, hoping both for trade expansion and the
elimination, through Russian influence and wire-pulling in the
khanates, of British competition in the textile trade. The idea was
prevalent that if the Russians did not forestall them, the British
would occupy Bukhara and Khiva from their outposts in India and
Afghanistan. In the '40s and '50s the idea of a British military and
economic threat to Central Asia aroused something of the same kind
of hysterical panic as the largely emotional fears in England of a
Russian threat to India. 'The tycoons, the bankers and indeed the
world of learning were vocal in their demand that the Government
should secure the conditions of trade. They could hardly have wished
for more willing co-operation than they got from the new headquarters staff in Turkestan which was itself crusading for the mastery
of the neighbouring markets "so that Russian goods might creep
forward over the Asian landmass as far south and as far east as
possible".'[2]

Trade agreements forced on Kokand and Bukhara in 1868 gave

---

[1] N. A. Khalfin, *Russia's Policy in Central Asia, 1857–1868*. A condensed version of the
original Russian by Hubert Evans (Central Asian Reseach Centre, London, 1964), pp.
15–16.   [2] Ibid. p. 76.

Russia many privileges and powers which enabled her to oust the 'dreaded competitor' Great Britain from these markets. Trade agencies were established in both khanates, duty was fixed at 2.5 per cent. of the value of goods and not 5 per cent. as formerly, and the old restrictions on freedom of movement and residence were abolished for Russian citizens. Bukhara's inclusion in the Russian customs system in 1895 led to both a sharp rise in trade with Russia and a corresponding fall in the import of British goods from India. This ousting of foreign competitors from the Central Asian markets began much earlier. It was achieved by political pressure and other manœuvres and was of direct interest to the Russian economy rather than entirely profitable to the native peoples. According to the Soviet economic historian, M. K. Rozhkova, the importation of foreign goods was prohibited in the Turkestan kray when the Siberian and Orenburg customs lines were abolished in 1868.[1] When the British Ambassador in St. Petersburg remonstrated with the director of the Asiatic department in 1869 about these measures 'squeezing out' British trade in Central Asia, the latter replied: 'England permitted freedom of trade having attained her industrial "majority" but we are far from that stage yet and however pleasant it would be for us to favour England and her trade, the requirements of our own trade and industry must come first with us.'[2] Native handicrafts and home industries suffered from the influx of certain Russian manufactured goods, for example, cheap cotton textiles, but there was also a considerable range of other Russian consumer goods which were not produced locally, like iron pots and pans, which had a ready sale.

By the Russian treaty of 1873 with the khanate of Khiva, the right bank of the Amu Dar'ya was incorporated into Russia. Russians were granted exclusive rights of navigation on this river and duty-free trade—both were valuable concessions and denied automatically to their competitors. On the whole, however, this area was less affected by Russian economic penetration than either Bukhara or Kokand though Russian trade with Khiva increased in the latter years of the nineteenth century.

The over-all economic results of Tsarist Russia's policy in Central

[1] M. K. Rozhkova, *Ekonomicheskiye Svyazi Rossii so Sredney Aziey 40–60–e gody XIX veka* (Iz. AN SSSR, Moscow, 1963) p. 99.   [2] Ibid. p. 99.

Asia have been favourably assessed by Soviet economic historians for ideological reasons. 'As a result of Central Asia's union with Russia', writes Khalfin, 'the development of capitalist relations went ahead more quickly.... Railways were built, enterprises were founded for the primary processing of raw materials and the exploitation of mineral resources was developed. All this naturally led to the growth of the productive forces of the country and to the development of a local proletariat. ... All these were positive developments. ... The British of course introduced similar measures in their colonies. ...'[1] That was a very different matter seen from the Marx–Leninist approach to history. 'Soviet historians', he continued 'are of the definite opinion that for Central Asia to have become part of the British colonial dominions would have been the greatest possible disaster for its peoples.' The crucial difference, according to Khalfin, was that through their inclusion in the Tsarist Empire, the Central Asian peoples 'participated with the Russian people, with the Russian working class in the mighty forces of revolution'.[2] With a complete disregard for the facts of history, Khalfin stresses 'the militant alliance' between the Russians and the Central Asian peoples and 'the close union between the working masses of Central Asia and the proletariat of Russia'.[3]

COLONIZATION AND SETTLEMENT IN TURKESTAN

Colonization followed the Russian flag in Turkestan as in Siberia and the Far East. In Turkestan, the possibilities were limited by the nature of the terrain and to a certain extent by specialization in

[1] Khalfin, op. cit. pp. 79–80.

[2] So little had these Russian peasants and workers ingratiated themselves with the natives of the 'borderlands' that the Kirgiz and Kazakh massive rising in the eastern borderlands of the Empire in 1916 was largely directed against Russian peasants settled on their expropriated lands. The urban Russians of Tashkent, the centre of the revolutionary movement in 1917, showed their concern for 'the national minorities' by refusing to allow any Muslims to participate in local government or in the crucial Third Congress of Workers' and Peasants' Deputies in 1917–18. Native Muslim feeling towards the transfer of power to the Bolsheviks in October 1917 was reflected in the resolution of the Third all-Muslim Congress simultaneously held in Tashkent *expressing hostility to the October Revolution*. 'The cleavage between the native and the immigrant Russian population at the outbreak of the Revolution remained broad despite progressive Westernization under Russian rule', to quote Professor Richard Pipes's *The Formation of the Soviet Union* (Harvard University Press, Cambridge, Mass., 1964), pp. 191–2. This subject is discussed in detail in chapter IV of his book.   [3] Khalfin, op. cit. p. 4.

3. Demobilized servicemen working on housing construction in Angarsk (east Siberia)

4a. The *Akademgorodek* (Academic city), Novosibirsk

4b. Members of the *Akademgorodek*

Left to Right: Academician Budker—the nuclear physicist; Professor Voroshtsov—Director of the Institute of Organic Chemistry; Professor Belyaev—the geneticist; Academician Voyevodsky—the physical chemist (d. 1967)

agriculture. The great nomadic deserts stretched for hundreds of miles east of the Caspian and defied Russian settlement. The fertile oases were already thickly populated by the sedentary Central Asian peoples who grew cotton and food crops. Here there was little or no Russian peasant colonization, the settlers came from the Russian artisan and trading classes who flocked into the towns and were a considerable element in the railway depots. The situation was very different in the Semirech'ye where a mass movement of peasant colonists was organized following the construction of the Trans-Siberian railway at the turn of the century.[1] This policy, framed in St. Petersburg by officials with little personal knowledge of the area, appropriated enormous tracts of Kazakh–Kirgiz land for settlement and was extremely unpopular with the nomads. It is estimated that up to 1914 some 41 million desiatines of land had been appropriated for the 'Land Settlement Fund' in the Steppe Kray. This amounted in Semirech'ye alone to 2.4 million desiatines from the Kazakhs and up to 4 million desiatines from the Kirgiz according to Soviet estimates.[2]

Russian settlers in Central Asia in 1912 (excluding the khanates) are estimated to have amounted to about 2 million in the whole of the Steppe Region and Turkestan. The hardships inflicted on the Kirgiz and Kazakh nomads by these misguided colonization policies and the brutality of the corrupt officials who administered them were sharply condemned by Senator Count Pahlen in his official report on Semirech'ye in 1908–9.[3] Some decades later further details of this situation were given by the Soviet economist Lyashchenko: 'Such a plundering colonization policy of Tsarism had a devastating effect on the position of the Kazakh and Kirgiz population and economy. The Kirgiz population fell between 1903–13 in the colonized areas by 7–10 per cent. and the number of cattle fell on an average by 27 per cent. The stock-breeding economy of the Kazakhs, requiring big tracts of land, and the systematic skilful utilization of pasture suffered in particular.'[4] There is, incidentally, unconscious irony in this lament for nomadic stock-breeding from a Soviet Stalin prize winner who later averts his eyes from the havoc wrought

[1] P. G. Galuzo, *Agrarniye Otnosheniya na yuge Kazakhstana v 1867–1914* (Iz. 'Nauka', Alma-Ata, 1965).   [2] Lyashchenko, op. cit. p. 515.

[3] Count K. K. Pahlen, *Mission to Turkestan (1908–1909)* (Oxford University Press, London, 1964), p. 174.   [4] Lyashchenko, op. cit. p. 515.

D

to the Kazakh population and their herds by Soviet official denomadization settlement and collectivization policies. Retribution for the Tsarist expropriation and settlement policies came in the 'horrible blood-baths and the wholesale slaughter of entire settler villages by the natives' in 1916.[1] This rising, provoked by a call-up of natives for labour duties in the army during the war, provided an outlet for years of pent-up bitterness among the nomads against the Slav settlers on their lands. Thousands fled in panic to Chinese Turkestan. In Turkestan, the rising was followed by further seizures by the European settlers who controlled the local Soviets. The day of reckoning came some years later under the Soviet land reform. The 'predatory Great Russian kulaks' and 'kulak colonists' were condemned by the Soviet Government in 1920 when official steps were taken to expel them and return the expropriated lands to the native Kirgiz, Kazakh, and Uzbek committees.

Confiscation of land above 'labour norms', under the land reform, from *bays*, kulaks, and monasteries throughout the entire area of Semirech'ye and the other provinces of Turkestan was estimated to amount to 1,696,970 desiatines by 1922.[2] In Semirech'ye *oblast*, 'the chief area of colonization under Tsardom, 900,000 d. was taken from the settlers' and distributed among poor households of Uzbeks, Kazakhs, Kirgiz, and Russians. Kazakhs and Kirgiz who fled after the suppression of the 1916 revolt to China returned to the Soviet Union at this time and were settled on the land, 'some in old places, some in new'.[3]

COMMUNICATIONS AND TRANSPORT

The economic aims of the Russian administration of Turkestan and the new relationship with the khanates urgently called for better means of communication with the Empire than was provided by the old caravans over the Kazakh steppes and the waterless deserts of the south. A system of post-roads and horse-relay stations for passengers and mail linking the main centres of government and trade, for example, Tashkent–Kazalinsk–Orenburg, was

---

[1] Pahlen, op. cit. p. 193.

[2] A. Tulepbayev, *Znacheniye Agrarnoy Politiki Partii dlya Perekhoda Sredney Azii k Sotzializmy'. Voprosy Istorii KPSS*, no. 3 (1965).

[3] V. P. Sherstobitov, *NEP v Kirgizii* (Frunze, 1964), p. 204.

soon organized. Telegraphic contact with these remote regions was established in 1869.[1] The problem of faster, more efficient transport of bulky goods and in the first place of a railway soon claimed attention. Great interest was shown by both Russian and foreign engineers and financiers in the construction of the railway line between Turkestan and European Russia. Many alternative schemes were proposed to the Government, including Ferdinand de Lesseps's grandiose plan to construct a railway from Calais to Calcutta via Orenburg and Samarkand.

The Transcaspian, the first line in Central Asia, was eventually constructed by a Russian military engineer of genius, General Annenkov. Originally the main object of this Transcaspian line was strategic, the transport of troops and supplies through the waterless desert east of the Caspian in the campaign against the Teke–Turkmen tribes, and its construction was a feat of great technical ingenuity and physical endurance. It ran from Uzun Ada on the Caspian shores to Kizyl-Arvat and Chardzhou on the Amu Dar'ya (1881–6). Samarkand was reached in 1888 and Tashkent in 1898. A couple of decades later the Tashkent–Orenburg railway was completed which directly connected Turkestan with the European Russian network. As in the case of irrigation, several important railway projects were under consideration on the eve of the 1914 war and these later came to fruition in the Soviet period. The most notable of these were the railway planned to link Semirech'ye with the Trans-Siberian line (the origin of the famous Turk–Sib railway) and bring Siberian grain to the expanding cotton plantations of Central Asia, and the south Siberian railway to develop the agricultural and industrial resources of the Kazakh steppe. The majority of the skilled workers employed on these railways were Russians while the semi-skilled workers were recruited from the native peoples of the country.

---

[1] Cf. Pierce, op. cit. p. 182.

II

The Economic Development of the Eastern Regions under Tsardom

RAW MATERIAL RESOURCES

The eastern regions of the Empire, i.e. Siberia and the Far East, Central Asia, and Kazakhstan, contained vast and valuable resources of raw materials for the development of power and industry. But, broadly speaking, industrial development before the Revolution was confined to the mining of coal and some valuable non-ferrous metals (gold, copper, lead, and silver), processing of agricultural raw materials like cotton in Central Asia, grain and timber in Siberia, and a small number of plants for the construction of agricultural machinery and railway equipment. The state of economic development is reflected in the fact that in 1913 Siberia and Central Asia with Kazakhstan only represented 3.9 per cent. of Russia's industrial production though these areas covered 75 per cent. of Russian territory.[1] The size of the area and the degree of development of its potential resources were in striking imbalance.

Lenin described these areas as colonies of European Russia because their exports consisted almost entirely of raw materials and minerals while they relied for their supplies of manufactured goods on European Russia. Large quantities of cotton, wool, raw silk, and leather were annually shipped 3,000–4,000 miles from Central Asia to the industrial towns of central Russia and St. Petersburg where there was a high concentration of Russian light industry in the pre-revolutionary period. Quantities of these raw materials were in turn sent back to the areas of origin as finished goods. Moreover, discriminatory transport rates on the railways were enforced to favour the European Russian producers of cotton goods and grain.

[1] R. S. Livshits, *Razmeshcheniye Promyshlennosti v dorevolyutsionnoy Rossii* (Iz. AN SSR, Moscow, 1955), p. 232.

Thus the rail transport rate on raw cotton to supply the central Russian mills was low, but cheap Siberian high-quality grain was subject to the so-called 'Chelyabinsk Barrier' or high railway tariff to prevent it from competing successfully with the dearer grain produced in the European regions.

Various factors worked against the more rapid development of these potentially rich areas. There was a great lack of domestic capital and unwillingness to risk it in the remoter areas of the Empire. Distances were vast, population sparse in Asiatic Russia, and raw material deposits were only partially, unsystematically prospected. One Soviet economist estimates that only 10 per cent. of the entire country had been covered by geological survey during the Tsarist period. 'But', he added, 'we now have large-scale geological maps of almost the whole territory of the SSSR.'[1]

Foreign capital, which had played a leading role in the economic development of European Russia, was far less active in Asiatic Russia. There were, however, considerable foreign investments in Siberia's mining industries and to a lesser extent in agriculture. The Soviet view that 'under capitalism these regions were white spots on the industrial map of the Russian Empire' contained a grain of truth but was far from the whole story. It is unlikely that the huge capital investment required for the forced development of Siberia and Central Asia as precipitated by the Soviet Five Year Plans would have been forthcoming under their predecessors until many more years had passed. There is no reason to doubt, however, the intention to develop trans-Uralian resources in time, especially if the Tsarist autocracy had been followed by a more liberal government. There was a definite trend in that direction but it was prematurely disrupted by World War I.

STRUCTURE OF INDUSTRIAL PRODUCTION IN SIBERIA AND TURKESTAN

Mining and the preparation and processing of agricultural products—flour milling, butter, meat—were the main Siberian industries in Tsarist Russia.

[1] I. Troshev, *Planirovaniye Razmeshcheniya Promyshlennosti v SSSR* (Moscow, 1960), p. 26.

Structure of Industrial Production of Siberia in 1908

(in per cent. of gross output)

Industrial enterprises	West Siberian	East Siberian
Food	84.1	74.1
Processing animal products	4.3	3.1
Metals (including gold)	3.7	12.2
Timber	2.2	4.5
Miscellaneous	5.7	5.8

Source: Livshits, op. cit. p. 220.

Various selective estimates of the number of industrial enterprises in pre-revolutionary Turkestan have been published in Soviet sources based on statistical archive material not available in the West. These estimates tend to stress the limited industrial development of the area when Soviet critics are attacking Tsarist policy and to enlarge both the number of industrial enterprises and the numbers employed in them when the aim is rather to prove the existence of a 'politically conscious proletariat' as a force supporting the 1917 Revolution. Whichever estimate is correct, there is no doubt that Russian immigrants monopolized positions requiring skill and that ownership of the small factory-mill industry was concentrated in Great Russian hands.[1] The lower estimates of the industrial proletariat, an example of which is given in the following table, are now challenged on the score that they were almost exclusively based on incomplete data which did not cover the whole of Turkestan or the extractive industries, such as coal, oil, salt, and fish.[2] This seems to be true, though in a tricky matter like selective statistics it is impossible to know exactly what the complete picture would be until all the available information is published.

According to the more complete statistical coverage shown in the table following, the number of factory-type enterprises engaged in the

[1] A. Park, *Bolshevism in Turkestan, 1917–1927* (Columbia University Press, New York, 1957) p. 254.

[2] R. A. Nurullin, 'On the Question of the Numbers of Industrial Enterprises and of the Working Class in Pre-Revolutionary Turkestan', *Obshchestvennyye Nauki v Uzbekistane*, no. 8 (1965).

Structure of Industry in Turkestan in 1914

Branch	Number of enterprises	Value of production in 000 roubles	Number of workers
Cotton ginning	197	96,177	7,626
Cotton oil pressing	19	12,381	1,720
Milling	46	3,982	472
Cocoon drying	28	3,136	2,198
Leather factories	72	324	422
Miscellaneous	340	16,887	8,487
Total	702	132,887	20,925

Source: Livshits, op. cit. p. 227.

Enterprises	Fergana	Syr Dar'ya	Samarkand	Transcaspian	Semirech'ye	Total for kray
Cotton ginning	167	41	31	15	—	254
Cotton wadding	3	6	—	—	—	9
Oil mills	18	3	5	56	2	84
Cocoon drying	27	—	1	—	—	28
Pomegranate	11	—	—	—	—	11
Tanneries	11	36	14	6	64	133
Soap	9	25	2	9	—	45
Entrail cleaning	5	5	3	9	4	26
Wool washing	—	4	1	—	12	17
Brick	9	7	4	—	—	20
Flour mills	17	21	5	16	6	65
Alcohol distilling	4	6	3	—	5	18
Distilleries and viniculture	2	6	24	4	3	40
Breweries	6	10	1	3	11	31
Typography and lithography	10	12	3	6	5	36
Electric stations	13	13	5	12	2	45
Others	30	80	32	25	32	199
Total	342	275	134	161	146	1061

Source: Nurullin, op. cit. p. 59.

processing industry of Turkestan should be 1,061 rather than 702 (or 852), the hitherto commonly accepted figure.

The extraction industries had also made some progress in Turkestan. In 1913 there were twenty-eight coal mines, more than ten oilfields, three copper mines, eight salt works, and several ozocerite quarries, as well as a considerable number of fisheries and a large number of small enterprises working in these fields. The latest estimate of the numbers employed in all these activities, many of which, no doubt, were of a handicraft nature, is 33,600, 28,079 in processing industry, and 5,408 in extractive industries.[1] Both the higher and the lower estimates show that far the greatest number of workers were employed in cotton-ginning plants. Thus though industrial development had not got beyond a rudimentary stage in Central Asia, the knowledge of simple tools and machines must have been pretty widespread in the towns among the settled native peoples. Their great skill in a wide range of handicrafts must also have been a useful lead-in to handling different materials and tools when introduced to industry after the Revolution.

COTTON

The acquisition of a cheap domestic source of cotton together with the now captive market of Turkestan were among the most valuable fruits of the Russian conquest. Before the 1860s only a relatively small percentage of Russia's raw cotton supplies came from Central Asia (7–10 per cent.), the main suppliers being the United States of America, India, and Egypt. The American Civil War in 1861 cut off American stocks and Russian manufacturers then turned towards Central Asia to supply the deficiency. Central Asian cotton was of coarser, inferior quality to American but it was cheaper. In the first years after the establishment of the Turkestan kray, the efforts of the Russian administration to improve quality met with little success but strains and cultivation were gradually greatly improved. As the Central Asian cotton was cheaper and trade conditions had so much improved, Russian merchants tried as far as possible to use it instead of the more expensive Egyptian and American varieties. Thus a sort of Central Asian cotton market was created which scarcely existed previously. By the end of the

[1] Nurullin, op. cit. p. 59.

century Turkestan was supplying 80 per cent. of Russia's raw cotton. Short staple cotton which had previously been grown in Central Asia was gradually replaced by good-quality American upland cotton. Cultivation was almost entirely in the hands of the Central Asian natives who had grown it with skill for centuries. The Russian peasant immigrants grew other crops such as grain outside the areas specifically suited to cotton cultivation in Bukhara and the Fergana Valley. Expansion of the cotton area was encouraged by the Tsarist administration through tax adjustments, favourable credit policy, attractive prices. As a result, it has been estimated from incomplete data that the area under cotton in Turkestan and the Bukhara and Khiva khanates increased from 41,400 to 541,900 desiatines between 1885 and 1915.[1] In Bukhara alone, the raw cotton exported to Russia rose from 410,000 poods in 1880 to 2,264,000 poods in 1915, and the total export from Central Asia in 1910 was over 3,500,000 poods.[2] This increase was typical of all the cotton-growing areas of Central Asia.

All Central Asian cotton was manufactured in the mills of central Russia or used for local handwoven cloth. No cotton mill existed in Turkestan or the khanates before the Revolution. Various arbitrary measures were taken by Russian manufacturers to protect their interests in the old textile regions of Russia and prevent the establishment of a competitive cotton industry in Turkestan and in this matter they had the full support of the Tsarist administration.[3] Nevertheless, there was a section of the merchant-manufacturers who saw the advantages of creating a local industry to compete with British goods in the neighbouring markets of Persia and Afghanistan. It was estimated that cotton manufactured in Central Asia would be cheaper because of the elimination of transport costs on the raw cotton to and finished goods from central Russia. But these arguments remained on paper, no cotton mills were established before the Revolution, and only cotton ginning developed.

IRRIGATION

In the arid regions of Central Asia, irrigation was an essential factor for enlarging the cotton plantations and the success of the

---

[1] Lyashchenko, op. cit. vol. II, p. 543.   [2] Holdsworth, op. cit. p. 20.
[3] Livshits, op. cit. p. 20.

expanding cotton market. Since time immemorial the Central Asian deserts had been rendered fertile by means of irrigation schemes and the native peoples had developed great skill in 'water economy'. The Russians realized that their plan of making Central Asia the cotton base of the Empire, thereby considerably reducing their foreign currency expenditure on imported cotton, depended on an active irrigation policy. This required both careful technical planning and considerable capital expenditure. Unlike their Soviet successors, the Tsarist administration did not interfere with the 'customary law' governing the crucial matter of water utilization, though they did retain control of some large new irrigation systems and the general direction of irrigation. The total area of irrigated land in Central Asia in 1910 (including Khiva and Bukhara) is estimated at about 4,758,000 desiatines, 'an insignificant result' according to the Soviet historian Lyashchenko and only representing 2.6 per cent. of the total area.[1] The irrigation problem was certainly not solved by 1914 but a great deal more interest was taken in it by the Tsarist administration than Soviet economists care to admit.

The Grand Duke Nikolay Konstantinovich, then living in exile in Tashkent, organized the first successful canals in the Hungry Steppe. The Murgab Imperial Domain was a large ambitious scheme of irrigation and reclamation in the desert lands along the Murgab River to which the Emperor Alexander III laid claim after the annexation of the Merv oasis. By 1914 it contained about 104,000 desiatines of land of which about 25,000 were under irrigation and growing cotton, cereals, and leguminous crops; the greater part of these lands were farmed by the natives. Some 11,000 natives and 4,000 Russians lived and worked in the Domain before World War I as lessees of the Tsar; Bayram-Ali, the administrative centre was laid out as a model village complete with a hospital, telegraph station, and electrically lit houses for the employees.[2] Russian engineers were keenly interested in the irrigation possibilities and problems of this area and a considerable expansion of irrigated land might have been expected if the projects then in the air had not been frustrated by the outbreak of war in 1914. Many of these plans remained in official pigeon-holes and in time formed the basis of such major Soviet

[1] Lyashchenko, op. cit. vol. II, p. 540.   [2] Pierce, op. cit. pp. 178–9.

irrigation projects as the Hungry Steppe[1] and the Great Kara-Kum Canal.

FUEL AND POWER

Since the days of Peter the Great there had been considerable interest in expanding the range of mineral 'treasures', from gold and other precious metals to coal, ferrous and non-ferrous minerals in Asiatic Russia. A good deal had been discovered about the location of major mineral deposits and in the first place about the coal pits of west Siberia, the Altay, and the Kazakh steppes since the eighteenth century. Siberian coal production was pushed up to supply the Trans-Siberian railway from the beginning of the twentieth century. Bituminous coal was known to exist in large quantities, but production methods were primitive and exports small and hampered by the lack of local communications. On the whole it did little more than satisfy local demand. The major deposits known in 1913 were at Kuznetsk, Cheremkhovo (opened up in 1898 for the railway), and Ekibastuz in north-east Kazakhstan.

Production of Coal in Siberia, 1897–1917

(in 000 tons)

Year	Cheremkhovo	Kuznetsk	Minusinsk	Total for Siberia
1897	—	10.0	—	10.0
1907	465.4	481.0	—	946.4
1913	470.3	773.8	21.4	1,265.5
1917	1,259.1	1,257.4	45.9	2,562.4

Source: cf. R. S. Livshits, op. cit. p. 223.

Farther east the deposits of bituminous and anthracite coals at Suchan in the Primor'ye were mined in small quantities for domestic purposes while the large brown coal deposits of Kamchatka were not exploited before the Revolution. In the fuel balance of the Empire, coal from Asiatic Russia was an insignificant quantity; the great Kuzbas coalfields, for example, only produced 3 per cent. of the

[1] *Osvoyeniye Golodnoy Stepi* (Moscow, 1963).

total Russian coal supply in 1913 compared to the 87 per cent. from the Donbas. This resulted in extremely long rail and water hauls of Donetz coal throughout the Empire. The lop-sided development of the Tsarist coal industry was also to a certain extent influenced by the domination of the fuel balance of the country by wood which formed 55–60 per cent. of the fuel consumption. As a result, the seemingly inexhaustible supply of timber reserves around the European towns had already been seriously depleted by 1913.

The concentration of production just noted in the case of coal was even more marked in the oil industry where over 97 per cent. of total Russian production came from the Caucasus, i.e. Baku, Maykop, and Grozny wells. Considerable oil deposits were known to exist in Central Asia but production in the Fergana, Emba (west Kazakhstan), and other Central Asian deposits was an insignificant quantity in the country's oil supply. No oil was known to exist in the Urals, Siberia, or the Far East apart from Sakhalin at this time. There seems to be good cause for the charges of manipulation of prices and supply by the Baku oil interests in order to maintain their monopolistic position on the Russian market and prevent development in Turkestan. In his memoirs[1] Count Pahlen tells an unpleasant story, from first-hand experience in Turkestan (1908–9), of the machinations of the Baku oil companies—Nobel, Mazut, Rothschild, and Lyanozov—against the young Turkestani oil industry. The Chimion oil wells in the Fergana area were doing well, he relates, under the management of two enterprising railway engineers. A pipeline had been built to the nearest railway station as well as a refinery to extract petrol and paraffin. The Chimion Company had secured a contract from the Central Asian railway for the delivery of fuel oil at 25 kopecks per pood of oil. This price was a boon to the railways which were previously paying the Nobel Company 50–54 kopecks for fuel hauled all the way from Baku across the Caspian. A second oil-producing district was also opened up at Namangan in spite of the opposition of the Baku industrialists. A third oil-bearing district which later proved the most productive was located at Cheleken Island in the Caspian. As a result of strikes and labour-production problems the Chimion oil industry fell on evil days. Then, in Pahlen's words, the large Baku oil companies 'struck like a

[1] Pahlen, op. cit. pp. 113–16.

shark', acquired a majority holding of the Chimion shares, and turned Chimion into a branch of the parent company in Baku. The Central Asian market was thus secured for the more expensive Baku oil and Chimion production was reduced to the minimum 100 poods per annum required by Russian law. The Fergana wells were allowed to stagnate artificially for the rest of the Tsarist period. The statistics in the following table for Fergana oil production in 1913 must therefore be assessed against this background:

Oil Production in Asiatic Russia,
1913

(in metric tons)

Far Eastern province (Sakhalin)	—
Ural–Emba region	117,641
Fergana	23,301
Transcaspian	129,500

Source: *Godovoy Obzor Mineral'nykh Resursov SSSR za 1925–26* (Leningrad, 1927) p. 652.

The spectacular development of electric power in Siberia before and especially after the last war has now largely obscured the story of its origins in the last century.[1] There is therefore a certain historical interest in excavating the details of how electricity first appeared in the mines and towns of Siberia, even though the economic results were on the whole meagre. Up to 1913 electrification had made relatively little progress in Tsarist Russia and was heavily concentrated in a few large cities of European Russia like St. Petersburg and Moscow. The position in Asiatic Russia reflected the low level of industrial development throughout the area. Still, Siberia had some remarkable electrification records to its credit which do not appear in the insignificant statistics of pre-Soviet Siberian electric power production and are worth recalling.

The first industrial hydro-electric station in Russia (based on the River Berezovka) was built at the Zyryanovsk mine in the Altay in

[1] *Predposylki Oktyabr'skoy Revolyutsii v Sibiri*, op. cit. V. V. Aleksiyev, *Pervyye Elektrostantsii v Sibiri*, pp. 243–53.

1892—a mine belonging to the imperial properties—and was a great success. Electric power was soon extended from the mining operations to the funicular railway and the plant for electrolysis of copper and silver. Living and working quarters at the mines were lit by electricity which was much cheaper and better than the former primitive lighting. The Altay mining industry was thus one of the first in Russia to use electrolysis for ore extraction and electrical mining discharge in the mines. A more powerful hydro-electric station was built in 1901 by the 'foreign capitalists' who now owned these mines, as the original station proved unequal to supply the mine's energy requirements.

The Lena gold industry soon followed up the initiative of the Altay. The mines, which were scattered over a large area, received the first current from a hydro-electric station based on the waters of the Nygra River in 1896, and were then linked by a high-voltage line. Thus the remote taiga of north Siberia was the site of Russia's first high-voltage line. The equipment for these progressive developments was supplied by German firms, but the first director of the station was a Russian engineer, A. K. Koksharov (who may also have supervised the construction of the Altay hydro-electric station). The Lena station was used for the electrification of the railway removing waste earth and the Lena gold mines were credited with being the first to employ an electric locomotive in the gold industry. Encouraged by this success, five hydro-electric stations were built on the Bodaybo River between 1900 and 1914. The total capacity of these six stations was 2,500 kW., at a time when the total capacity of all hydro-electric stations of Tsarist Russia was 16,000 kW., i.e. the Lena gold-fields accounted for about 15 per cent. of Tsarist Russia's capacity. They were the most highly electrified branch of the economy in pre-revolutionary Siberia and managed to keep the hydro-electric power stations going throughout the year. As a reserve against fluctuating hydro-current in the Siberian freeze-up, a thermal power station of 600 kW. was built and worked on one grid with the Bodaybo HES—this was the first attempt in Russia to unite electric power stations in an energy system.

From the beginning of the twentieth century electricity began to appear in the coal and salt industries of Siberia. The first record of the employment of electric motors is in 1901 in the Cheremkhovo coal basin, near Irkutsk. The pits were connected with Cheremkhovo railway station by an electric locomotive and later by an electric tram. Following the initiative of the mining industry, electricity gradually penetrated other branches of Siberian industry but did not play a significant role in this field until after the Revolution. In rural districts power was limited to some distilleries, butter factories, and mills.

It was natural that electrification should make most progress in the mining industry, which was itself the most important industry in Siberia. The development of electric power by the municipal authorities was slow, and enterprising businessmen were in many cases ahead of them. The question of constructing municipal electrical stations for general purposes arose comparatively early in Siberia, about the same time as they were appearing in London, Paris, and St. Petersburg. The proposal to give Irkutsk electric light was mooted in 1886 but fell through for lack of funds. The first Siberian municipal central electrical station for general purposes was built in 1895 in Tomsk with a capacity of 200 kW. Similar stations came into operation between 1899 and 1908 in Biysk, Chita, Sretensk, Verkhne-Udinsk, Kansk, and Tyumen'. The construction of electric power stations in Siberia as elsewhere in Tsarist Russia was much delayed by the lack of electric–technical equipment and well-qualified specialists. The need was especially acute in Siberia. The Irkutsk (1908) and Krasnoyarsk (1912) stations were built by the respective municipal *dumas* using Russian technicians and foreign equipment. The poor performance of both aroused much local criticism. The Krasnoyarsk newspaper *Sibirskaya Mysyl* wrote ' . . . the inhabitants are not fully satisfied. They expected that bright electric light would illuminate their streets but it did not happen. The weak twinkle of small electric bulbs is insufficient. . . . The inhabitants are disappointed.'[1] A number of thermal electric stations were constructed between 1912 and 1915, the largest of which was at Yakutsk, in the frozen earth of north-eastern Siberia. By the introduction of electric power, Yakutsk was at last relieved of the heavy burden of the age-old 'kerosene crisis' caused by the difficulties and expense of transporting oil products to the wilds of Yakutia.

[1] *Predposylki Oktyabr'skoy Revolyutsii v Sibiri*, op. cit. p. 246.

Before being utilized in industry, electricity was used in Siberia for domestic lighting and largely provided by enterprising local businessmen to boost trade in their shops and warehouses. They often entered this field before the municipal authorities, hampered by conservatism and red-tape, were prepared to follow suit. The first Siberian electric station began to operate in Krasnoyarsk, a go-ahead mid-Siberian trade centre, in the 1880s at the same time as the first stations appeared in St. Petersburg. It lit the residential quarters and shops of the merchant Gadalov and served as a kind of advertisement for his business. Street lighting was introduced in Irkutsk, 'the capital of Siberia', by a prosperous local merchant, A. Vtorov, in 1896. Other private entrepreneurs then began to specialize in the production of electrical power and undertook the lighting of the Irkutsk General Assembly building and the Dramatic Theatre and the adjacent area of the city. Competition in this field was keen. In 1910 it is estimated that there were six small private electric stations in Krasnoyarsk, at least ten in Irkutsk, and even more in Tomsk. Subsequently their role diminished with the development of municipally owned and operated stations.

In connexion with the construction of the Trans-Siberian railway, a number of electric stations were built at important junctions such as Omsk, Krasnoyarsk, Irkutsk, and Chita, in 1896–1907.

The great water-power resources of the Siberian rivers, the Irtysh, the Ob', the Yenisey, the Angara, and the Lena, were frequently studied pre-1913, but mainly from the point of view of transport; relatively little thought was given to their utilization for power.

In Russian Turkestan, electric power was in a rudimentary state of development before the Revolution. The great water-power resources of the southern regions of Central Asia now known as Tadzhikistan and Kirgizia had not been studied even to the meagre extent of Siberian power. The total capacity of all the small stations in Russian Turkestan was 3,000 kW. and the largest power unit was one erected by Belgian engineers to drive the Tashkent trams. There was only one 'dwarf' power station (50 kW.) in the whole of the Bukhara emirate and that was attached to the emir's summer palace.[1]

---

[1] *Narodnoye Khozyaystvo Sredney Azii*, no. 9 (1965), p. 19.

Uzbekistan's contribution to the total Russian output of 1,949 million kWh. of electric power was only 3.3 million kWh., and the total capacity of all electric stations in Russian Turkestan was 3,000 kW.[1] The situation was thus ripe for the expansion of electric power which, as will be shown below, was initiated in the first Soviet planned period, pre-war, in the Central Asian republics.

MINERALS AND METALLURGY

Iron had been mined in the Urals since the days of Peter the Great and earlier. And up to the last quarter of the nineteenth century, before the discovery of a method of producing pig-iron with mineral fuel, the Urals were the chief and practically the only base of ferrous metallurgy in Russia. But subsequently this industry, with its charcoal fuel base in default of local coking coal, primitive equipment, and the low productivity of its badly paid workers, rapidly declined in favour of the better equipped and organized new metallurgical industry of the south based on Krivog Rog iron ore and Donbas coal.[2]

The east Siberian iron works at Petrovsk-Zabaykal'skiy, Abakan, and Nikolayevsk on the River Angara were even more primitive and of purely local significance at this time, though the natural resources for development existed in valuable iron and coal deposits. At their maximum production in 1898 these Siberian mines only produced 10,000 tons of metal.[3] Pre-1913, there were at least two schemes to develop a metallurgical industry based on Kuznetsk coal on the lines later adopted by the Soviets, using Kuzbas coal and local iron ore, but neither came to anything. The second scheme arose in 1913 from the concession of 'cabinet lands' in the Kuzbas granted to a company backed by foreign capital: the Kuznetsk coal mines limited company. It planned to develop the valuable Kuzbas coal mines and build a metallurgical plant.[4] This scheme was eventually revived after the Revolution in the form of the Soviet West Siberian Iron and Steel Works.

---

[1] Cf. *Central Asian Review*, vol. I, no. 3, p. 28.
[2] S. S. Balzak, *Economic Geography of the USSR*, translated from the Russian by Chauncy D. Harris (Macmillan, New York, 1949), pp. 117–22.
[3] Livshits, op. cit. p. 222.   [4] Ibid. p. 222.

E

The non-ferrous mining industry, especially the mining of gold and copper, was better and more widely developed in the eastern regions than the mining of ferrous deposits. It had attracted a considerable amount of foreign capital in the nineteenth and early twentieth centuries. In 1727 a member of the well-known Russian merchant family Demidov started to work the rich Altay copper and silver deposits and built smelters under state franchise. Some years later an Englishman named Philip Ridder, who had been working the Crown mines as an overseer, discovered very rich silver and lead mines near Ust'-Kamenogorsk in the Altay at a place now known as Leninogorsk which long bore his name and is still a major producing area.

Early in the nineteenth century Siberian merchants began to buy mining properties in north and east Kazakhstan and to work them in a rather rudimentary fashion. In this way mines of note like the Uspenskiy and Dzhezkazgan copper mines and the Karaganda coal mine were bought for derisory sums from the nomadic Kazakh owners. The Russians, however, were not successful in this field and some of the best mines in central and north Kazakhstan, including the Spasskiy–Dzhezkazgan–Akbazar properties, were sold in 1905 to a British concessionary group, the Spasskiy Copper Mine Company. The Spasskiy group also worked the Karaganda colliery, which provided coal for ore smelting and mining purposes. It was situated about twenty-six miles from Spasskiy on the Petropavlovsk road. British investments played a major role in the non-ferrous industry of Tsarist Russia amounting to 70 per cent. in the gold–platinum and 56 per cent. in the copper industries. The enterprises in which British capital was invested were mostly located in the eastern regions.[1] Owing to Russian legal requirements these companies were usually mixed and were obliged to have Russian managers as well as foreign managers, the former being legally in charge while as a rule the latter were in actual control of mining staff and operations.

Soviet propaganda consistently rails about conditions in these pre-revolutionary, foreign-run mines and attacks the companies for receiving high profits 'as a result of the merciless exploitation of workers who frequently fought to improve their conditions'.

[1] *Predposylki Oktyabr'skoy Revolyutsii v Sibiri.*

The various extant accounts by former foreign managers and engineers of life in these mines go far to disprove these charges and to show that the Russian officials were much more insistent on regulations being observed by the foreigners than by Russian mine owners. A British engineer, Mr. Wardell, who worked in the Spasskiy mining settlements, has written a detailed account of life at Spasskiy.[1] It is worth recalling because Mr. Wardell's patent sincerity gives the lie to Soviet clamour about how these properties were run. Spasskiy had a population of about 3,000 in 1914, of which 1,500 Kazakhs and 300 Russians worked for the company. The British staff numbered 18. It was a self-contained little place with Russian and foreign staff quarters, a Russian church, a bazaar, a school, a hospital, and a 'Tatar Traders' settlement'. In view of the remoteness of the mines from the Trans-Siberian railway and centres of supply, the concessionaires provided many amenities for the workers. They also had a farm to supply oats and hay for the transport animals. Living was cheap and all servants of the company, both staff and workmen, had free quarters, light, coal, water, and medical attendance. They were able to make most of their purchases at the company stores where goods were supplied wholesale plus 10 per cent. to cover expenses. This does not sound exorbitant and is far from the usual Soviet charge of 'exploitation of the workers' through the company's stores and supplies.

After the British took over the copper mine at Uspenskiy, systematic development and exploration of the deposits was started. The high-grade ore was smelted at Spasskiy, and a mill was erected at Sary Su to treat the low-grade ore, and a reverberatory furnace built at Spasskiy to smelt the concentrate. The smelting plant was thus capable of producing 410 tons of copper per month. From 1909 to 1914 approximately 149,000 tons of ore averaging 19 per cent. copper were raised and 21,815 tons of copper produced from the rich Uspenskiy mine. It was already recognized that the Karaganda colliery was exceptionally large and rich but at this time when there was no railway in the vicinity, as there is now, it was only worked by the Russian and British owners for the requirements of the mining camps and produced about 80,000 tons annually.

[1] John Wilford Wardell, *In the Kirghiz Steppes* (The Galley Press, London, 1961).

The claim areas of the company's properties were:

Uspenskiy copper mine	9.80 square miles
Sary Su concentrator	1.75 square miles
Sasik Kara Su iron area	1.75 square miles
Karaganda colliery	22 square miles
Spasskiy smelting works, etc.	46.20 square miles
Total area of five claims	81.50 square miles

The Sary Su concentration plant built in 1916 was the first of its kind in this area. The company also operated the Atbazar property some 500 miles south-west of Uspenskiy, comprising the great Dzhezkazgan copper mine, one of the richest in the world, and a colliery at Baykonur. Obscure Baykonur has now become famous as the launching site in 1960 of the first Soviet astronaut. The company was virtually self-supporting, as iron ore and limestone for flux, and quartz and fireclay for all kinds of bricks were also to be found within their claims. The only imports were machinery and technical supplies and manufactured goods for domestic purposes.

Mr. Wardell's opinion of the Russian and Kazakh workmen employed by his company on the eve of the Revolution is of interest: 'The Kazakhs had a large capacity for work if it were on contract, otherwise they were much inferior to the Russians. Some however were ambitious and capable and if put into positions of trust they were very reliable and got the last ounce of work out of their men.'

Gold had been mined since ancient times in Asiatic Russia. Commercial production started in the 1870s in the Barguzin district of the Buryat-Tungus taiga. Unlike other mining industries, the gold industry was relatively well organized pre-1913 and Asiatic Russia supplied much the largest part of Russian gold, or 83 per cent. of the total Russian output of 37,486 kg.[1] The Lena gold-fields headed the list of gold-mining concerns; output was 14,256 kg. in 1914 according to academician Obruchev.[2] This enterprise controlled mining properties in the Altay and the Urals, but its major interests were in the gold-fields stretching for hundreds of

[1] *Godovoy Obzor Mineral'nykh Resursov SSSR*, op. cit.
[2] *Sibirskaya Sovetskaya Entsiklopediya* (Zapadno-Sibirskoye Otdeleniye Ogiz, Moscow, 1932), vol. 3, p. 81.

miles north of Barguzin on Lake Baykal, the headquarters of the industry, to the Bodaybo deposits on the River Vitim (a tributary of the Lena), 1,200 miles from Irkutsk, where 7,000 workers were employed in 1913–14.[1]

There were many smaller gold-fields in Siberia, for example, 'Yenisey Gold' and in the Far East the Bureya and Zeyskiy fields which were worked by more primitive methods. The small enterprises in the Far East contained a large number of Chinese 'adventurer prospectors' who often succeeded in smuggling gold out of the country. The Lena–Vitim gold industry was worked on a very different commercial scale. It operated its own building and transport organizations including the Bodaybo railway. It had a complicated existence both before and after the Revolution (when a new and short-lived concession was granted to an English company by the Soviet Government in 1925).[2] It started its operations as a Russian limited liability company, 'The Lena Gold Industry', in 1896. As this company was unable to provide the necessary financial capital for development, an English company was duly registered to operate the mines and sell the products. A further reorganization took place in 1908 when, with a considerable increase of capital (£1,405,000), the 'Lena Gold-Fields Corporation' was formed.[3]

An excellent account of conditions in the Lena mining camps and life in Barguzin is given by a former member of this mining community, Mr. M. A. Novomeysky, in his fascinating book, *My Siberian Life*.[4] According to Mr. Novomeysky gold was extracted in a primitive manner and the first dredger only reached the Lena gold-fields in 1914 after an extraordinary journey by sea, river, road, and train from England. He noted that the dredgers already operating in the gold-fields of Australia, New Zealand, and California, and even in the Yenisey region, never had to tackle frozen soil (permafrost) such as existed throughout the Lena gold-fields. The introduction of mechanical methods was thus extremely complicated in the Barguzin region, but the difficulties were eventually overcome and the dredger, combined with boilers, steam-spraying

[1] Ibid. p. 82.
[2] S. A. Bernstein, *The Financial and Economical Results of the Working of the Lena Goldfields Co. Ltd.* (The Blackfriars Press, London, 1930).
[3] Lyashchenko, op. cit. pp. 367–8.
[4] M. A. Novomeysky, *My Siberian Life* (Max Parrish, London, 1956), pp. 112–19.

equipment, and everything needed for washing the gold sludge and extracting the precious metal, was in order by the end of 1914. The mine managers had learned how to cope with the harsh climate and lived in 'excellent well-maintained houses' (thus putting to shame the conditions and especially the housing in many Soviet mining camps some decades later).

The difficulties experienced at various times by the Lena gold-fields were largely caused by the complicated position in which they were placed by Russian legislation which forbade foreign companies to work mineral resources. This prohibition was sidetracked by the creation of a fictitious Russian concern and the transfer of its shares to an English holding company. A Russian agent had to be appointed with full powers of attorney to satisfy Russian officialdom. The result was that in practice two authorities controlled foreign companies in Russia, the foreign board residing in the foreign country concerned, which represented the interests supplying the capital and receiving their share of profits, and the Russian agents or board on the spot, which alone was legally recognized by the Russian authorities, and thus was responsible in the eyes of the Russian Government for the management and administration of the company. The Lena Gold-Fields Company has been savagely attacked by the Soviets as a British capitalist concern for exploitation of the workers and the unhappy events of the 1912 riot and massacre.[1] The real cause of the trouble, the responsible Russian officials who had systematically underpaid and ill-housed their employees and bribed the local officials to keep quiet about their misdoings, is never identified in these attacks. When the outraged workers at last came out on strike against these abuses of the law, the Russian officials requested the local military forces to crush the revolt. This they did most ruthlessly. The British board had, of course, a moral obligation to see how things were run in the Lena gold-fields but they were far away and thus full responsibility for the bloody events of 1912[2] can scarcely be laid at their door as it usually is in Soviet writing.

Another British company which operated on the same lines as the

---

[1] *Bol'shaya Sovetskaya Entsiklopediya*, cf. article on the 'Lena Gold-Fields'; *Sibirskaya Sovetskaya Entsiklopediya*, cf. article, 'Lenskiye Sobytiya', p. 67.

[2] Price, op. cit. pp. 242–5.

Lena Gold-Fields was the Russo-Asiatic Corporation. It was established in 1913 with a basic capital of £300,000 to finance the operation of the Nerchinsk lead–zinc–silver mines, the Ridder lead–silver mines in the Altay, and the Ekibastuz coal properties on the Irtysh River. War and revolution soon brought its activities to an end.

Far south of Siberia in the Chinese borderlands of present-day Kirgizia, beyond Osh, many valuable minerals were reported to exist, though the area had not yet been geologically surveyed. 'The earth here is so full of treasures that any enterprising man could easily make his fortune', a local prospector told Count Pahlen during an inspection tour of the area.[1] Pahlen himself actually visited a cave of high-quality uranium deep in the mountains above Osh. The ore was brought in containers to St. Petersburg where the uranium was separated from the other components. For the rest there were many reported sources of gold and other precious metals throughout Turkestan, but prospecting pre-1913 had done little more than scratch the surface of the considerable mineral wealth which lay buried in the ground.

PRE-SOVIET DEVELOPMENT PROJECTS

The Soviet thesis that the natural resources of Asiatic Russia were not and could not be developed by 'Tsarist capitalism' leaves out of account the progress made by the Tsarist economy as a whole during the last decades of the Tsarist régime with the assistance of foreign capital and expertise and its emergence as a 'developed' economy. The interest shown by Russian and foreign banking groups in railway construction projects east of the Urals reflects the growing awareness at home and abroad of the great economic possibilities of this area and belief in its future. In 1909, for example, the following main railway projects were under consideration (and later provided the technical basis for many Soviet constructions): Ural'sk–Semipalatinsk–Barnaul–Biysk (2155 versts); Orenburg–Semipalatinsk–Barnaul–Biysk (2395 versts); Omsk–Pavlodar–Semipalatinsk–Barnaul (1135 versts); Novo-Nikolayevsk (Novosibirsk)–Barnaul–Semipalatinsk (762 versts); Arys-Vernyy (Alma-Ata)–

[1] Pahlen, op. cit. pp. 110-11.

Tokmak (1029 versts); Turkestan–Siberian line (partly constructed pre-1917).[1]

There were also plans for the development of a metallurgical industry in mid-Siberia based on Kuznetsk coal. As has been shown the gold industry in Siberia and the Urals was thriving while foreign capital was actively interested in the poly-metallic mines (in the first place copper) of the Altay and Kazakhstan. Russian engineers were working on electrification schemes in Siberia and planning further irrigation in Turkestan so as to expand the area of arable land for crops and in particular cotton, while many learned tomes had been and were being written by Russian scientists about the natural resources of both areas. Though prospecting and exploration of the Asian territories were still far from complete, much sound work had been done in this field before the Revolution.

Siberia's poorly developed manufacturing industry contrasted strongly with the growing prosperity of Siberian market towns like Omsk, Tomsk, Irkutsk, Krasnoyarsk, Barnaul, or Tyumen', where trade in agricultural products was brisk and flourishing until it was destroyed by war and revolution. The 'dormant colossus' was stirring, albeit slowly. Even if the Soviets had not come to power there are good grounds for believing that Siberian industry would have developed under the impetus of the go-ahead Sibiryaki, not perhaps at the pace made possible by the ruthless Soviet methods of capital accumulation and political coercion, but more gradually, normally, and probably with the assistance of Western capital.

[1] G. Cleinow, *Neu-Siberien* (Verlag von Reimar Hobbing, Berlin, 1928), p. 55.

PART TWO

The Economic Development of Central Asia and Kazakhstan under the Soviets (1917-45)

III

The Soviet Approach to the Development of the Eastern Regions (1917-45)

THE POLITICAL–ECONOMIC BACKGROUND

After the collapse of Tsardom in 1917, the economic life of Siberia and Central Asia[1] was disrupted by civil war and revolution. The strife was particularly bitter in Central Asia where the Russian Bolsheviks, the spearhead of the Revolution, met strong racial-religious opposition to their concepts of government, social relations, industrialization, and collectivization from the native Turkic-Muslim peoples. It is not necessary here to retrace the early history of the Sovietization of Central Asia by which native institutions and the native pattern of economic life were destroyed. It is not directly relevant to this study, and has been admirably done by others.[2] But it is important to clarify the peculiar relationship between the centre and the periphery of the Soviet Union, i.e. 'the Eastern borderlands', as a result of which it was possible to launch areas of more or less rudimentary economic development into the general pattern of Soviet industrialization in a few decades.

The all-Union Constitution of 1924 contained a number of measures of crucial importance for the shape of things to come in the eastern regions as elsewhere in the Soviet Union. The old administrative divisions of Central Asia were replaced by the Uzbek SSR and the Turkmen SSR which thus became fully fledged Union republics; the Kazakh and Kirgiz autonomous republics of the RSFSR (which only attained full republican status in 1936); and

[1] Central Asia is the usual English term for the area known in Russian as 'Srednyaya Aziya' or Middle Asia covering the Soviet republics of Uzbekistan, Tadzhikistan, Kirgizia, and Turkmenistan. It does not include Kazakhstan.
[2] Richard Pipes, *The Formation of the Soviet Union*, 1964. A. Park, *Bolshevism in Turkestan, 1917–1927*, 1957. Geoffrey Wheeler, *A Modern History of Central Asia*, 1964.

the Tadzhik ASSR (part of the Uzbek SSR until it attained full republican status in 1927). This 'national delimitation', as the new territorial-administrative arrangements were officially designated, went far to split areas and people which traditionally formed one unit, especially in the rich Fergana Valley which was divided between the Uzbeks, Kirgiz, and Tadzhiks. The Constitution confirmed 'the socialist system of economy and the socialist ownership of the instruments and the means of production', i.e. the nationalization of the land, its mineral wealth, waters, forests, mills, factories, mines, and all means of communication throughout the entire Soviet Union. The Central Government was thus in a position to direct development of the economic resources of the Central Asian republics in accordance with its long-term aim of building up the economic power of the Soviet Union on Marxist socialist principles. Other clauses of the Constitution made such far-reaching concessions to the Central Government in regard to international and domestic decisions as to reduce their nominal 'national sovereignty' to a legal fiction.

At the time when these vital decisions were being taken in Moscow the representation of the Central Asian peoples in the Party and Soviet hierarchies was negligible, both being dominated by Russian Bolshevik majorities. In 1922 native Communists from Turkestan represented a tiny fraction of the Russian Communist Party, Uzbeks—0.54 per cent., Kirgiz—1.32 per cent., compared to Russians—72 per cent.[1] In Tashkent, the centre of Russian power after as before the Revolution, the Russians had antagonized the native elements of the population by their assumption of a privileged position and the exclusion of Muslims from the Tashkent Soviet and all government posts. Thus Soviet power and the Soviet economic system were foisted on the people of Central Asia by completely unrepresentative bodies at the centre and locally. Soviet historians are forced by the tenets of the Leninist nationalities policy—which assumed the automatic acceptance of socialism by all the Russian nationalities once they were freed from Tsarist oppression—to deny the protracted struggle of the Central Asian people against Sovietization. The intervention of the Red Army which finally 'pacified'

---

[1] Statistics based on the 1922 Party Census in I. P. Trainin, *SSSR i National'naia Problema* (Moscow, 1924), quoted by R. Pipes, op. cit. p. 278.

this area is therefore inadmissibly embarrassing for Moscow though it was admitted by some contemporary Soviet sources.[1] The 1924 Constitution and the Stalin Constitution of 1936 (which is still operative) established a façade of representative institutions for the government of the Central Asian republics and the other republics of the Soviet Union. Each republic is (and has been since 1936) empowered to elect its Supreme Soviet or parliament and its Council of Ministers or chief executive body. The national republics are also represented in the highest all-Union organs, the Soviet of Nationalities and the Soviet of the Union which together form the Supreme Soviet of the USSR. Real power, however, does not reside in these nominally independent government institutions but in the Communist Party of the Soviet Union by which they are dominated. There are also republican party organs but their function is to execute the policies and decisions of the Central Party authorities, not to act as independent national parties. The all-Union Party is highly centralized and through its principle of 'democratic centralism' all decisions of the Central Party organs are binding on the republican and all lower party organs in the system. The Communist Party of the Soviet Union has thus a monopoly of political power in this one-party State.

In the economic field, the powers granted to the republican and government organs have oscillated between the complete centralization favoured by Stalin, and varying degrees of decentralization and recentralization under Khrushchev and the present Soviet Government, in the constant search for a magic formula for the effective operation of the economy. In 1957 the country was divided into a number of economic administrative regions each containing a *sovnarkhoz* or council of national economy (CNE) to manage its industry and construction (but not agriculture) and this promised a fair measure of decentralization. After several changes in the local administration in Uzbekistan, by 1960 each of the four Central Asian republics had one *sovnarkhoz* while Kazakhstan had nine. This system of partial decentralization was apparently not found satisfactory and by 1962 Khrushchev was already thinking again

[1] Cf. G. Safarov, *Kolonial'naya Revolyutsiya: Opyt Turkestana* (Moscow 1921). Ye. Kozlovskiy, *Krasnaya Armiya v Sredney Azii* (Tashkent, 1928), p. 31. 'The Red Army in Turkestan 1917–1920', *Central Asian Review*, no. 1 (1965), gives a detailed analysis of these books and others on the same subject.

in terms of recentralization. The Party was reorganized on a production basis. Under this scheme separate committees of the Party
(and Soviets) were established for industry and agriculture by which
the powers of the republican governments (including control of
investment) were severely restricted. At the same time, following
Mr. Khrushchev's visit to Central Asia, the individual Central Asian
sovnarkhozes were abolished and new joint supra-national agencies
were set up consisting of a joint Central Asian Bureau directly
subordinate to the Central Committee of the CPSU and four joint
Central Asian economic agencies: the Central Asian *Sovnarkhoz*
(CNE), the Central Asian Construction Agency (subordinate to
Gosstroy USSR), the Central Asian Directorate for Cotton Growing, and the Chief Directorate for Irrigation and the Construction of
Sovkhozy (subordinate to Gosstroy USSR).[1] The snub to local
amour propre implied by this subordination of the local economy
and administration to the central organs must have been aggravated
by the appointment of Russians to the chief posts in these new
bodies. The chairman of the new Central Asian Bureau and his two
deputies were Russians, as were the chairmen of the Central Asian
CNE and of the other joint economic agencies.

The timing and nature of this reorganization strongly suggests
that Khrushchev took a poor view of local officialdom during his
visit to Central Asia, and created the joint Central Asian Bureau as
Moscow's watch-dog. There had been a series of economic scandals
in these republics and many charges of 'localism' or 'getting together'
among native officials to defraud the State or otherwise by-pass
Gosplan's orders were reported in the Press. It is therefore not
surprising that *Pravda Vostoka* (22 February 1963), the Uzbek
Party newspaper, stated that the aims of the Central Asian CNE 'will
be to help to overcome localist tendencies, attempts to build a closed
economy and (prevent) the dispersal of material and manpower
resources'. 'The formation of a single Central Asian Economic
Region created favourable conditions for a powerful rise of productive forces and accelerated development of the economy of the
Central Asian fraternal republics and still more strengthens the
unbreakable friendship between our peoples', exclaimed the journal

---

[1] This subject is treated in greater detail in *Central Asian Review*, nos. 1–3 (1965).

of the Planning Commission and the *Sovnarkhoz* of the Central Asian Economic Region.[1]

There was little time for these new agencies to prove their worth or achieve these aims for they were abolished by the new Government soon after Khrushchev's fall in December 1964. At the same time separate *sovnarkhozy* were re-established in each of the four Central Asian republics. Though these moves had considerable local interest, there was no local comment and they were surrounded with a secretiveness that must have puzzled Central Asian citizens as much as the outside world. A brief notice in *Pravda* (23 December 1964) and the Central Asian republican Press stated that the Central Asian Economic Region and the Central Asian *Sovnarkhoz* had been abolished. No mention was made then nor subsequently of the fate of the Central Asian Bureau of the Party or of the other joint agencies though it was inferred from internal evidence (including the appointment of their chairmen to other posts) that they had also been disbanded. The motivation of these moves by Khrushchev's successors is still rather obscure. They may have been inspired by a desire to gain favour in Central Asia where the agencies are believed to have been unpopular, or simply part of the general dismantling of Khrushchev's organization of the Party and administration initiated by the new Government. There is no evidence, however, that the Central Asian governments themselves had any voice either in the establishment or dissolution of these supra-national bodies.

The whole territorial *sovnarkhoz* system of industrial planning and administration set up by Khrushchev in 1957 was scrapped by decree of the Supreme Soviet in October 1965.[2] Accordingly, the former centralized administration of industry and planning by all-Union and Union-republican ministries was restored but with greater flexibility and other badly needed reforms. In Professor Nove's graphic words, the *sovnarkhozy* 'had been a cause of increasing confusion, crossed wires and irresponsibility'.[3] 'Regionalism', which was perhaps a stronger 'deviation' in Central Asia than in other parts of the Soviet Union, flourished under the *sovnarkhozy*. It may be more effectually repressed under Kosygin's centralized ministerial controls.

[1] *Nar. Khoz. S. A.*, no. 5 (1964).   [2] *Pravda*, 3 October 1965.
[3] Alec Nove, *The Soviet Economy* (George Allen & Unwin Ltd., London, 1965), p. 331.

THE IDEOLOGICAL BACKGROUND TO THE INDUSTRIALIZA-
TION OF THE 'UNDER-DEVELOPED BORDERLANDS'

The Bolsheviks approached the problem of development in the under-developed 'eastern regions' from ideological positions to which they attached great importance but which contained inherent contradictions more easily ignored than resolved in practice. Lenin had devoted much sound and fury to denouncing Tsarist neglect and exploitation of the 'national borderlands' of the Empire, Siberia, as well as Central Asia and Kazakhstan, solely as sources of raw materials. The criteria he used to condemn Western imperialism applied equally in his view to the colonial territories of imperial Russia: i.e. concentration on agriculture, rudimentary industry, opposition of metropolitan magnates to the development of industry in the periphery based on local raw materials, and the monopoly of industrialization by the metropolis. Early in 1918 he formulated his sketch of a 'Plan of Scientific–Technical Tasks'[1] in which he briefly outlined principles for the reorganization and the rational location of industry for the guidance of the Academy of Sciences' plan of economic development. Industry must, accordingly, be brought nearer to the sources of raw materials and long-distance freight hauls reduced as much as possible. His idea was to get away from the old concentration of industrial power in central Russia and open up the resources of the under-industrialized hinterland of the 'eastern regions' of the country.

These ideas inspired and took more definite form in GOELRO (the State Plan for the Electrification of Russia, 1920) and the first Soviet plan for the reconstruction of the national economy. It recognized the need for 'a rationalization of our industry . . . by a significant transfer of industry to the East' and the primary role of electrification as a means of developing the country. Subsequently, both the Tenth (1921) and the Twelfth (1923) Party Congresses emphasized the importance of promoting the economic and cultural progress of Turkestan and the other national borderlands as intrinsic points of the Soviet nationalities policy. The Tenth Congress called *inter alia* for the 'systematic elimination of all remnants of national inequality in all branches of public and economic life. . . . It is the

[1] V. I. Lenin, *Sochineniya* (Moscow, 1950), vol. 27, p. 288. Signed 6 April 1918. First published in *Pravda*, 4 March 1924.

Party's task', it declared, 'to help the toiling masses in the non-Russian nations to overtake central Russia which has forged ahead. . . .'[1]

These resolutions had a strong propaganda appeal but there were nevertheless sound economic and strategic grounds for broadening the industrial base of Russia by developing the great natural resources of Asiatic Russia. The idea that the under-developed territories of Russia could be brought to 'overtake' the more developed parts of the country was, however, economic nonsense—unless European Russia conveniently stagnated while the under-developed areas were 'catching up'. There was also an inherent contradiction in the Leninist injunction to bring industry close to raw material sources and consumption centres because under Russian conditions many valuable sources of raw materials were located in uninhabited wildernesses remote from the most highly populated European centres of consumption. Nature has been almost equally lavish in her allocation of Russia's share of the world's stock of raw materials and irrational in her location of many of them in singularly difficult or inaccessible terrain, for example, gold, diamonds, copper, nickel, and tin in the permafrost soil of northern Siberia, oil in the waterless Central Asian deserts and the uninhabited roadless Khanty–Mansiyskiy tundra–taiga wilderness.

Moreover, as Professor Holland Hunter has pointed out in his interesting examination of 'Locational Objectives and Problems', 'the emphasis on rapid expansion of heavy industry and the emphasis on large production units both tended to deflect energy away from the even spread of industry into backward, interior regions of the USSR that was called for by the leading slogans of the party'.[2] The very urgency of the first plans of economic development inevitably inclined the planners to install new works and plants in areas where there were skilled workers and other facilities for construction rather than in the industrial wilds where everything including skill had to be imported and time was an essential factor in laying the basis of industrialization. It is therefore not surprising that, according to the record, Soviet development in the 'eastern

---

[1] *Vsesoyuznaya KP v Resolyutsiyakh i Resheniyakh S'ezdov, Konferentsii i Plenumov Ts. Komitetov*, Part I, 1898–1925 (Moscow, 1954), p. 559.

[2] Holland Hunter, *Soviet Transportation Policy* (Harvard University Press, Cambridge, Mass., 1957), p. 25.

F

regions', in spite of the undoubted achievements in some forty years of Soviet power, proceeded relatively slowly up to World War II and that 'the old centres of European Russia have usually received more attention than outlying regions'.[1]

Though national disparities in the location of natural resources, population, and skilled workers cannot be spirited away by decrees or exhortation, the Leninist principles of 'the shift to the east' and a 'more rational location of industry' have been potent forces in shaping all the Soviet Five Year Plans up to date and forcing production 'outwards and eastwards'. Professor Peter Wiles's down-to-earth view that 'natural resources are all too often unemployable and it is only right to leave them so'[2] would be incomprehensible to many Russian Bolsheviks to whom the notion of a 'white spot' or undeveloped area on the map, irrespective of the relatively much higher costs and difficulties of development, is positively shameful. This fits in neatly with the Bolshevik obsession with autarky.

The First and Second Five Year Plans could justly claim to be actively concerned with 'the technical reconstruction of the national economy of the country', i.e. the restoration and expansion of industry in European Russia, 'the creation of a new location of the productive forces', and 'the liquidation of the economic and cultural backwardness of the national regions inherited from Tsarist Russia'.[3] But the extreme backwardness of a 'national region' like Central Asia meant that only the first steps in industrialization could be taken (as will be shown in detail below) while the great frenzied effort in 'relocation of productive forces' was concentrated on the creation of a second coal–metallurgical base in the east, the Urals–Kuznetsk combine.

The Eighteenth Party Congress (1939) which approved the Third Five Year Plan gave a big impetus to the 'eastward shift' by creating 'duplicate enterprises' in a number of branches of engineering, oil refining, and chemical industries in the eastern regions.[4] Owing to the strained relations with the Japanese at this time, the Soviet Far Eastern Kray received special mention in this Plan even to the extent

[1] Hunter, op. cit. p. 23.
[2] P. J. D. Wiles, *The Political Economy of Communism* (Basil Blackwell, Oxford, 1962), p. 153.
[3] *Vtoroy Pyatiletniy Plan Razvitiya Narodnogo Khozyaystva SSSR*, Tom. 2 (Gosplan Moscow, 1954), p. 3.
[4] P. N. Stepanov, *Geografiya Promyshlennosti SSSR* (Moscow, 1955), p. 48.

of optimistic prognostications of achievements which have not yet materialized. Thus the text of the Plan runs: 'The Far East should provide from its own resources everything necessary for fuel, and as far as possible metals and engineering, cement, timber and building materials as a whole, as well as the majority of bulky food and light industrial supplies.'[1] This Plan repudiated the construction of 'giant plants' (*gigantomania*) which had sprung up often in clusters in the big industrial centres of European Russia and the Urals but not to any extent 'east of the Urals'.

After World War II and the restoration of the devastated areas of European Russia and the Ukraine, the 'shift to the east' was taken up enthusiastically by Khrushchev and other Party leaders at the Twentieth and Twenty-First Party Congresses. Khrushchev's imagination, it would seem, was fired by a vision of the 'enormous resources of the eastern regions' containing, he reported, '75 per cent. of all Soviet coal reserves, up to 80 per cent. of hydro-energy and four-fifths of the lumber wealth, basic supplies of non-ferrous and rare metals, and great resources of chemical raw materials, iron ore, and building materials', and the fact that coal and electric power could be produced more cheaply in the east than in the European part of the USSR.[2] With typical verve he produced statistics to prove the economic advantages of production in Siberia, the apex of which was the giant Bratsk hydro-electric power station which 'will produce 22 milliard kWh., annually as much as the two most powerful stations in the European part of the USSR. . . . The annual cost of power produced at Bratsk will be 200 million roubles lower than at the Kuybyshev and Stalingrad HES. That, Comrades, is how advantageous it is to master the energy resources of the east. . . .' Characteristically, in this peroration Khrushchev ignored the real costs of the Bratsk power station (which were enormous if the capital investment were included) and to what purpose its huge capacity out in the wilds could be put in the early stages of operation, nor did he mention any of the major difficulties confronting construction projects in metallurgy, mining, or engineering in east Siberia, for example, labour or supply problems.

[1] V. Molotov, 'Doklad i Zaklyuchitel'noye Slovo na XVIII S'ezd VKP (b)', *Tretiy Pyatiletniy Plan Razvitiya Narodnogo Khozyaystva* (Moscow, 1939).

[2] 'Questions of the Correct Location of Productive Forces', *S'yezd Kommunisticheskoy Partii Sovetskogo Soyuza 14–25 February 1956, XX*, Sten. Ochet (Moscow, 1956).

In his report to the Twentieth Party Congress on the Sixth Five Year Plan Bulganin further expatiated on the eastern regions and their value to the country's economy: 'This vast wealth of our eastern regions must be made to serve the national economy to a much greater degree than hitherto. Accordingly, capital investment in these areas is to be more than doubled under the new plan and will amount to about half of the total for the whole of the USSR. In 1960 the eastern areas should produce more coal and iron than the whole of the USSR produced in 1950 and considerably more power and cement than was produced throughout the country in 1954. More than 100 engineering factories will be built in the east in these five years.'[1] Clearly, 'the Party's central committee and the Government . . . attach special importance to the economic development of Siberia', he said. Reflecting the First Secretary's optimism the Twentieth Party Congress approved the directives of the Sixth Five Year Plan. Not surprisingly, many of the inflated targets of the Sixth Five Year Plan, in Asiatic Russia as elsewhere, were found to be unfeasible. It made inglorious history by being the first Five Year Plan to be overtly scrapped and was replaced in 1959 by the Seven Year Plan. These increased investments in the eastern regions under the Sixth Five Year Plan represented a rise of 150 per cent. in west Siberia, 180 per cent. in east Siberia, and 170 per cent. in the Kazakh Republic compared to those of the previous Five Year Plan. The investment planned in the other Central Asian republics was considerably less than in Kazakhstan; Turkmenistan, for example, was allotted 7.2 milliard roubles compared to Kazakhstan's 78 milliard roubles.[2] But as the Sixth Five Year Plan was prematurely scrapped these figures do not represent actual investment so much as the Soviet Government's intent to develop the eastern regions.

In his report to the Extraordinary Twenty-First Congress of the CPSU called to consider the control figures of the new Seven Year Plan in 1959, Khrushchev specifically stressed the 'important step forward' in major construction plans made since the Twentieth Party Congress by the eastern regions and the increased share in all-Union production of coal (50 per cent.), steel (48 per cent.), copper

[1] Directives of the Sixth Five Year Plan of the USSR 1956–60 and report by N. A. Bulganin to the Twentieth Congress of the CPSU, *Soviet News Booklet*, no. 5 (London, 1956), p. 47.

[2] J. Barth, 'Verlagerung des Wirtschaftlichen Schwergewichts nach Osten', *Osteuropa*, no. 3 (1956), p. 258.

refining (88 per cent.), aluminium (71 per cent.), cement (42 per cent.), lumber (52 per cent.), paper (32 per cent.), to be achieved by them in 1965. At a moment when the 'Virgin Lands of Kazakhstan' had run into serious trouble from 'dust-bowls', erosion, and other phenomena arising from incorrect cultivation of these dry farming lands, he gave the Congress no hint of these problems, referring sanguinely to 'the successes being consolidated in the conquest of the virgin and long fallow lands'.[1] The text of the Seven Year Plan (1959) reiterated Khrushchev's emphasis on the importance of economic development in the eastern regions: 'The main shifts in distribution of production', it ran, 'in the forthcoming seven year period, were conceived primarily along the lines of accelerated development of the country's eastern regions. More than 40 per cent. of all capital investment in 1959–65 will go towards the development of the eastern regions, including the Urals, Siberia, the Far East, Kazakhstan, and Central Asia.'[2]

Finally, the new Party programme adopted at the Twenty-Second Party Congress in 1961 set its authoritative seal on the increasingly important role in the national economy and the expansion of 'industry in the areas to the east of the Urals'.[3] But in the same breath it stated: 'The economy in the European part of the USSR which contains the bulk of the population and where there are great opportunities for the increased industrial output will make further substantial progress', thus striking a realistic note in the east–west economic balance often forgotten in over-exuberant estimates of the eastern regions. Obviously the resources of both parts of the country must be regarded as interlocking and interdependent for many years to come, with the east supplying an ever-rising share of such basic raw materials as coal, iron, and oil to supplement expendable western resources.

In the latest phase of comment on the problems of the location of industry and notably since the removal of Khrushchev, the former stress on development of 'the inexhaustible natural riches of the eastern regions' regardless of costs and difficulties is more and more

[1] *Vneocherednoy XXI S'yezd Kommunisticheskoy Partii Sovetskogo Soyuza*, Sten. Otchet (Moscow, 1959), pp. 42–44.
[2] Control Figures for the Development of the USSR National Economy in 1959–65 (*Pravda*, 8 February 1959).
[3] Programme of the Communist Party of the Soviet Union, 1961, p. 60.

tempered by considerations of profitability, costs of capital investment, and production. This accords with the more professional
economic approach of Khrushchev's successors and also of many
individual economists. A recent article entitled 'The Rational
Specialization of Engineering in the Eastern Regions of the USSR'
in *Voprosy Ekonomiki* (no. 10, 1965), p. 54, may be taken as typical
of this attitude. 'In 20 engineering enterprises of the Far East',
it states, 'capital investment on construction exceeds 18 million
roubles or 30 per cent. of the cost of these factories, if they had been
constructed in the European part of the USSR. The expenditure on
one rouble of commercial production in engineering and metal-
working in the Far East is 20 per cent. and the cost of many types of
machine-manufactured articles 30–36 per cent. and more above that
in the European part of the USSR.' These conditions have apparently given rise to a controversy on the subject and some economists are even asking the fundamental question: 'Is it advisable to
develop those items of engineering production the importation
of which is cheaper than production locally?' 'Some economists
answered in the negative', we are informed by *Voprosy Ekonomiki*'s
correspondent. It is a far cry to the 'thirties when criticism of the
astronomical costs of constructing the Ural–Kuzbas metallurgical
base earned castigation as the work of 'an enemy of the people'.[1]

DEFINITION OF THE 'EASTERN REGIONS'

Some attempt must now be made to define the eastern regions
which have already been mentioned briefly. This is far from easy as
the term has no fixed connotation in Russian economic literature,
nor is it always clear where the boundary between west and east
lies; the eastern regions may even refer to all the territory between
and including the Volga, Bashkiria, and the Far Eastern region or
equally arbitrarily may include or exclude the Volga basin or Bashkiria and include or exclude the Caucasus. Thus in the Second Five
Year Plan the eastern regions are explicitly defined as the Urals,
Bashkiria, west Siberia, east Siberia, the Far Eastern region, Kazakhstan, Central Asia, and Transcaucasia.[2] As the concept of the eastern

---

[1] B. Stepanov, *Razvitiye i Razmeshcheniye Proizvoditel'nykh Sil SSSR v Tretey Stalinskoy
Pyatiletke* (Leningrad, 1939), p. 51.   [2] *Vtoroy Pyatiletniy Plan*, p. 313.

regions always implied the under-developed national borderlands, the Urals and the Volga areas, which are highly industrialized areas of the RSFSR, are often omitted for that reason. Thus the *Economic Geography of the USSR*[1] divides Asiatic Russia, i.e. the eastern regions, into four parts: Siberia; the Far East (rarely grouped with Siberia); Central Asia; Kazakhstan. The grouping of the official *Statistical Yearbook*,[2] however, omits Transcaucasia but is otherwise identical with the Second Five Year Plan definition. Professor Holland Hunter writes of this ambiguous term: 'Identification of the Russian "east" is probably just as nebulous in Russian minds as is the "west" in the United States.'[3] There is also a pertinent comment on this confusing term from a Soviet author sponsored by Gosplan. 'The division of the country into western and eastern regions not only does not correspond to the tasks of perspective planning but also does not satisfy its current requirements', he says. 'More and more often, for example, the Urals economic region is separated from the eastern regions and the geographical concept "regions to the east of the Urals" is used, mention of which is made in the 1961 Programme of the CPSU: "Industry in the regions to the east of the Urals will expand greatly". '[4] Finally, the directives of the Twenty-Third Congress for the Five Year Plan, 1966–70, in the section (VII) dealing with the location of productive forces and the development of the economy of the Union republics group 'the European part of the RSFSR and the Urals'[5] together, which is at last a clear recognition, in 1966, of a relationship which has existed since the planned periods started. This imprecision in the definition of 'East of the Urals' and the frequent shifts in the economic regions are most confusing and make exact comparisons of production (or other items) in specific areas over a period of time often almost impossible.[6]

I should therefore explain that the 'eastern regions' throughout this study are generally taken to mean: east and west Siberia, the

[1] Balzak, op. cit. p. 573.
[2] *Narodnoye Khozyaystvo SSSR v 1963* (Moscow, 1965), p. 131.
[3] Hunter, op. cit. p. 33.
[4] *Voprosy Razmeshcheniya Proizvodstva v SSSR* (Gosplan SSSR, Moscow, 1965), p. 24.
[5] *Pravda*, 20 February 1966.
[6] Before 1965, the Yakut ASSR, for example, was part of the east Siberian region but was then attached to the Far Eastern region. This change does not make much difference statistically owing to the insignificant level of Yakut production (which does not include valuable non-ferrous products and gold, statistics of which are not published).

Soviet Far Eastern region, the four Central Asian republics, and Kazakhstan, i.e. the areas 'to the east of the Urals' or Asiatic Russia. These are developing areas in the sense that the Urals region is not. In this study I have been interested to discover how they have developed under Soviet power and what has been and is their contribution to the build-up of the Soviet economy. These natural geographical terms represent areas with more or less stable boundaries and are therefore preferable to the fluctuating lines of demarcation of the economic regions (large and small) as a guide to the territorial divisions of the Soviet Union.

SOVIET PRE-WAR PLANS (1928–41)

When the planned era was initiated with the launching of the First Five Year Plan in 1928, Stalin's obsession with security and the

Total Capital Investments in State Industry (planned) for the five year period 1928/9–1933 (selected areas)

(in million roubles at 1926–7 prices)

Republics and regions	*Total amount*
USSR	16,548,1
A. RSFSR	10,494,1
Central industrial region	2,998,1
Urals *oblast*	1,949,6
Leningrad *oblast*	1,055,1
Siberian kray	662,5
Kazakh ASSR	345,7
Far Eastern kray	310,5
Kirgiz ASSR	37,1
Yakut ASSR	6,2
B. Ukrainian SSR	4,521,3
C. Transcaucasian SR	1,139,9
D. Uzbek SSR	340,8
E. Turkmen SSR	81,9

Source: *Pyatiletniy Plan*, Tom Tretiy (Gosplan SSSR, Moscow, 1930), p. 568.

need for a second metallurgical base far from Russia's vulnerable Western European frontier dominated the plan directives and not the immediate needs of the population for better supplies of food, clothing, and other consumer goods, or the requirements of the under-developed regions. The capital investments allocated for the Central Asian republics, Kazakhstan, and the Far Eastern region were relatively modest compared to the mobilization of resources for the build-up and reconstruction of southern Russia and the great new industrial base in the Urals.

The Urals industrial district covers an area about 500 miles square and contains the famous iron deposits of Magnitogorsk and an exceptional wealth of other materials including copper, gold, lead, zinc, and platinum. Only good coking coal was lacking for the cluster of new industries, metallurgical, chemical, and engineering, planned on a grand scale to be completed in frenzied haste from north to south of the Urals. Regardless of the expense or the heavy strain on the railways, it was decided to import coking coal from the Kuzbas mines in west Siberia, 1,300 miles farther east. 'A quarter of a million souls—Communists, Kulaks, foreigners, Tartars, convicted saboteurs and a mass of blue-eyed Russian peasants—made the biggest steel *combinat* in Europe in the middle of the barren Ural steppe. Money was spent like water, men froze, hungered and suffered but the construction work went on with a disregard for individuals and a mass heroism seldom paralleled in history', wrote John Scott who took part in this work.[1] The Ural–Kuznetsk Combine (as it was called) contained 'a galaxy of engineering and armaments plants' which saved Russia from disaster when the old heavy industry centre in the Ukraine had been largely lost or destroyed, and justified Stalin's ruthless foresight in creating a second arsenal, the Magnitogorsk of 1933. Side by side with this feverish activity in the Urals and Kuzbas, capital construction and electrification proceeded on a still larger scale in central Russia and the Ukraine in the decade before World War II. Thus in spite of the emphasis on the 'eastern regions' in the Soviet Plan literature of the time, the shift in the national distribution of the production of iron and steel, though considerable, was much less than might have been expected.

[1] John Scott, *Behind the Urals* (Secker & Warburg, London, 1942), p. 76.

It was not until World War II and subsequently that decisive changes occurred in the locational pattern of the iron and steel industry.[1] The discovery and operation (1935) of the rich Gornaya Shoraya iron deposits south of Kuznetsk gradually reduced the expensive hauls of Urals iron ore for the Kuznetsk works while Karaganda coal was increasingly used in the Urals after the new railway line, Karaganda–Akmolinsk–Kartaly, was built and coal

Regional Distribution of Iron and Steel Production in the USSR

Region	1913	1927–8	1940
Pig iron (in million metric tons)			
Southern	3.1	2.4	9.9
Central	0.2	0.2	0.9
Eastern	0.9	0.7	4.2
Steel			
Southern	3.2	2.5	11.2
Central	0.1	0.8	1.2
Eastern	0.9	1.0	5.9

Source: Harry Schwartz, *Russia's Soviet Economy* (Prentice-Hall, New York, 1954), p. 250.

could be transported direct to the Urals and farther north. Owing to the intensive work of thousands of forced labourers, the Karaganda coal mines had stepped up production to nearly 7 million tons in 1940.[2] Thus both industrial centres became more and more independent of each other though neither was fully self-contained by 1940.

The development of industry in and beyond the Urals was accompanied by a great increase of electric power capacity and many new power stations were built in the eastern regions. Two of the biggest power stations constructed pre-war in this area were at Kemerovo in west Siberia (50,000 kW.) and at Kuznetsk (100,000 kW.). The former concentration of electric power in European Russia gave place to a wider distribution of power and it became

[1] Schwartz, op. cit. p. 250.
[2] *Narodnoye Khozyaystvo Kazakhskoy SSR* (Alma-Ata, 1957), p. 36.

available in many areas where it was hitherto non-existent. The following table shows the planned changes in the regional distribution of electric power under the Second Five Year Plan.

Percentage of Regional Power Capacity to Total Soviet Capacity

Regions	1932	1937
SSSR	100	100
Old industrial regions (Leningrad, Moscow, Ivanov provinces)	28.99	26.76
Volga area (Tatariya, Middle Volga, Lower Volga, Gor'kiy kray)	10.54	10.23
Ukrainian SSR	29.93	21.88
UKK regions (Urals, Bashkiria, west Siberia, Kazakhstan)	13.06	18.26
East Siberia and the Far Eastern kray	1.03	2.50
Transcaucasia	4.54	6.03
Central Asia	0.92	3.38

Source: *Vtoroy Pyatiletniy Plan Razvitiya Narodnogo Khozyaystva SSSR* (Moscow, 1934), vol. I, p. 312.

Hydro-electric power development lagged at this time because the huge water power resources of the eastern regions had not yet been adequately studied.

According to the Second Five Year Plan: 'The general shift of industry to the East and the high tempi of the industrialization of the national republics is specially clearly characterized by these shifts in the location of the main energy base of the USSR.'[1] This was a characteristic exaggeration. There was a new trend eastwards but no 'general shift of industry'.

FERROUS METALLURGY

Soviet economic geographers tend to overrate the extent of the development of ferrous metallurgy in the eastern regions under the first three Five Year Plans, playing down the state of this industry in the Tsarist period. For example, the standard Soviet geography 'for use in institutions of higher learning' published in 1940 states that 'Siberia produced neither pig-iron nor rolled metal pre-1913',

[1] *Vtoroy Pyatiletniy Plan,* op. cit. vol. I, p. 312.

but 'in 1937, 1,510,000 tons of pig-iron or 10.3 per cent. of all Soviet production came from here'.[1] The achievement obviously gains against that background. A more scholarly work published in 1964 springs to the defence of the development of heavy metallurgy in pre-Soviet Siberia and states that there are frequently errors 'in books and pamphlets'.[2] According to this essay on the 'Heavy Metallurgy of east Siberia in the second half of the nineteenth and the first half of the twentieth century', the three Siberian iron-works the Petrovsk pig-iron foundry, the Abakan, and the Nikolayevskiy works in Irkutsk between them produced 6,852,321 poods of iron in 1885–1909.[3]

After the completion of the Second Five Year Plan in 1937 Siberia produced 1,510,000 tons of pig-iron, i.e. 10 per cent. of Soviet production. Most of this Siberian metal came from the new Stalinsk (Novokuznetsk) metallurgical plant on the River Tom using the local iron deposits of Tel'bes, Temir Tau, Tashtagol, and Gornaya Shoriya. Of the total State investment in Siberia under the Second Five Year Plan 67.5 per cent. was allocated for the development of the Kuznetsk coal basin and the Stalinsk engineering–metallurgical base. Farther east a new plant was built at the old site of the Petrosvk-Zabaykalskiy iron-works to replace the largely obsolete original plant.

Two major regional developments in pre-war metallurgy were the establishment of *Amurstal'*, the first steel and rolling mill in the Far East, at Komsomol'sk-on-the-Amur, and the first Central Asian steel plant at Begovat in Uzbekistan. *Amurstal'* was based on coal from the local Suchan mines, local scrap, and imports of pig- and scrap-iron from Manchuria. It had no blast furnaces. The aim was to reduce the long hauls of Urals and Ukrainian metal on which the Far East had hitherto been dependent. The V. I. Lenin Uzbek Metallurgical Plant at Begovat (now Bekabad), on the Syr Dar'ya Uzbek border with Tadzhikistan, was under construction before World War II but did not start production until about 1941. As there was no convenient ore base, the plant had to work on local scrap-iron. It consisted of three small, open-hearth furnaces and some

[1] Balzak, op. cit. p. 250.
[2] I. N. Komogoryzev, 'Chernaya Metallurgiya Vostochnoy Sibiri vo Vtoroy Polovine XIX i Nachale XX vv', in *Predposylki Oktyabr'skoy Revolyutsii v Sibiri*, op. cit. p. 101.
[3] Ibid. p. 114.

vacuum-electric furnaces. It was created with the aim of supplying Central Asia with its own metal, but with a production of about 200,000 tons of steel and 180,000 tons of rolled metal per annum it could only satisfy a small percentage of the needs of this developing area which therefore remained heavily dependent on imports.

NON-FERROUS METALLURGY

In Tsarist Russia, and until the end of World War I, non-ferrous metals headed the list of Russia's imports of minerals. The non-ferrous metals—copper, zinc, lead, aluminium, nickel, tin, and their alloys—were of basic importance for the Soviet industrialization and electrification plans owing to their use in the manufacture of high-grade steel, and in the electrical engineering, chemical, automobile, and other industries. Their development was therefore a key target of the Five Year Plans from the outset and geological prospecting was generously subsidized to discover and prove new non-ferrous reserves. Copper, lead, and zinc had been mined in a rudimentary way before the Revolution in deposits scattered throughout the Urals, Siberia, Kazakhstan, and the Far East (whence the polymetallic ores of the Tetyukhe region were exported as raw material to other parts of the Soviet Union).

The need to improve the technical level of the non-ferrous metals industry was early recognized by the Soviet planning authorities and considerable sums were invested in new mining machinery and much more precise prospecting of reserves. Urgent planned directives demanded and obtained increased production of these metals, especially of copper, in order to make the Soviet Union independent of foreign sources of supply. The main smelting area in the 1930s was the Urals though the copper reserves were known to be greater in Kazakhstan. Copper production rose impressively between 1934 and 1943 in the Urals and the Kazakh mines, with the latter rapidly overtaking the Urals where production gradually declined owing to the exhaustion of the smaller deposits and inefficient use of equipment.[1]

In Kazakhstan large and expensive copper plants were built at

Demitri B. Shimkin, *Minerals: A Key to Soviet Power* (Harvard University Press, Cambridge, Mass., 1953), p. 112.

Kounrad (the Balkhash Copper Refinery) and Dzhezkazgan and an electrolysis plant at Karaganda to handle black copper from both sources.[1] The high losses in concentration and smelting of copper in the Urals and Kazakhstan were officially constantly attacked in these years. The technical level of Soviet non-ferrous mining and refining was low, and recoveries in the concentration of bauxite and lead and smelting of copper, lead, and zinc was poor.[2] In spite

Soviet Mine Output of Fire-Burned (Black) Copper, 1934–42

(in metric tons)

Economic regions	1934	1937	1943
Urals	36,607	76,400	64,400
Kazakhstan	3,945	8,900	56,000
Dzhezkazgan	3,945	(6,400)	30,800
Kounrad	—	(2,500)	16,800
Other	—	—	8,400
Transcaucasus	3,529		
Alaverdi	2,140	5,450	18,000
Zangezur	1,389		
Total	44,081	90,800	140,000

Source: Shimkin, op. cit. p. 110.

of these deficiencies production of non-ferrous metals rose to levels unknown in pre-Soviet days and there was also a great diversification in the range and location of deposits in the eastern regions.

Kazakhstan became a major source of copper as well as of zinc and lead, silver and polymetallic ores. Domestic production of copper was not yet sufficient to meet the strain on resources caused by World War II when large Lend-Lease imports from the United States of America and Canada eased the situation.

Large-scale mining of zinc and lead was pushed forward under the first three Five Year Plans in the rich Ridder mines of the Altay. By 1937 and the completion of the Second Five Year Plan, 42.5 per cent. of all Soviet zinc was mined in the Altay and over 23 per cent. in the Salair deposits in Novosibirsk province for which a new zinc

[1] Shimkin, op. cit. p. 112. [2] Ibid. p. 95.

plant was constructed at Belovo (1934). About 10 per cent. of Soviet zinc at this time came from the Tetyukhe mines in the Maritime Province of the Far East. Both Tetyukhe and Altay zinc concentrate were sent hundreds of miles west for smelting to the large zinc plant at Konstantinovka in the Ukraine.

Smelting capacity did not keep pace with mining production in the pre-war period. No zinc, for example, was smelted at this time in the Altay.[1] The lack of adequate electric power before the construction of the large hydro-electric power station of Ust'-Kamenogorsk (started under the Third Five Year Plan) retarded the development of the Altay as a centre of non-ferrous metallurgy. In south Kazakhstan, the 'giant' Chimkent lead plant, with an annual capacity of 60,000 metric tons, operated on ores from the Achisay deposit in the Karatau mountains, to the north of the region. As these were soon found to be insufficient to supply a plant of this capacity, Chimkent drew on the more distant Tekeli lead deposits (in Alma-Ata province) and others still further removed from the plant. Nevertheless, the supply situation here remained unsatisfactory in the pre-war period.

Recognition of Kazakhstan as a major centre of Soviet non-ferrous industry was reflected in the large capital investment in it in the Second and Third Five Year Plans. For example, the Second Five Year Plan allocated 701 million roubles or 31.4 per cent. of the total Union investment in this industry to Kazakh non-ferrous development, which represented 17.3 per cent. of investment in Kazakhstan as a whole. Moreover, 18.4 per cent. and 11.1 per cent. respectively of the total funds allocated for geodetic–geological prospecting throughout the Soviet Union were devoted to more exact investigation of the still relatively little known natural resources of Kazakhstan.[2]

No tin was produced before the Revolution in the Soviet Union. Intensive geological surveys between 1928 and 1940 successfully located tin reserves in east Siberia and the Far East. The first mine to be operated was at Olovyannaya in Transbaykalia. The Far East deposits were situated in the extremely remote districts of Yakutia and Chukotka and were very difficult of access and to operate.[3]

---

[1] Balzak, op. cit. p. 262.   [2] *Vtoroy Pyatiletniy Plan*, op. cit. vol. 2, pp. 162, 477.
[3] Further developments in this field are discussed in detail in chapter VI: 'The Soviet Far East'.

Tin remained throughout the pre-war period 'a tight place' in the Soviet economy. During World War II large imports were necessary from Britain and the United States of America. Other deficient minerals in pre-revolutionary Russia were nickel and aluminium. Discoveries made during the Second and Third Year Plans brought to light important sources of domestic supply of both minerals. Nickel was found at Noril'sk in the permafrost Arctic zone of Siberia, in the Urals (where the first Soviet nickel was produced in 1934), and in the Kola Peninsula.

The operation of the Noril'sk nickel deposits was complicated by the permafrost soil, and the remoteness of the area from any inhabited centres. It did not get going until about 1940 and was almost entirely dependent on concentration camp labour; the first Soviet nickel was produced by the Urals plants at Ufaley and Rezh in 1934. The Noril'sk combine expanded during and after the war, working on a deposit estimated to be the largest in the Soviet Union.[1] Platinum and copper were also associated with the nickel deposits in Noril'sk. Tsarist Russia was much the largest producer (over 80 per cent.) of platinum in the world, but platinum from the main Urals mines was all exported as raw platinum. During World War II production from Noril'sk began to dominate Soviet production of platinum while Urals production 'seems to have declined steadily'. A refinery was built at Noril'sk and it was connected by a new railway with the port of Dudinka on the lower Yenisey. The major developments in this extremely rich area of nickel, copper, and platinum belong, however, to the post-war years.

The development of electric power capacity in the eastern regions in turn facilitated the slow growth at this time of the Soviet aluminium industry. Owing to poor domestic bauxite resources and the low level of aluminium technology, it did not assume importance in the area 'to the east of the Urals' until after World War II. Over half of all Soviet aluminium came from Allied sources during the war.

ENGINEERING INDUSTRIES

The development during the first three Five Year Plans of mining and metallurgy in west Siberia provided a basis for a local engineering

[1] Shimkin, op. cit. p. 79. The data on nickel, platinum, and aluminium in this section are substantially based on this work.

industry which had scarcely existed before. The Urals dominated this picture but east of the Urals many new types of machinery and equipment were gradually added to the nomenclature of industrial production. This was common sense economically, but also in line with 'the principle' that engineering works should as far as possible align their production with regional demand for machinery. West Siberia, a large grain and metallurgical centre, started manufacturing tractors and other agricultural machinery at Omsk and Novosibirsk in the heart of the Siberian 'granary' during the three pre-war plan periods. Mining machinery plants were also set up to supply the coal and iron, gold and non-ferrous mines of west and east Siberia in Kemerovo, Stalinsk (now Novokuznetsk), and the industrial complex centred on the Kuzbas. Irkutsk and Blagoveshchensk (Far East) also produced gold-mining equipment such as dredges. Transport machinery plants building locomotives and carriages, and repair shops were distributed along the Trans-Siberian railway at Tomsk, Krasnoyarsk, Stalinsk, Irkutsk, Ulan-Ude, Cheremkhovo, and Vladivostok (automobile assembly plant).

Two plants of major importance for the development of industry in Central Asia were built under the First and Second Five Year Plans in Tashkent. *Tashsel'mash*, the agricultural engineering plant, was built (1929–35) on the most up-to-date lines to produce agricultural and other special machinery for the cultivation of local cotton. At the same time a huge cotton textile combine was being constructed to manufacture cotton cloth from Central Asian cotton (200,000 spindles). As the first cotton mill in Central Asia it represented a landmark in the Russian cotton industry. Both plants were originally almost entirely staffed by Russians. Neither employed Uzbeks or other native people until after the war.[1] In the 1940s, during World War II, another large cotton combine began to operate in Stalinabad (Dushanbe), also with a predominantly Russian staff. The establishment of these Central Asian mills was taken as proof by some Soviet economic geographers that climatic conditions should not be used as an argument (as they had been in Tsarist times) against their location in Asia. 'Modern equipment overcomes the unfavourable position, i.e. dryness of the atmosphere, by the use

---

[1] 'Regional Economic Policy in the Soviet Union: The Case of Central Asia.' *U.N. Economic Bulletin for Europe* (Geneva, 1957), p. 54.

of artificial humidity', wrote one of them.[1] Knitted goods factories were set up in many Central Asian towns like Tashkent to produce stockings and knitwear for local requirements. Nevertheless, imports from European Russian factories continued for many years owing to the inadequate Central Asian production. Only a small percentage of local Central Asian cotton was woven or spun in these new mills.[2] As formerly, the greater part of Central Asian cotton continued to be processed in the old Russian mills.

CHEMICAL INDUSTRIES

Geological research under State auspices was very actively directed in the first planned periods (and even before) towards the

Expenditure on Scientific Research

(in millions of roubles)

	From Budget	From ministries	From econ. orgs.	Total
Five Year Plan (1928–32)	877	95	613	1,585
(1933–37)	3,015	303	2,040	5,358
(1938–42)	5,818	230	3,244	9,292
1943	1,079	40	739	1,858
1944	1,551	50	913	2,514
1945	2,127	50	851	3,028
Total in 1928–45	14,467	768	8,400	23,635

Source: Serge N. Prokopovicz, *Histoire Economique de L'URSS* (Flammarion, Paris, 1952), p. 287.

discovery of new mineral deposits to make the Soviet Union independent of foreign supplies of chemicals (as of most imported commodities). This research was subsidized by regular and generous subsidies from the State budget, ministries, and economic organizations, and it paid high dividends.

The Russian chemical industry in the pre-Soviet period was insignificant in relation to the requirements of a large country like

[1] P. N. Stepanov, op. cit. p. 232.
[2] *U.N. Economic Bulletin for Europe*, op. cit. p. 61.

Tsarist Russia, while many branches of the industry did not exist at all. There was a massive rise in the investment in the chemical industry in the three pre-war plans and production also rose rapidly. The eastern regions had only a modest share in this expansion though a start was made to establish the chemical industry in Uzbekistan, Siberia, and Kazakhstan.

The production of superphosphates, for example, before 1913, depended largely on imported raw materials and was concentrated in European Russia, because at this time the reserves of raw materials for basic chemical products like sulphuric acid and mineral fertilizer had not yet been systematically prospected. The discovery of phosphate deposits in 1936 at Karatau in south Kazakhstan (Dzhambul *oblast*), which are among the richest in the world, was very important for Central Asian agriculture. Production of mineral fertilizer at the new plant did not begin until 1946.[1] A small artificial fertilizer plant was built in 1936 at Aktyubinsk in north Kazakhstan based on local phosphate deposits. As these supplies were insufficient to keep the plant running, apatite from the distant Kola peninsula had to be imported. Chirchik, on the river of the same name 50 km. from Tashkent, has an important place in both the development of hydro-electric power and the fertilizer industry of Central Asia. During the Second Five Year Plan a combine was established at Chirchik to produce ammonium nitrate fertilizers by fixation of atmospheric nitrogen and the manufacture of hydrogen from water.[2] The result was a large-scale industry producing fertilizer primarily for the cotton fields of Uzbekistan. Simultaneously, a hydro-electric power station (capacity 100,000 kWh.) was built on the Chirchik River which, with its canals, was the first river to be tapped for power in the region and facilitated the development of local industry.

It was originally planned to produce about 42 per cent. of Central Asia's requirements in fertilizer locally.[3] But this planned aim for satisfying the needs of the cotton-growing republics with local fertilizer did not succeed in the decade before the war. The cotton industry, however, got more than its fair share of scarce Soviet fertilizer supplies at a time when fertilizer production lagged badly

[1] Shimkin, op. cit. pp. 258–61. [2] *Central Asian Review*, vol. I, no. 3, p. 31.
[3] *Pyatiletniy Plan*, op. cit. p. 336.

behind the planned goals.[1] Nitrogenous fertilizers, so important for the cultivation of cotton and many other Soviet crops, were produced in this period only at Kemerovo in the Kuzbas but not in Central Asia.

The Central Asian republics and south Kazakhstan had a large share in the new natural rubber industry created after the Revolution on the basis of the wild rubber-bearing plants *kok-sagyz* and *tau-sagyz* of the Central Asian deserts. This domestic rubber was soon eclipsed by a branch of the chemical industry producing synthetic rubber which supplied the greater part of Soviet needs for raw rubber together with imports. Neither Central Asia nor Siberia participated in this industry, at this time.

TIMBER AND WOOD-PROCESSING INDUSTRY

The enormous forest areas of the Soviet Union stretch across the northern regions of European Russia and Asiatic Russia to the Far East. About 75 per cent. of these reserves are estimated to be in the Siberian zone, i.e. west and east Siberia and the Far East, and a high percentage are in very difficult terrain for logging and export. Commercial production of timber has long been most unequally distributed between the eastern and western Russian areas. It is estimated, for example, that only 1 per cent. of the Siberian forests were worked pre-1913, the major share of production coming from the European north.[2] The Soviet Government's efforts to extend the area of logging and increase the Siberian share in production were perfunctory. They did not include to any great extent such essential measures as the building of railways and roads into the eastern forested area, or adequate provision of suitable equipment for the harsh Siberian climate. The backwardness of the timber industry was recognized by the Eighteenth Party Congress which called for general and complex mechanization and an end to the prevailing unsatisfactory state of affairs.[3] Then the war supervened and the timber industry showed no dramatic improvement.

In spite of Russia's timber reserves, the paper and furniture

[1] N. Jasny, *The Socialized Agriculture of the USSR* (Stanford University Press, California, 1951), p. 496.
[2] *USSR Handbook* (Victor Gollancz, London, 1934), p. 235.
[3] Balzak, op. cit. p. 303.

Industries were poorly developed before the Revolution and were located near the western metropolitan centres. In Siberia, the saw-mill industry was mainly concentrated along the Trans-Siberian line. New mills were built in the '30s and old mills expanded or re-equipped at Omsk, Novosibirsk, Krasnoyarsk, Kansk, Irkutsk, Chita, and Khabarovsk. Lumber was brought from Igarka and other saw-mills on the Yenisey and Ob' rivers. The *Amur-Zeysk* (Blagoveshchensk), *Primorles* (Vladivostok), and *Middle Amur* Timber Trusts were established in the Far East with an eye to the possibilities of developing trade with the Pacific market and with large timber-importing countries like China, Japan, Australia, and India. Tsarist Russia had a long-established timber trade with Japan. This trade began to decline in the '20s owing to competition from America and Japanese imports of timber from Karafuto (south Sakhalin) where the local Manchurian cedar, pine, larch, and fir closely resembled the varieties offered by the Soviet Far Eastern Trusts.[1]

Lack of organization and co-ordination in the paper industry pre-1913 had produced an absurdly uneconomic state of affairs. Domestic production of wood pulp only satisfied 40 per cent. of the requirements of the industry. The greater part had to be imported while pulp wood, the material from which wood pulp and cellulose are produced, was exported pre-1913 in 'enormous quantities'.[2] None of the paper factories built under the first Five Year Plans (1928–40) were in the areas east of the Urals.

Forced labour produced the greater part of the lumberjacks employed in the timber industry of Asiatic Russia (as of European Russia) until the death of Stalin in 1953 and the closing of the con-centration camps about 1956. 'The most important assignment of this labour, rating higher than any of the listed projects, was lumbering', reported David J. Dallin and Boris I. Nicolaevsky in their authoritative report on Soviet concentration camps.[3] The Soviet Government rounded up thousands of people to work in the appalling conditions of the northern forests so as to push up timber exports to replace the diminishing exports of grain. The introduction of forced labour into the lumbering industry did not send production

[1] Cf. Violet Conolly, *Soviet Trade from the Pacific to the Levant* (Oxford University Press, London, 1935), p. 45.   [2] Balzak, op. cit. p. 298.
[3] David J. Dallin and Boris I. Nicolaevsky, *Forced Labour in Russia* (Yale University Press, Connecticut, 1954), p. 215.

soaring as was expected in the Kremlin. 'It seems certain', writes Professor S. Swianiewicz, 'that this productivity was lowered, first by the inadequate living conditions, in particular by inadequate food, and secondly by putting people to work to which they had not been accustomed. If a shoemaker or a trader were sent to cut trees he was certainly less proficient than a professional woodsman.'[1]

TRANSPORT

The Turk–Sib was far the most important railway constructed to the east of the Urals under the first three Five Year Plans. This bold conception linking the Trans-Siberian railway with the Central Asian network was one of the many projects to be taken out of Tsarist files. The surveys had been made and the line started on the northern sector from Novosibirsk in 1912 and it had reached Semipalatinsk in the north in 1916 when work was halted by the war. It was restarted from both ends in 1927 and was completed in record time over a very difficult route with the aid of forced labour in 1930. This trunk-line between Lugavoy in southern Kazakhstan and Novosibirsk, 1,442 km. long, was intended to carry grain and timber to the cotton-growing areas of Central Asia which were deficient in both commodities, while cotton for the new textile mills in Barnaul and Novosibirsk would be sent up from Central Asia. Such was the plan, but in practice things did not work out so smoothly. In their exuberance over this 'triumph of socialist labour' the Soviet leaders overlooked, at least in their public statements, the greatly increased costs of construction and many constructional defects of the line.[2]

Party pressure for increased cotton production squeezed out subsistence farming in the Central Asian republics but supplies of grain did not arrive as planned by the Turk–Sib railway to feed Central Asian cotton farmers and their families. There was local competition for Siberian grain and it was also more expensive than had been anticipated owing to high transport costs.[3] There were also difficulties about supplies of Siberian timber for Central Asia because

[1] S. Swianiewicz, *Forced Labour and Economic Development. An Inquiry into the Experience of Soviet Industrialization* (Oxford University Press, London, 1965), p. 202.

[2] Georg Cleinow, *Roter Imperialismus* (Verlag von Julius Springer, Berlin, 1931), pp. 180–3.

[3] Ibid.

the available exports were reduced by the quantities required for the many new constructions in Siberia.

There had been hopes at this time that the Turk–Sib would give a spurt to the Soviet trade with Sinkiang. Before the appearance of the railway Sinkiang was far from the Russian railway system. Now the Turk–Sib passed within reasonable distance of the Sino-Soviet frontier, though the projected spur from Aktogay to the frontier itself did not materialize until after World War II, while the projected railway on the Chinese side of the frontier has not yet been built to link up with the Turk–Sib.

At the time of construction, the stretch of this railway running through Semirech'ye and the controversial Ili Valley gave Russia a strategic advantage over China, where the nearest railhead was 2,668 km. distant from the frontier at Kalgan. Meanwhile, as will be shown later, the whole situation in this area has changed politically and economically owing to the Sino-Soviet conflict.

Other railways built in the '30s marked the new importance attached by the Soviet Union to isolated reserves of Kazakh and Siberian raw materials, primarily minerals, and also to providing better communications between them and industry. Thus the Karaganda colliery was linked in the north with Petropavlovsk on the Trans-Siberian railway and in the south with the 'Giant' Balkhash copper smelter 504 km. distant in south-east Kazakhstan, so as to provide the smelter with fuel and an outlet for its copper, and this was also the case with the Dzhezkazgan copper mine. The Rubtsovsk–Ridder railway, a spur of the Turk–Sib in north-east Kazakhstan, opened up the rich non-ferrous areas of the Altay and greatly facilitated their development. The Gur'yev–Kandagach line (518 km.) connected the industrial districts of the Urals with the Emba oilfields in west Kazakhstan.

The main railway construction (after the Turk–Sib) in the eastern areas centred on the massive development of the second Urals–Kuznetsk metallurgical base. In both centres a network of interconnecting mine and factory lines was built at great speed. The shuttling of coal, coke, and ore for the Urals–Kuznetsk combine imposed 'a staggering burden' on the main Trans-Siberian line. The existing capacity was also heavily overtaxed by planned developments in east Siberia and the Far East, involving greatly increased shipments of oil and industrial equipment to the east as well as the traditional east–west freight of animal products, foodstuffs, and tea for European Russia. There were also heavy shipments of military supplies along this line during these years. The result of all this strain was 'mounting backlogs of unshipped assignments and a sharp rise in accidents and wrecks',[1] due to the failure to allocate capital funds for much needed improvements and rolling stock to this vital east–west artery. Matters began to improve under the tough administration of Lazar M. Kaganovich who was appointed Commissar of Communications in 1938. The overworked rolling stock was reinforced and the busiest sectors of the line between the Urals and the Kuzbas double-tracked.

A large plant for building and repairing locomotives went into operation at Ulan-Ude in Buryat Mongolia and other repair workshops were built in Stalinsk (now Novokuznetsk). The preoccupation with defence and economic development in the Far East and the need to bring these remote regions into closer contact with western European Russia was reflected in the double-tracking in 1933–6 of the 1,687-mile-long line between Ulan-Ude and Khabarovsk (with forced labour crews), and the linking of Khabarovsk with the new town of Komsomol'sk-on-the-Amur.[2] On the eve of World War II a new line, 213 miles long, was constructed (also with forced labour) from Ulan-Ude to Naushki (near the old caravan-tea entrepôt of Kyakhta) thus for the first time connecting Outer Mongolia with the Russian railway system.[3] The second and third Five Year Plans mentioned the construction of the BAM (Baykal-Amur) 'magistral' or trunk-line planned to run through the desolate taiga, mountain, and marsh terrain north of the Amur River between Tayshet on the Trans-Siberian railway and Komsomol'sk (about 1,800 km.) or an undesignated port on the Soviet Pacific coast. The 'Lena' sector from Tayshet to Ust'-Kut via the now famous Bratsk hydro-electric station was completed and is marked on the Soviet maps. Forced labour crews also worked on the other end of the mysterious BAM, transferred for this purpose from the ill-starred Belomor (White Sea Canal).[4] According to the text of the

---

[1] Tupper, op. cit. pp. 415–20.   [2] Ibid. pp. 419–20.   [3] Ibid. p. 420.
[4] The references here to forced labour in the construction of railways are from Swianiewicz, op. cit. pp. 290, 301.

Second Five Year Plan: 'It will transverse little investigated regions of the Amur and the Primor'ye and bring to life a new enormous territory and its colossal riches—timber, gold, coal, and also make possible the cultivation of great tracts of land suitable for agriculture. Two-thirds of the BAM will go through the Far Eastern kray, the length of which is 1,800 km. The line will be completed in the Third Five Year Plan.'[1] As there was no further public mention of the progress of this grandiose scheme the most likely supposition is that construction was stopped by the war (it would seem to have been revived in the *Sevsib* project in 1966).

In the southern Central Asian republics no railway of national significance on the scale of the Transcaspian or the Tashkent–Orenburg lines was built under the three pre-World War II plans. New lines of some local significance connected the Lenger coal-fields with the big lead-refining and cotton-ginning town of Chim-kent, the capital of south Kazakhstan, and Stalinabad (Dushanbe) and its large cotton combine (1942), and with Kurgan Tyube in the Vakhsh Valley, one of the largest cotton-ginning centres in the Soviet Union.

Some factories, as has been mentioned above, were built before the war in Central Asia, but in general the insistence on the principles of the priority of heavy industry and the production of capital goods in the planned development of the more advanced regions of Russia were not and could not be maintained in the early stages of Soviet industrialization in the Central Asian republics.[2] The natural resources of this area had not been adequately studied and as a result 'erroneous impressions were widespread about the poverty of Central Asia in fuel-energy resources', and cadres for industrial employment (especially skilled cadres for heavy industry), or even the rudimentary development of heavy industry, were lacking. Moreover, the creation of heavy industry required much greater funds for a longer period than other branches and it was thus primarily located in areas where it would yield the best economic results.[3] The industrialization of

---

[1] *Vtoroy Pyatiletniy Plan Razvitiya Narodnogo Khozyaystva SSSR 1933–7*, Tom 2, p. 186.

[2] R. Rakhimov, 'The Development of Industry of the Central Asian Economic Region', *Iz. AN Tadzhikskoy SSR*, no. 3 (38) (1964), p. 35.

[3] G. Ya. Kurtser, 'Basic Results of the Socialist Industrialization of Tadzhikistan', *Iz. AN Tadzhikskoy SSR*, no. 3 (38) (1964), p. 66.

Central Asia therefore started in the first Five Year Plans with the development of light industry, and in the first place the processing of cotton and other local raw materials, for example, silk, leather, and wool. It was promoted by financial and technical assistance, equipment, and apparatus from more highly industrialized regions of the Soviet Union.

In the pre-war years (1932–40) the bases for further industrial progress and for the development of heavy industry were laid by a considerable expansion of electrification and geological research especially in regard to the fuel-energy and mineral raw material resources. These measures, it is claimed by Soviet sources, significantly raised the proportion of industry in the national economy of the Central Asian republics. In Uzbekistan, the most highly industrialized of the republics, for example, the proportion of agriculture in the national economy fell from 68 per cent. to 30 per cent. between 1913 and 1940 while industry rose from 32 per cent. to 70 per cent. The following table shows how these changes affected the formerly pastoral-handicrafts economy of Kirgizia:

Branch Structure of Industry of Kirgizia

(in per cent.)

	1913	1933	1940
Fuel extraction	13.3	12.7	6.3
Metal working	6.6	6.7	13.3
Building materials industry	0.0	0.9	1.8
Woodworking	3.1	1.6	3.0
Leather and footwear	5.0	2.4	2.8
Textiles	10.5	20.7	16.5
Clothes	19.8	3.1	4.4
Food	34.8	40.4	46.3
Sugar	—	3.7	7.4
Meat	No data	10.9	10.2

Source: Rakhimov, op. cit. p. 39.

In these years the main lines of development in Tadzhikistan were in the light and food industries, but the basis of heavy industry was also laid as natural resources were explored for developments, transport was developed, and the skilled labour cadres were expanded. By 1940 the energy, metal-working, building materials, and mining industries were playing a significant role in the Tadzhik economy. In this period the development of water power, the chief energy resource of Tadzhikistan, began. The Varsob GES was constructed in 1937, the first-born of the projects for the utilization of the colossal power potential of the rivers of this lofty Republic. It laid the basis for the development of the production of electric power which in the near future, with the construction of the most powerful GES in Central Asia (Nurek), would be a special feature of the Republic. Though all the Tadzhik power stations including the Varsob could only increase the percentage of the production of electric power in the total industrial production of the Republic from 0.1 per cent. to 0.2 per cent., this step had great significance for the Republic itself where electric light only made its appearance during the years of the first Five Year Plans.[1]

The progress of industry in the Central Asian republics by 1940 compared to 1913 (according to Soviet statistics) and the emergence of hitherto unknown branches of industry is shown in the following table:

Production of the Most Important Branches of Industrial Production in Central Asia in 1913–40

Branch of industry	Unit (of measurement)	1913	1940	1940 in % of 1913
Steel	ooo tons	—	11.4	—
Coal	ooo tons	158	1684.7	1066.3
Oil	ooo tons	152	760	500
Gas (including associated)	million cu. metres	0.3	12.1	4033.3
Electric power	million kW.	5.8	678.5	11698.3
Metal-cutting lathes	units	—	139	—
Cement	ooo tons	—	267.3	—
Cotton-fibre	ooo tons	196.5	692.6	352.5
Cotton textiles	million metres	—	117.34	—
Woollen cloth	ooo linear metres	—	254	—
Silk	ooo linear metres	—	6305	—

Source: *Narodnoye Khozyaystvo SSSR v 1958.* Quoted by Rakhimov, op. cit. p. 41.

[1] Kurtser, op. cit. pp. 72–73.

The rate of growth of capital investments in industry throughout the Central Asian region during the pre-war and war-time periods also reflected the industrial progress of the area. These investments rose from 27.5 per cent. of the total capital investment in the national economy of Central Asia in the Second Five Year Plan years to 31.5 per cent. in the third planned period and 54 per cent. during the war.[1]

AGRICULTURE

Collectivization of land and livestock was introduced into Central Asia and Kazakhstan in 1929, after a decade of civil war, bitter opposition to Sovietization, and economic chaos. The process of rounding up the individual peasants and homesteads was not completed until about 1938. The agrarian reform decrees of 1920 and later, by which Russian settlers were ordered to return the land expropriated from Muslim peasants, mainly in Semirech'ye, brought no enduring peace to Turkestan.[2] These measures were soon followed by a general redistribution of land and of water rights on a class-war basis, the real aim of which was to dispossess the land-owners, set the 'haves' against the 'have nots', and destroy the traditional social basis of the country.[3] Moreover, lands already communally owned by tribes or family groups as, for example, in Turkmenistan, were also arbitrarily split up to the angry bewilderment of the native people. The economic situation was aggravated by these social upheavals and by the break-down in the production of grain in Siberia and European Russia, the usual sources of supply, which led to an acute food shortage. The peasants returned to subsistence farming and reduced the acreage under cotton to provide food for their families, but the food situation remained critical.

Collectivization brought havoc in its train in Central Asia because of the methods used and the predominantly rural character of the country. Though the southern republics were subtropical and ideally suited to the cultivation of cotton, rice, tobacco, and fruit in which they specialized, they also possessed large numbers of livestock: cattle, sheep, and goats. In the north and north-east of the country, the Kazakh and Kirgiz inhabitants of the steppes with their immense

---

[1] Rakhimov, op. cit. p. 41.   [2] Park, op. cit. p. 323.   [3] Ibid. pp. 325-7.

flocks of sheep, goats, and horses had lived a nomadic existence for centuries, geared to their peculiar pastoral methods of stock-breeding, requiring them to move from winter to spring, to summer and winter pastures. Thus before the Revolution Central Asia had considerably more livestock per head of population than the Russian Empire as a whole.[1]

The ruthless methods used to force the settled peasants of the southern republics and the Kazakh-Kirgiz nomads into collective farms led to great human misery and to an enormous reduction of the livestock numbers throughout Central Asia and Kazakhstan. Bread imports were reduced and bread was even withheld from peasants refusing to join the collectives so that many died from starvation during this terrible campaign.[2] The government policy was to settle the steppe nomads in collective farms and expropriate the land and beasts of the better-off elements or *bays* so that they would be more amenable to Sovietization. This was fiercely resisted by the Kazakhs, who slaughtered their herds, starved, or fled to China rather than submit to a policy which spelt death to nomadic stock-breeding. Kazakhstan and Kirgizia, which had 20 per cent. of all Soviet sheep and goats in 1928, are estimated by Naum Jasny to have lost more than five-sixths of their herds during the next five years. Between 1928 and 1933 the other Central Asian republics and west Siberia lost almost 45,000,000 sheep and goats or nearly four-fifths of their stocks. While the decline in sheep and goats was large in all areas of the Soviet Union, it was not so dramatic as in these nomadic or semi-nomadic areas.[3]

Nomadism was anathema to the Bolsheviks, settled agriculture being regarded as a higher form of economic organization irrespective of the land or type of agriculture practised. Roaming nomads also presented many problems of political control and subjugation so they were doomed. In the conditions of the Kazakh steppe it was economically senseless to try to replace the traditional methods of stock-breeding by settled agriculture, especially before proper buildings or other arrangements had been made to receive the Kazakhs and their herds. This was later ackowledged as being a

---

[1] Cf. *U.N. Economic Bulletin for Europe*, p. 57.

[2] Cf. B. Hayit, *Turkestan im XX Jahrhundert* (C. W. Leske Verlag, Darmstadt, 1956), p. 281.   [3] Jasny, op. cit. p. 633.

fundamental error but only when it was too late to repair the damage done to Kazakh life and animals. Between the censuses of 1926 and 1939 the Kazakhs declined in numbers from 3,968,289 to 3,098,764 and the rural population declined from 5,518,018 in 1926 to 4,404,057 in 1939.[1] Even at the slow rate of increase in all the USSR, the Kazakhs should have numbered 4,600,000 in 1939.[2] This decline was caused by the annihilation of virtually all their livestock —their only livelihood—in connexion with the collectivization drive. The drastic reduction in livestock is clear from the following table and the fact that even by 1954 Kazakhstan had not caught up with pre-collectivization levels.

	1928	1934	1935	1940	1954	1961	1964
			(millions of head)				
Sheep and goats	19.2	2.26	3.6	7.0	18.4	28.7	29.5

Sources: *Nar. Khozyaystvo Kazakhskoy SSR*, op. cit. p. 141; *Nar. Khozyaystvo SSSR*, 1960, p. 455; *Kazakhstanskaya Pravda*, 4 February 1965.

No hint of these happenings in Kazakh animal husbandry appeared in the official *Itogi* (results) of the First or Second Five Year Plans and there was also a strict censorship on news of this Kazakh tragedy reaching the outside world. The *Itogi* of the First Five Year Plan published in 1934 in the midst of the Kazakh collectivization tragedy refers to Kazakh agriculture in the following terms: '. . . the organization of large livestock and grain farms, the collectivization and introduction of highly mechanized equipment caused profound reconstructive improvements in agriculture.' It was years before the significance of these 'reconstructive improvements' in Kazakh agriculture became known in the West.

The American mining engineer John D. Littlepage, one of the very few foreigners to witness the devastation caused by de-nomadiza-tion, i.e. forced settlement of the Kazakh nomads, has left a grim picture of what he actually saw at this time in Kazakhstan.

On this trip, however, as we pushed along day after day through these pastured plateaux, brilliant with green grass and sprinkled with multi-coloured wild flowers, my sympathies went out to those nomads who had forcibly resisted their conversion into 'proletarians'. . . . It was a queer

---

[1] Cf. 1926 and 1939 Soviet censuses.   [2] Cf. Jasny, op. cit. p. 323.

sensation to push through this beautiful, almost deserted country following empty camel trails which had once been heavily travelled at this time of year. . . . We caught frequent glimpses of smoke rising lazily from the ruins of adobe villages once occupied by herders. These villages had been set on fire during the struggle between the nomads and Communist reformers and were still burning months later.[1]

Collectivization also had disastrous effects on the home industries of Central Asia, the varied handicrafts of which supplied the local population with many of the ordinary articles of clothing and domestic utensils. The peasants had always been the largest market for these handicrafts. But as a result of collectivization and industrialization under the First Five Year Plan the links between the peasants and the handicraft producers were sundered. The State became a sort of middleman between the two groups. The handicraft workers were obliged to seek their raw materials from the State trade organs whose policy was to starve the private industries of raw materials and to collectivize them. Thus the private weavers obtained no cotton and the handicraft workers in leather or silk were also deprived of raw materials and forced out of business. Their only choice was either to enter collective farms or become part of the industrial proletariat in the towns. Handicrafts in all industrialized countries had been gradually superseded by manufactured goods. But the centuries-old and extremely skilled handicrafts of Central Asia, examples of which can still be seen in the museums of Tashkent and Khiva, were killed more swiftly and deliberately by a ruthless Government than happened elsewhere in the world.

Cotton

It was clear from the directives of the First Five Year Plan that the Soviets would continue and intensify the Tsarist policy of cotton expansion in Central Asia. The four Central Asian republics and the southern cotton belt of Kazakhstan were, in the words of the plan, 'to be the main cotton base of the Soviet Union'. 'The role of the Central Asian republics in the all-Union division of labour is to serve mainly as an area of cotton fibre production, silk, karakul, one of the biggest if not the biggest areas of garden and vine produce

[1] John D. Littlepage, *In Search of Soviet Gold* (Harcourt, Brace & Co., New York, 1937), pp. 185–6.

and one of the basic areas of other technical crops and animal raw materials.'[1] When the first Five Year Plans went into operation, projects for developing food crops in the Central Asian republics capable of satisfying local requirements were not mentioned. The Soviets were determined to make the country independent of imported raw cotton in the shortest possible time so as to save scarce foreign currency. In spite of their condemnation of Tsarist policy in making Central Asia a 'cotton colony', they continued this policy themselves (with a greatly extended programme of education, public health, and economic development). There was no question of consulting the cotton growers on the expanded cotton programme. The note of command was clear: 'Central Asia was called to free the Soviet Union from dependence on foreign cotton or foreign cloth.'[2]

In the early planned years the Soviet authorities made serious mistakes in regard to cotton prices, fertilizer supplies, and the need to grow cotton in rotation. The result was a sharp decline in yields in spite of the increased acreage under cotton in irrigated areas of Central Asia (from 9 quintals per ha. in 1925–8 to less than 7 quintals in 1931–2) and widespread discontent among the cotton farmers.[3] Until 1935 cotton producers were paid prices little differing from the pre-collectivization prices. Then, in compensation for the rapid inflation in prices of all consumer goods in the early '30s, they received seed, fertilizer, tea, sugar, and bread grain at low prices to encourage production of cotton. Advances in money and goods were also made. Another reason for providing grain was to prevent cotton growers from using their irrigated fields for grain rather than cotton—which they were prone to do when uncertain of government food supplies. After 1 January 1935 the delivery of grain to cotton growers was discontinued (and they had to pay the prevailing high prices for it) but, simultaneously, the procurement prices of cotton were raised in Central Asia to almost four times the level of 1926–7. As a result, cotton yields rocketed and production was improved by generous government supplies of fertilizer to the cotton industry at relatively low prices. Moreover, the Government

---

[1] *Pyatiletniy Plan Narodnokhozyaystvennogo Stroitel'stva SSSR* (Moscow, 1930), Tom 3, p. 327.

[2] *Itogi Vypoleniya Pervogo Pyatiletnogo Plana Razvitiya Narodnogo Khozyaystvo SSSR* (Moscow, 1934), p. 227.   [3] Jasny, op. cit. p. 566.

offered huge premiums for cotton delivered in excess of the planned yield,[1] a clear proof that under the prevailing conditions the Central Asian farmers were not being overpaid for their labours though relatively speaking they were a good deal better off than the famished peasants of European Russia. The concessions were made to the cotton producers because the Government wanted to be sure of supplies. It was dealing with an area which had very recently been seething with discontent and even open hostility against Sovietization and could not afford to risk further dissatisfaction on the score of cotton prices. As a result of improved conditions and prices cotton plans were often over-fulfilled and the Government decided to stabilize the acreage in irrigated cotton at the 1933 level of 1,677,000 ha. or more than 60 per cent. above that reached before collectivization. From being a heavy importer of cotton in Tsarist times, the Soviet Union became for the first time self-sufficient in cotton in 1931[2] and a net exporter of cotton by 1937 (42,000 tons).[3] This much-publicized 'self-sufficiency' was, however, achieved only at the expense of pitifully low domestic consumption of cotton goods held down by high prices and scanty supplies.

The then accepted Soviet thesis that 'the specialization of Soviet agriculture differs radically from the specialization of agricultural regions in pre-revolutionary Russia' determined by 'costs of production and market prices' had little or no foundation as far as the cotton crop was concerned.[4] In both the Tsarist and Soviet periods cotton was grown where it was most favoured by climatic conditions (and thus incidentally where it was economically most profitable for the 'market'). The disastrous results of Khrushchev's obsession with the 'nation-wide cultivation of maize' irrespective of climate or soil and the short-lived attempts to grow cotton in non-irrigated lands of the Ukraine and the north Caucasus prove the nonsense (if proof were needed) of this kind of jejune Soviet theorizing.

After the initial fumbling the pre-war record shows that the Soviet Government tackled the cotton problem on a broader basis and more effectively than their predecessors in the Kremlin. Not only were fertilizer supplies assured to the cotton industry at a time when other crops were starved of them but a new fertilizer industry was

---

[1] Jasny, op. cit. p. 382.   [2] *Itogi Vypoleniya Pervogo Pyatiletnogo Plana*, p. 147.
[3] Jasny, op. cit. p. 96.   [4] Balzak, op. cit. p. 356.

H

established at Chirchik near Tashkent with a hydro-electric power station (110,000 kW. capacity) by the First Five Year Plan. This was a considerable advance even if, in the words of the plan, 'it must only be regarded as a beginning and will only suppy 42 per cent. of Central Asian requirements of mineral fertilizer'.[1] A large engineering works, the *Tashsel'mash*, for the construction and repair of agricultural and especially cotton cultivation machinery, was also constructed under the First Five Year Plan in Tashkent. The plans for this plant were drafted by Muscovites and Leningraders and many big industrial cities like Moscow, Leningrad, Kiev, and Kharkov helped to build it. The *Itogi* of the First Five Year Plan announced the introduction of tractor and horse-implements into the cotton industry and so began the long process of replacing primitive hand implements by mechanization which, though far from complete in 1965, gradually transformed the techniques of Central Asian cotton cultivation.[2] Good-quality American upland cotton was widely grown under government auspices instead of the short-staple variety traditionally cultivated in Central Asia.

Unlike the system in grain farms, the procurements of cotton were based at this time on contracts to deliver the whole crop from a given area to the government authorities and the MTS. And as government policy put increased pressure on the cotton collectives to produce more cotton, food crops were squeezed out; the Government's problem was to keep the price right and ensure good supplies to the cotton farmers. Failure on either score (as happened later under Khrushchev's régime) inevitably affected production.

During World War II there was a decline in the irrigated cotton acreage and in the cotton yields owing to the lack of labour to operate the irrigation facilities and fertilizer. Food crops were grown to feed the war-time population swollen with evacuees and compensate to some extent for the absence of supplies from the occupied European Russian granary. Some supplies of grain were, however, made to the cotton growers at privileged prices and this continued to 1953.[3]

These developments in cotton cultivation were accompanied by the creation of a Central Asian cotton textile industry. This step

[1] *Pyatiletniy Plan*, p. 336.   [2] *Itogi*, op. 148.
[3] Jasny, op. cit. p. 382.

was directly inspired by Lenin's thesis on the local processing of the raw materials of 'the neglected borderlands of Russia'. In this case, a huge cotton textile combine was set up in Tashkent during the First Five Year Plan, the first wing of which was in operation in the early '30s,[1] and others followed in Dushanbe (then Stalinabad), Fergana, and Ashkhabad. The Tashkent combine was expected 'to satisfy in the first place local requirements and partly the requirements of neighbouring countries'.[2] In fact, as will be shown later, in spite of Lenin's theorizing and the existence of a group of local cotton mills (some large even by international standards, like the Tashkent and Dushanbe combines), local cloth requirements could not be supplied by these mills and by far the largest part of the Soviet cotton textile industry remained in European Russia close to the chief centres of population and consumption, as of old.

In the early years these Central Asian mills were almost entirely run by Russians. The staff at the Tashkent combine was completely Russian in the pre-war years and even later and the situation was the same at the *Tashsel'mash*.[3] Women usually formed the majority of workers in cotton mills, but it was extremely difficult to draw the veiled Muslim women into this or any other industry in the early years of Sovietization. Later, when many Muslim women did enter the factories, it was generally as a result of intensive party propaganda, prodding, and preaching amounting at times to unpleasant administrative pressures.

Irrigation[4]

Before the onset of the first Five Year Plans in 1928–9, the Soviet Government was faced by a dangerous situation in the cotton areas of Turkestan owing to the advance of the desert upon the arable land and to the contraction of the irrigation systems following chaotic conditions during the Revolution and civil war. The breakdown in the traditional food supplies had caused many small cotton farmers to revert to subsistence farming and neglect the irrigation canals. The new water codes also added to the confusion

[1] *Pyatiletniy Plan*, p. 336.
[2] *Itogi Vypoleniya Vtorogo Pyatiletnogo Plana*, 1939, p. 54.
[3] *U.N. Economic Bulletin for Europe*, p. 54.
[4] In this section I am greatly indebted to the articles on irrigation in *Central Asian Review*, vol. VIII, nos. 1 and 2; vol. V, no. 3.

by proclaiming the principles of public ownership and controls of water supplies. The traditional system and distribution of water rights on the principle of the 'labouring use' was thus destroyed and water rights were restricted or annulled to the non-toiling elements of the population.[1] In order to get cotton production going again, the Government spent considerable sums on a programme of reconstruction of the old irrigated areas in the early 1920s. Uzbekistan, the main cotton-growing area of Central Asia, was the largest beneficiary in this programme.

The chief water resources of Central Asia for irrigation purposes are the Amu Dar'ya, the Syr Dar'ya, and Irtysh rivers and the smaller but locally important Vakhsh, Varsob, Chu, Murgab, Sary Su, and Zeravshan rivers. The national importance and interconnexion of the irrigation and cotton expansion plans in this area of desert, semi-desert, and tropical climate was clearly stressed in the words of the First Five Year Plan: 'The anticipated increase in the irrigated lands and the cotton area is linked with development of the irrigation system and cotton cultivation in Central Asia and Kazakhstan as adopted in the plan. Non-fulfilment of the works mentioned in the plan ensuring growth in these areas would cause a decline in the cotton cultivation plans. Thus the projected task of forced development of irrigated works not only for Central Asia and south Kazakhstan but for the USSR as a whole is a task of primary national importance.'[2] The Soviets claimed that as a result of the 'reconstruction process' the irrigated area of Central Asia and Kazakhstan amounted to about 92 per cent. of the pre-World War I level or some 3,332,000 ha. in 1927–8, on the eve of the First Five Year Plan.[3] The easy means of extending irrigation had been exhausted and large new irrigation works had to be undertaken so as to ensure the success of the cotton programme.

All the Central Asian republics and Kazakhstan had a share in the irrigation programmes laid on by the First Five Year Plan. The first of these large-scale projects was the Vakhsh Valley Canal Project in Tadzhikistan (Vakhshstroy) which was announced by the First Five Year Plan. The Vakhsh Valley was ideal from the point of view

[1] Park, op. cit. ch. VII, 'The Revival of Agriculture', pp. 311–20.
[2] *Pyatiletniy Plan Narodnokhozyaystvennogo Stroitel'stva SSSR*, Tom 3, p. 343.
[3] Ibid. p. 340.

of climate for the cultivation of fine long-staple Egyptian cotton, though little cotton had previously been grown there. Russian workers were used for skilled or semi-skilled jobs—'Kulaks' from Siberia and the Caucasus are reported to have been imported as forced labour—while American technicians supervised the whole project.[1] The area was ridden by malaria and many people perished from it in the early stages of the work before prophylactic work exterminated it. The canal had a total length of 13,000 km., with its system of feeder canals. The main canal and the head works on the Vakhsh were finished in 1933. Uzbeks and Tadzhiks, Russians and Ukrainians from over-populated areas were settled on the new lands opened up by the Vakhsh irrigation scheme. The electrification of the valley, the second part of the scheme, did not start until 1954.

The Fergana Valley, the largest in Central Asia (300 km. from east to west and 140 km. from north to south), is one of the most fertile areas of Central Asia producing cotton and silk and containing many branches of industry: oil, engineering, chemicals, and textiles have been established there. It was the scene in 1939 of a new type of 'mass manual' irrigation construction (*vse-narodnyy stroy*). Some 160,000 collective farmers, students, intellectuals, and workers of every kind from Uzbekistan and the adjacent republics turned out (under strong propaganda stress) to lend a hand in building the 270 km. long Fergana Canal in record time (an extension of 60 km. was simultaneously made by Tadzhik farmers).[2] Other examples of the 'mass construction' type of irrigation canal built in 1939–40 were the Great Zeravshan Canal in Samarkand *oblast*, and the North and South Fergana Canals. There seems to have been an element of genuine enthusiasm among the native people constructing these canals (in spite of the Party pressures) because they realized they were building something of permanent value to the areas in which they lived.

The whole Fergana irrigation system is dependent on the Syr Dar'ya River and its head waters, combined with the Naryn and the Kara-Dar'ya rivers. Land reclamation running into millions of hectares quickly followed these irrigation schemes. In 1939–40, in

[1] B. Yakovlev, *Kontsentratsionnyye Lageri SSSR*, Institute for the Study of the USSR (Munich, 1955), p. 140.
[2] S. M. Mamarasylou, *Irrigatsiya Uzbekistana* (Tashkent, 1964), p. 19.

Uzbekistan it was officially reported that the expenditure on this work alone amounted to 442 million roubles.[1]

In the Gissar Valley (in Tadzhikistan) the Molotov Canal was opened in 1942 and brought more than 10,000 ha. under cultivation. In Kirgizia there was also a considerable development of irrigation in the pre-war years. Old systems were reconstructed and new networks laid down. Between 1937 and 1940 the irrigated area rose from 450,000 ha. to 750,000 ha. Works of great local importance centred on the Chumysh Dam (begun in the early '30s), the Orto-Tokoy Reservoir, and the Great Chu Canal begun in 1941.[2] In the extreme west of the country some of the most arid desert lands are to be found in Turkmenistan. Here it was reported that between 1924 and 1938 the irrigated area had almost doubled.[3] Many irrigation canals in Turkmenistan were fed from the great Amu Dar'ya River including the Bosaga–Kerki Canal which was the starting-point in later years of the famous Kara-Kum Canal, and in the south other canals issued from the Tedzhen River to irrigate the orchards and cotton-fields of Ashkhabad *oblast*.

Extensive irrigation work was done in south Kazakhstan, notably in the barren lands of the Hungry Steppe (Golodnaya Step') which covers an area of about 10,000 sq. km. lying between the Tashkent and Samarkand oases, and in the western region of the country the Ural–Kushum Canal irrigated 5,000 ha. of cultivated land. The Golodnaya Step', or Hungry Steppe (so called because it offers neither food nor water to man or beast), had a long history of alternate irrigation and desiccation since ancient times. It was early an object of special attention by the Soviet Government intent on utilizing it for cotton cultivation. Until 1963 the Hungry Steppe was divided between Uzbekistan, Tadzhikistan, and Kazakhstan but the Kazakh portion, which will be dealt with later, was then transferred to Uzbekistan. The first State cotton farm (*Sovkhoz*), the 'Pakhta-Aral' or 'Cotton Island' in the steppe, was established in the early '20s and by 1928–9, 68,000 ha. had been brought under cultivation in this formerly barren steppe. By 1939, 95,000 ha. were under irrigation and 4,000 workers were attached to the Pakhta-Aral farm.[4]

[1] Mamarasulov, op. cit. p. 20.
[2] V. F. Pavlenko and S. N. Ryazantsev, *Kirgizskaya SSR* (Moscow, 1956), p. 46.
[3] *Kommunist Turkmenistana*, no. 2 (1956).
[4] *Osvoyeniye Golodnoy Stepi* (Moscow, 1963), p. 7.

All this complicated irrigation work was not done without complaints in the Soviet Press of many shortcomings and defects. There was dissatisfaction over negligence in construction of the canals, wastage of water, and the fact that insufficient advantage was taken of new techniques and machinery. But the overall impression at the time was of satisfaction that the cotton area had been so far extended as to provide a base for greatly increased cotton production in the future.

WAR-TIME EVACUATION AND INDUSTRIAL DEVELOPMENT

The evacuation of industrial plant from European Russia during World War II gave a great impetus to industry in the 'eastern regions'. Nikolay A. Voznesenskiy, then Chief of the State Planning Commission, dramatically described this operation: 'There was a period during the history of the war economy of the USSR when a large part of war industry was moving eastwards. Tens of thousands of machine tools, hammers, presses, and turbines were on the move. It was a distinct period of re-location of the productive powers of the USSR to the east. Thousands of workers, engineers and mechanics were migrating. The evacuated industries were reconstructed, thanks to the heroic efforts of the working class and technicians under the leadership of the party of Lenin-Stalin.'[1] The mobilization of the economic resources of the country, including the location of the evacuated plant, was directed by the 'War Economic Plan' of August 1941. The eastern economic regions of the country became the primary supply base for the front and the war economy. Voznesenskiy reports that 'in 1943, the output of all industry in the regions of the Volga, the Urals, west Siberia, Kazakhstan and Central Asia was 2.9 times as large as in 1940 and their share in the total industrial output of the USSR increased more than threefold'. The Urals were transformed in the course of the war into the basic and most powerful industrial region of the country.[2]

The direction of 'the great re-location of productive powers of the USSR' was partly based on the existence in the sites selected of skilled workmen capable of continuing production as quickly as

[1] N. A. Voznesenskiy, *The Economy of the USSR during World War II*. Translated from the Russian (Public Affairs Press, Washington, 1948), p. 4.   [2] Ibid. p. 26.

possible, but in many cases plant and skilled staff were evacuated together. Voznesenskiy states that 455 enterprises were evacuated to the Urals, 210 to west Siberia, and 250 to Central Asia and Kazakhstan, in all 1,360 large enterprises (where the others went is not stated).

In order to cope with the greatly increased rail traffic between Siberia, the Urals, and central Russia and between the Central Asian republics and central Russia, several new lines were built in the eastern areas and the traffic capacity of operating lines was increased. The following new railways were constructed: Akmolinsk–Kartaly, Orsk–Kandagach–Gur'yev, and Komsomol'sk–Sovetskaya –Gavan' (in the Far East).

Professor Hunter utters a warning (with which I completely agree) against a literal acceptance of Voznesenskiy's 'official chronicle of this period' and believes that 'the role of the Russian east has been considerably exaggerated'. 'Two devices', he says, 'have been employed—a shift of the dividing line from east to west that transfers certain districts from west to east and a simple failure to discuss developments in the territory lying between Nazi-occupied areas in the west and the true eastern regions.'[1]

Owing to its important raw material, technological, and mining resources Kazakhstan became the main reception area for evacuated heavy industrial plant in Central Asia while light industry gravitated farther south to the four Central Asian republics which were less developed industrially than Kazakhstan, but already familiar with some light manufacturing industries.

The loss of the highly developed metallurgical industry of the Ukraine resulted in the creation of some new industries in the eastern regions and in an intensive search for new sources of strategic raw materials. Thus largely on the basis of evacuated plant an industry producing quality steels, ferro-alloys, and rolled steel was rapidly developed in the Urals and introduced into west Siberia. A 'Commission of the all-Union Academy of Sciences for the Mobilization of the Resources of the Urals, west Siberia, and Kazakhstan for the Needs of the War' under the leadership of the President of the all-Union Academy, V. L. Komarov, assisted by Academician Bardin, was entrusted with the direction of raw materials, technological,

[1] Hunter, op. cit. p. 33.

power, and agricultural problems arising from the mobilization for defence of the eastern regions.[1] As a result of their activities, improved techniques for the production of copper, lead, nickel, and the poly-metallic ores of the Altay were worked out, the resources of the Karaganda coal basin and the coal and metals of the Orsk–Aktyubinsk area were more thoroughly investigated, and new sources of strategic raw materials were discovered, for example, the big Blagodat iron mines in the Urals and several manganese mines in the Urals, western Siberia, and Kazakhstan were used to replace the German-occupied Nikopol (Ukraine) source of supply.[2]

The poorly developed coke–chemical industry of the Urals was greatly reinforced by the evacuated equipment of the Krivoy Rog and the Donbas coke–chemical plants. Central Asia was also a reception centre for some evacuated plants from Leningrad and Moscow, for example, the Ivanovo (Moscow) non-ferrous plant was moved to the Balkhash copper site in Kazakhstan.

The evacuation of engineering plant led, in some cases, to the creation of new industries, in others it reinforced an already existing industry, thus the equipment of the Rostov agricultural machine plant evacuated to Tashkent in 1941 was the basis of the very important textile machine-building plant (*Tashtekstil'mash*) which was equipped with new textile shops in 1942. From 1941–5 it also produced metal-cutting lathes and spare parts for textile equipment and in 1946 went over completely to serial production of spinning and textile machines of many types.[3] Then the Kharkov tractor plant, evacuated to the Altay at the beginning of the war, was converted to war production but subsequently was the basis for the development of a powerful new tractor plant at Rubtsovsk.

Together with the Urals, 'the chief arsenal of the USSR' during the war, evacuated and reinforced local plants and factories forged ahead in western Siberia, Central Asia, and Kazakhstan with the production of armaments essential for Russia's war effort. Some large and important new constructions were put up such as the Magnitogorsk blast furnaces nos. 5 and 6 (the biggest in Europe), the Chelyabinsk metallurgical plant and thermal electric station, and the

---

[1] M. K. Kozybaev, 'Iz Istorii Deyatel'nosti "Komissii AN SSSR po Mobilizatsii Resursov Urala, zapadnoy Sibiri i Kazakhstana na Nuzhdy Oborony" ', *Iz. AN Kaz. SSR*, no. 1 (18) (1962), pp. 62–69.

[2] Lyashchenko, op. cit. vol. III, p. 512.   [3] *Bolshaya Entsiklopediya*, p. 112.

above-mentioned Uzbek metallurgical and steel works at Begovat, the first in Central Asia.[1] With the evacuation to the east of so many enterprises and the construction of new plants the problem of adequate power to run them became acute. The capacity of existing electric power stations had to be greatly reinforced and many new stations were built. Electric power in Uzbekistan, which before the war lagged behind the needs of industry, was substantially increased to meet the new demands of evacuated industry. A series of hydro-electric power stations were built at Ak-Kabak, Ak-Tepe, Salar, Farkhad on the Syr Dar'ya, and in the Tashkent power system alone production of electric power rose from 210 million kWh. in 1940 to 882 million kWh. in 1943.[2]

The other Central Asian republics also increased their power capacity but to a somewhat lesser degree. The so-called 'People's Constructions' method of mass manual labour which first received publicity in the construction of the Great Fergana Canal in 1939–40 was used to build the Farkhad GES in 1943, 'where 70,000 collective farmers tackled the earthworks and 20,000 people worked on the actual construction of the station'. The Ust'-Kamenogorsk GES on the River Irtysh was also a 'People's Construction' in which 'representatives of collective-farmers, workers, and the intelligentsia of various provinces of Kazakhstan participated'.[3] This station, 'not finished until after the war', had far-reaching effects on the development of industry in east Kazakhstan and on the great mineral wealth of the Altay.

During the war Kazakhstan became one of the main all-Union sources of supply for the front not only in agricultural produce such as grain, meat, fats, leather, wool, but also industrial goods—armaments and heavy and light metallurgical products.

These war-time developments in the eastern regions involved heavy capital investments. Voznesenskiy reports that during the four years of the war, the volume of capital investments in the Urals amounted to 16.3 billion roubles or on the average 55 per cent. per year more than was invested in the economy of the Urals during the pre-war years. The speed-up in the industrialization of west Siberia at this time is also reflected in the rise, during the four war years,

[1] Lyashchenko, op. cit. vol. III, p. 519.   [2] Ibid. pp. 521–2.
[3] Ibid. pp. 523–4.

in the level of capital investment by 74 per cent. above the pre-war years, amounting to 5.9 billion roubles. The role of the Central Asian republics and Kazakhstan in the industrial production of the USSR increased considerably, gross output of industry amounted to 4.8 billion roubles in 1940 and 6.6 billion roubles in 1945.[1] The greatest war-time development in this area took place in the metallurgical and fuel industries chiefly in Kazakhstan.

The effects of evacuation of trained personnel and equipment on Tadzhikistan, then taking its first steps in economic development, were notable in several respects. As the Tadzhiks had some experience of light industry pre-war, many food and light industrial plants were evacuated with or without their staffs to 'the deep rear' of Tadzhikistan. 'Tens of thousands of evacuees were received fraternally', we are told.[2] Some of these evacuated mills, factories, and plants were accommodated in existing enterprises of a similar type, for others special accommodation had to be arranged. Thus the equipment of the Feodosiya conserve factory was installed in the Kanibadam conserve factory. The Moscow soap factory and part of the Kharkov soap factory were evacuated to the partly constructed Dushanbe (Stalinabad) soap factory. The Leninabad silk combine and silk-weaving mill received the important Moscow silk-weaving mill, the equipment of which cost 2,800,000 roubles to assemble. About ninety wagons of unassembled equipment reached the unfinished Dushanbe textile combine from the Lyuberetska mill (Moscow region), forty-seven wagons of equipment having already arrived from the Pavlo-Pokrovskiy factory. Not surprisingly, difficulties arose in the primitive country in connexion with the housing of so much machinery and so many evacuees. The building materials and qualified workers available were inadequate for the big tasks imposed upon them. On the other hand, the workers and especially the engineering technical staff evacuated to Central Asia from the more economically advanced, industrialized areas of European Russia helped to raise technical skills among the native peoples where they worked during the war. This was notably so in Tadzhikistan

---

[1] Voznesenskiy, op. cit. pp. 26–28.

[2] Details regarding the evacuation of enterprises to Tadzhikistan are given in an article by L. P. Sechkina: 'Iz Istorii Razmeshcheniya Evakuirovannykh Predpriyatii na Territorii Tadzhikskoy SSR v Gody Velikoy Voiny Otechestyennoy', *Iz. AN Tadzhikskoy SSR, Ot. Obshchestvennykh Nauk*, 3 (38) (1964), p. 86.

where no manufacturing industry existed before the Revolution. The process was facilitated by the evacuation of the Odessa Technological Institute of the canning industry to Tadzhikistan. It trained technicians for the local canning enterprises, the produce of orchards and vineyards being an important element in the Tadzhik economy.[1]

Apart from the expansion of local plant with evacuated equipment, some Central Asian enterprises continued to expand on their own as already planned. A good example of this was the second section of the important Chirchik chemicals plant in Uzbekistan which was opened in 1944. The development of Kazakhstan as a metallurgical and chemical centre continued with the expansion of the range of products manufactured at the Aktyubinsk chemical plant begun in the '30s and the construction of a non-ferrous metals plant in the same town, producing its first ferro-chrome alloys in 1943.[2]

In Kirgizia, war-time evacuation of factories also greatly expedited the then rudimentary level of industrialization. These covered a wide range of industrial activities; among others there were the agricultural engineering plant from Osipenko in the Ukraine, the knitwear factory from Kursk, the footwear factory from Rostov-on-the-Don, the hemp–jute factory and four leather factories from Odessa, and some sugar factories chiefly from the Ukraine; some were re-established as independent enterprises, some attached to already existing concerns,[3] mostly in the south of the Republic. In 1942 the equipment of the Rakhmanovsk spinning–weaving plant was evacuated from Moscow to Osh and attached to the local silk combine. In general, the productive base of Central Asian industry and in particular the food and textile industries was broadened during the war. Decisions about the retention or return of these evacuated factories at the end of the war varied according to the national importance of the individual works. Thus the Rostov tractor works transferred to Tashkent (and the basis of the important new textile machinery plant) was returned to Rostov, but much of the manufacturing capacity producing consumer goods, for example, textiles, footwear, and glass, was retained.

[1] Sechkina, op. cit. p. 92.

[2] A. Nove and J. A. Newth, *The Soviet Middle East—A Communist Model for Development* (Allen & Unwin Ltd., London, 1967), p. 49.

[3] I. G. Grishkov, *Elektrifikatsiya Sovetskogo Kirgizstana* (Frunze, 1965), pp. 39–48.

PART THREE
Economic Development (1945-66)

IV

Soviet Central Asia and Kazakhstan

NATURAL FEATURES AND RESOURCES

The 'geographic distinctiveness' of the Central Asian republics and Kazakhstan has exercised a decisive influence on their history and also on the economic life of this large region.[1] Within its boundaries are to be found extremes of aridity and fertility in the fearsome Kara-Kum and Kyzylkum deserts covering between them large areas of south Kazakhstan, Uzbekistan, and the greater part of Turkmenistan and the lush oases of the south. Historically famous oasis cities like Tashkent, Samarkand, Fergana, and Bukhara owe their prosperity to the vivifying waters of the Amu Dar'ya and Syr Dar'ya rivers, the Oxus and Jaxartes of the Greeks, and other lesser streams like the Zeravshan or the Chirchik, while an ever-growing network of irrigation canals based on this river system enables cultivation to be greatly expanded beyond the riverine cultivated strips. All Central Asian cotton is grown on irrigated land which also yields excellent crops of other tropical produce, notably fruit and vegetables.

The southern and eastern areas of Central Asia are bounded by the mighty mountain chains of the Tyan Shan and the Pamirs, the source of many swiftly flowing, turbulent streams with enormous hydro-power which is now being harnessed in accordance with the planned industrialization and electrification of the republics.

North of these oases stretch the huge Kazakh steppe lands providing ideal pasturage for cattle, sheep, and goats. These former homelands of the nomadic Kazakh stock-breeders are now worked as State or collective farms and since the inception of Khrushchev's 'Virgin Lands' scheme an increasing area has come under the plough.

[1] For a fuller description of the natural features of the Central Asian republics and Kazakhstan, cf. Olaf Caroe, *Soviet Empire* (Macmillan & Co., London, 1953), p. 13, and Wheeler, op. cit. p. 1.

As a result of a peculiarly dynamic early history of conquest, invasion, and migration, the population of Central Asia presents many distinctive features and sharp differences in trends and composition, for example, from that of European Russia. It is mainly an amalgam of Turkic, Mongol, Iranian, and Slav peoples and in the framework of Central Asia industrialization, the trends and problems of this 'human material' are important.

POPULATION AND LABOUR PROBLEMS

The post-war years saw many changes in the populations of the republics of Central Asia and Kazakhstan. Russification trends which had already been apparent in the pre-war period were intensified by large-scale migrations of Slav peoples: Russians, Ukrainians, and Belorussians who by race and way of life differed sharply from the traditionally Muslim native peoples of Turkic-Iranian stock. These Central Asian peoples are characterized by their high birth-rate which is much above the Soviet average. In 1961 the average birth-rate in the Soviet Union was 23.8 per thousand, but in the Uzbek SSR 38.5 per thousand, in the Turkmen SSR 41 per thousand, and in the Tadzhik SSR 34.4 per thousand.[1] This difference is partly due to the earlier marriages among these nationalities. This factor, and the large-scale immigration from European Russia, has led to a great increase in the population of all the Central Asian republics between the 1939 and 1959 censuses, by almost 3,000,000 (21.5 per cent.) as against 23,700,000 or 14 per cent. for the Soviet Union as a whole. Since 1959 it is estimated that the increase has been even greater, 27 per cent. or almost three times that of the USSR where the population increased by only 9.7 per cent. The Central Asian republics are the most populous in the country. The population rose 40 per cent. between 1939 and 1961 compared to the 13 per cent. Union average.[2]

Most of the peoples of the multi-national Soviet State are also to be found among the indigenous inhabitants of these republics, including Tatars, Poles, Koreans, Jews, Germans, Mordvinians,

---

[1] *Itogi Vsesoyuznoy Perepisi Naseleniya 1959*, Sbornik po SSSR (Moscow, 1962). Quoted in A. A. Isupov, *Natsional'nyy Sostav Naseleniya SSSR* (Moscow, 1964), p. 25.

[2] *Nar. Khoz. S.A.*, no. 5 (1964), p. 13.

Chuvash, Uygurs, Kurds, Georgians. For example, in Kazakhstan 101 nationalities are working 'side by side'.[1] But by far the largest element among the immigrant settlers are the Slavs. The Slav migration to the Central Asian republics is closely connected with the industrialization plans though the settlement of Slav peasant colonists, especially in the Kazakh borderlands and the former Semirech'ye province, long preceded industrialization. It has been steadily on the increase since the inception of the Five Year Plans in 1928 and was much intensified during the war with the evacuation of technical-managerial staffs, teachers, and other workers.

Population Increase in Soviet Central Asia, 1913–65

	1913	1926	1939	1959	1965
Uzbek SSR	4,366,000	4,565,000	6,440,000	8,261,000	10,180,000
Kirgiz SSR	864,000	1,002,000	1,458,000	2,066,000	2,600,000
Tadzhik SSR	1,034,000	1,032,000	1,484,000	1,981,000	2,430,000
Turkmen SSR	1,042,000	998,000	1,252,000	1,516,000	1,870,000
Total	7,306,000	7,597,000	10,634,000	13,824,000	17,080,000
Kazakh SSR	5,565,000	6,074,000	5,990,000	9,154,000	12,000,000
Total Central Asia	12,871,000	13,671,000	16,624,000	22,978,000	29,080,000

Sources: *Nar. Khoz. SSR 1963 g.* (Moscow, 1965), p. 9: *Izvestiya* 30 January 1963 and the reports of the Central Statistical Offices of the Union Republics on the population of 1 January 1965. Quoted from Y. P. Mironenko, *Population Trends in Soviet Central Asia* (Munich, 1965).

Non-native experts mostly from European Russia are still an important element in the Central Asian and Kazakh economies in spite of the great strides made in higher education among these Muslim nationalities, especially the Uzbeks, since 1940.[2] According to the following statistics the Russians account for a considerably larger number of specialists in the Central Asian republics than their percentage of the relevant populations would warrant:

---

[1] *Kaz. Pravda*, 1 April 1966.

[2] 'Some Statistics on Higher Education in the Muslim Republics', *Central Asian Review*, vol. X, no. 3 (1962) p. 229, contains a useful analysis of statistics on higher education in the Muslim republics based on a very informative Russian work: *Vyssheye Obrazovaniye v SSSR* (Moscow, 1961).

I

Specialists in Central Asian Economy

(in per cent.)

	Population 1959	Specialists in economy 1960
Uzbekistan		
Uzbeks	62.2	36.9
Russians	13.5	30.2
Kazakhstan		
Kazakhs	30.0	24.0
Russians	42.7	53.2
Kirgizia		
Kirgiz	40.5	30.0
Russians	30.2	46.0
Uzbeks	10.6	4.6
Tadzhikistan		
Tadzhiks	53.1	34.0
Uzbeks	23.0	10.7
Russians	13.3	35.9
Turkmenistan		
Turkmens	60.9	44.0
Russians	17.3	32.7

Source: *Central Asian Review*, vol. X, no. 3 (1962), p. 229.
The population figures are taken from the 1959 official Soviet
census returns. The percentage of specialists is based on
figures in *Vyssheye Obrazovaniye v USSR* (Moscow, 1961).

Official Soviet census statistics show how great Slav immigration
has been and how far-reaching its effect on the position of the native
population of the five Central Asian republics. In 1926, for example,
there were 2,650,000 Slavs (Russians, Ukrainians, and Belorussians) living in Central Asia and Kazakhstan, of which Russians
alone amounted to 1,670,000. By the time of the 1959 census the
Russian population had grown to 6,220,000, the Ukrainians to
1,041,000, Belorussians to 125,000. An immediate effect of this
massive Slav immigration was to lower significantly the percentage
of the titular nationality in each of the Central Asian republics though
the percentage varied from republic to republic. Generally speaking,
the Slav migration was greatest to the towns and mining settlements
throughout the area where it helped to construct and manage the

new industrial and mining enterprises and initiate the native peoples into industrial life and skills.

This influx was most noticeable in the capital cities of the republics. In Tashkent, for example, in 1959, only 308,000 out of a population of 912,000 were Uzbeks, while 401,000 or 44 per cent. were Russians. In the capitals of the Kazakh and Kirgiz republics, Alma-Ata and Frunze, the Slavs formed a non-Asian element of much greater strength. Thus Alma-Ata, according to the 1959 census, had a population consisting of 359,000 non-Asians (Russians, Ukrainians, and Belorussians), but only 39,410 Kazakhs and 31,341 other Asian inhabitants. Accordingly, the Kazakhs formed about 8.5 per cent or a relatively small minority of the population in their 'home town'. From 1959 to 1965, the population of Alma-Ata has rapidly increased from 456,000 to 620,000. There is no doubt (though no official breakdown of the national composition of this latest increase has yet been published) that the Slav element is mainly responsible for it as hitherto. The Slav element also largely outnumbers the native population in Frunze, the Kirgiz capital. In 1959, out of a total population of 220,000, 151,000 or more than 68 per cent. of all the inhabitants were Russians, with the Kirgiz numbering only 21,000 or 10 per cent. of the total population.

The relative importance of the Slav element was somewhat less among the Tadzhiks than among the Kazakhs and the Kirgiz. Thus Tadzhiks and other native peoples formed 18.8 per cent. of the Dushanbe population in 1959, but 82 per cent. of the total Tadzhikistan population consisted of Tadzhiks while immigrants from European Russia were 16 per cent. The national composition of the urban population of Tadzhikistan revealed a different relationship between the Tadzhiks and the non-Asian immigrants, with Tadzhiks forming only 31 per cent. or 205,000 out of a total urban population of 605,000.

The intensive development of the economic resources of Kazakhstan will call for increased migration during the current Five Year Plan. According to the Chairman of the Kazakh Council of Ministers, M. Beysebayev, during this period 'the annual growth of the population will be not less than 500,000 mainly through the influx (of workers) to newly developing areas: Mangyshlak Peninsula oil deposits, the poly-metallic deposits of Orlovka, Nikolayevsk,

Karagayly, the copper mines at Sayak, Kachar, the phosphorus mines at Kentau, and also the new sheep *sovkhozy* organized in the desert and semi-desert zones'.[1] This 'influx' will inevitably increase the Slav element in Kazakhstan.

Information about the national composition of the labour force on particular sites is not generally made available in Soviet sources.

Nationality Composition of the Labour Force in September 1964

(in per cent.)

Nationality	Nurek hydro-station	Dushanbe textile mill
Tadzhiks	27.8	15.2
Uzbeks	1.7	10.1
Russians	51.8	55.7
Ukrainians	7.3	2.3
Belorussians	1.9	1.0
Tatars	4.2	7.4
Mordvinians	1.0	2.4
Others	4.3	5.9
Total	100.0	100.0

Source: V. I. Perevedentsev, 'The Influence of Ethnic Factors on the Territorial Redistribution of Population', *Iz. AN SSSR Seriya Geograficheskaya* (1965), no. 4, pp. 31–39. A translation of this article is published in *Soviet Geography* (American Geographical Society, New York, October, 1965), pp. 40–50.

The details published in 1965 of the nationalities engaged in two major construction schemes in Tadzhikistan, the Nurek hydro-electric station and the Dushanbe textile mill, are therefore of great interest. The Nurek hydro-electric station is being built in a high mountain gorge near the new town of Nurek in a densely populated rural area of central Tadzhikistan inhabited almost entirely by Tadzhiks. Nevertheless, Tadzhiks form only a little more than one-fourth of the labour force. Tadzhiks are also in a minority at the

[1] *Pravda*, 7 April 1966.

Dushanbe textile construction site, the largest industrial enterprise in the Tadzhik capital, but their small numbers almost correspond with the ethnic composition of the city itself—15.2 per cent. Tadzhik and 55.7 per cent. Russian.[1] The cause of this disparity between Russians and Tadzhiks was frankly admitted by the Personnel Department of the project to be the poor knowledge of Russian, 'the main language used at work', among the young Tadzhiks of the countryside.[2] It does not seem to have struck the authorities that the Russians should learn Tadzhik so as to be able to instruct the native trainees in their own language. On the contrary, both at Nurek and Dushanbe, they took the alternative course of importing skilled workers from European Russia, Siberia, and elsewhere in the Soviet Union, regardless of the cost and their failure to live up to Party slogans about technical training of nationalities such as the Tadzhiks. The situation at Nurek was the same as at Dushanbe. Among the skilled workers (drill erectors, blasters, tunnel workers, excavators), a large proportion consists of people transferred from other construction projects and coal and ore mines. The small number of Tadzhiks among engineers and technicians on the site makes it impossible to find instructors who could conduct the training courses in Tadzhik. Experienced workers from Siberian hydro-projects and new workers trained at the building workers' school attached to the Novosibirsk hydro-station are to be found on the Nurek site either on transfer or 'voluntarily'. At a time when Siberia itself is suffering from an acute shortage of skilled workers this north–south movement is thoroughly 'irrational' and reflects the general disarray in the Soviet distribution of labour. However, the Nurek management, according to Perevedentsev, is interested in recruiting more local workers because they are better able to support the high summer temperatures of the site.

It is not suggested that the Dushanbe–Nurek situation is typical of conditions throughout Central Asia. There is, in fact, too little detailed information on this point to warrant any general conclusions, though clearly the position varies greatly from region to

---

[1] According to V. I. Perevedentsev efforts are made to attract Tadzhiks from the mountain areas where the labour surplus is greatest to the combine's technical-industrial college but they find it difficult to support the heat and high humidity of the mill's shops and soon leave the combine.   [2] Perevedentsev, op. cit.

region. Thus an investigation carried out in Uzbekistan revealed that the rapidly developing industrialization there and the need for qualified workers had led to a swift rise in the numbers of Uzbek workers with 'definite production qualifications' at three important works. This is shown by the figures compiled as a result of the investigation at the *Tashsel'mash*, *Uzbeksel'mash*, and *Chirchiksel'-mash* plants:

	Total number of workers	
	Uzbeks	*Russians*
	620	602
Stokers	63	72
Locksmiths	92	102
Moulders	46	14
Electric welders	18	23
Others	391	375

Source: F. A. Aripov, 'O Formirovanii Kadrov Promyshlennykh Rabochikh v Uzbekistane', *Ob. Nauki v Uzbekistane*, no. 8 (1965), p. 25.

The investigation apparently only covered rather low-grade skilled workers, and made no mention of the division of managerial jobs between Russians and native nationalities. In the *Tashsel'mash* and *Uzbeksel'mash* plants 84 skilled Russian workers individually trained 300 workers, including 131 from local nationalities, 140 Russians, and others. At the same time 72 skilled Uzbek workers trained 244 workers, of which 118 were from local nationalities, 113 were Russians. The report concludes that 'Russian workers and workers of local nationalities are almost equal in their degree of mastering techniques and qualifications'.[1] The situation thus apparently differs among the more industrially advanced Uzbeks and their Tadzhik neighbours.

The publication in 1965 of a list of government awards for good work in different fields of activity in Central Asia seems to contain a much higher percentage of non-indigenous workers than of native workers judging by the names of the recipients:[2]

[1] Aripov, op. cit. p. 29.
[2] *Vestnik Verkhovogo Soveta*, no. 5 (1966); no. 33 (1965); no. 29 (1965).

Government Awards

1. *Prospecting, etc., Muruntau gold mine in Uzbekistan*
   Non-indigenous 36   (30 specialists, management, etc., and 6 workers)
   Indigenous   12   (4 specialists, management, etc., and 8 workers)
2. *Militia awards*
   Uzb. SSR Non-indigenous 12   Indigenous 38
   Kaz. SSR   49   36
   Kir. SSR   5   7
   Tad. SSR   2   8
   Turk. SSR   4   6
3. *Construction of titanium–magnesium works in Ust'-Kamenogorsk*
   Non-indigenous 173   (56 specialists, management, etc., 117 workers)
   Indigenous   25   (3 specialists, management, etc., Secretary Ust'-
                         Kamenogorsk gorkom, Secretary East Kaz-
                         akhstan obkom, chief engineer, and 22
                         workers)
4. *Outstanding miners' brigade in Karaganda*
   Non-indigenous 18   (3 or 4 Germans or Balts, including head of
                       brigade)
   Indigenous   3
5. *Construction of Uch-Kurgan GES, Kirgizia*[1]
   Non-indigenous 21   (12 specialists, management, etc., and 9 workers)
   Indigenous   19   (3 works superintendents and 16 workers)
6. *Construction of Pavlodar aluminium works, Turgay bauxite mines, and Pavlodar
   TETs*
   Non-indigenous 80   (22 specialists, management, etc., and 58 workers)
   Indigenous   19   (all workers)

Clearly a prominent part is still played by the non-indigenous
elements and mainly by the Russians and Ukrainians in the development of the Central Asian republics, because of the lack of native
cadres. Even in the most highly industrialized of the republics,
Uzbekistan, the Chairman of the Gosplan, S. Ziyadullayev, complained of the lack of qualified workers and specialists and the need
to train them. 'For a number of skills [*spetsial'nost*] in spite of great
demand, training is not organized here', he said.[2]

In spite of the advances in industrialization and urbanization since
the end of World War II, the populations of the Central Asian
republics, with the exception of Kazakhstan, are still predominantly

[1] *Vestnik Verkhovogo Soveta*, no. 21 (1965); no. 16 (1965).
[2] *Ekon. i Zhizn'*, no. 10 (1965), p. 12.

rural and are likely to remain so in view of the numbers required to work the cotton plantations or until mechanization there proceeds at a more rapid rate than hitherto. In this, they differ sharply from the Soviet Union as a whole where the rural population is gradually declining under the pressure of expanding urbanization and industrialization.

The situation in Kazakhstan as a result of the forced rate of industrialization and the 'Virgin Lands' project has several points of considerable demographic interest. According to the Soviet census figures only 3,200,000 or 35 per cent. of the 9,300,000 inhabitants of Kazakhstan were natives, Russians, Ukrainians, and other peoples from European Russia amounting to 6,100,000 or 65 per cent. of the population. The high population of Russians in Alma-Ata has already been mentioned and corresponds to the many industrial enterprises, civic and scientific institutions located there. Russification is also taking place in varying degrees in the different provinces of Kazakhstan. Thus the development of the 'Virgin Lands' in the five northern provinces of Kazakhstan was speeded up by the settlement of millions of young Russians, Ukrainians, and other non-Asian nationalities from 1954 onwards when the scheme was inaugurated by Khrushchev. By 1959 the Kazakhs only amounted to 18 per cent. of the population of the 'Virgin Lands', while the percentage was even lower (12 per cent.) in the north Kazakhstan province. The huge 'Virgin Lands' kray formed in 1960 (which reverted to the original five constituent *oblasts*: Kokchetavskaya *oblast*, Kustanayskaya *oblast*, Pavlodarskaya *oblast*, north Kazakhstan *oblast*, and Tselinogradskaya *oblast* in 1965) is now virtually a Russian enclave in north Kazakhstan. With the continuous planned stress on the further development of the rich natural resources of Kazakhstan, more intensive Russification may be expected to take place in the years ahead.

Moscow had gilded the pill of Russification with several euphemisms such as '*Druzhba narodov*' (Friendship of the peoples) or 'Internationalism'. While large-scale migration of Russians and other Slav peoples was undoubtedly necessary for the industrialization of Kazakhstan and the other Central Asian republics at the pace dictated by Moscow, there is also fairly strong if indirect evidence of native resentment about this Slav invasion of these countries. Thus criticism of the Government's migration policy in Kazakhstan is clearly at the root of the following admonition: 'There are still people who do not wish to take into account such a natural phenomenon as the increasing rate of influx of cadres as a result of which the population of the Republic is becoming increasingly mixed in its composition. One must first of all be a communist and internationalist and then a Russian, Kazakh, Ukrainian, or Uygur.'[1] Again, speaking at the Agricultural Conference in Alma-Ata in 1961, Khrushchev thought it necessary to remind his audience: 'You should be proud that in your Republic representatives of 100 nationalities and peoples of the Soviet Union live and work amicably and are drawn together [sblizheniye] politically and morally as in one family.'[2] 'It is important to explain to the Kazakhs', observed Kazakhstanskaya Pravda (16 January 1963), 'that on their own they could never have developed the vast resources of the Republic.' Relations between the Russians and the Kazakhs would scarcely be sweetened by this kind of supercilious comment from the organ of the Kazakh Communist Party.

The same obtuseness to national sentiment is also shown by the Soviet Press in its tributes to the policies of 'Internationalism' or 'Druzhba narodov' and the 'multi-national labour forces' on important constructions while the titular nationality of the site only appears in a mixed list of 'heroic workers'.

In the official pep talks on production, the Kazakhs are most frequently attacked for 'residual nationalism' as an obstacle to progress. In plain English this probably means little more than that there are still Kazakhs who hanker after the old days of free roaming in the steppes and resent the 'forced' pace of industrialization and the ever-increasing 'progressive' Russian presence in their midst.

The so-called mobility of labour which is plaguing the construction sites in Siberia and the Far East has more recently made its appearance in some of the excessively torrid and insalubrious areas of Central Asia. In the north the problem is caused by temperatures far below zero and the permafrost, and in the south by the lack of water and the intolerable dry heat. In both cases, the workers find

---

[1] Kaz. Pravda, 16 January 1963.
[2] Stroitel'stvo Kommunizma v SSSR i Razvitiye Sel'skogo Khozyaystva (Moscow, 1963), vol. 5, p. 263.

the situation unbearable largely because of the failure of officialdom to make adequate preparations for workers living in these climates. As a result, thousands of skilled workers, disgusted with the poor living conditions and erratic supplies, throw up their jobs, thus disorganizing construction plans, and flee to more temperate areas of the Soviet Union (as soon as they have saved up enough money to do so). The relatively mild type of pressure that can be applied locally is not sufficient to hold these 'flitters', now that the fear of imprisonment or other sanctions that existed in Stalin's day have been abolished.

Partiynaya Zhizn' Kazakhstana[1] frankly discussed the causes of the turnover of labour in the new oil industry of Mangyshlak in western Kazakhstan, in spite of high pay. Man does not live by bread alone, it said. 'People need well-arranged living conditions and opportunities for cultural development. . . . The swift growth of the population in Mangyshlak requires an expansion of the network of children's centres, hospitals, schools, cinemas, and also baths and hairdressers.' In view of the desert conditions, remoteness from civilized centres, and lack of water, the author of the article thought that there should be a 1.6 to 2.2 differential added to regular working wages in the area and that the differential should be tied to the length of work on the peninsula so that workers remaining one year should not get the same pay as those working five.[2] From what this article reveals there seems to be a yawning gulf between the 'treasures of Mangyshlak' and living conditions for the workers there.

Strong criticism of the delays in equipping living quarters for the oil workers 'with cultural-service facilities' was also expressed by *Kaz. Pravda* (8 July 1965). 'The recruitment of staff is one of the worst bottle-necks in the west Kazakh oil industry. . . . Rapid growth of population requires a sharp rise in living conditions.' *Pravda* (21 May 1965) also joined the chorus of complaints about Mangyshlak living conditions which are apparently causing as much concern (because of the flight of workers) as the technical difficulties of processing and shipping the excessively waxy oil. 'The process of putting the oil and gas deposits of Mangyshlak into commercial

[1] No. 8 (August 1965), pp. 35–36.

[2] According to *Stroitel'naya Gazeta* (29 April 1966), a a differential of 1.7 is paid in addition to the ordinary wages in Mangyshlak. 'Practice has shown, however, that it does little to keep the workers there.'

exploitation is being retarded by the serious delays in housing, cultural-domestic, and oil industrial construction', it stated.

This labour problem also engaged the attention of the Turkmen deputy, M. Gapurov, at the September 1965 session of the Supreme Soviet. 'It is necessary', he said, 'at the present time to restore the differential pay for Turkmen workers and employees in the harsh climatic conditions of some places in Turkmenistan so as to get rid of the evil of labour mobility.'[1] The references made in the above statement to the necessity to restore the pay differentials raises the question of when they were abolished (if they were) in Central Asia. It has not been possible to discover when the original decrees on differentials for workers in harsh climates were altered though occasional references to amendments in labour legislation, both in Siberia and Central Asia, have been noted.

Clearly, the arrangements made (or in fact not made) by the Soviet Government for the workers in the inhospitable sands of either Mangyshlak or Turkmenistan cannot compare with the air-conditioned housing, water supplies, refrigerated food, and other amenities organized by the big American oil companies for oil workers in similar conditions in Arabia.

The 'Virgin Lands' of Kazakhstan is another area which has suffered from a large turnover of labour among groups of young Komsomols who answered Krushchev's appeal to 'Go East' in 1954–6. Not all were sturdy enough to stand up to the extremely primitive conditions of the Kazakh steppe where only tents awaited them in the mid-winter of 1954 and they had to build everything from scratch in the uninhabited steppe lands. '140,000 left the "Virgin Lands" including experienced mechanics; life is too hard there', reported *Kaz. Pravda* (22 January 1960). These 'flitters' continued to leave the 'Virgin Lands' and on 15 July 1962, *Sel'skaya Zhizn'* stated that 180,000 machine operators had left this area because of difficult living conditions, poor food supplies, the severe climate, and low pay.

Between 1 January 1963 and 1 January 1964 there was a drop of 15,000 in the rural population of the Tselinnyy kray and a drop of 31,000 between 1 January 1964 and 1 January 1965. If natural increase is taken into account, this means that in 1963 72,000 more

[1] *Pravda*, 3 October 1965.

people left the rural areas of this kray than arrived and that in 1964 83,000 more people left than arrived.[1] 'The trouble is not that the number of settlers arriving is small', observed *Pravda* (17 October 1966), 'but that so many depart.'

The high labour turnover was so serious in Kazakhstan that the Kazakh Planning Commission decided to investigate the problem.[2] A spot check on workers who had left their jobs showed that the main reasons were: (1) inadequate pay arising from low professional qualifications; (2) unsatisfactory living conditions.

While labour turnover haunts the less attractive construction sites of Central Asia, the problem of the under-employed rural masses is causing more worry to the republican governments. There are apparently wide differences between successful and unsuccessful farms. It has been suggested that a portion of these surplus labour resources, which may be expected to grow with the high birth-rate and the development of mechanization and electrification, should be removed, if possible to more labour-absorbing branches of industry or to less inhabited areas of Uzbekistan. All the republics are, in fact, clamouring for new 'labour intensive' industries to mop up their 'abundant labour reserves'. Under these circumstances the anomaly of large-scale immigration of Slavs is an aggravating feature and openly criticized as such.

The Kirgiz Academy of Sciences, which seems to have devoted special attention to this problem in Kirgizia, briefly summarized the position as follows:

> The importance of the problem of a fuller and more rational utilization of labour resources for our Republic is intensified by the fact that in the immediate future and in the next twenty years it is expected that the growth of population including the able-bodied sector will be approximately twice as fast as the USSR average. . . . This will be due both to the high rate of natural increase of the population and also to the influx of people from other economic regions and Union republics. Migrants are attracted to Kirgizia by the favourable natural and climatic conditions and also by the rapid rates of economic–cultural construction in the Republic.
>
> It is expected that in the nearest and more distant future the influx of

---

[1] *Nar. Khoz. SSSR v 1962, 1963, 1964.* Natural rates of increase for 1963 and 1964 are given in the statistical handbook for 1964, pp. 38–39. In the computation the rate for 1960 has been used for 1959 and the intermediate figures between those of 1960 and 1963 for 1961 and 1962.   [2] *Izvestiya*, 4 November 1963.

population to Kirgizia from other regions, especially from Siberia, the Far East, and Kazakhstan, which are characterized by a lack of labour, will appreciably diminish. A diminution of the role of migration in the growth of population of Kirgizia will enable the planning–economic organs to concentrate their main attention on a better utilization of the labour forces of our Republic.[1]

Though not explicitly expressed, there is no mistaking the Academy's desire to see the end of migration in Kirgizia. Uzbek and Tadzhik journals in the last few years have also constantly stressed the need to find better outlets for their rising populations.

Another labour problem that is frequently discussed in the Central Asian Press is the under-employment of women in industry, though the number has been constantly rising in the post-war period. In 1965–6 it was stated that not more than 41 per cent. of the women of Uzbekistan were occupied in the national economy, the remainder being engaged in the private sector and household duties.[2] The percentage is lowest in Turkmenistan where there are still great difficulties in going against native custom by employing women in the factories.

The general impression gained from statements by Party and Government leaders and numerous comments in the local journals is that in Central Asia (as in Siberia) a real need exists for an all-Union organ specially charged with responsibility for the co-ordination and direction of labour and that the problem is likely to grow in Central Asia as a result of the high birth-rate, the increasing mechanization of cotton cultivation, and the lack of systematic technical training. When arguing in favour of the location of new industries in their republics Central Asian economists frequently mention what they call 'the favourable labour situation',[3] which might be employed to better advantage, actually a euphemism obscuring a considerable labour surplus in some rural areas and in smaller towns owing to the lack of industry and increasing difficulties in finding jobs for school leavers.[4] As unemployment is an inadmissible concept in the Soviet Union it is usually obliquely inferred

---

[1] *Razvitiye Proizvoditel'nykh Sil Kirgizskoy SSR v Perspektive* (Frunze, 1966), pp. 62–63.
[2] *Ob. Nauki v Uzbekistane*, no. 1 (1966), p. 30.
[3] *Nar. Khoz. S.A.*, no. 5 (1964), p. 13.
[4] This subject is analysed in an excellent article by Ann Sheehy: 'Labour Problems and Employment in Kazakhstan and Central Asia', *C.A.R.*, no. 2 (1966), p. 164.

rather than frankly discussed though there is obviously growing concern about it and about the imbalances in the distribution of manpower, in informed circles.[1]

PATTERN OF POST-WAR INDUSTRIALIZATION

The impetus given to industrialization by the war-time evacuation of men and machines from European Russia has continued and been reinforced in all the Central Asian republics since the end of World War II. Industrialization is now moving forward on a firmer basis and the hesitant rudimentary advances of the pre-war years are almost a thing of the past. More precise prospecting has revealed that the natural resources of the Central Asian republics had previously been underestimated in regard to fuel, power, and many useful minerals. The area long believed to have a deficient fuel balance was found to be rich in natural gas, oil, and water power. Gas strikes in Uzbekistan and west Turkmenistan in the early '60s (and later in west Kazakhstan) were of all-Union importance and were a major factor in increasing the proportion of gas in the fuel balance of the country.[2] Soviet reserves of natural gas are now estimated to be the third largest in the world after those of the United States of America and the Middle East. The Soviet oil industry is, however, regarded by foreign oil experts as being far behind that of the USA in general efficiency and particularly in the quality of its deep drilling equipment.[3]

A wide-diameter dual pipeline has been laid to carry the gas to the Urals (2,500 km.) and others are being built to transmit it to Moscow and other cities of European Russia. The difficulties encountered by Soviet industry in making this 40 inch wide diameter pipe, accentuated by the export ban of the NATO countries on the type of quality steel required for this purpose, seem to have been largely overcome by new technological processes and the reported construction of special mills for making this steel.[4]

[1] V. I. Perevedentsev, *Liternaturnaya Gazeta* (10 March 1966).

[2] Soviet gas consumption, for example, rose from 6.4 per cent. in 1958 to 20.2 in 1966 according to '*L'Industrie du Pétrole et de la Chimie* (September 1966), p. 52.

[3] Cf. *Impact of Oil Exports from the Soviet Bloc*. A Report of the National Petroleum Council (Washington, 1964).

[4] Ibid. p. 93. *Petroleum Press Service*, no. 4 (April 1966), p. 132.

The young Central Asian chemical industry has been greatly invigorated by the shift to natural gas as a feedstock. The largest chemical combine in the country now being built at Navoi in the Bukhara *oblast* will be based on local Gazli natural gas. It will also be used by the Uzbek GRES, the most powerful Soviet thermal electric station (capacity 4–4.5 million kW.) and the big Navoi thermal electric station, both of which are now under construction. Domestic gas needs within the Central Asian Kazakh area are to be supplied by the Bukhara–Tashkent–Frunze–Alma-Ata trunk pipeline, which reached Tashkent in 1965 and was scheduled to reach both Frunze and Alma-Ata about 1967.

The question of the correct distribution of Central Asian natural gas aroused a lively local controversy in Tashkent which was marked by frankly nationalist overtones. Dissatisfaction was expressed in some quarters that more than half of the 60–65 milliard cu. m. of natural gas planned to be produced in 1970 would be transmitted outside the region with nefarious domestic results. The argument was summarized in the following terms: 'If the quantity of gas required by the thermal electric power stations of Central Asia is transferred to the power needs of the Centre of the USSR, it will be necessary to increase production of coal for power.... It is more economical to use gas in Central Asia for power fuel.... Is it therefore not clear that it is more advantageous to direct gas in the first place to the power needs of Central Asia than to those of the European area of the USSR?'[1] The writer's conclusion was that the transfer of natural gas to the power needs of the European part of the USSR would be rational when the requirements of the national economy of Central Asia as a base for chemical raw materials and technological and power fuel were satisfied. The same critical spirit is shown about the planned development of the Central Asian textile industry. Objection is taken to the 'irrational location' of 85 per cent. of the textile industry in the non-cotton growing RSFSR and only 8.2 per cent. in the cotton-growing areas of Central Asia.[2] These economic grievances will be discussed in greater detail in later sections of this chapter.

[1] I. B. Desyatchikov and I. Mints, 'We Consider the Problem of the Fuel Balance of Central Asia', *Nar. Khoz. S.A.*, no. 12 (1964), p. 7.

[2] 'On Prospects of Developing Cotton Textile Industry in Uzbek SSR', *Ob. Nauki v Uzbekistana*, no. 3 (1965).

It was confirmed in 1965 that the deposits of natural gas and oil in the waterless Mangyshlak desert of west Kazakhstan were among the largest in the Soviet Union though extremely difficult to operate owing to the waxy content of the crude oil and the lack of water in the area. The creation of new oil and gas centres in west Kazakhstan was picked out as 'a most important task' by the draft directives of the 1966–70 Plan and clearly a major effort should now be made to overcome the initial difficulties of extraction in this area.

Oil and gas were not the only treasures yielded up after hundreds of years to the geologists searching the Central Asian deserts for minerals. Under the shifting sandhills of the central Kyzylkum at Muruntau, in Uzbekistan, one of the biggest gold mines in the Soviet Union was discovered in 1965.[1]

The realization during the Seven Year Plan period (1959–65) that the water-power resources of Central Asia were much greater than was previously known may have important results in conjunction with Siberian resources not only for Central Asia but also for European Russia and the Caucasus where the deficit in fuel and electric power is expected to increase and cannot be covered by their own energy resources.[2] In spite of the disparity in resources, the greater part of Soviet energy is still produced and consumed west of the Urals and integrated into the European grid[3] owing to the great concentration of industry in European Russia. Central Asia and Kazakhstan (with east and west Siberia) can offer by far the cheapest electric power in the country on account of the comparatively low cost of investment and production. (See following table.) This fact is frequently used as an argument by writers in Central Asian journals for a greater share of the Soviet energy-intensive, chemical, and other industries.[4]

According to provisional estimates the eastern regions will supply about 30 per cent. of the Soviet electric power (one-fifth Central Asia), 12 per cent. oil (one-half Central Asia), and 28–30 per cent. natural gas (about three-quarters Central Asia) in 1970.[5]

Under the 1966–70 Draft Plan directives, industrialization is to be

[1] *Ekon. i Zhizn'*, no. 11 (1965).
[2] *Voprosy Razmeshcheniya Proizvodstva v SSSR, Iz. Nauka AN SSSR, Gosplan SSSR* (Moscow, 1965), p. 226.
[3] David Hooson, 'Soviet Industrial Growth—Where Next?', *Survey* (October 1965), p. 115.
[4] *Nar. Khoz. S.A.*, no. 5 (1964), p. 19.   [5] Ibid. p. 13.

still further intensified in Kazakhstan, already the giant industrial power in Central Asia. Investments are to rise to 19 milliard roubles. Kazakhstan, a primary Soviet producer of lead, zinc, copper, and poly-metallic ores, will build new non-ferrous plants in Ust'-Kamenogorsk, Dzhezkazgan, and Balkhash by 1970, and otherwise improve and expand this metallurgical industry.[1]

Economic region	Capital investment (roubles per kW.)	Cost (kopeks per kWh.)
North Caucasus	90	0.16
Urals	90	0.30
Transcaucasus	100	0.35
Volga-Vyatskiy	110	0.35
West Siberian	70	0.13
East Siberian	70	0.10
Central Asian	60	0.10
Kazakhstan	80	0.14

Source: *Voprosy Razmeshcheniya Proizvodstva v SSSR*, p. 225.

Industrial progress in Uzbekistan, the most developed of the Central Asian republics, always excepting the Kazakh 'giant' republic to the north, was marked by some exceptional developments in the post-war period. In the first place there was the big natural gas strike at Gazli which could materially change the former deficit fuel balance in Uzbekistan. Moreover, gas became the base for expansion in the chemical, electrical, metallurgical, and other industries. It facilitated the gasification of the chief towns and is gradually making its way to the rural districts of Uzbekistan.

Uzbekistan ranks fifth for industrial production among the Union republics (1964). In 1964 it produced 3.9 times more electric power than the whole of pre-revolutionary Russia[2] and is now building some large thermal power stations. It has an important non-ferrous industry, notably the Almalyk copper plant, the Altyn-Topkanskiy lead–zinc–copper combine, and the Ingichkinskiy wolfram mine (which are all to be expanded according to the 1966–70 Plan directives). Uzbek engineering plants make all the machinery

---

[1] Kazakh ferrous industry is dealt with in chapter VI because of its closer connexion with Siberia than with Central Asia.

[2] *40 Let Uzbekskoy Sovetskoy Sotsialisticheskoy Respubliki* (Tashkent, 1964), p. 25.

K

for the local cotton textile and cotton cultivation industries and a wide range of other machines. The Tashkent cotton textile combine is one of the biggest in the USSR. It is a reflection of this many-sided industrial development that Uzbek exports are now stated to be second only to those of the RSFSR in value and distributed to fifty-eight countries of the world among which are the United States of America, England, France, the Scandinavian countries, India, Indonesia, and others.[1]

Tadzhikistan made considerable progress in industrialization after the war. Light industry which had formerly been predominant attained its highest level (58.9 per cent. of the total industrial output) in 1955 when industrialization in Tadzhikistan, following the conventional Soviet pattern, began to give priority to heavy industry. It accounted for 22 per cent. of the gross industrial product in 1963,[2] and is increasing owing to the construction of the big power schemes, the chemical combine at Yavan, and the production of light and non-ferrous metals.[3]

Water power dominates the natural resources of Tadzhikistan. This small southern outpost of Central Asia occupies second place among all the regions of the Soviet Union for its hydro-electric resources. Electric power is the pivot of the new diversified structure of industry in Tadzhikistan. It is a country of great mountain ranges with many swiftly flowing rivers pouring into the valleys. More than 57 per cent. of the potential reserves of Tadzhik hydro-energy is concentrated in the following rivers: the Pyandzh, Vakhsh, Surkhob, Kafirnigan, Zeravshan, Bartang, Gunt, Varsob and Yagob. Though it is impossible at the present time to utilize fully the potential water power of Tadzhikistan owing to unfavourable topographical and geological conditions and unwillingness to flood country containing valuable minerals, many hydro-electric stations have already been built, for example, the Kayrak-Kum GES on the Syr Dar'ya, the 'Perepadnaya' and 'Golovnaya' on the Vakhsh, as well as the Dushanbe thermal electric station.

A bigger development of Tadzhik hydro-electric power is foreseen with the construction of the 'giant' Nurek GES (2.7 million kW.) now under way on the Vakhsh and the still larger

[1] 40 Let Uzbekskoy Sovetskoy Sotsialistichesky Respubliki, p. 28.
[2] Kurtser, op. cit. p. 68.   [3] Ibid. p. 75.

projected Nizhne-Rogunsk GES (3.2 million kW.), also on the
Vakhsh. Some of this great power capacity will be taken up eventually by important new power-consuming industries, for in spite
of her energy potential Tadzhikistan actually produced far less
electric power than the Soviet average per head and 30 per cent.
ess than the Central Asian region average in 1964.[1] The first section
of the Yavan electro-chemical combine (the largest so far in the
country) and the Regar aluminium plant, both based on Nurek
power, are scheduled to start operation in 1968[2] though there may
be delays in this timetable owing to the many complaints of 'lagging'
and inefficiency at the Nurek construction site.[3] The Yavan combine
is an impressive project for a small country like Tadzhikistan and
will be equipped to produce a wide range of chemical products:
caustic soda, synthetic resins, plastics, and nitrogenous fertilizers
for the Tadzhik cotton industry. The production of aluminium
and magnesium and the development of the Dzhizhikrutskiy
antimony and mercury deposits in northern Tadzhikistan under the
1966–70 Plan will place the non-ferrous industry of Tadzhikistan,
which has hitherto been regarded as of little importance, on a new
footing.

An analysis of the performance of Tadzhik industry in 1964–5 by
he Tadzhik C.P. Congress revealed so many failures and deficiencies
as to suggest that the Tadzhiks may be somewhat out of their depth
in their swift progress from agriculture to the complicated techniques
of modern industry.[4] Planned targets for the extraction of gas
and oil, production of spare parts for automobiles, bricks, prefabricated concrete units and looms, silk and cotton fabrics were not
fulfilled in 1965. In many enterprises machinery was badly used,
scientific and technical improvements seldom installed, labour
discipline was poor, and there was a great loss of working time.
According to this report, the quality of building materials, fabrics,
boots and shoes, and clothes left much to be desired. The pride of
the Republic's light industry, the Dushanbe textile combine, only
fulfilled its annual plan by 85 per cent. and every sixth worker failed
to fulfil his work norm. Cases of loafing were common. From this

[1] D. Rasulov, *Tadzhikistan, god 1970. Nar. Khoz. S.A.*, no. 5 (1964), p. 7.
[2] Ibid.   [3] *Kom. Tadzhikistana*, 27 November 1965 and 23 January 1966.
[4] *Pravda*, 9 March 1966.

catalogue of failures it seems that Tadzhikistan has a lot of leeway to make up before it can operate its young industrial potential efficiently.

Kirgizia, which was very low in the industrial scale pre-war made some notable strides in industrialization subsequently. It now ranks in Soviet sources as 'an important economic region' Industrial production increased by 100 per cent. in the 1959–6 period. New industries such as electrical engineering, electronics and instrument making are to be further developed under the 1966–70 Plan and an automobile industry created.[1]

Frunze now possesses the first worsted cloth combine in Central Asia. In the course of 1966–7 the Frunze electrical engineering works is to be reconstructed to become a major producer of transistors and transistorized equipment.

The development of heavy industry in the four Central Asian republics which Soviet economists tend to stress should not obscure the fact that agriculture still plays an important role in all of them. Thus in the total production of industry and agriculture, the share of the latter amounts to almost 43 per cent. And this is also reflected in the structure of industry, branches based in the main on the processing of agricultural raw materials occupying a leading place in the economy. The total production of the light and food industries amounted to about 70 per cent. of the total volume of industrial production in the (then) Central Asian economic region in 1963–4.[2]

In spite of the general spread of industrial development throughout these republics, they are still largely dependent on imports for commodities such as heavy metals, mineral fertilizers, oil products, coal, and cement. It is planned to change the great excess of imports over exports (23 and 12 million tons respectively in 1960)[3] and achieve a better balance by 1970 through larger domestic production of some of these commodities. Such, at least, is the plan.

Following this broad outline of economic development in the Central Asian republics and Kazakhstan, the problems and prospects

[1] *Pravda*, 23 January 1966.
[2] Rakhimov, op. cit. p. 50. The statistics in the paragraph are taken from this article.
[3] *Nar. Khoz. S.A.*, no. 5 (1964), p. 18.

n the main branches of industrialization: fuel and power, chemicals, minerals and metallurgy, engineering, manufacturing industries, and transport must now be examined more closely so as to see where these republics actually stand, economically. The construction of 'giant' plants and the establishment of new industries is only the beginning of the story. Soviet statistics cannot always be taken at their face value and are often most misleading. Thus statistics of cubic metres of factory or housing space built, for example, can mean little or nothing until more is known about the state of these buildings—whether roofs leak, plumbing is in order, there is lighting and drinking-water, and the buildings are normally habitable. Much digging and delving is often necessary to discover what is the real state of affairs behind Soviet statistics and beguiling general descriptions.

FUEL AND POWER

Oil and Gas

Oil and natural gas deposits are widely distributed throughout Central Asia and knowledge of their whereabouts has been vastly increased by intensive prospecting during the Seven Year Plan period and earlier. Even Tadzhikistan, long believed to lack both natural gas and oil, now claims to possess both, though oil production is still only a trickle compared to that of Kazakhstan, Turkmenistan, or Uzbekistan.[1] Some natural gas is also produced in Tadzhikistan.

The largest oil deposits are in Kazakhstan, with important gas deposits in Uzbekistan and smaller oilfields in Turkmenistan and Uzbekistan. Prospecting for new deposits of oil and natural gas is very active in this area and the situation may always change from year to year as impressively as it has done recently.

According to the Five Year Plan directives 16 per cent. of the total Soviet oil production should come from the area east of the Urals. Of this it is estimated that 37.5 million tons will be produced by Central Asia and probably approximately as follows:

[1] U. Kh. Kletsel'man, 'Rol' Toplivno-Energeticheskoy Promyshlennosti v Sovershenstvovanii Otraslevoy Struktury Promyshlennosti Tadzhikskoy SSR', *Iz. AN Tadzhikskoy SSR*, no. 3 (38) (1964); *Pravda*, 19 January 1966.

(in million tons)

Kazakh SSR	15	(c. 12 million tons from Mangyshlak peninsula—the balance from Emba fields)
Turkmen SSS	15	
Uzbek SSR	3–3.5	
Tadzhik SSR	0.5–1.0	

Source: Draft Five Year Plan and Soviet Press.

These targets represent a considerable increase over the 1964 production figures:

Crude Oil Production, 1964

(in tons)

Turkmenistan	8,539,000
Uzbekistan	1,806,000
Kazakhstan	1,631,000
Kirgizia	320,000
Tadzhikistan	28,000

Source: *Nar. Khoz. SSSR v 1964*, p. 166.

Until the discovery in 1961 of large oil and gas deposits in the southern part of Mangyshlak peninsula on the remote and desolate western shore of the Caspian, Kazakh oil reserves were limited to the small but high-quality oilfield at Emba in the north Caspian region. Emba had been in production since before the Revolution and shipped its oil for refining to the Orsk refinery and also later to the refinery and petro-chemicals plant built at Gur'yev during World War II.[1]

Mangyshlak oil was given the industrial all-clear in 1965 after several years of experimental drilling and examination. The first five train-loads of Mangyshlak oil arrived at Gur'yev refinery in July 1965.[2]

Estimates still fluctuate about the size of the Mangyshlak reserves of oil and gas, as new wells are constantly being drilled and knowledge of this new area expanded. The indications are, however, that

[1] R. E. H. Mellor, *Geography of the USSR* (Macmillan & Co., London, 1964), p. 236.
[2] *Pravda*, 16 January 1966.

west Kazakhstan is one of the richest oil-bearing regions of the world.) More than forty oil-bearing structures are reported so far. Writing in *Pravda* (21 May 1965), the First Deputy Chairman of the then State Committee of the oil extraction industry estimated the Uzen' field, the first in production, to contain 'some hundreds of millions of tons'. The other main field now in production is at Zhetybay and is also credited with big oil reserves. Probes at Tenge in the same area proved the existence of abundant reserves of gas also which are reported to amount to almost 50 per cent. of the Gazli wells. But the high waxy content of the oil has created many problems in production and transport.

The production target for the Mangyshlak fields in 1970 fluctuates between 10 million and 20 million tons of oil[1] and 100 million tons has been mentioned for 1980 (or about 14 per cent. of Khrushchev's original Twenty Year Plan for the Soviet oil industry). Only 334,000 tons were produced in 1965 and uncertainty about the production situation is reflected in the targets of 1 million tons[2] and 2 million tons[3] published in Soviet sources, for 1966.

Transport and refining of Mangyshlak oil present many difficulties. Shevchenko, formerly a tiny settlement, is being built up as the new administrative centre of this oil industry and is connected by a 706 km. line, built in record time, with Makat on the Kandagach–Gur'yev railway, and is thus linked with the Gur'yev refinery and the Kazakh, Urals, and central industrial regions. A new asphalt road has been built between Shevchenko and the largest oilfield at Uzen'. Construction of the oil terminal at Aktau port near Shevchenko is nearing completion.[4] As there are no refineries in the peninsula itself, the only refinery to have received this oil in any quantity is Gur'yev, which is trying to refuse further deliveries since it cannot cope with its high paraffin wax content (20–25 per cent.).[5] Towards the end of 1965, five other refineries were listed as possible future recipients of Mangyshlak oil—Krasnovodsk, Orsk, Volgograd, Grozny, and Baku;[6] all these plants would, however, need special de-waxing facilities to deal with it. Until this problem is solved the transport facilities for large bulk cannot be

---

[1] *Kaz. Pravda*, 13 March 1966.

[2] *Nar. Khoz. Kazakhstana*, no. 11 (1965).

[3] *Trud*, 3 April 1966.

[4] Russian radio, 14 October 1966.

[5] Moscow Home Service, 18 March 1966.

[6] *Nar. Khoz. Kazakhstana*, no. 11 (1965).

constructed, and it seems that there must be considerable delay in the huge production increases planned for the next year or two at least.

The technical problems created by the high wax content of Mangyshlak oil are serious and complicated. It solidifies below 34° C. (93° F.), and unless kept above this temperature it tends to block the pipeline. Glass-lined pipes would considerably lessen this problem, but the glass tends to break and experiments are now being carried out with resin linings. Another proposed solution is to heat the pipeline and this method was used in the 130 km. long pipe already laid from Uzen' to Shevchenko; unfortunately, owing to an oversight, it could not be tested because the outlet runs straight to the bay whose waters feed the intake for the desalination plant which provides the town's fresh-water supply, and tankers loading oil would inevitably have polluted it. It is still apparently planned to construct a pipeline to Gur'yev, and possibly on to Volgograd, by 1970,[1] whatever the technical means. This is a difficult but not insoluble problem and it is interesting to note that it was encountered and solved in the case of the Libyan oil deposits which also have a high wax content.

The operation of the Mangyshlak oil–gas deposits is fraught with other complications. Work has been hampered by great delays in the construction of living quarters, and the organization of amenities for the workers in this waterless semi-desert. 'It is necessary to establish proper conditions of work', declared *Partiynaya Zhizn' Kazakhstana* (August 1965, p. 35). *Kaz. Pravda* (8 July 1965) warned that in view of the state of construction-assembly work in the oilfields the volume of oil extraction set for 1970 could not be guaranteed and that the targets should be revised more realistically. The Soviet Press, moreover, has severely criticized the slow progress in prospecting, drilling, and development of this oil industry.[2] Prompted, no doubt, by reports of inefficient planning and bad management in Mangyshlak, *Stroitel'naya Gazeta* sent a special correspondent to the peninsula to find out what was happening there. The results of the correspondent's investigations published in *Stroitel'naya Gazeta* (27–29 April 1966) confirmed the worst suspicions of wholesale muddle and technical incompetence in

---

[1] Ecotass, 2 June 1966. [2] *Pravda*, 21 May 1965.

Mangyshlak. The main criticisms made in this report were that there was no co-ordinated management, no comprehensive plans, no estimates for the development of Mangyshlak, and that 'it has not yet been decided who is to create the base for the capital construction without which the main problems cannot be overcome. There exists a completely negligent attitude towards questions of housing, and the everyday domestic and cultural needs of the workers.' As there is no construction base, all the building materials have to be imported hundreds of kilometres, though there is apparently plenty of local limestone which could be used for construction purposes. 'Owing to the negligent attitude to the construction work regulations which lay down that a production base should be developed in advance, living conditions are intolerable', concluded *Stroitel'naya Gazeta*.

The crucial problem of water for the workers and for industrial purposes is being tackled in various ways since it was found that the Mangyshlak water desalination plant was quite inadequate to supply local demand for drinking water. Construction of a nuclear reactor was begun in 1965 at Shevchenko and according to the Russian wireless (22 July 1965) will be the world's first nuclear plant to be used in a dual capacity: to produce electricity and to convert salt water into fresh. Large underground sources of fresh water have been discovered and are being tapped.[1] But the problem is not yet solved and Shevchenko is reported to be acutely short of water.

Turkmenistan had a small pre-revolutionary oil industry located at Nebit-Dag and Cheleken on the Caspian. The Republic's fuel position was greatly changed by important post-war oil and gas discoveries in the heart of the Kara-Kum Desert near Kushki, on the shores of the Caspian, and in the Amu Dar'ya Valley. The indications are that Turkmenistan has still bigger reserves of oil and gas awaiting exploitation beneath the Kara-Kum sands where many parties of geologists are now actively prospecting. One of the largest oil refineries in the Soviet Union and the largest in Central Asia is in the Caspian port of Krasnovodsk. It is not for nothing that the Turkmen national emblem contains an oil derrick. But Turkmenistan, the third biggest oil producer in the USSR after the RSFSR and Azerbaydzhan in 1960, should be overtaken and even eclipsed by Kazakhstan if the present difficulties in Mangyshlak can be overcome.

[1] Russian radio, 6 January 1966.

Huge natural gas deposits have also been discovered at Darvaza, Bayram Ali, and other places in the Kara-Kum Desert. The centre of the Kara-Kum gas and oil industry at the present time is at Darvaza where the drillers work in conditions of extreme heat and cold without water, described as 'hellish'. They are mostly young people who get their training in practical work 'on the drill': Russians, Ukrainians, Moldavians, Azerbaydzhanis. A complicated industrial settlement has grown up round the Darvaza oilfields with two electric stations, electric motors, and the usual appurtenances of an oil-drilling centre. The workers remain twenty days in the desert and then have five days home on leave.[1]

Having mastered the roadless desert and the shifting sandhills of Turkmenistan in search of oil and gas, the search is now continuing beneath the western shores of the Caspian Sea. Oil has been discovered some kilometres below the seabed by the crews living on the new 'steel islands' which correspond to similar structures off the Baku coast.[2]

A new pipeline is being laid across the Kara-Kum Desert from Darvaza to Krasnovodsk. It is expected that when it is in service it will be able to meet all Turkmenistan's requirements for liquid gas. A major trunk pipeline is to be built during the 1966–70 Plan period to carry Turkmen oil from Darvaza to central Russia which will link up on the way with the Bukhara–Centre pipeline.

There have been complaints in the Press that the speed of development of the Turkmen oil industry has been hampered by underfulfilment of drilling norms, still too frequent accidents in boring, serious defects in subterranean repair of wells and in the introduction of new equipment. The construction of deep wells and the quality of construction–erection work in drilling were also said to be often below standard.[3] The Turkmen oil workers are not the only group to get this criticism. Most exploratory oil-drilling teams throughout the Soviet Union seem to suffer from the same defects.

Uzbekistan has huge natural gas deposits in the Bukhara *oblast* but her oil industry is insignificant compared to the swift development of the gas industry since 1959. The first fields to be worked were at Gazli where the deposits, estimated at 583 milliard cu. m., are said

[1] *Turk. Iskra*, 20 October 1965.　　　[2] Ibid. 7 November 1965.
[3] Ibid. 26 May 1965.

to be the largest in the country.[1] The gas is relatively near the surface and easy to produce, making it the cheapest in the Soviet Union. It is dry, contains no sulphur and is about 90 per cent. methane. Production has made great strides since 1959 when the first Bukhara gas entered the 767 km. Dzharkak–Samarkand–Tashkent pipeline. Up to 1965 the chief fields exploited were at Gazli and Dzharkak but in the 1966–70 Plan period the new deposits at north and south Mubarek, Uchkyr, Yangi-Kazgan, Karabair, Urtabulak, Kultak, and other places in the area are to be brought into operation.[2]

According to Soviet sources *Bukharaneftegas* produced 16.5 milliard cu. m. in 1965 or an increase of 80 per cent. over 1964. This amounted to 12 per cent. of the total Soviet gas production.[3] In the first year of the new Five Year Plan gas output is to be further increased by 8 milliard cu. m. and to rise to 24 milliard cu. m.[4]

Utilization of Bukhara gas is being promoted in Uzbekistan itself and outside the Republic by an impressive gas pipe construction programme. A mammoth dual gas pipe (40 inch), started in 1961, will carry this gas to the Urals. The first string of this Urals pipeline reached Nizhniy Tagil in the north Urals in 1965 and a second string has got as far as the borders of Kazakhstan and the RSFSR. The combined length of the two strings is more than 4,500 km. Before the construction of the Bukhara–Urals pipeline the Trans-Canadian gas pipe was considered the biggest in the world (3,670 km.). Now the Soviets claim that it has been left far behind by the Bukhara–Urals pipe,[5] but this is only so if the dual pipeline is taken as one.

Other pipelines planned for construction in 1966–70 are the great Central Asian–Centre trunk pipeline (3,300 km.), the first 300 km. of which were laid in 1965, the Mubarek–Tashkent-Alma-Ata pipeline, the first section of which should go into service in 1966, the Bukhara pipeline which should reach Frunze in 1967, and many other domestic pipelines. The Central Asian–Centre pipeline is supplied from three main sources: Darvaza, Bayram Ali, and Gazli. It will run through Kungrad–Makat–Aleksandrov–Gay to cross the Volga above Saratov, and past Penza and Ryazan' to

[1] *Ekon i Zhizn'*, no. 9 (1965), p. 19.   [2] Ibid. p. 25.
[3] Tass, 12 February 1966.   [4] *Pravda Vostoka*, 18 January 1966.
[5] *Ekon. i Zhizn'*, no. 9 (1965), p. 20.

Moscow. The southern trace of this line passes through sultry desert, salt and arid steppe where shifting sandhills, sand and dust storms, and blistering heat are daily occurrences. The success of this enormously complicated task obviously depends on the most careful organization of equipment, transport, supplies, and living conditions, especially drinking water for the workers.

The Central Asian gas industry, like the Soviet industry as a whole, may be hampered by a lack of pumping and compressor facilities on the pipelines which has prevented full capacity utilization of the Soviet system as well as by the inability of the USSR to develop compressors adequate for use on large-diameter pipelines and other special equipment.[1]

The problem of the correct distribution and utilization of Bukhara natural gas has aroused a lively local controversy judging by the diverging views expressed in Central Asian journals. Obviously much thought has been given to the best way to determine a scientific fuel-energy base for Uzbekistan in view of the prospective effect of the new gas reserves on this formerly fuel-deficient area. The issues raised are too technical and complicated to be judged here but the fact that they have been raised is in many ways interesting. Both sides admit that the use of gas would be more economical than coal and would reduce the heavy expenditure on coal imports to the four Central Asian republics from Karaganda and the Kuzbas and farther afield amounting to about 4,000,000 tons annually up to 1968. But other factors enter into this argument about gas. 'Gas is in the first place a chemical raw material and not a fuel', argues one article on the fuel balance of Central Asia in reply to another which urged that it should be based on gas.[2] 'At the present time 50–55 per cent. of the gas produced in our area is used for power, about 35 per cent. for technological purposes and only 8–8.5 per cent. as chemical raw material. The creation of a big chemical industry in Central Asia demands that the use of gas for various chemical products should be increased and its use as a fuel reduced to a minimum.' Such in brief is the position of the opponents of gas as fuel. Other critics object to the large transfer of gas to the European

---

[1] *Impact of Oil Exports from the Soviet Bloc*, pp. 94, 113.

[2] B. Kireyev and A. Khimatov, 'Ugol' v Toplivnom Balanse Sredney Azii', *Nar. Khoz. S.A.*, no. 5 (1964), p. 29; Ya. Mazover and A. Probst, 'Gaz, Neft', Ugol' ', *Nar. Khoz. S.A.*, no. 4 (1964).

areas of Russia and a note of apprehension appears in many articles lest Central Asia should be drained of valuable gas supplies before its own requirements are fully met. 'More than half of the gas produced in 1966–70 in Central Asia will be transferred to the centre of the country and the Urals. From the national economic point of view this ratio', complains the writer, 'cannot be regarded as reasonable because large industrial consumers of fuel are concentrated there'. (The inference is that they will consume too much Central Asian gas.) Central Asian critics of this gas distribution policy are clearly averse to helping the European areas of the USSR and the Urals to overcome their fuel deficiency when 'our economic region will have a fuel deficit in 1970 of 7.5–13 million tons of conventional fuel'.[1] 'With a possible gas production of 55–60 milliard cu. m. in Central Asia in 1970', objects another critic, 'its use there will stand at about 12–17 milliard cu. m. which is clearly inadequate to satisfy the requirements of the economic region itself. In this case, the fuel balance of Uzbekistan and other Central Asian republics will be formed with a big deficit.'[2]

Problems have also arisen in connexion with the industrial and domestic use of natural gas within Uzbekistan itself. The industry is so new that it is not surprising that it should have run into initial difficulties. One of the major complaints is that gas is being uneconomically used and that there is great wastage. 'The supply must be restricted to enterprises already supplied with gas', reported *Ekonomika i Zhizn'* (no. 3 [1965], p. 39). In the Tashkent GRES alone the over-consumption of gas early in 1965 amounted to 100,000 cu. m. in twenty-four hours. Much of this wastage is due to the inefficient equipment employed for laying on the gas and the discrepancies between the correct types of burners and stoves, for example, and those actually installed.

Great losses of fuel also occur through gross engineering defects in the installation and manufacture of equipment. For example, at the *Tashkentkabel'* works there was no thermal installation on steam pipelines more than 3 km. long. At the Chirchik combine of building materials and ferro-concrete constructions the loss of steam

[1] Kireyev and Khimatov, op. cit. p. 31.
[2] K. Kim and N. Niyazov, 'Nekotoryye Voprosy Razvitiya Toplivnoy Promshlennosti Uzbekistana', *Ob. Nauki v Uzbekistane*, no. 7 (1964), pp. 14–15.

in the steam chambers was such that the electric motors went out of action through heightened humidity in the premises. Much heat is also lost in winter because windows, doors, and entrances are kept open and the thermal screens work unsatisfactorily. The consumption of fuel (gas) is not standardized in particular industrial operations and whereas in some plants the consumption is normal, in others it fluctuates and is excessive. According to *Ekonomika i Zhizn'*, the planning organizations (in their eagerness to find consumers for the newly won gas) have no precise idea of the correct quantities of gas which should be utilized or of the advisability of an order of priority for different categories of consumers. The result is a sharp difference between the growth of gas production and the preparation of the national economy for the utilization of natural gas with the maximum efficiency.

The tariff rates for the use of gas are allegedly uneconomical and need revising. For example, the cost price of a cubic metre of gas in Uzbekistan is one kopek but this low selling price does not in fact reflect the cost of production and should be greatly increased.[1] This low cost does not stimulate an economic use of gas. If the present wastage continues, it is even feared by local Uzbek experts that it will lead to exhaustion of the reserves of this valuable fuel. 'The burning of gas in the fire boxes of boilers and stoves with increased losses is equivalent to the barbarous destruction of milliards of cubic metres of fuel.' In 1963 alone the 'unproductive loss of gas in the Uzbek Republic exceeded a milliard cubic metres'.

There have been many complaints that the exploratory drilling teams have consistently failed to reach footage targets in their search for additional deposits of natural gas and oil in Uzbekistan, Turkmenistan, and Kazakhstan. Gross carelessness in drilling deep wells in the Central Asian deserts has also been criticized in the Press.[2] The speed of exploratory drilling during the seven year period only amounted to 54.1 per cent. of the planned target for Central Asia while costs of drilling per metre exceeded the planned costs 2.2 times.[3] The plans for increasing exploitable reserves of oil and gas in the seven year period were not fulfilled in Uzbekistan (nor in the USSR as a whole). The conclusion drawn by a Moscow commentator

[1] *Ekon. i Zhizn'*, no. 3 (1965), p. 41.   [2] *Ekon. i Zhizn'*, no. 9 (1965), p. 14.
[3] Ibid. pp. 14–15.

was that the means allocated by the State for this purpose were not spent to the best advantage. It appears that the geologists were not provided with the necessary gear or machinery for sinking wells and it was thus impossible to carry out extra-deep drilling.[1]

According to the Turkmen First Party Secretary, 'the further development of the oil and gas industry is hampered by inefficient management of exploratory drilling on the part of the *Turkmenneft*'. ... It has had an excessive number of breakdowns and too much idling of equipment, its drilling speeds are low, drilling costs are high, and it has failed to utilize wet gas'.[2] In fact *Turkmenneft* seems in a pretty bad state.

Apart from its prolific Central Asian natural gas supplies, the Soviet Union is also developing the natural gas deposits of northern Afghanistan. Soviet drilling crews first discovered the deposits at Haga Gugerdagh in 1961 and others subsequently. According to a Soviet–Afghan technical-assistance agreement concluded in 1963 (implementation of which was delayed until 1965) Soviet engineers are to build a 255 mile long, big-inch pipeline (the exact diameter has not been stated) to move the gas from Shibarghan to Kelif on the Soviet Amu Dar'ya frontier and beyond.[3] It is scheduled to be connected with the Central Asian gas pipeline system in 1967[4] but the direction of this pipe after it crosses the Soviet frontier is not clear, as it has been variously mentioned in Soviet sources as going north to join the Central Asian system near the Murbek gas-field and as following a route to Dushanbe via Kelif-Termez.[5] Possibly pipes may in the end be laid in both directions. When this gas is flowing, the Soviet Union will import 3.5 milliard cu. m. annually.[6] The gas not imported by the Soviet Union would be partly consumed by the important new Afghan nitrogenous fertilizer plant at Mazar-i-Sharif and a new 36,000 kW. power plant there.[7]

---

[1] Moscow Home Service, 18 October 1965.   [2] *Turk. Iskra*, 25 February 1966.
[3] *The Oil and Gas Journal*, 24 January 1966.
[4] Tass in Russian for Abroad, 11 November 1966.   [5] Russian radio, 4 August 1966.
[6] Tass in English, 9 February 1966.
[7] *The Oil and Gas Journal*, op. cit. Oil and gas agreements have also been concluded with Iran, and the Soviets are to build a pipeline to carry natural gas from southern Iran to the Caspian Sea whence it will be transmitted to the Caucasus. In this way they have obtained considerable control of natural gas deposits south of the Central Asian frontier.

Coal

Until recently coal, *guẓa-paya* (cotton stalks), and oil were the main fuels used in Central Asia. The situation changed sharply with the discovery of natural gas in Uzbekistan, the output and consumption of which has greatly increased in a few years.

Estimated Fuel Balance in Four Central Asian Republics in 1965

(in per cent.)

Natural and associated gas	44.4
Energy coal	29.3
Furnace crude oil	9.0
Guẓa-paya	11.0
Other fuels	6.3

Source: *Nar. Khoẓ. S.A.*, no. 5 (1964), p. 30.

But the growth of the oil and gas industry has not kept pace with industrial requirements in the southern Asian republics. Some 2,000,000 tons of coal are still annually imported from Karaganda and the Kuzbas.[1] Uzbek experts have complained (and apparently with reason) that 'gas is in the first place a chemical raw material and not a fuel' and they oppose its use for this purpose.[2] Others argue in favour of the intensive use of gas so as to eliminate the Central Asian fuel deficiency and the expenditure on imports of coal. In spite of the rapidly increasing use of gas, coal is still a matter of considerable interest to the area.

Kazakhstan is by far the main coal producer of this area and exports coal both to the Urals and to the southern Asian republics. Otherwise coal deposits of purely local significance are found scattered through the four southern republics which are deficient in coal supplies.

The chief Kazakh coal mines are at Ekibastuz and in the Karaganda coal basin, which contains a sixth of the total Soviet coal reserves;[3] combined they are among the largest coal producers in the Soviet Union and production has risen from 6,972,000 tons in 1940 to 41,196,000 tons in 1964. The major part of this production is deep mined (27,283,000 tons). Coal mined at the north Kazakh

[1] 'Ugol' v Toplivnom Balanse Sredney Azii', *Nar. Khoẓ. S.A.*, no. 5 (1964), p. 29.
[2] Ibid.　　　　　[3] *Voprosy Raẓmeshcheniya Proiẓvodstva*, op. cit. p. 45.

deposits at Ekibastuz is opencast mined and cheaper than Karaganda coal. It is producing about 15,000,000 tons a year, but there are plans for opening new mines and reconstructing old ones so that Ekibastuz should yield about 69,000,000 tons a year by 1975 if these plans mature. Both the Karaganda and the Ekibastuz coals can be used for coking. Ekibastuz coal is the fuel base for the powerful new thermal electric power station at Yermak and the two Ekibastuz GRES.

The Angren coal mines in Uzbekistan are the most productive in the four Central Asian republics, and supply not only Uzbekistan but also some of the neighbouring republics and south Kazakhstan, though a shortage of coal particularly for domestic consumption has been reported. The Uzbek coal industry has not done well in the five year period 1961–5, during which it 'failed to supply the national economy with 6,200,000 tons of coal, as scheduled'.[1] Plans for developing new productive capacity at the Angren and Shargun mines were fulfilled four to five years behind schedule, and capital investment at Angren was only taken up by 90 per cent. Other measures for the concentration and grading of Angren coal have been hanging fire since 1963 and work has been disorganized by delays in dealing with the intrusion of the Angren River into the mines. The fuel production balance of Uzbekistan in 1965 consisted of 78 per cent. gas, 11.8 per cent. oil, and 9 per cent. coal. Coal has thus dropped heavily in the Uzbek fuel balance and may be expected to drop still further if the present plans for the intensive utilization of natural gas materialize. The Angren coal mines are conveniently situated in the heart of industrialized Uzbekistan, about 90–100 km. from Tashkent. Production started here during the last war and though there have been many complaints about these mines they have no doubt played an important part in the economic development of Uzbekistan. A large part of the coal at Angren is mined opencast though there is also some deep-mined coal. By 1970 coal extraction is scheduled to rise to 5.8 million tons compared to 4.3 million tons in 1964. The Angren GRES, the Almalyk TETs, and various industrial enterprises of Tashkent, as well as the Achisay combine, the Dzhambul superphosphate plant, and some enterprises in Kirgizia and Turkmenistan use Angren coal (though they may eventually shift to gas)

[1] *Ekon. i Zhizn'*, no. 9, pp. 14–15.

L

and it is widely used for domestic purposes. (Better quality coal is found in the south of the republic at Baysya and there are coal deposits in the Surkhandar'ya *oblast*, but they are among the most expensive in the country to work.[1]

The largest coal mines in the four Central Asian republics are in Kirgizia (at Kyzyl-Kiya, Sulyukta, and Kok-Yangak, all brown coal). But coal production in Kirgizia labours under many drawbacks: it is mostly deep mined and more expensive than coal imported from Karaganda, the Kuzbas, or Uzbekistan. The Kirgiz mines, in view of these drawbacks and the priority now being given to opencast mining,[2] would not seem to have much chance of large-scale development at present.) There has been a good deal of local controversy about development. Some local representatives argue that

Coal Production in the Central Asian Republics and Kazakhstan and Targets for 1966–70

(in ooo tons)

	1964	1970 Plan
USSR	553,997	665–676,000
Kazakh	41,196	68–69,000
		(of which 32,000 opencast)
Uzbekistan	4,498	Not available
Kirgizia	3,314	4,500
Tadzhikistan	831	Not available

Source: *Nar. Khoz. SSSR v 1964 g.*, p. 164. Targets from Soviet Press reports

it would be worth while (in spite of the expense), while others argue that it would be more economical to buy coal as previously from Karaganda.[3]

(In spite of the relative unimportance of this coal industry local mining–economic experts are of the opinion that in order to satisfy the requirements of the Central Asian economy, coal output should reach 15–20 million tons a year.[4] They believe that this is perfectly feasible because most of the coal is opencast mined and there are possibilities of lower costs of production and raising productivity through up-to-date mining technology.) But whether these are sound estimates or inflated by local patriotism, it is impossible to say.

[1] *Voprosy Razmeshcheniya Proizvodstva v SSSR*, p. 266.

[2] The advantages of opencast mining were mentioned at the Twenty-Third Party Congress 1966, by Kosygin.

[3] *Sovetskaya Kirgizia*, 12 November 1964.   [4] *Nar. Khoz. S.A.*, no. 5 (1964), p. 3

Electric Power

The fifth and sixth post-war Plans pushed forward the expansion of electric power in the Central Asian republics, the development of which was already a marked feature of the pre-war industrialization. The hydro-power of this area ranks second only to east Siberia and has a high all-Union value, amounting to about one-fifth of the total Soviet hydro-energy resources.

From 1958 to 1962 the rate of growth of electric power in these republics was higher than for the USSR as a whole. Electric power grew in the USSR during this period by 56.9 per cent. while in Central Asia it increased by 62.6 per cent. Moreover, there was a better distribution of the electrical industry and the former concentration of electric power in Uzbekistan was more evenly distributed. The Uzbek share of the production of electric power in 1940

Rate of Growth of Production of Electric Power in Central Asia in percentage to 1958

Republic	1958	1959	1960	1962
Uzbek SSR	100	110.3	125.5	160.6
Kirgiz SSR	100	105.7	115.1	197.5
Tadzhik SSR	100	133.9	149.8	132.7
Turkmen SSR	100	111.6	126.6	172.5
Central Asia as a whole	100	112.9	127.5	162.2

Source: *Iz. AN Tadzhikskoy SSR*, 3 (38) (1964), p. 46.

was 70.9 per cent., Kirgizia 7.6 per cent., but in 1962 the Uzbek share had fallen to 67.3 per cent. and that of Kirgizia risen to 13.4 per cent. This meant that in the republics which formerly had an insufficient energy base, a more rapid rate of development of this essential branch of industry was taking place.[1]

Some of the major power schemes in the Central Asian republics are centred on harnessing the swift mountain rivers of the southern areas of Central Asia, the Vakhsh and the Pyandzh in Tadzhikistan, the Naryn in Kirgizia, the Chirchik and Syr Dar'ya in Uzbekistan. Kazakhstan, otherwise so favoured in natural resources, is poor in hydro-energy and relies on thermal power for its electricity. Only

[1] *Iz. AN Tadzhikskoy SSR*, 3 (38) (1964), p. 46.

the Irtysh River in east Kazakhstan is capable of providing hydro-power in any quantity. There is also a great disparity in the power potential of the rivers of Turkmenistan and its eastern neighbours, in the first place Tadzhikistan. The rivers running down from the Kopet Dag Mountains as a rule have relatively small hydro-power potential compared to the powerful flow of rivers rising in the heights of the Pamirs or the Tyan Shan system like the Vakhsh, the Chu, or the Naryn.

Throughout the four Central Asian republics and Kazakhstan many thermal stations were built based on coal, oil, and in the latest seven year period an increasing number on natural gas. As a result of the construction of these hydro-electric and thermal power stations the production of electric power in all the republics has greatly increased since 1940, as is shown in the following table:

Production of Electric Power in the USSR and Central Asian Republics and Kazakhstan

(in million kWh.)

	1940	*1958*	*1964*
USSR	48,309	235,350	458,902
Uzbek SSR	482	4,687	9,266
Kazakh SSR	632	8,525	16,917
Kirgiz SSR	52	757	2,174
Tadzhik SSR	62	860	1,751
Turkmen SSR	83	593	1,270

Source: *Nar. Khoz. SSSR v 1964 g.*, p. 158.

Central Asia shares with east Siberia the advantage not only of having the greatest hydro-energy resources in the country but also of being the area where the cheapest electric power in the Soviet Union will be produced in the future. At the present time, however, the level of development of electric power lags behind the all-Union level, though 15 per cent. of the Union's most useful power sources, i.e. hydro-energy and gas, are estimated to be located in these four republics.[1]

The largest hydro-energy resources in Central Asia are in Tadzhikistan and Kirgizia. Uzbekistan, which lacks hydro-power

[1] *Voprosy Razmeshcheniya Proizvodstva v SSSR*, p. 240.

sufficient for her power requirements, has built some of the most powerful thermal stations in Central Asia: the Angren, Tashkent, Navoi, and Uzbek (Bekabad) GRES. In assessing the power resources of Central Asia, the relatively high cost of transmission lines crossing the many mountainous regions must be taken into account. It is therefore more economical to establish big hydro-electric and thermal power stations in the vicinity of energy-consuming industries. For example, it has been recommended that large energy–industrial complexes might be established in future in south Tadzhikistan (in the Vakhsh Valley) like the Yavan chemical combine, and in south-west Kirgizia. Central Asia also has a part to play in making good the energy deficiency of neighbouring areas like south Kazakhstan and in time perhaps also the Caucasus, by means of underground cables beneath the Caspian Sea.[1]

Agriculture has also benefited by the introduction of electric power in Central Asia, though, as will be seen below, not to the extent that is required. The regulation of water flow in the new reservoirs and artificial lakes, and the construction of canals with the aid of electrification, has increased irrigation, especially for cotton cultivation, on a large scale.

There are many important plans afoot for the construction of hydro-electric and thermal power stations (mostly based on natural gas) during the new Five Year Plan and a considerable extension of long transmission lines is scheduled in all the Central Asian republics and Kazakhstan. When these plans mature, the capacity of a unified Central Asian energy system will be greatly increased and it is hoped to abolish many small uneconomic electric stations and to promote industrial development.

In spite of the enormous potential resources and construction of large hydro-electric power stations like the Nurek and Farkhad stations, the volume and rate of development of the power industry in the Central Asian republics is still regarded by local experts as insufficient. Transmission lines within the republics were greatly extended in the seven year period and grew from 2,222 km. to more than 6,000 km. at the end of 1965, in Uzbekistan. For the most part these lines are intended to serve agriculture.[2] Transmission lines now cover Uzbekistan from Fergana to Tashkent with an outlet to south

[1] Ibid. p. 238.   [2] *Ekon. i Zhizn'*, no. 1 (1966), p. 8.

Kazakhstan, and from Tashkent to Bukhara and Karshi with an outlet to Chardzhou in Turkmenistan, while a 220 kW. line from the Tadzhik energy system through Denau to the Sherabad machine irrigation pumping station ensures electric power in the south Surkhandar'inskaya *oblast* of Uzbekistan.[1] In spite of the abolition of the Central Asian economic council, interchange of electric power between the republics by means of inter-republican systems continues and is planned to expand.

Uzbekistan

In the early post-war years about 85 per cent. of the electric power in Uzbekistan was generated by hydro-electric power plants. These plants were centred mainly on the Syr Dar'ya River (the big Farkhad plant opened in 1948), and the inter-republican Kayrak-Kum hydro-electric power station, construction of which started in 1956, through the combined efforts of the Uzbek and Tadzhik workers in the Leninabad *oblast* of Tadzhikistan,[2] and the cascade of smaller plants on the Chirchik River which produced 40 per cent. of Uzbek power in 1965.[3] Many hydro-electric power stations were also built on the rivers and irrigation canals of the Fergana Valley. In Uzbekistan the development of electric power is closely connected with irrigation works owing to its large cotton belt where cotton is entirely grown by irrigation, and this of course applies to all the Central Asian cotton-growing areas. Hundreds of hectares of land are irrigated by the inter-republican Farkhad, Kayrak-Kum, and Chirchik systems. Many smaller electric power stations have also been built on collective and State farms, chiefly for irrigation canals. Nevertheless, reporting to the Uzbek Republican Party Congress in March 1966, Rashidov said that the use of electricity in rural areas was still very limited.[4] Consumption of electric power in agriculture was, however, scheduled to rise by 33 per cent. in 1966.[5]

Uzbek power-generating capacity increased by 1,226,000 kW. between 1961 and 1965 but *per capita* consumption (not surprisingly in view of the relative lack of large-scale, power-intensive industries) is still lower than the all-Union average.

[1] *Ekon. i Zhizn'*, no. 2 (1966), p. 21.
[2] 'More Power for Central Asia', *Central Asian Review*, vol. IV, no. 3 (1963), p. 269.
[3] *Pravda Vostoka*, 22 December 1965.   [4] Ibid. 4 March 1966.
[5] Ibid. 25 December 1965.

During the seven year period 1959–65 electric power capacity was greatly increased by the construction of some powerful new thermal stations based on Uzbek gas and by the increased capacity of other stations.[1] The chief stations started and partly completed in this period, mostly based on cheap Angren coal and natural gas, were the Angren GRES (present capacity 600,000 kW.), the Navoi GRES (present capacity 600,000 kW., to be raised to 1,100,000 kW.), the Tashkent GRES (planned capacity 1,800,000 kW. and the largest in Central Asia when it was started in 1961). The Navoi gas turbine station (capacity 350,000 kW., 1965) was the first to operate on gas in Uzbekistan; owing to its proximity to the Bukhara gas-fields its economic value is considerable in this developing area. Great importance for irrigation is attached to the expansion of the Takhiatash GRES (full capacity 2,500,000 kW.) and the Charvak HES. The Takhiatash thermal GRES system to be completed in 1968 is situated on the lower reaches of the Amu Dar'ya River in the Karakalpak ASSR, and is economically important for the Khorezm *oblast* and the Tashauz *rayon* of the adjacent Turkmen Republic where it could promote the irrigation of about 500,000 ha. of new land.[2] The Charvak HES (started during the Seven Year Plan and due to be completed in 1969) is the centre of a large hydro-electric system based on the Chirchik River, with a dam, a reservoir of 1.2 milliard cu. m. capacity (known as the Charvak Sea), and a powerful electric station (680,000 kW.). Apart from its great value for irrigation (over 500,000 ha. is envisaged), the Charvak hydro-system is intended to preserve the Tashkent Oasis from flooding and drought when completed, as the Chirchik power stations should then be able to work round the year without interruptions.

The 'giant' construction of the new Five Year Plan in Uzbekistan and one of the most powerful thermal electric stations in the world, the Uzbek GRES is to be built at Bekabad, the site of the only steel plant in Central Asia. It is scheduled to start construction in 1966, will have a capacity of 600,000 kW. by 1971, and when completed a capacity of 4.4 million kW. It is intended that this plant will eventually (but not until after 1971) be in a position to make good the short fall of power in winter of the Toktogul, Nurek, and other hydro-power stations with uneven power generation owing to

---

[1] *Ekon. i Zhizn'*, no. 2 (1966), pp. 20–23. [2] Ibid. no. 10 (1965), p. 11.

the freezing of their high mountain sources. The first stage of the Bekabad plant will go on load in 1969. When fully operating it will generate more than three times the power generated by all Uzbek stations in 1964.

Plans for the development of Uzbek electric power in the next Plan period are impressive. According to Kurbanov, Chairman of the Uzbek Council of Ministers (1966), 25 milliard kWh. is to be generated, which is 13.5 milliard kWh. more than in the previous Five Year Plan period.[1] Consumption of electricity in the rural areas of the country is to increase by 400 per cent. he said, and 5,700 km. of electric grid is to be built. As a result of construction during the Seven Year Plan period the Uzbek grid system stretched over 6,000 km. But it is recognized in Uzbekistan that rural electrification is still far below requirements. It is therefore intended to improve the situation by constructing more than 45,000 km. of electric transmission lines in the current Five Year Plan period.[2]

Tadzhikistan

Post-war electric power development has centred on the upper and lower reaches of the Vakhsh (the wild or fearful) River. This powerful stream rises in the 'Roof of the World' mountains of west Kirgizia, flows through the Pulisangin Gorge to the steamy southern areas of Tadzhikistan where it joins the Pyandzh to form the great Amu Dar'ya River. Electric power generation in Tadzhikistan is mainly based on hydro-energy which has produced more than four-fifths of its electric power in recent years. The great hydro-power resources of this remote mountainous country (representing the second largest reserves in the Soviet Union[3]) are still largely untapped though some major power plants are now under construction.

It has been estimated that the potential annual generation of hydro-electric power in Tadzhikistan was 240 times greater than the amount actually consumed in 1961.[4] There are still serious obstacles to the full utilization of this power potential: the mountainous–geological conditions where it is located which are unpropitious for modern technology, inadvisability of flooding areas with valuable raw materials, fertile lands, and dense population. The result of

[1] PV, 5 March 1966.   [2] Ekon. i Zhizn', no. 2 (1966), p. 23.
[3] Kletsel'man, op. cit. p. 82.   [4] Ibid.

these handicaps is a substantial reduction in the much-vaunted Tadzhik hydro-resources which an expert of the Tadzhik Academy of Sciences has estimated to be industrially only 30–40 per cent. of the potential capacity.[1]

The lower Varsob HES which supplies the city of Dushanbe with power and light was the first post-war construction and was completed in 1949. It supplemented the older Varsob plant (completed in 1937). In the north, Leninabad receives electricity from the Farkhad power plant in Uzbekistan.

Hydro-resources of the Tadzhik SSR

(Main rivers)

Rivers	Average annual capacity (in 000 kW.)	Average annual generation of electric power (in m. kWh.)	
Zeravshan	1,354	11,750	Tadzhik section
Yagnob (Fan-Dar'ya)	396	3,469	
Pyandzh	5,568	48,776	
Vakhsh	5,130	44,939	
Surkhob	1,679	14,708	
Kafirnigan	1,423	12,465	
Varsob	438	7,837	
Murgab (Bartang)	965	8,453	
Gunt (Aligur)	940	8,234	
Total	17,893	160,631	

Source: Kletsel'man, op. cit. p. 82.

The Vakhsh power resources were first developed at Perepadnaya in the southern part of Tadzhikistan, chiefly with a view to irrigating this valley which has unique climatic conditions for growing fine-staple cotton. During the early '60s another station on the south Vakhsh River, the Golovnaya (210,000 kW.), was finished and at the time was the most powerful HES in Central Asia.[2] These stations, which are very useful locally in so far as they have greatly extended the irrigated cotton-growing area, have been eclipsed by the 'giant' Nurek hydro-electric station. It is being built in the deep

[1] Ibid. p. 83.
[2] I. G. Grishkov, *Elektrifikatsiya Sovetskogo Kirgizstana* (Frunze, 1965), p. 106.

mountain gorge of Pulisangin, 70 km. from Dushanbe. With a capacity of 2.7 million kW. it will be one of the largest in the Soviet Union when completed. Construction work in this gorge for the future plant involved building a diversion tunnel owing to complicated geological factors and frequent caving in. There were also angry complaints in the Tadzhik Press of the unnecessary delays, chaotic working conditions, 'scandalous waste of building materials', 'poor labour discipline', and deplorable incompetence on the part of the *Gidrospetsstroy*.[1] However, the tunnel was finally completed in March 1966.[2] 'Mobility of labour' also had a serious effect on the progress of the Nurek construction because according to *Izvestiya* (24 March 1966) 'the Party, Komsomol, and Trade Unions take little interest in improving living and labour conditions'. The Nurek plant was scheduled to be completed in 1966 but as conditions did not improve sufficiently a postponement of this date was necessary.

The construction of the large Nurek plant is only the beginning of a colossal plan of electrification including a cascade of HES with a capacity of 10 million kW. and generation of 36 milliard kWh. on the Vakhsh,[3] and the development of the Pyandzh, 'another most powerful water source of Central Asia'. The Rogunskaya HES and its 20 milliard cu. m. reservoir in the Palangpara Gorge (capacity 3.2 million kW.) will be the first of the new series of plants in the Vakhsh cascade to be constructed under the new Five Year Plan when power generation in Tadzhikistan should rise over 200 per cent.

An analysis of the comparative costs of development of hydro-power on the Vakhsh cascade stations and the Pyandzh cascade shows that they are marked by low capital investment per kilowatt of established capacity and low cost per kilowatt-hour of electric power. For example, it is estimated that the capital investment required per kilowatt of established power at the Nurek HES is almost four times as low as at the Lenin Volga HES and even lower (though not so much) than on the construction of important HES in east Siberia such as the Bratsk and Krasnoyarsk stations, while the

---

[1] *Kom. Tadzhikistana*, 27 November 1965; 10 December 1965; 23 January 1966.

[2] *Pravda*, 23 March 1966.

[3] E. I. Polyarush and N. Shatskikh, 'Ob Osnovnykh Napravleniyakh Kompleksnogo Razvitiya Narodnogo Khozyaystva Tadzhikistana', *Iz. AN Tadzhikskoy SSR*, 1 (39) (1965), p. 5.

cost of Nurek power will eventually be almost twice as low as these Siberian plants. Thus economically the development of Tadzhik water power should be extremely advantageous to the Soviet Union. The low costs are explained by the steep fall and great water-carrying capacity of the Tadzhik rivers. The Vakhsh, for example, according to the head of water, exceeds not only the powerful rivers of Central Asia, but also the Volga, the Angara, and the Yenisey: it rises at a height of 3,600 m. above sea level and drops 3,160 m. before reaching the Vakhsh Valley.[1]

The development of cheap power from the Nurek and other projected stations on the Vakhsh opens enormous possibilities for irrigating new land with mechanically lifted water. It would enable the area under cotton, vineyards, and orchards to be increased by 200,000 ha. in Tadzhikistan alone and up to 1,000,000 ha. if lands in the adjacent *oblasts* of Uzbekistan are included.

The favourable aspects of the production of Tadzhik water power are considerably diminished if it is used outside the Republic where it becomes much more expensive owing to the high costs of transmission especially over the surrounding mountain chains. This aspect of the industry, however, reinforces the Tadzhik arguments in favour of establishing many more energy-intensive industries than already exist in Tadzhikistan to absorb surplus energy. The most likely industries for this purpose are certain non-ferrous (in the first place aluminium) and chemical industries, both large energy consumers.

Apart from the above-mentioned hydro-electric constructions, work has started on the Yavan thermal station in south Tadzhikistan, the capacity of which will be 220,000 kW. It is planned to start generating electricity in 1968 and to supply power to the new town of Yavan and the important electro-chemical works where construction started in 1966.

The power situation in this small Republic has been analysed at some length because of the industrial expansion ideas seemingly cherished there for a much broader industrialization, including a metallurgical and big textile industry based on greater electrification and the development of Tadzhik minerals with a much better utilization of abundant Tadzhik manpower.[2] This latter point is frequently

---

[1] Kletsel'man, op. cit. p. 84.   [2] Polyarush, op. cit. pp. 8–9.

stressed in Tadzhik economic studies and it seems to irritate some analysts of the Tadzhik economy (possibly better 'nationalists' than economists) that this manpower is not put to work to develop the natural resources of the country to which Tadzhik energy is the key.

Kirgizia

Though the potential power resources of Kirgizia are large, little more than a start was made to harness the Republic's powerful rivers and provide power for industry and agriculture until the Seven Year Plan (1959–65). Hitherto the Republic's power deficit was to a considerable extent supplied by Uzbekistan. During the war some hydro-electric power stations were built to supply defence and other evacuated industries in the Frunze area and power capacity increased 3.5 times between 1940 and 1950. The Voroshilov (later Lebedinov) HES was built on the Great Chu Canal in 1943. Many difficulties were experienced in getting the equipment for this station to distant Kirgizia under war-time conditions. A turbine and generator from Karelia were actually installed at the Lebedinskaya HES in 1941 and other machinery from Baku, Sverdlovsk, and Karaganda also arrived. In order to supplement the still inadequate supplies of electricity to Frunze, another station, the Alamedinskaya HES No. 1, was built at this time on the Chu Canal (i.e. No. 1 of the Alamedinskiy cascade).[1] The largest thermal station in the country, the Frunze Heat and Power Station, was started in 1957 but not completed until 1963 'owing to many delays in supplying equipment and bad labour organization'.[2] Until the Frunze station was built there was an acute lack of power in the capital and in the Chu Valley where new industries were being established. In order to supply these needs new capacity was added to the Frunze station bringing it to 300,000 kW. in 1965. It is now known as the 'energy heart of Kirgizia'.[3]

The Seven Year Plan envisaged a large expansion of Kirgiz electric power capacity. As a result, the rate of growth of electric power during this period was above the Soviet average. The completed Uch-Kurgan HES (begun in 1956, capacity 180,000 kW.) and the Frunze Heat and Power Station were much larger than any power stations previously existing in Kirgizia; several smaller plants

[1] Grishkov, op. cit. pp. 41–47.   [2] Ibid. p. 88.   [3] *Pravda*, 23 January 1966.

were built at Przheval'sk (6,500 kW.), Osh (50,000 kW.), Naryn, and other inhabited places in the central Tyan Shan.[1]

This electrification programme did not run smoothly during the first three years (1959–61); there were delays in getting new plants on load and the capacity of some plants was badly utilized.[2] The Frunze station went on load in 1963 and extended its capacity to 300,000 kW. in 1965. Apart from supplying power to industry it provided domestic heat and hot water in the city. The Uch-Kurgan plant, the first of a cascade of electric stations planned 'to tame' the Naryn, was completed in 1962. This river, one of the most tempestuous in Central Asia, winds its way across the high Tyan Shan Mountains and rushes down with great velocity into the Fergana Valley where it joins the Kara-Dar'ya to form the Syr Dar'ya. The Naryn electrification scheme includes the eventual construction of seventeen hydro-electric power stations with a total capacity of 6.4 million kW. The site chosen for the Uch-Kurgan station was on the rapids of the river before it emerges into the Fergana Valley. The power plant construction was declared 'a shock Komsomol construction' and hundreds of young people from the Ukraine, White Russia, Uzbekistan, and other parts of the Soviet Union, with little or no previous experience of building power stations, toiled to build it. They were aided by about one hundred young boys and girls from the Bulgarian National Republic. The job was completed in 1962 and solved some serious power problems in Kirgizia and also brought large areas of new lands into cultivation through irrigation.

The decision of the Twenty-Second Party Congress to build the Toktogul HES (the second station of the Naryn cascade on the lower course of the river north of Uch-Kurgan), with a capacity of 1,200,000 kW., was of great importance not only for the Kirgiz economy but also for the other Central Asian republics and south Kazakhstan. The question had been more than once raised by the Kirgiz Party, Government, and Gosplan with the Union planning organs.[3] Work started on this project, which included a large artificial reservoir (265 cu. km.) and a 230 m. high dam, in 1962. Some 3,500 workers of thirty-seven nationalities were employed on the job and the Komsomols were also active here. A motor-road

[1] Grishkov, op. cit. p. 83.   [2] Ibid. p. 87.   [3] Ibid. p. 108.

(10 km. long) was built from Frunze to Osh to transport supplies to the construction site. The Toktogul power system is scheduled for completion in 1968. An important stage in its construction was reached in January 1966 when the Naryn River was channelled into the diversion tunnel (800 m. long) in the course of building the dam.[1]

As a result of this large electrification programme, Kirgiz production of electricity increased by over 200 per cent. in the Seven Year Plan period and *per capita* production in 1965 was 60 per cent. higher than in 1958 according to the Kirgiz First Party Secretary's report to the Kirgiz Party Congress in March 1966. In the next planned period (1966–70) power generation is to rise 1.7 times in Kirgizia.[2]

In Kirgizia (as in the other Central Asian republics) the progress made with rural electrification to date is not regarded as satisfactory.[3] It is specially mentioned for expansion under the new plan. The centralization of all Kirgiz energy in a unified power system is now making headway with the aim of linking it eventually with the unified Central Asian and south Kazakhstan grid and ultimately to an all-Union power system. In general, the development of energy and electric power is still below the requirements of the Kirgiz economy and of the population for electric power. According to an assessment of the Kirgiz Academy of Sciences, the average *per caput* of electric power generated was only 787 kWh., compared to the Soviet average of 1836 kWh. This was not due to any lack of hydro-power in Kirgizia as its hydro-power potential is 3.4 times larger than the Soviet average *per caput*.[4] It is, however, somewhat absurd, at the present state of development, to suggest that Kirgizia should produce the Soviet average output of power.

Kazakhstan[5]

Kazakhstan is the largest generator of electricity in Central Asia at the present time and the largest consumer, being the most highly

[1] *Sov. Kirgizia*, 7 January 1966.
[2] *Pravda*, 20 February 1966.   [3] Grishkov, op. cit. p. 96.
[4] *Razvitiye Proizvoditel'nykh Sil Kirkizskoy SSR v Perspektive*, p. 23.
[5] Useful articles on the development of electric power in Kazakhstan appeared in the *Central Asian Review*, vol. III, no. 1 (1955), p. 55, and vol. IV, no. 3 (1956), p. 272. The subject is fully treated in S. A. Neyshtadt, *Ekonomicheskoye Razvitiye Kazakhskoy SSR* (Alma-Ata, 1960).

industrialized of these republics. None the less, it is poorly supplied with electric power in relation to its enormous area, the requirements of its constantly developing industry, and the development of its great natural resources. Most of the electricity pre-war was supplied by low-powered thermal stations in the towns and rural electrification was virtually non-existent. The post-war plans involved the reconstruction of the existing thermal stations at Karaganda, Alma-Ata, Semipalatinsk, and other towns.

Electrification in Kazakhstan is complicated by the location of its energy resources. Although these resources, according to the calculations of the Energy Institute of the Kazakh Academy of Sciences, should be sufficient to cover all the requirements of the Republic, they are so unequally distributed throughout the territory of Kazakhstan as to create serious discrepancies and other problems. Thus 94 per cent. of all stone and brown coal reserves are concentrated in the north-east, the central, and north-west areas, while 78.5 per cent. of the hydro-energy resources are in east Kazakhstan and the southern regions. North-east and central Kazakhstan suffer from lack of hydro-power and east and south Kazakhstan operate on imported coal.

These factors and problems were taken into account in the projects of the Sixth Five Year and the Seven Year Plans of electrification which envisaged large-scale developments in Kazakhstan and a rate of growth of power 2.5 times that of European Russia by 1965. Schemes already begun in the '50s were to be completed and the construction of important new power stations such as the Balkhash, the Dzhezkazgan, and Alma-Ata industrial stations were started under the Seven Year Plan (1959–65).

The harnessing of the power of the Irtysh River in east Kazakhstan began pre-war with the construction of the Ust'-Kamenogorsk station, completed in 1953 (capacity 425,000 kW.). The Irtysh is the main source of water power in Kazakhstan and this was the first of many important hydro-electric stations erected on its waters. The site chosen for the Ust'-Kamenogorsk power station was ten miles upstream at Ablaketh, an ideal site in the centre of the Altay ore fields. Both the Ust'-Kamenogorsk and its successor, the Bukhtarma HES (some 80 km. upstream from Ust'-Kamenogorsk), aimed primarily at providing cheap power for working the rich poly-metallic mines of the Altay. In fact, cheap power from these stations revolutionized the production processes of non-ferrous metals in which the Altay is so rich.[1] The Ust'-Kamenogorsk plant started to operate in 1953 and the Bukhtarma, after many delays, went on load in 1961.

In the south-east of Kazakhstan, the River Ili, after flowing some 600 km. through west Sinkiang, makes its way across the semi-desert regions of Semirech'ye to Lake Balkhash. The first of a number of power stations to be built on the Ili is the Kapchagay HES (capacity 400,000 kW.), construction of which started in 1956, in the Kapchagay Gorge, 70 km. north of Alma-Ata. This large electri-fication project, which includes an enormous artificial lake or sea, has been a long time under construction. It is now specifically mentioned in the Draft Five Year Plan for completion by 1970. The Chardara Reservoir, on the Syr Dar'ya, the biggest in the Soviet Union, is now being filled. But when the Kapchagayskoye Mor'ye (sea) is completed it will be five times larger than the Chardara Dam.[2] Through irrigation based on the Kapchagay scheme a large area of desert in the Balkhash region will receive 'new life and water'.

Apart from these hydro-electric schemes, the enormous coal reserves of north Kazakhstan are to be the base of a huge programme of thermal electrification to serve the industrialized areas of Kara-ganda and Temir Tau and also the adjacent 'Virgin Lands'. A specialists' headquarters has been set up at Pavlodar to direct this new development. Construction will start during the Five Year Plan period (1966–70) on the Ekibastuz GRES (No. 1) and the Ekibastuz GRES (No. 2), each with a capacity of 3,000,000 kW. The first stage of the important Yermak GRES (capacity 1,500,000 kW. but planned total capacity 2,400,000 kW.) is to be completed during the present planned period. The Kazakh Press proudly points out that the Ekibastuz GRES (No. 2) will be more powerful than all the hydro-electric stations on the Dnieper. By 1970 electric power in the Irtysh area is scheduled to increase by thirteen times, and thermal power 3.5 times.[3] Heat and power stations are also to be expanded at Petropavlovsk, Ust'-Kamenogorsk, Karaganda, and other industrial

[1] *Central Asian Review*, no. 3 (July–September 1953); vol. II, no. 1 (1954).
[2] *Trud*, 11 March 1966.   [3] *Kaz. Pravda*, 14 April 1966.

towns. The final plans for the Ekibastuz area between 1965 and 1973 which are now being prepared envisage three to four stations with a total capacity of 15,000,000–16,000,000 kW.[1]

In the southern area a large GRES is being built at Dzhambul (total planned capacity 1,200,000 kW.) and will be the first in Kazakhstan to operate on Uzbek natural gas. Dzhambul power will be used to feed the Kazakh chemical industry in the town.[2]

According to Beysebayev's report to the Twenty-Third Party Congress,[3] installed generating capacity in Kazakhstan increased during the past seven year period 2.9 times, and by 1970 annual electricity generation in the Republic will have risen to 40 milliard kWh., representing an increase of 100 per cent. Even now, he said, Kazakhstan will not yet be self-sufficient in power and the deficit will be made up by transmission of power from the Urals and the Uzbek SSR. In the opinion of the Kazakh Prime Minister, the transmission of more than 3 milliard kWh. of electric power to the Kustanay *oblast* from the Urals was inefficient and it was therefore intended to construct an electric transmission line from Yermak–Ekibastuz–Tselinograd to Sarbay. A transmission line from Ekibastuz to Dzhambul should also be constructed in the current five year period so as to link the power system of north and south Kazakhstan eventually with that of Central Asia. In all, some 25,000 km. of power lines are to be built in the Republic in this period. As a result of the Ekibastuz electrification scheme, plans are also being prepared for a 2,500 km. transmission line to be erected during the five year period to bring Kazakh power to the Urals and eventually to the European part of the USSR. According to the Director of the All-Union Power Systems and Supply Lines Institute, the erection of these lines is becoming an economic necessity. By 1980, according to the estimates of this Institute, the thermal power stations based on the brown coal-fields of Siberia and Kazakhstan will be sending 125 milliard kWh. annually to the western regions of the USSR. This is part of the great electric transmission line Siberia–north Kazakhstan–Centre construction on which it is hoped to start in the present Five Year Plan.[4] 'Nothing similar to this transmission of current yet

[1] *Kaz. Pravda*, 14 March 1966.   [2] Ibid. 16 January 1966.
[3] *Pravda*, 7 April 1966.   [4] Ibid. 10 May 1966.

M

exists in any country in the world.'[1] It is interesting to note that
per kilowatt-hour of power, energy transmitted to the Centre will
be 30 per cent. cheaper than power based on coal from the Don,
according to the estimates of the chief engineer of the 'Pavlodar
Energy Directorate'.[2] These far-ranging electrification projects
in Kazakhstan reflect as well as any other indicator could the exciting
industrial and agricultural prospects before this Republic and its
important place in the Soviet economy. The importance attached
to electrification in connexion with the constantly expanding
industrialization of Kazakhstan is also reflected in the fact that
capital investment in electric power stations will be 56.6 per cent
more in the new Five Year Plan period than in the preceding five
years.[3]

MINERALS AND METALLURGY

(Kazakhstan is the richest source of ferrous and non-ferrous
minerals and the largest producer of metal in Central Asia.) The
development of ferrous metallurgy in Kazakhstan is dealt with in
the next chapter because of its close connexions with the Siberian
industry. Kazakhstan, as has been shown, was already before the war
a primary producer of copper, chrome, lead, zinc, gold, and silver
and is regarded as occupying first place in the Soviet Union for the
reserves of most of these non-ferrous metals. It is undoubtedly one
of the richest ore-bearing regions of the USSR. Geological pros
pecting in the post-war period has greatly added to knowledge of
Kazakh mineral resources and confirmed their extent and richness
In Kazakhstan and the Central Asian republics (as in the USSR as a
whole) it is difficult to assess the progress of the non-ferrous industry
because of the continuing Soviet refusal to publish absolute figure
of production. The percentage figures of growth (mainly from an
unknown base) are on the whole a very unreliable substitute for
absolute production figures.

Apart from Kazakhstan, ferrous metallurgy is poorly developed
in Central Asia owing to the lack of iron ore reserves. The only steel
plant is at Bekabad (formerly Begovat in Uzbekistan) which only

[1] *Kaz. Pravda*, 10 April 1966.   [2] Ibid. 14 April 1966.
[3] *PV*, 12 March 1966.

supplies 15 per cent. of the region's metal requirements including those of south Kazakhstan.[1] It started as a scrap collection plant to make steel from war scrap collected from the battle-fields. But it was not completed until 1946 when the first steel was produced. Meanwhile the works (non-integrated) have been constantly expanding and since 1950 it has been known as the Uzbek Metallurgical Works. It still works mainly from scrap owing to the lack of iron ore. It now consists of three open-hearth furnaces but there are no electric furnaces which would be ideal for a plant working on scrap. The open-hearth furnaces are reported to be 'antiquated and the rolling equipment technically backward'.[2]

Bekabad is situated on the banks of the Syr Dar'ya River about 128 km. south of Tashkent city, and is supplied with power by the Farkhad plant on the opposite bank of the Syr Dar'ya. It is now producing about 200,000 tons of steel and 180,000 tons of rolled metal. Locally it is not considered advisable to attempt to increase production of steel at Bekabad by constructing electric furnaces because 'there is not sufficient power in Uzbekistan and we have no charge [raw materials] of the required quality'.[3] Production cannot be stepped up much more with the present equipment which was installed in 1944–5. Apart from conversion to natural gas in 1961, and the introduction of a continuous casting plant in 1962, with some minor modifications to increase efficiency, there has been no further capital investment in Bekabad.[4] Gross output of the plant and productivity per worker increased and costs were lowered following conversion to gas, according to a local report.[5]

Metal has still to be imported in large quantities to Central Asia from the Ukraine, the Urals, and west Siberia at a cost of 6.7–7 roubles a ton, averaging about 12 million roubles per annum, while surplus scrap is sent to the Urals. Central Asian metal requirements are continually rising as a result of the expansion of the engineering and electrical industries. It is estimated that by 1970 Central Asian requirements of small and medium types of rolled metal will have sharply risen and that Bekabad 'will not be able to satisfy them even by half'[6] while surplus scrap in 1965 already amounted to more than

[1] *Ekon. i Zhizn'*, no. 10 (1965), p. 8.   [2] *Ekon. Gazeta*, no. 46 (16 November 1963).
[3] *Ekon. i Zhizn'*, no. 3 (1966), p. 46.   [4] *Ekon. Gazeta*, no. 46 (16 November 1963).
[5] *Ekon. i Zhizn'*, no. 3 (1966), p. 44.   [6] Ibid. p. 45.

300,000 tons and should reach 1,080,000 tons by 1970. This metal is dispatched to the Urals and re-exported to Central Asia as rolled metal. In order to cut down this wasteful process, the Chief Engineer of Bekabad has suggested that a fourth Marten furnace should be constructed and other equipment reconstructed.[1] Moreover, the Chairman of the Uzbek Gosplan has described the Uzbek metal problem as 'extremely urgent' and stressed the need to abolish the present 'irrational crosshauls' of metal and scrap by increasing the capacity of the Uzbek metallurgical plant.[2]

Since the war there has been a great expansion of the Kazakh non-ferrous industry and its output is of increasing industrial importance to the Soviet Union. Kazakhstan has been confirmed as the chief non-ferrous base of the Soviet Union.[3] It holds first place in the world for its reserves of chrome and vanadium,[4] its polymetallic ores (including the important copper element) are the richest in the Soviet Union, while it also holds first place for lead smelting. Both the Seven Year Plan and its current successor devote special attention to the development of the Kazakh non-ferrous industry which is heavily concentrated in the Altay, central and south Kazakhstan. Some important plants which were started between 1959 and 1965 are scheduled for completion during the new Five Year Plan: the Dzhezkazgan ore-mining and metallurgical combine; expansion of the Balkhash mining and metallurgical combine; operation of the Leninogorsk zinc works at full capacity by 1969. Furthermore, the Ust'-Kamenogorsk lead and zinc combine is to be expanded and will produce argon for the first time in Kazakhstan. A special argon section was being installed in 1965. When it is in production, it will be possible to supply completely the Ust'-Kamenogorsk titanium and magnesium combine's requirements of argon which had formerly to be imported from the Urals. Lead extraction is to be increased by expansion of the Chimkent lead works and more intensive exploitation of capacity at the Leninogorsk lead works and the Ust'-Kamenogorsk lead and zinc combine.[5] In order to increase Kazakh raw material supplies for these plants it is planned to put the Tishinka lead and zinc mines, the Sayak copper

---

[1] *Ekon. i Zhizn'*, no. 3 (1966), p. 47.   [2] Ibid. no. 10 (1965), p. 8.

[3] Neyshtadt, op. cit. p. 163.

[4] G. Kh. Burambayev and N. I. Yanios, *Rastsvet Ekonomiki i Kul'tury Kazakhskoy SSR* (Moscow, 1958), p. 11.   [5] *Kaz. Pravda*, 13 March 1966.

mines, and the first sections of the Nikolayevka and the Orlovka mining and concentration plants into operation and to increase the capacity of Tekeli lead and zinc, Zyryanovsk lead, and the Irtysh and Achisay polymetals combines.)

The Altay received an important addition to its wide range of metallurgical resources by the completion of the Ust'-Kamenogorsk titanium and magnesium combine early in 1965 and of the Union's largest installation for the extraction of lead and zinc from slag which was put into operation later in the year.

If the Kazakh Five Year Plan is to be fulfilled in regard to the non-ferrous industry, Beysebayev, Chairman of the Kazakh Council of Ministers, stressed at the Party Congress in March 1966 that it would be necessary to eliminate such existing defects as slowness in developing ore-fields and making use of planned capacity, losses of metal before concentration and during metallurgical processing, and what he called the inadequate use of the achievements of science and technology. There have also been complaints of wastage in the extraction processes because valuable ore had become contaminated through the introduction of foreign matter, resulting in a decline in the quantity of lead and zinc produced annually.[1]

The development of Kazakh copper reserves (the largest in the country) is of the greatest significance to the Soviet economy. The major reserves are at Dzhezkazgan (estimated at one-fourth of total USSR reserves and yielding 50 per cent. of Soviet production), Kounrad, Boshchekul', and the Altay. There are copper smelters at Karsakpay, west of Dzhezkazgan (estimated annual output 220,000 metric tons), and Balkhash (estimated annual output 165,000 metric tons). It was reliably considered that largely owing to Kazakh (and Urals) copper supplies, the Soviet Union would be at least self-sufficient in copper by 1966 though it is impossible to forecast what the position may be subsequently. Development of the big Bosh-chekul deposits (in Pavlodar *oblast*) was pushed forward during the Seven Year Plan and prospects there are said to be excellent.[2] They are situated near the Maykubinskiy coal mines in an area which also contains iron ore, chrome, nickel, and magnesite.

Soviet reports state that the Dzhezkazgan, Kounrad, and Zyryanovsk plants have been modernized and mechanized and that

[1] *Partiynaya Zhizn'*, 11 January 1966.   [2] Neyshtadt, op. cit. p. 277.

productivity has been increased because of more advanced technology in the Leninogorsk and other Altay mines. Though automation and mechanization are advancing in this industry, there are still many unsolved technical problems.

(It seems that the Soviet Union continues to regard copper as a deficit metal, in spite of the discovery in the last few decades of additional Soviet reserves, and it is trying to substitute aluminium (though later than other countries) for various types of production requiring copper. The result has been an urgent quest for new sources of bauxite or other raw materials to expand the Soviet aluminium industry.) The Pavlodar aluminium plant was completed during the Seven Year Plan and works on bauxite from the Turgay bauxite mines in the Kustanay *oblast*; its alumina production section is to be completed shortly and a second Pavlodar alumina works to be put into operation by 1970.[1] Other Central Asian countries are now participating or trying to participate in this expansion of the aluminium industry. (A new aluminium plant is to be constructed hundreds of miles away in south Tadzhikistan. It is to be constructed at Regar, and the first wing is scheduled to start production in 1968) power will be supplied by the Nurek hydro-power station, and as its capacity increases it is expected eventually to draw additional power from the huge new Nizhne-Rogunsk hydro-electric station also on the Vakhsh.

There has apparently been some competition among the republics about the location of this first Central Asian aluminium plant. The arguments in favour of locating it in Tadzhikistan rather than in the Tashkent area or north Kirgizia are that the cost of transmitting power from Nurek to Tashkent would be much higher per ton of metallic aluminium than the cost of transporting alumina, for production of a ton of aluminium, from Angren to the vicinity of Nurek. Transmission of electric power from Nurek would also involve much larger capital costs than the transport of alumina to Tadzhikistan, according to this analysis.[2] These economic considerations, therefore, weighed the scales in favour of locating the new plant in south Tadzhikistan. It is also estimated that the cost of metal there will be 2.5 times lower than that actually produced at

[1] *Kaz. Pravda*, 13 March 1966.
[2] Polyarush, op. cit. pp. 6–7.

the big Dnieper plant and 10 per cent. lower than at the projected Bratsk plant.[1]

Efforts are also being made in Uzbekistan and Kirgizia to produce alumina. Work has begun at Almalyk in Tashkent *oblast* on a pilot installation to produce alumina from kaolin which has been found in large quantities in the Angren coal-fields. Although kaolins are regarded as leaner materials for alumina production, the Uzbeks claim that alumina produced from Angren kaolins will be among the cheapest in the USSR.[2] The Kirgiz have no bauxite but have put forward a rather lame case for developing their nepheline deposits as a basis for an aluminium industry. Their argument is that the chemical composition of their nepheline syenite, 'admittedly not of high quality', is similar to that of the nepheline syenite on which the Armenian mining–chemical combine was established at Razdan, that there is the necessary limestone in the vicinity of the nepheline deposits, cheap electric power, and adequate water resources.[3] Nothing has yet come of this proposal.

Kirgizia's strongest asset in non-ferrous resources is mercury, for which she holds first place in the country. She also produces high-quality antimony and a work sponsored by the Kirgiz Academy of Sciences states that the prospect of the development of tin and gold in the Republic is 'of all-Union significance'.[4] Many rare metals, including uranium, are known to exist in the Republic but nothing is published about their output.

The Uzbek non-ferrous industry, second in importance in Central Asia to that of Kazakhstan, is heavily concentrated in the Angren–Almalyk–Altyn–Topkan area. Almalyk, 'the heart of the Uzbek mining territory', has been greatly developed in the post-war years and from a mere hamlet in the '30s is now a town of 70,000 inhabitants. The Almalyk poly-metallic deposits contain copper, lead, and zinc and are one of the chief Soviet sources of copper. There is also an important copper refinery at Almalyk. During the new five year period (1966–70), the whole cycle of copper production will become possible for the first time at Almalyk from ore extraction to finished rolled metal.[5] Early in 1966 a deoxidized copper-wire

[1] Ibid.   [2] Tass in English, 5 January 1966.
[3] *Razvitiye Proizvoditel'nykh Sil Kirgizskoy SSR v Perspektive*, op. cit. p. 30.
[4] Ibid. p. 31.
[5] Cf. Kurbanov's speech at the Republican Party Congress, March 1966. *PV*, 5 March 1966.

bar shop started to operate at the Lenin metals combine in Almalyk, the first shop of its kind in Central Asia. The furnace is fired by natural gas. Uzbek output of copper is expected to increase swiftly (1966–70) while the high return on capital investment and profitableness of copper is stressed as a basis for local optimism about the industry's future.[1] According to First Party Secretary Rashidov's report to the Uzbek Party Congress in March 1966, Uzbek output of copper concentrate and of molybdenum increased by over 800 per cent. in the last four and a half years of the Seven Year Plan, while prospecting increased by over 50 per cent.[2]

A major project set before the Uzbek non-ferrous industry by the draft plan directives is the completion by 1970 of a zinc plant at the Altyn–Topkan combine; with the completion of this zinc plant a full metallurgical cycle of zinc production will be possible for the first time in Uzbekistan.

Great excitement was aroused in Uzbekistan in 1965 by the sensational discovery of gold at Muruntau in the depths of the Kyzylkum Desert. Thus ended a long hunt by tenacious geologists drawn on by ancient lore and legend about desert gold and by expert examination of the terrain. The exceptional nature and extent of these gold deposits was confirmed by a detailed survey of the gold-field in 1965 and by the expert testimony of Academician Shcherbakov. He described the Muruntau gold deposits as 'colossal' and not to be compared to the Klondyke gold-fields which lay in river valleys and were quickly exhausted whereas the Muruntau contained lode gold-mines which might be considered 'inexhaustible'.[3] The mines were only 2–3 m. beneath 'one's feet' in the sand. They would thus have the great economic advantage, he said, of being the first in the world experience of gold-mining to be worked by open-cast methods. Another Soviet writer stated that Muruntau contained the largest gold deposits in the Soviet Union, surpassing the gold resources of Siberia, the Far East, or any other gold-bearing area of the country.[4] Though this may be an over-exuberant estimate (which there is no means of checking), there seems no doubt of the great importance of the Muruntau gold-mines. Commercial

[1] *Ekon. i Zhizn'*, no. 10 (1965), p. 8.   [2] *PV*, 4 March 1966.
[3] *Kom. Pravda*, 26 February 1966.
[4] P. Kovalev, 'Treasure House of the Red Sands', *Ekon. i Zhizn'*, no. 11 (1965), p. 65.

production was not expected to start until 1967 while prospecting continues as it is thought that there may be other deposits in the area. *Pravda Vostoka*, 7 April 1966, reported that the first ore had been produced from an experimental quarry in 1966. A refinery is also planned near Muruntau. Experts believe that Muruntau may yield as much as ten tons per annum by 1970. A new town called Zolotogorsk is being built for the miners but supply conditions in this desert region are extremely difficult.

CHEMICAL INDUSTRIES

There has been a considerable expansion in the capacity and range of products of the chemical industry in the Central Asian republics and Kazakhstan throughout the post-war period. The effect of Khrushchev's 'Big Chemistry' programme of 1959 also penetrated to Central Asia resulting in the construction of some large chemical plants and the expansion of others during the Seven Year Plan period. Mineral fertilizers for the Central Asian cotton-fields are the chief product of the industry. The major producer in the area

Production of Mineral Fertilizers by Union Republics

(in conventional units: 000 tons)

	1940	*1950*	*1958*	*1960*	*1963*	*1964*
USSR	3,238	5,497	12,419	13,867	19,935	25,562
including:						
RSFSR	2,164	3,093	6,420	7,169	10,543	13,787
Ukrainian SSR	1,012	1,536	3,375	3,853	5,380	5,784
Belorussian SSR	13	—	—	—	195	943
Uzbek. SSR	2	522	1,005	1,121	1,419	1,679
Kazakh. SSR	—	22	475	477	568	707
Georgian SSR	—	—	230	247	416	447
Azerbaydzhan SSR	—	—	—	—	36	423
Latvian SSR	47	177	315	324	332	333
Armenian SSR	—	58	194	211	203	107
Turkmen SSR	—	—	—	—	228	250
Estonian SSR	—	78	405	465	615	774
Lithuanian SSR	—	—	—	—	—	328

Source: *Nar. Khoz. SSSR v 1964 g.*, p. 176.

is Uzbekistan (also the major raw-cotton producer), which ranks third in the Soviet Union for mineral fertilizer output after the RSFSR and the Ukraine, with 8 per cent. of all-Union production[1] in 1960, falling below 7 per cent. in 1964.

Since the discovery of the Bukhara natural gas deposits, a lively interest has been aroused in Central Asia in the location of a chemical industry based on the deposits. Great advantages are claimed for the location of this chemical industry in Central Asia rather than in European Russia. As a writer in the local monthly *Narodnoye Khozyaystvo Sredney Azii* (no. 5, 1964) put it:

In comparison with the developing centres of the chemical industry in the European part of the USSR, Central Asia possesses great advantages. It has unique raw material and fuel-power resources . . . and is well supplied with labour. Unfortunately the planning organs still do not properly value the favourable possibilities of the eastern regions of the country. In deciding problems of the location of the chemical industry, they follow the beaten track and continue to site chemical enterprises in the European part of the USSR.

It is also argued that it is more economical to establish the chemical industry and especially products of organic synthesis (organic chemistry) requiring a large quantity of gas in Central Asia than to transmit gas to the European part of the USSR for chemical production.[2] Thus the cost of transporting chlorine rubber is allegedly 4–5 times less than the cost of transmitting gas required for its production and the same applies to other chemical products like polyacrylon nitrile, cellulose acetate.[3] The only reservations these Central Asian economists have about a large expansion of the chemical industry based on natural gas is the scarcity of water in Central Asia.[4]

[1] The Soviets only publish distribution and production statistics for mineral fertilizers as a whole, not distinguishing the various types of fertilizer. The statistical handbook for 1964 published production figures for the Union republics for the first time.

[2] This was also the line taken by V. Moskvin, Director of a group of laboratories of energy at the Institute of Technical–Economic Researches of the Chemical Industry, in a critical analysis of the mistakes in the location of Soviet chemical plants in *Pravda* (21 December 1964): 'As a result of the extremely irrational location of enterprises of the chemical industry we lose hundreds of millions of roubles annually. As economic calculations show, it is more advantageous to transport the finished energy-consuming chemical product or the basic by-product than an equivalent amount of fuel used in its production. It is much more advisable to locate energy-consuming chemical production in the eastern regions of the country and to export the finished product to the European part of the USSR. This would make it possible to lessen the very great strain of the fuel-energy balance in the European part of the country and effectively to raise the national economic result by using the cheap energy resources of Siberia and north Kazakhstan.'

[3] *Nar. Khoz. S.A.*, no. 4 (1964), p. 52.   [4] Ibid. no. 5 (1964), p. 21.

The Central Asian phosphorus industry should by now have a local raw material base. Very large deposits of phosphorus rock (only second in size to the Khibiny apatite mines in the Kola Peninsula) were discovered in the Karatau Mountains in south Kazakhstan in 1936 but were not exploited until after the war. The development of these Karatau deposits has lagged far behind the planned schedules with the result that large quantities of Kola apatite rock are still hauled by rail to feed some of the Central Asian and Kazakh superphosphate plants. There were also great delays in getting the local Chulak-Tau concentration plant into production but it was reported to be operating in 1963. All Soviet phosphate rock has to be processed in a concentration plant before delivery to the superphosphate factories, so great importance was attached to the completion of the Chulak-Tau plant.

There are also considerable phosphate reserves at Aktyubinsk in east Kazakhstan which are processed at the Aktyubinsk chemical combine (production began about 1952). The announcement that a contract was signed between the Soviet trading organization *Tekhmashimport* and the West German firm of Friedrich Uhde GmbH of Dortmund to develop the phosphate industry of Kazakhstan with the aid of German equipment at a total cost of DM 65 million (£6 million) and that two units had already been built in Kazakhstan by Uhde and K. Knapsack AG reflects the urgent Soviet need to improve production at Karatau and Aktyubinsk, the two chief Kazakh phosphate centres, in order to increase supplies for Central Asia.[1] Most of the sulphur required by the Central Asian superphosphate plants is produced by the Gaurdak mines in Turkmenistan[2] and the by-products of the metallurgical plants.

In the post-war period as formerly, the Uzbek chemical industry has continued to lay chief stress on the production of fertilizer for the cotton plantations while latterly initiating a new range of products based on the Republic's natural gas deposits. The Uzbek plants producing superphosphates are at Kokand and Samarkand. The Kokand plant started production as a small-scale preparation works in 1947. It was converted to a large-scale superphosphate plant by the addition of new facilities in 1959 and 1961 and is to be

---

[1] *The Times*, 24 October 1966.
[2] S. G. Freykin, *Turkmenskaya SSR* (Moscow, 1957).

switched over completely to ammoniated superphosphate production. About five hundred workers are employed on three shifts. Kokand has its own sulphuric acid plant. It works on phosphate ore from Karatau, liquid ammonia and nitric acid from Tashkent, and sulphur from copper extraction plants in Kazakhstan.

The oldest and for a long time the only plant producing nitrogenous fertilizer in Central Asia was the Chirchik electro-chemical combine in Uzbekistan, situated about 50 km. from Tashkent. 'This firstling of the Uzbek chemical industry' started to operate in 1940 and celebrated its twenty-fifth anniversary with considerable local rejoicing in 1965. Reconstruction of the plant began in 1959 and new capacity for ammonia and urea production was added during the seven year period. A large carbamide shop went into operation in 1964. Chirchik now produces ammonium nitrate, compound fertilizers, liquid fertilizers, and urea for the cotton industry; the first synthetic ammonia was made here in 1965.[1] The plant was converted to natural gas in 1960–3. It is claimed locally that the Chirchik combine was a pioneer in devising and introducing new technology into the Uzbek nitrogenous industry,[2] and that it has done much to train cadres for other chemical plants.

The Central Asian chemical industry will be greatly strengthened when the important Fergana nitrogen fertilizer plant and the Navoi chemical combine, both working on natural gas, are completed. Construction on the Fergana plant began in 1959, certain units came into operation in 1961, and ammonium nitrate production began in 1962. Its performance so far has been disappointing and much criticized. Output of potassium nitrate was less than planned in 1965. Mistakes and miscalculation in design, failure to make use of existing capacity, and increased costs greatly above the original estimates were also alleged in regard to the new plant.[3] Probably the most serious defect was the underfulfilment of the ammonia plant 'which in turn brought the distribution of mineral fertilizer to a standstill'.[4] Kommunist Uzbekistana (no. 2, 1965) complained that 'the workers were badly trained and that the Trade Unions did not concern

---

[1] Ekon. i Zhizn', no. 10 (1965), p. 65.

[2] Ibid. The Chirchik electro-chemical plant is one of several chemical plants equipped with foreign machinery in Central Asia. The Dutch supplied machinery for Chirchik.

[3] PV, 28 July 1965; 20 October 1965.   [4] Kom. Uzbekistana, no. 2 (1965).

themselves with cultural–living conditions. So in 1963 five hundred workers melted away.'

The Navoi chemical combine, the largest in Central Asia, started production in 1965 (construction began in 1961). It was built in the village of Kermine (now renamed Navoi) in east Bukhara where the former Emir of Bukhara had his summer palace. A new town is being built round the combine and the architects are said to be taking great care 'to avoid monotony in its appearance'. The combine will work on Gazli natural gas. The main product is nitrogenous fertilizer but it is also designed to manufacture synthetic fibres and other chemical products. The first thousand tons of granulated ammoniated nitrate were produced from ammonia of its own production in 1965.

In the past four and a half years (to March 1966), the Uzbek chemical industries' output increased at an average annual rate of nearly 20 per cent., and output of mineral fertilizers was 110 per cent. greater than before the onset of the Seven Year Plan period. Investment rose seven times in the chemical industry between 1959 and 1966.[1] Nevertheless the Uzbek chemical industry is still far from being able to satisfy the needs of the Republic's economy. Mineral fertilizers, toxic chemicals, defoliants, synthetic resins, plastics, and other chemical products have to be imported in considerable quantities from other regions of the country. Automobile tyres are not yet manufactured in Uzbekistan (or elsewhere in Central Asia) and there is an acute need of polymer materials for agriculture, irrigation, the engineering, electric, and radio industries.[2] In treeless Central Asia, the use of polymers is most advantageous. A plant processing plastic materials for domestic and municipal construction went into production at Akhangaran for the first time in 1964. When completed, its capacity is expected to be equal to satisfying the requirements of the other Central Asian republics as well as Uzbekistan.[3] But this industry is still in its infancy. The only factory in the whole of Central Asia making viscose silk is in Namangan and production of other chemical fibres is to be expanded during the next Five Year Plan period.

A large programme of expansion has been scheduled for the Uzbek chemical industry by the new Five Year Plan. The output

---

[1] *PV*, 4 March 1966.   [2] *Ekon. i Zhizn'*, no. 9 (1965), pp. 11–12.
[3] Ibid. no. 11 (1965), p. 65.

of mineral fertilizer is to reach 4,500,000 tons by 1970, an increase of 100 per cent. A plastics and a chemical fibre manufacturing industry are to be established in the Republic. The second part of the Fergana nitrogenous fertilizer factory and of the Navoi chemical combine are to be completed and the Chirchik electro-chemical combine is to be further expanded.[1] It is hoped that as a result of these plans Uzbekistan, in the first place, will be fully able to supply her needs for mineral fertilizer and have some to spare for her neighbours.[2] But the accomplishment of these aims will largely depend on the extent to which an end can be put to the constant stoppages of machinery, the incorrect installation of equipment, the under-utilization of plant, and other defects which have clogged progress in the last planned period.[3]

Uzbekistan's great northern neighbour, Kazakhstan, has mineral fertilizer (superphosphate) plants at Aktyubinsk, Dzhambul, and Chimkent (phosphate salts). The hopes of greatly increased production based on the development of the Karatau phosphates deposits have not yet materialized because of the muddle and gross inefficiency reported in both the 'Karataukhimstroy' (Karatau chemical construction trust) and the Karatau mining–chemical combine. According to *Pravda* (11 June 1965) things were in poor shape in both enterprises in mid-1965. As a result of this state of affairs, the original production target of 15,000,000 tons of phosphorite ore annually intended to satisfy the requirements in phosphorous mineral fertilizer not only of Central Asia and Kazakhstan but of the Middle Urals, Siberia, and the Far East is still far from being realized. At the Aksay mine of the Karatau mining–chemical combine the cost of removing the overburden is much higher than in other open-cast mines; the planned capacity of the mine is 2,000,000 tons a year, but because of mistakes in planning, deliveries of ore will be considerably less, and in 1966, it was stated, the mine would deliver only 512,000 tons, due to idle equipment and high production costs. The construction plan at Karatau was not fulfilled in 1964 and early in 1965 plan fulfilment was almost half that in the corresponding

[1] Cf. speech by Kurbanov, Chairman of the Council of Ministers at the Uzbek Republican Congress, *PV*, 5 March 1966.

[2] *Ekon. i Zhizn'*, no. 9 (1965), p. 13.

[3] *Kom. Uzbekistana*, no. 2 (1965). Uzbekistan has hitherto annually imported about 800,000 tons of mineral fertilizers for cotton cultivation.

period of the previous year. This inevitable problem in all construction sites of the eastern regions crops up here also, i.e. 'inattention to the living needs of the workers and employees which
in fact led to great instability of the labour force'.[1]

The Kirov chemical combine at Aktyubinsk in east Kazakhstan
supplies superphosphate, trace fertilizers, and toxic chemicals for
grain farms in Kazakhstan and cotton farms in Uzbekistan, Tadzhikistan, and other republics. It seems to be doing well and was
awarded the Order of the Red Banner for fulfilling the Seven Year
Plan ahead of time, installing new equipment and advanced technological processes in 1966.[2] Owing to the still inadequate production
of ore from the Aktyubinsk mines, apatite from Kola has also to be
hauled long distances by rail to supplement local Aktyubinsk supplies.[3]

Simple superphosphate with low phosphorous content (15 per
cent.) is the basic fertilizer made in Kazakhstan because of the lack
of sulphuric acid, 'although inexhaustible stocks of raw material for
the manufacture of sulphuric acid are available in the by-product
gases of the non-ferrous industry'.[4] It was later reported that the
Ust'-Kamenogorsk lead and zinc combine had produced the first
thousand tons of sulphuric acid in 1966.

Up to the present, production of nitrogenous fertilizer is limited
to a small output of by-product ammonium sulphate from the Temir-
Tau metallurgical plant. A project for a nitrogenous fertilizer plant
to be built at Temir-Tau has been on the stocks for some time but
construction has not started yet as far as can be ascertained.

The capacity of the Kazakh chemical industry is planned to
expand very considerably, 200 per cent. between 1966 and 1970.[5]
New chemical plants are to be constructed and a wide range of
products manufactured for the first time. In particular, new capacity
is planned for the production of phosphorus, phosphates, and
polyethylene. The Chimkent phosphate works when completed
will be the largest undertaking of its kind in the Soviet Union;
its products will be used mainly to replace edible fats in the manufacture of detergents and mineral fertilizers.[6] Other important new

[1] *Pravda*, 11 June 1965.   [2] Ibid. 5 June 1966.
[3] *Partiynaya Zhizn' Kazakhstana*, no. 2 (February 1964), p. 17.   [4] Ibid.
[5] Moscow Home Service, 6 May 1966.
[6] Speech by Beysebayev, Chairman of the Kazakh Council of Ministers at the Republican
  Supreme Soviet, 21 December 1965.

projects are the Dzhambul double superphosphate works and the new Pavlodar chemicals combine. Pavlodar is scheduled to make over fifty different types of products, many of which will appear for the first time in the Soviet Union. Rubber goods, paint, and lacquer are to be manufactured in two large chemical plants to be constructed side by side at Saran' in the Karaganda *oblast* and planned to form a single industrial unit. The variety of products to be made by these new factories is illustrated by the yeast factory under construction at the Kzyl-Orda cellulose and cardboard combine to produce fodder yeast from reed cellulose. The young Kazakh pharmaceutical industry represented by the Chimkent chemical and pharmaceutical works is to be reinforced by a new plant in Alma-Ata scheduled to be put into operation in 1966. Among other products Chimkent manufactures cortisone derived from the local deadly nightshade plant, and is the sole works in the Soviet Union producing ephedrine and codeine. In order to finance these plans, capital investment in the development of the Kazakh chemical industry is to increase to 662 million roubles or 190 per cent. more than between 1961 and 1965. On past performance it will be surprising if these far-reaching plans are fulfilled according to the five year timetable. But they do hold out prospects of a great expansion sooner or later of the Kazakh chemical industry for which there is urgent need especially in agriculture, in this rapidly developing, huge area.

The Tadzhik chemical industry is still in the early formative stage. It is directly linked with the development of Tadzhik hydroelectric power now in progress. The two main projects under construction at the present time are the Vakhsh nitrogen fertilizer works and the Yavan electro-chemical 'giant' plant. Construction of the Vakhsh chemical works (in Dushanbe), the first in Tadzhikistan, was started in 1963 and completion was reported to be 'not far off' in 1965.[1] The works will be supplied with power from the Golovnaya GES and will use natural gas from the Vakhsh Valley; the mechanical repair shop and the construction shop are already in operation. Some cryptic remarks about the location of a 'chemical combine ... in the Nurek HES zone' in an article in *Pravda* (21 November 1964) suggested that some Soviet experts did

[1] *Pravda*, 2 November 1966.

not approve of the site: 'To supply it with heat it would be necessary to build a powerful heat and power station and to supply it with power a trunk gas pipeline of 700 km. would have to be laid. The economic advisability of choosing this place for a chemical combine arouses great doubts.' The scheduled commissioning of this plant in 1966 is now threatened by lack of equipment and funds. The buildings were ready to start production of urea in mid-1965 but the necessary equipment was not available from the suppliers (including some all-Union firms) 'who unjustifiably failed to keep their contracts'. The funds allocated for the purchase of equipment were also insufficient 'while a flow of new decisions disrupted work on the site'.[1]

The Yavan electro-chemical combine is being built in the humid steppe of south Tadzhikistan. It is to be a very large enterprise and will produce 'dozens of different types of chemical products from caustic soda to calcium chloride, synthetic resins, plastics, and nitrogenous fertilizers'.[2] A new town to accommodate 100,000 people is to be built over the next five years and it is also hoped, as described above, to irrigate the 57,600 ha. of land in the Yavan and Obi-Kiik valleys. Nurek power, local natural gas, and dolomite deposits will be used. Time alone will show how far these ambitious plans for the Tadzhik chemical industry will succeed or how soundly they are based. At the present time Tadzhik requirements of fertilizer are supplied by imports from other regions of the Soviet Union. In 1962, 300,000 tons (in conventional units) was supplied, i.e. 24,400 tons of nitrogenous fertilizer, 84,700 tons of phosphorus and potash. More than 57.3 per cent. of the nitrogenous fertilizer was supplied by the Kemerovo works in west Siberia and the remainder came from plants as far distant as the Urals and the Ukraine. Kazakhstan was Tadzhikistan's main supplier of phosphorus fertilizer and the Urals supplied 100 per cent. of the potash fertilizer. Transport costs on these imports amounted to more than 3,000,000 roubles annually.[3]

Some of the chief sources of chemical minerals and production in Turkmenistan are in west Turkmeniya and have been worked

[1] Ibid. 22 July 1965.   [2] *Nar. Khoz. S.A.*, no. 5 (1964).
[3] U. Kh. Kletsel'man, 'Mezhrayonnyye Svyazi', *Iz. AN Tadzhiskoy SSR*, no. 3 (41) (1965), p. 30.

N

throughout the Soviet period and before. The harsh climate and relative inaccessibility of many of these deposits delayed development on modern lines. The mirabilite (glauber salts) deposits of the Kara-Bogaz-Gol have long been famous and a new plant has been built to produce various chemical products based on these salts. The port of Bekdash on the northern tip of the Kara-Bogaz-Gol has been expanded to deal with these chemicals. The ozocerite of Cheleken which is used in the manufacture of insulation tape, cables, artificial wax, and cerasin employed in the manufacture of waterproof fabrics has been worked since before the Revolution. But the bases of an advanced chemical industry in Turkmenistan were only laid after World War II. During the Seven Year Plan period the capacities of the Cheleken iodine and bromide works and the Kara-Bogaz-Gol chemical combine were considerably increased and both were radically reconstructed.[1] Carbon black produced at Cheleken now goes to twenty tyre and paint-lacquer factories in the Soviet Union and from the annual production at Cheleken 1,200,000 tyres are made.[2]

A new superphosphate plant was completed at Chardzou in 1963 (having been under construction since 1957). It works on Karatau phosphorite and Gaurdak sulphur, and the first sulphuric acid was produced in 1960. Single superphosphate production started in 1961. Compound fertilizers including ammoniated superphosphate are now also manufactured at Chardzhou. This fertilizer is specially important for the cotton-growing districts in the Amu Dar'ya basin because the Amu Dar'ya water is poor in phosphorus salts.[3] The Gaurdak sulphur mines are one of the largest sources of natural sulphur in the Soviet Union. Construction of these mines started in the '50s and they are linked by rail and river with the Chardzhou phosphorus plant. The Gaurdak sulphur combine was built at the end of the Seven Year Plan period and is eventually to produce sulphur, sulphuric acid, nitrogenous fertilizers, and other chemicals.

Although the Turkmen chemical industry developed considerably during the last two years of the Seven Year Plan, the account of its present position given in the report of the First Party Secretary,

---

[1] *Pravda*, 25 November 1964.   [2] *Turk. Iskra*, 7 November 1965.
[3] Freykin, op. cit. p. 73.

Ovezov, at the February 1966 Republican Congress was far from satisfactory. According to Ovezov, its plant had not been used to capacity, mainly because of the failure to use productive capacity at the Gaurdak sulphur combine and the big Kara-Bogaz-Gol combine. He also complained that maintenance of equipment in Turkmen chemical enterprises was unsatisfactory, technical instructions were not observed, and production capacity was left idle. The position at the Kara-Bogaz-Gol sulphate combine was also the subject of scathing criticism from its own general manager. He deplored the fact that 'the inexhaustible wealth of the Kara-Bogaz-Gol raw material resources about which so much had been written could not be realized. In scope and equipment production at the combine was much the same as in 1939–40. Equipment is obsolete and production is based mainly on manual labour.'[1] But in 1965, he added more hopefully, the process of sulphate extraction was partially mechanized and by 1966 it was proposed to extend mechanization and compression for transport which should to some extent increase profitability.

During the current five year period 150 million roubles is assigned for the development of the Turkmen chemical industry. This is important for a republic lacking ferrous and non-ferrous resources. Among the new projects listed for this period are the construction of a large mineral fertilizer works to be based on the Karlyuk potassium deposits (in the Chardzhou region south of Gaurdak in the extreme south-western corner of Turkmenistan).[2] As the first potash plant in the Central Asian republics, this should be a valuable addition to their fertilizer resources. Soviet potash comes mainly from the Solikamsk deposits in European Russia and plants in the Ukraine and Belorussia.[3] The development of these Karlyuk potash deposits was long held up because of the lack of roads in the mountain area where they are situated and the deficiency of fresh water, both of which were overcome when the neighbouring Gaurdak sulphur mine was developed.

It is expected that with the expansion of the Turkmen natural gas and oil industries the young petro-chemical industry now

---

[1] *Turk. Iskra*, 5 March 1966.
[2] 'Tyazhelaya Promyshlennost' Respubliki na Novom Etape', *Turk. Iskra*, 12 March 1966.
[3] Mellor, op. cit. pp. 219, 260.

associated with the large oil refinery at Krasnovodsk will also expand in the current five year period. Owing to the lack of building stone or construction timber in Turkmenistan, it has been decided to establish a local plastics industry. A start is to be made during the current plan period with a plastics factory at Mary working on Turkmen natural gas. Power is to be provided by the projected Mary GRES (which is not yet operating) and water by the Kara-Kum Canal.[1]

There is no chemical industry to speak of in Kirgizia and at various levels from the Kirgiz Academy of Sciences[2] to the daily Press, dissatisfaction has been expressed on this score. 'Although Kirgizistan has sufficient sources of raw materials, power, and manpower, there is not yet a single large-scale chemical undertaking in the Republic', complained *Sovetskaya Kirgizia* (25 February 1966). 'There are only small undertakings, making such things as pigments and industrial rubber goods, using materials from outside the Republic and employing obsolete methods. Would it not be rational to build a homogenized cellulose works at Shamaldy-Say or a nitrogen fertilizer works in the Chu valley?' How feasible all this is, it is hard to judge but there is no mistaking the resentment against Gosplan for not promoting a Kirgiz chemical industry.

ENGINEERING

The engineering and metal-work industries throughout Central Asia and Kazakhstan have expanded from small origins before the war to a position of increasing importance in the national economies of these republics in the post-war period. The concentration of heavy machine building in European Russia, the Ukraine, and the Urals has, however, scarcely been affected by this development though it is of considerable local importance. The distribution pattern of the engineering industries in these regions tends to correspond to the requirements of the local natural resources though in certain cases, such as the new electronic industry in Kirgizia, the domestic development of electrification would scarcely in itself justify this location. Thus cotton textile machinery is manufactured in the cotton-growing republics of Uzbekistan and Tadzhikistan, agricultural

[1] *Turk. Iskra*, 12 March 1966.
[2] *Razvitiye Proizvoditel'nykh Sil Kirgizskoy SSR v Perspektive*, op. cit. pp. 10–11.

machinery for the cotton-fields is made in Uzbekistan and also in the grain areas of the 'Virgin Lands'. Coal-mining equipment is made in north Kazakhstan, where there is a big coal industry, and metallurgical and energy machinery in east Kazakhstan.

In Kazakhstan the engineering and metal-working industries virtually originated during the last war. There is no heavy concentration of this industry in one place; the works are scattered throughout the Republic. Kazakhstan has abundant ferrous and non-ferrous metals to supply these engineering industries. Though they are relatively young, there is now a growing diversity of production, but the output of the engineering industry is still far below the requirements of this rapidly developing Republic. Large capital investments were sunk in the engineering industry during the Seven Year Plan period so as to encourage expansion and technical progress, including the introduction of many new branches of engineering, among which were: instrument and electro-technical production, electric motors and electro-vacuum appliances, cables, and welding equipment.

In order to carry out these plans an engineering plant was built at Ust'-Kamenogorsk, a cable factory at Taldy-Kurgan, a plant to manufacture refrigerators and other equipment at Pavlodar, and an excavator factory in Kentau (in Chimkent *oblast*) which makes general-purpose machines to dig trenches and to lift loads.[1] The *Kazakhsel'mash* works in Tselinograd was expanded to make new types of agricultural machinery and spare parts for automobiles and tractors. One of the largest plants in the Soviet Union was built in Pavlodar to manufacture harvesting equipment.

The 1966–70 Plan for the Kazakh engineering and metal-work industries contains higher targets for the increased output of excavators (by 110 per cent.), transformers (by 30 per cent.), metal-cutting lathes (by 120 per cent.), motor vehicle components (by 150 per cent.) during this period. But the new plan is more concerned with the completion of unfinished buildings begun under the Seven Year Plan and bringing others up to planned production capacity than starting new enterprises. In his speech to the Kazakh Party Congress in March 1966,[2] Chairman Beysebayev listed a number of major projects which had not been finished on time. They were the Alma-Ata

[1] Neyshtadt, op. cit. p. 289.   [2] *Kaz. Pravda*, 13 March 1966.

heavy engineering works; the Alma-Ata foundry and engineering works; Karaganda no. 1 engineering works; Ural'sk and Semipalatinsk fittings works; Tselinograd pump works; Kentau transformer works; the agricultural machinery works (unidentified), and the Dzhambul components works. It is therefore not surprising that with so many constructions unfinished, the list of new construction in the 1966–70 Plan for Kazakhstan is relatively small and concentrated in the rapidly growing Karaganda–Pavlodar industrial area. A steel-casting works is to be built in Karaganda, an accumulator works in Yermak, and the Pavlodar engineering works is to be converted into the Pavlodar tractor works by 1968. This new industry is to have a capacity of 80,000 DT-75 tractors a year. It will be supplied with engines by the Altay tractor works, and gearboxes and other equipment will be made by a specialist works to be developed simultaneously with the tractor works.[1]

The engineering industry in Kazakhstan was sharply criticized by the Kazakh First Party Secretary, Kunayev, at the Republican Party Congress in 1966 for what he called 'an intolerable attitude to design and the study of technological processes, the number of overdue building sites and clumsy inefficient decisions about equipment'.[2] He laid the blame for much of the unfinished work on shortages of building materials. In order to increase the supply of building materials some new plants were mentioned in 1965, including a large asbestos–cement combine on the outskirts of Chimkent consisting of six factories for the production mainly of asbestos pipe, tiles, mineral wool products, and bricks; in planned capacity and variety of products for the building industry this is the largest factory in Central Asia. Another factory has been built at Atbasar to manufacture wall panels for house and industrial construction, and arbolit panels from crushed reed, cement, and water-glass.

The light and food industries of Kazakhstan on which the welfare and comfort of the people so largely depend seem to be in a bad state. 'An alarming situation prevails in Kazakhstan, particularly in the case of the light and food industries, in regard to completing new production capacity', reported *Kaz. Pravda* (22 June 1965). 'Not a single industrial project in Tselinnyy kray has been equipped with materials, machinery, or instruments.' A very gloomy picture was

[1] *Kaz. Pravda*, 27 March 1966.　　[2] Ibid. 11 March 1966.

given of the state of affairs in this industry by the Chairman of the Council of Ministers, Beysebayev, at a republican conference of workers in the light and food industries in May 1965.[1] Though there had been a considerable increase in the production of consumer goods (since 1958) Beysebayev listed many 'serious failures' in consumer goods production: output of furniture was increasing too slowly. The production plan for children's bicycles, household utensils, and electric irons, to mention only a few items, was not completed in 1964. A lime-packing factory making many consumer goods, which produced 166,000 fibre mats in 1962, produces none now, nor does it produce any metal or silk sieves, household or paint brushes though it used to manufacture large quantities of all these items. The practice of importing increasing quantities of even the simplest type of manufacture should be eliminated. Beysebayev also stressed the enormous losses allowed to occur at meat combines and the inefficiencies in the dairy industry. The products of light industrial undertakings are often down-graded or returned as rejects. In the first quarter of 1965, the Alma-Ata fruit-canning association was unable to sell 12,000,000 tins of jam, fruit, vegetables, and juices though in the same period similar products were being obtained in large quantities from the Ukraine, Moldavia, and other republics. Beysebayev's list of inefficient enterprises continued over practically the whole range of light industry, but enough has been said to show that 'the main consumer goods industries are far behind the general level of the Republic's economic development'.

In mid-1965 the first stage of the large Alma-Ata cotton textile combine was completed, and the combine is planned to turn out 60,000,000 m. of various textiles working at full capacity. This should help to improve the textile situation in Kazakhstan. Five thousand women workers are to be employed and it is thus hoped to absorb some of the surplus female labour in the metallurgical, mining, and chemical industries which have limited opportunities for employing women.

Uzbekistan has had a long start over the other Central Asian republics in the engineering industry and some important works producing agricultural and textile machinery as well as other manufacturing industries were well developed pre-war. In the

[1] Ibid. 26 May 1965.

post-war years the agricultural and textile engineering works have been expanded and special attention given to the production of machinery for the main cotton crop. The centre of the engineering industry is Tashkent; there are also works in other towns: Chirchik, Samarkand, Fergana, Kokand. Many of the older factories have been completely reconstructed or new works built. During the Seven Year Plan alone, according to First Secretary Rashidov, more than two hundred new types of more modern machines, instruments, and appliances were made.[1] Engineering is one of the most important sectors of Uzbek industry and accounted for 23 per cent. of gross industrial production in 1964–5.[2]

During the current Plan period, priority is given to producing equipment for the complete mechanization of the cotton industry and other branches of agriculture, especially irrigation. Equipment for road construction, electric power, and the chemical, oil, and gas industries will also be manufactured. The chief enterprises producing agricultural machinery in Uzbekistan are: *Tashsel'mash'*; *Uzbeksel' mash'* in Tashkent; *Chirchiksel'mash'* in Chirchik; and *Krasnyy Dvigatel'* in Samarkand. The *Tashavtomash'* in Tashkent specializes in making equipment for transporting cotton from the fields to the packing stations. Mechanization of cotton harvesting has a high priority so as to cut down on the low productivity of the large amount of casual labour recruited annually from the urban population, teaching institutions, industrial enterprises, and other organizations for this work.[3]

The success of the cotton harvest also largely depends on the production of adequate supplies of irrigation machinery, as all Central Asian cotton is grown on irrigated land. With the expansion of irrigation in Uzbekistan (and the other Central Asian republics) there is a growing need for excavators, bulldozers, and such-like equipment. Local supplies at the present time come chiefly from the reconstructed Andizhan irrigation machinery plant. It is also proposed to build a new plant in the centre of the Hungry Steppe. As highly efficient machinery is frequently held up for lack of spare parts, there is a great need for a specialist works to make spare parts for cotton-harvesting machines.[4]

[1] *PV*, 4 March 1966.
[2] *Ekon. i Zhizn'*, no. 9 (1965).
[3] Ibid. no. 9 (1965).
[4] *Pravda*, 19 April 1966.

The development of the Uzbek chemical industry has in turn necessitated expansion of the Republic's chemical equipment production. The 'Uzbekkhimmash' and the Kokand 'Bolshevik' plants now produce this equipment and some is also made at the 'Sredazkhimmash' in Chirchik. But more is needed and the Uzbek Prime Minister Kurbanov urged the Soviet Government at the Twenty-Third Party Congress to include irrigation and chemical engineering plants in the Plan directives for 1966–70 as already stipulated, he said, in 1964. But it is not yet known how this matter has been decided.

The Uzbek textile-machinery industry is now of all-Union importance. Uzbekistan produces 68 per cent. of all the spinning and all the roving machines made in the Soviet Union.[1] Spinning and twining machines for asbestos are also now being produced at the 'Tashtekstil'mash' works.[2] The situation has indeed changed since the '30s when all the machinery for the Tashkent cotton mill was made in European Russia.

MAJOR MANUFACTURING INDUSTRIES

The establishment of the Uzbek cotton textile industry in 1935 was regarded as a national event of importance when the Tashkent textile combine, the largest textile mill in the world, was opened. It was also the first cotton mill in Central Asia. But this industry has not lived up to local expectations and there have been repeated grumblings in the two chief cotton-growing republics, Uzbekistan and Tadzhikistan, about the discrepancy between the volume of raw cotton grown in Uzbekistan and the Uzbek production of cotton textiles. The Chairman of the Uzbek Council of Ministers criticized the central authorities very bluntly at the Twenty-Third Party Congress for not allocating a larger percentage of the industry to his Republic: 'It must be said that in the location of the production forces of the country Gosplan SSSR has made not a few mistakes. How otherwise explain the fact that in Uzbekistan, which is the main cotton base of the country and disposes of large labour reserves, about 150 million metres of cotton textiles and a large quantity of knitted goods are annually imported. The Republic occupies one

[1] *Ob. Nauki v Uzbekistane*, no. 3 (1966), p. 30.   [2] *Uzbekskaya SSSR*, p. 169.

of the last places in the country for the production of knitwear and the production of cotton textiles per head of the population has even decreased in the last few years. In the Republic there are all the objective conditions for the creation of a big centre of the textile–knitwear industry of all-Union significance. This in our opinion should find a place in the Congress directives.' Kurbanov was, of course, directly echoing Lenin's well-known views on the subject of locating industry close to the sources of raw materials. And after all the platitudes which were uttered at the time of the opening of the Tashkent textile mill contrasting Soviet with capitalist practice on this point, it is curious to note that the follow-up, in Central Asia, to this original mill was so insignificant.

Kurbanov's attack on the location of the Soviet cotton industry has been repeated in many of the Uzbek journals where the case for the location of a major cotton textile industry in Uzbekistan is argued with a great deal of supporting evidence. I. Iskanderov in *Ekonomika i Zhizn'* (no. 3, 1966), for example, came out strongly for a 'second textile base for the country'. He stated that the level of production of textiles in Uzbekistan was behind the growing needs of the population and that considerable quantities of clothing and household cloths and many decorative cloths were not made at all in Uzbekistan, while production of calico, satin, and shirt cloths was insufficient. 'The most deplorable fact is', he said, 'that the central planning organs should have considered the established situation and not have noticed the disproportions in the location of the cotton industry.' He rounded on certain economists who tried to justify the structure of the production of raw cotton and ready-made cloth on the grounds that transport of fibre is more advantageous than cloth. He produced statistics to show that this was not so and that the railway tariffs were more favourable for the transport of cotton fibre to the Centre than for cotton cloth to Central Asia, i.e. Central Asian consumers, he implied, were being unfairly taxed, as a sort of captive market for Russian textiles. In spite of some improvements in recent years, he said, 'the Russian Federation, as formerly, remains the basic producer while Uzbekistan occupies an insignificant place in Union production'. Iskanderov also stressed that it was much cheaper to produce cotton cloth in Central Asia than in the Centre, costs being much higher in all the Moscow *oblast* mills. Moreover, the American practice of moving textile mills to plantation areas was quoted by him in support of the argument that the Soviet cotton textile industry should be located in cotton-growing areas. 'Every year, Uzbekistan imports about 134 million metres of cotton cloth. . . . At least, production should increase so as to be able to supply the requirements of the Uzbek and partly the Kazakh and Turkmen republics, i.e. rise to 646 million linear metres by 1970', argued another journal.[1] 'Only 4 per cent. of the cotton produced is processed in the cotton-growing republics', stated *Ekonomicheskaya Gazeta* (29 September 1965). It is clear from the tone of this continuing controversy that there is deep resentment in the cotton-growing centres of Central Asia about the heavy concentration of the Soviet cotton textile industry in European Russia, especially at a time when the problem of absorbing 'the abundant labour reserves' in the countryside and some small towns is a matter of concern to the Central Asian authorities.

However unsatisfactory the situation, it must nevertheless be stated that the production of cotton cloth has risen steadily in all four Central Asian republics and Kazakhstan since 1940 as is shown by the following table (in million linear metres):

	1940	*1950*	*1958*	*1960*	*1963*	*1964*
Central Asian region	117.3	188.7	286.9	311.3	341.3	356.2
Uzbek SSR	107.4	161.2	219.9	234.7	246.7	256.6
Kirgiz SSR	0.04	0.4	0.9	1.5	1.7	1.8
Tadzhik SSR	0.2	16.6	43.7	51.5	70.5	76.8
Turkmen SSR	9.7	10.5	22.4	23.6	22.4	21.0
Kazakhstan	0.1	4.9	18.5	20.4	20.2	21.9

Source: *Nar. Khoz. SSSR v 1964 g.*, p. 210.

In many parts of Central Asia silkworm breeding and hand-weaving of silk are traditional industries. A silk-manufacturing industry was set up in Uzbekistan for the first time after the Revolution. The biggest silk mill of this now important industry which has almost completely replaced the old hand-woven product is in Namangan and there are several other silk mills in Uzbekistan. Apart from silk, Uzbek light industries include leather, boot and shoe

[1] *Ob. Nauki v Uzbekistane*, no. 3 (1965), p. 34.

factories, furniture, food processing, with a large production of vegetable oil, and fruit and vegetable canning. The quality of many of these Uzbek products is reported to be extremely low.[1] This is notably so, apparently, of boots and shoes and clothes, from 14 to 58 per cent. of the output of some factories in Tashkent, Samarkand, and Namangan being returned as defective for repairs. Though output in these industries is expanding, it is still far below local requirements and large quantities of footwear, clothing, textiles, and knitwear have to be imported. At the same time there are complaints that considerable quantities of raw materials which might be processed locally are exported to central Russia which 'itself lacks a raw material base for cotton textile, silk, and woollen cloths'.[2]

The construction materials industry based on local resources of limestone, gypsum, asbestos, marble, and gravel, for example, stepped up production considerably in order to meet the demands of the many new construction sites in Uzbekistan in the post-war period. Output of important materials such as cement, wall and roofing materials, bricks, and reinforced concrete blocks was also greatly increased. Large cement factories were built in Bekabad, Kuvasay, Kuvsa, and Angren, and one of the largest cement combines in the Soviet Union started production at Akhangaran (Tashkent *oblast*).[3] Production of cement in 1964 in Uzbekistan was 2,152,800 tons.[4] Special attention was devoted to the production of reinforced concrete in the Seven Year Plan period. This is a new industry in Central Asia; production started in Uzbekistan in 1955 and output was 1,321,100 cu. m. of reinforced concrete prefabricated units in 1963. In order to speed up house-building, mechanized plants for prefabricated units were set up in Tashkent and in all the *oblasts* of the Republic.

Nevertheless, the construction materials industry has not been equal to the demands of industrial and domestic construction during the Seven Year Plan period. According to the Chairman of the Uzbek Gosplan, output of bricks was very unsatisfactory and not equal to the growing demand while lack of wall materials paralysed capital construction. He considered that the Akhangaran cement

[1] *Ekon. i Zhizn'*, no. 11 (1965), p. 40.   [2] *Ob. Nauki v Uzbekistane*, no. 3 (1965).
[3] *Uzbekskaya SSR*, p. 178.   [4] *Nar. Khoz. SSSR v 1964*, p. 201.

factory should be expanded and a new factory built in Navoi in order
to increase supplies of cement.[1]

Since the war the diversification of industry and the importance
of heavy industry (including engineering and metal-working) which
was noticeable during the war has steadily increased in Tadzhikistan.
The share of capital investment in heavy industry has also steadily
increased and from the middle '50s was gaining on the former
predominance of the light and food industries.[2] But the readily
available resources of Tadzhikistan were poor as a basis for engineering or metallurgical industries compared to either Kazakhstan or
Uzbekistan. Reserves of coal are expensive to develop and though oil
and gas are suspected to exist neither has been proven commercially
in any quantity. In spite of these handicaps Tadzhikistan has
developed an engineering industry, and the large Dushanbe textile
combine, started during the war, has been considerably expanded.
In Tadzhikistan, as in the other Central Asian republics, the rate of
growth of the gross output of these industries has been higher than
that of industry as a whole, as shown in the table below:

Comparative Rates of Growth of Production of all Industry and of Engineering and Metal-working Industries

| | 1958 in per cent. of 1955 | | 1962 in per cent. of 1958 | |
| | | Of which | | Of which |
Republics	All industry	engineering and metal-working	All industry	engineering and metal-working
Uzbek SSR	119.0	159.0	137.2	175.0
Kirgiz SSR	134.0	169.0	145.7	222.2
Tadzhik SSR	129.6	110.2	147.7	250.0
Turkmen SSR	116.0	123.0	124.0	165.0

Source: Iz. AN Tadzhikskoy SSR, p. 47.

Some small engineering repair shops including works making
spare parts and metal-working shops preceded the establishment
of a number of important new enterprises during the Seven Year
Plan period. The first enterprise of the Tadzhik engineering industry,
the 'Tadzhiktekstil'mash' (Tadzhik textile machinery works)
produced the first automatic looms in 1960. It was followed by the

Ekon. i Zhizn', no. 10 (1965), p. 9.   [2] Iz. AN Tadzhikskoy SSR, no. 3 (38), p. 44.

Dushanbe 'Tadzhikkabel' plant, a low-voltage apparatus factory in Adrasman (in north Tadzhikistan), an electrical equipment plant in Isfara (also in north Tadzhikistan), and a transformer factory in Kurgan-Tyube (in south Tadzhikistan on the Vakhsh).[1] A group of works was also built producing spare parts for tractors, agricultural machines, automobiles, and for the equipment of the oil, cotton-ginning, and textile industries, and also facilities to repair them.[2]

The Tadzhik construction industry was reinforced by a large cement works and the first and second units of a house-building combine. New food-processing factories, including the first sector of the Dushanbe oil and fats combine and milk and meat combines in Leninabad, were built. A new furniture and a cotton wadding factory were also opened in Leninabad. The asbestos–cement pipe works completed in Dushanbe in 1965 is one of the largest works producing irrigation pipes in Central Asia.

The claim is proudly made in Tadzhikistan that the products of its new engineering plants are widely known at home and abroad. Thus the automatic looms of 'Tadzhiktekstil'mash' are reported to be operating in mills in Leningrad, Kherson, Voronezh, and Engel's, and the products of the electro-technical industry of the Republic 'are familiar to the Grodno, Urals, Leningrad, and other factories in Kazakhstan, Siberia, and the Far East. . . . Exports are also increasing to foreign countries. At the present time, oil equipment from the Ordzhonikidze plant is known in twenty-six foreign countries, the young African governments receive the "Tadzhikkabel" factory products, and the products of the Dushanbe "Traktordetal" (tractor components) factory are sent to the socialist camp countries.'[3]

One of the latest developments announced is the production of the 'Pamir' domestic refrigerator at the Dushanbe factory, which is using plastics to reduce the weight. It has been especially welcomed in the humid heat of south Tadzhikistan where there is a great demand for such a refrigerator. When the factory is working to full capacity, it is scheduled to produce 140,000 refrigerators a year.[4]

No major engineering projects on the scale of the new chemical and aluminium plants are mentioned for Tadzhikistan in the new

[1] K. P. Marsakov, 'Slavniyy yubiley', *Iz. AN Tadzhikskoy*, no. 3 (38) (1964), p. 7.
[2] *Ekonomicheskiye Rayony SSSR* (Moscow, 1965), p. 541.
[3] Marsakov, op. cit. p. 5.   [4] *Pravda*, 19 January 1966.

Draft Plan. The cotton textile and knitting factories are to be finished and light industry is to be built up with a number of new factories. Tadzhikistan has no domestic metallurgical industry. The development of its new industries, especially the new engineering industries, has necessitated large imports of metal from such remote areas as the Ukraine, the Urals (which supply 54.1 per cent.), and Kazakhstan (less than a third) of the heavy metal requirements. As these imports involve large transport costs, it has been suggested that she should switch deliveries from the Urals and the Ukraine to Karaganda, the nearest source of supply, thus reducing transport by 3,200 km. and transport time by five to six days.[1]

The development of the cotton textile industry in Tadzhikistan, the second largest cotton-producing country in the Soviet Union, is a more natural process than engineering. The same complaints are made in Tadzhikistan, as already noted in Uzbekistan, about the low percentage of cotton textiles produced in the Republic. In fact, only 10 per cent. of the cotton fibre grown in Tadzhikistan is processed there while 80 per cent. of Tadzhik cloth requirements are supplied by imports from other regions.[2] 'It would be more rational from the point of view of reducing transport costs and the better utilization of the labour force to process an ever-increasing quantity of raw materials locally so as to export ready-made cloth to other regions.'[3] This attitude to the cotton industry is common in critical articles in Tadzhik journals today. In particular, the need to create new industries to absorb surplus population constantly emerges in these articles and reflects apprehension about surplus labour arising from the high birth-rate. 'At the present time a considerable percentage (26 per cent.) of the labour forces in the Republic is not occupied in social production', according to a Tadzhik analysis of the situation. 'In the near future, the labour forces will increase at a higher rate. By 1970, they will have increased about 30 per cent. which is somewhat higher than in the other Central Asian republics. The abundance of labour reserves and the presence of considerable unemployed reserves of labour makes it advisable to develop labour-intensive industries more widely as one of the chief aims in the development of the productive forces. In the conditions of the

[1] Kletsel'man, 'Mezhrayonnyye Svyazi', pp. 29–30.   [2] Polyarush, op. cit. p. 8.   [3] Ibid.

Republic, these branches are light industry, especially cotton textile, precision (non-metal intensive) engineering, cotton cultivation, horticulture, and viticulture.'[1]

In spite of the development of heavy industry in Tadzhikistan, in gross output and the numbers of workers employed the light and food industries still have a leading if declining place, 79.85 per cent. of the gross output and 57.63 per cent. of the labour force compared to 18 per cent. gross output of heavy industry with 39.62 per cent. of the labour force. The low percentage of the heavy industrial branch is partly attributed by some local economists to the fact that Tadzhik resources of fuel, power, and minerals have so far been little studied.[2]

Tadzhikistan produces high-quality fruit and vegetables which are now being canned and exported in large quantities to other areas of the Soviet Union. The canning industry is one of the most successful in the country. In Pendzhikent in north Tadzhikistan the capacity of the fruit and vegetable canneries is to be greatly increased and new canneries built in Isfara, Zafarabad, and Shaydar (the latter is nearing completion).

Tadzhikistan's northern neighbour, Kirgizia, where industry had scarcely penetrated pre-war, has also made a big leap into modernity and industrialization since the war. A number of sophisticated industries have been established, some directly the outcome of war-time evacuated enterprises, some entirely new, like the electronic industries established during the Seven Year Plan period. The fact that the population of the chief towns of Kirgizia is predominantly Russian may explain what looks like a near industrial miracle on the part of the Kirgiz nomads of yesterday. Engineering and metal-working is now one of the leading branches of Kirgiz industry, accounting for 17.2 per cent. of the gross industrial product and coming third after light and food industries in the national economy. Kirgizia specializes in the production of instruments, automobile spare parts and assembly, agricultural machinery, electronics, and lathe production. It is surprising to note that on the basis of her young industries she produced 98 per cent. of the metal-cutting lathes, 67 per cent. of the instruments, and 7.5 per cent. of the items

---

[1] Polyarush, op. cit. p. 13.
[2] U. Kh. Kletsel'man, *Iz. AN Tadzhikskoy SSR*, no. 3 (38), pp. 78–79.

of the electronics industry of the Central Asian economic region in 1962.[1] It is expected that these industries will develop further in response to the growth of demand in the Central Asian republics, the neighbouring districts of Kazakhstan, and the Soviet Union as a whole. Specialization is regarded as essential in the Kirgiz engineering industry and owing to the lack of a domestic metallurgical base, it is to concentrate on low metal consuming branches of the industry. Local Kirgiz publications pleading for an expansion of this or other industries in the Republic inevitably refer to the problem of finding employment for the Republic's rising population.[2]

The most important Kirgiz engineering works are the Frunze electrical engineering works, the 'Kirgizmash' works (Frunze), the Mayli-Say (south Kirgizia) electric lamp works, and the 'Kirgizkabel' works in Kainda on the Dzhambul–Frunze railway. The Frunze electrical engineering works began mass production of electrical vacuum equipment for the first time in the Soviet Union in 1965. During 1966 a new building was to be added to the works which will become a large producer of transistors and transistorized equipment and another building where automatic conveyors will be made is to be put up under the new Five Year Plan. According to local reports, the 'Kirgizmash' works is becoming one of the country's largest producers of motor vehicle radiators. New shops are being built and equipment modernized and its radiators have been exported as far afield as the Kutaisi motor works and L'vov bus works.[3] It has also begun serial production of gear-boxes. The automobile assembly works now being built will be the first unit of the automobile industry in the Central Asian republics and will specialize in the production of lorries and spare parts. The main line of production at the Osh electro-mechanical works, founded in 1959, is artesian electric pumps. The Osh and Kishinev plants are reported to be the sole producers of these pumps in the Soviet Union.[4]

The Mayli-Say works, under construction since 1962, has attracted great attention in the Kirgiz Press. With a production capacity of a million electric bulbs a year, it will be one of the largest

[1] *Razvitiye Proizvoditel'nykh Sil Kirgizskoy SSR v Perspektive*, p. 27.
[2] Ibid.; *Naseleniye i Trudovyye Resursy Kirgizskoy SSR* (Frunze, 1965).
[3] *Pravda*, 6 March 1965.   [4] *Elektrifikatsiya Sov. Kirgizstana* (Frunze, 1965), pp. 85–86.

Soviet plants producing electric bulbs when completed. Most of the production processes will be automatic and the equipment will be made partly in Frunze, Saratov, and Hungary. The Frunze agricultural machinery works specializes in harvesting machinery (tractor-drawn rakes, pick-up balers, and beet-loaders), 80 per cent. of its output being exported outside the Central Asian economic region. In the development of agricultural engineering it is intended to concentrate on the requirements of agriculture in the Central Asian republics and south Kazakhstan while taking into account the specialization of the Uzbek agricultural engineering industry in machinery for the cotton industry.[1]

Reporting on Kirgiz economic progress during the seven year period to the Republican Party Congress in March 1966, Usubaliyev, the First Party Secretary, said that the engineering and metal-working industries had risen by 320 per cent. since 1958 (admittedly the start was very low). Good progress was made by the non-ferrous metallurgical, coal, building materials, light, and food industries. But due to serious flaws in industrial management and failure to put new production capacity into production, the Republic's gross industrial output fell short of the Seven Year Plan target. In spite of the fact that Kirgizia is one of the Union's main mercury and antimony producers, extensive reserves remained untapped and the geological directorate failed to organize proper prospecting work. Many undertakings, according to Usubaliyev, failed to make efficient use of mechanization and were working at a loss.

The light and food industries are also important in Kirgizia but, like her sister republics, Kirgizia has a grievance about the low proportion of cotton and wool processed in the Republic. Thus in 1962, 45,800 tons of raw cotton was produced and only 3,300 tons manufactured. 'The rest of the raw material was exported.'[2] The only cotton-textile mill in the country is a spinning–weaving works. The cotton-textile combine now being built in Osh will use 30,000–35,000 tons of Kirgiz cotton fibre when operating at full capacity.

The situation regarding Kirgiz wool is still more unsatisfactory. Kirgizia occupies third place in the Union and first place in Central Asia for the production of fine and semi-fine wool. But the Republic

[1] *Razvitiye Proizvoditel'nykh Sil Kirgizskoy SSR v Perspektive*, p. 28.
[2] Ibid. p. 37.

does not have a single enterprise for the primary processing of wool.[1] All its wool is exported to wool-washing enterprises outside the country. The situation will, it is hoped, improve when the factory now being constructed in Tokmak is completed in 1970, with a capacity corresponding to the total deliveries of Kirgiz wool. The chief consumer of wool in the Republic is the worsted-cloth combine in Frunze constructed during the Seven Year Plan period, which is scheduled to produce 6–7 million metres of woollen cloth in 1970. According to the above-cited Kirgiz work, knitted goods are the 'most progressive' and profitable section of the textile industry because of their volume and the low amount of raw materials required. Output of the chief types of knitted goods is planned to rise sharply during the new Plan period.

The production of sugar occupies a leading place in the food industry of Kirgizia. Kirgizia has the highest sugar-beet yield per hectare of the sugar-beet producing republics of the Soviet Union, higher than either Kazakhstan or the Ukraine (the other leading producers). By 1970 production of sugar is planned to rise 1.5 times above that of 1964 and it is hoped thus to satisfy the growing sugar requirements not only of Kirgizia but of Central Asia as a whole. Owing to the lack of a sugar refinery, Kirgizia has to import large quantities of refined sugar annually. This is also the position in the other Central Asian republics and involves high transport costs. The Kirgiz believe 'it would be advisable to construct a refinery at one of the six sugar factories of Kirgizia and thus avoid the present irrational long cross-hauls of sugar'.[2] Meanwhile the same situation exists in Central Asia as in the West Indies before Independence when all their sugar was refined in the United Kingdom. One inevitably remembers that the first Soviet gesture to independent Jamaica was the offer of a sugar refinery so as to show up the former 'colonial exploiter'. But at home the Soviet Union has another code of behaviour.

In spite of rapid industrial development Kirgizia is still much behind the all-Union level of industrial production. Thus the proportion of industry in the social product of the national economy of the USSR as a whole is 64.5 per cent. and in the Kirgiz SSR only

[1] Ibid.
[2] Ibid. p. 43.

52.2 per cent. 'The backwardness of the industrial development of Kirgizia is also shown by the fact that the national income in our Republic per head of the population is twice as low as in the rest of the country. Therefore the equalization of the economic level of the Republic demands a further development of industry in Kirgizia and at a more rapid rate than in the rest of the country', comments the Economic Institute of the Kirgiz Academy of Sciences.[1] It is amusing to find the Kirgiz trying to force Moscow's hand about a more rapid rate of industrialization with the old Leninist slogan of 'equalization of the economic level of the Republic' (presumably to the level of the more advanced parts of the country?).

Turkmenistan has no engineering industry of any significance. The industry is mostly limited to some metal-working shops, railway and ship repair works, and enterprises for the repair of oil equipment, agricultural and earth-moving machines, automobiles, and diesel locomotives. The metal-working centres are at Ashkhabad (where works making oil equipment and cables were recently started), Chardzhou, Krasnovodsk, Kazandzhik, Kizyl-Arvat, and Mary.[2] Geological prospecting, which has been active and successful in the oilfields, has not so far revealed either coal or iron in the Turkmen deserts to provide a metallurgical base for engineering.

Light industries and notably carpets, textiles, and the production of some construction materials (chiefly glass and cement) head the list of manufactures. The favourable oasis conditions of the Ashkhabad area have made it a centre of economic development in a country containing over 80 per cent. desert within its boundaries. Ashkhabad has a textile combine and its large new glass factory has made Turkmenistan the largest glass producer in Central Asia. Cement production at the Bezmein factory near Ashkhabad grew from 9,600 tons in 1950 to 325,700 tons in 1963.[3] But in the last few years 'it failed to produce 93,000 tons of cement and put construction workers in an extremely difficult position'.[4] It is interesting to note in this earthquake area (Ashkhabad was destroyed by an earthquake eighteen years ago) that the Bezmein combine is

[1] *Razvitiye Proizvoditel'nykh Sil Kirgizskoy SSR v Perspektive*, p. 22.
[2] *Ekon. Rayony*, p. 550.   [3] *Nar. Khoz. S.A. v 1963 g.*, p. 83.
[4] *Turk. Iskra*, 25 February 1966.

the only one capable of producing panels withstanding force nine tremors, the highest ever recorded in the Soviet Union. This combine is therefore to make pre-cast components for the new housing projects in earthquake-rent Tashkent.

In his report on Turkmen industry in 1966, First Party Secretary Ovezov stated that the cotton-textile and building materials industries had heavily over-expended their allowances. He also complained of the low quality of clothing and footwear and the high percentage of defective output of both.[1] It is not surprising that Turkmen industry is not flourishing since Ovezov stated that the Minister of Construction was completely inefficient and failed to correct the poor organization, extensive idling of equipment and labour, and the lack of co-ordination between the construction and installation organizations. According to Ovezov's allegations the planning organs 'made serious errors in planning capital investment. Plans and specifications often include projects about which there is no information and for which there is no money.'[2] In addition to these discrepancies, 'more than half the directors of industrial enterprises have neither high nor middle special training, only a fourth of the planning–economic and accountancy workers have special training'. It is no wonder that Turkmen industry is in a muddle and did not fulfil its Seven Year Plan target for increasing industrial output while during the last two years about a third of the Republic's industrial undertakings have not made profits.[3]

The harsh desert climate and relative lack of amenities in Turkmenistan do not make it an attractive country for migrants. In fact the net balance of in-migration between 1963 and 1965 was only 7,000, which is very much lower than that in any of the other Central Asian republics.[4] It is therefore tempting to speculate about the possible link between the absence of Russian skilled migrants and the shortcomings of Turkmen industry. Apart from the oil and chemical industries, there are relatively few openings to draw the usual influx of Slavs who so largely man the industries of the other Central Asian republics.

[1] *Turk. Iskra*, 25 February 1966.   [2] Ibid.   [3] Ibid. 4 March 1966.

[4] Cf. *Nar. Khoz. SSSR v 1962–1963–1964.* Natural rates of increase for 1960, 1963, and 1964 are given in the statistical handbook for 1964, pp. 38–39, and in the computation the rate for 1960 has been used for 1959, and intermediate figures between those of 1960 and 1963 for 1961 and 1962.

AGRICULTURE

The main subjects of all-Union national importance in the agricultural economies of the Central Asian republics and Kazakhstan in the post-war period were: (1) the struggle to increase cotton yields and production in the cotton-growing republics; (2) the 'Virgin Lands' development scheme in Kazakhstan; (3) livestock and meat production in Kazakhstan.

Cotton Production

In the post-war years as hitherto the Soviet Government continued and even intensified its demands for increased production of cotton in the Central Asian cotton belt. This struggle between the native cotton farmers, who, in spite of the inroads of industrialization, still form the largest element in the population of the cotton-growing republics,[1] and Moscow, has many angles of interest, economic and political, which call for more detailed comment than can readily be found in Western or Soviet sources on Central Asia.[2]

Efforts are made to increase production both through larger acreage and higher yields. But there are limitations in both spheres. Almost all of the Russian 'cotton belt' lies north of the northern limits of the United States cotton-growing areas. This means a short growing season and inability to obtain full benefits from improvement in cultivation practices, for example, the use of fertilizer. Also, new areas brought under cultivation require irrigation involving considerable capital outlay and labour. Yields in Central Asia average only about half those in the United States where cotton is grown under irrigation.

Cotton is grown by collective and State farms in Central Asia. The majority of the cotton farms are collectives but the percentage of State farms growing cotton has risen from 6 per cent. in 1940 to 20 per cent. in 1964.[3] The average size of a cotton farm is now very large, about 1,450 ha., since the amalgamation of farms in 1950–3, with some 400 families per farm.[4] The cotton farmers and

---

[1] 'The overwhelming majority of Uzbek citizens are cotton growers.' *Izvestiya*, 11 March 1965.

[2] There is, of course, valuable information in a few specialist works like the Report on the E.C.E. Delegation's visit to Central Asia in 1957 or that of the cotton exchange group of the U.S. Department of Agriculture in 1958 but such works are few.

[3] *Nar. Khoz. SSSR v 1964 g.*, p. 252.

[4] Cf. *U.N. Economic Bulletin for Europe*, p. 55.

their families mostly continue to live in the old villages which are often far from their work in the huge cotton plantations. In the early post-war years (1949–53), cotton production rose considerably above the pre-war peak in response to the Government's attractive price for cotton. There was a large increase in the area sown to cotton but yields also rose owing to improved equipment, good supplies of fertilizers, and a large expansion of irrigation, as appears from the following table:

Central Asia

	1940	1950	1953
Area sown to cotton (000 ha.)	1244	1442	1599
Cotton production (million tons)	1894	2964	3358
Cotton yield (centners per ha.)	15,0	20,0	21,0

Source: *Nar. Khoʐ. S.A. v 1963 g.* (Tashkent, 1964).

The increase in the national average yield may also in large part have been due to the fact that cotton cultivation on about 2.5 million acres of unirrigated land in European Russia (where yields were very low) was abandoned after the German occupation[1] and new areas were brought into production in Central Asia under irrigation. All Soviet cotton is now grown on irrigated ground. In comparing Soviet and American yields and claiming higher yields, Soviet writers tend to overlook the fact that a large share of American cotton is grown on non-irrigated ground which makes a valid comparison extremely difficult; but the yields per unit of labour on American farms are much higher than on Soviet. This point was stressed by both the Economic Commission for Europe delegation to Central Asia (1957) and the cotton exchange group of the American Department of Agriculture which visited Uzbekistan and Tadzhikistan in 1958 to study the Soviet cotton industry. 'The manpower of Uzbekistan and throughout the areas of the USSR we visited', states the American cotton exchange report, 'appeared to be unlimited. The labour force is composed mainly of women and is short of men aged 35 to 50. The use of manpower would seem to be such as to indicate surplus labour in many cases since there was

[1] Jasny, op. cit. pp. 563–6.

constant evidence of people doing what appeared to us as minor or completely unnecessary jobs just to be busy.'[1]

The U.N. Delegation was also struck by the high input of labour on the farms with the highest yields and the great differences in yields between the different farms. 'The group of farms with the highest yields use nearly 50 per cent. more labour and their money expenditure on other inputs is about two-thirds higher per hectare than in the lowest group', it reported.[2] It was also surprising to learn from this delegation that the present use of labour on most farms exceeds the amount which was considered normal before the Revolution when 1.6 ha. under cotton was assumed to be the maximum one man could cultivate, and beyond what was deemed necessary in 1925 before mechanization had started.[3] It seems therefore that the increased yields per hectare where they occurred were due to an exceptionally extravagant use of manpower per unit of land and not to any great increase of productivity in the land. Two cotton bushes were not growing where one had grown before.

The advantageous position long enjoyed by Central Asian cotton farmers owing to the relatively high prices paid by the Government for tropical produce, in the first place for cotton before and after the war, changed in the '50s when cotton prices remained almost stationary and other procurement prices and retail prices for food and many items of mass consumption rose.[4] The very high premia-increments paid to farms that exceeded their targets or obtained high yields, introduced in 1935 as incentives to stimulate cotton production, were abolished in 1958. At the same time the counter-sales of grain and other goods to the cotton collectives were stopped.[5] The dissatisfaction caused by these measures was reflected in sagging cotton production and regular failures to fulfil cotton production or yield targets. Where there was an increase in production it was chiefly due to an increase of the sown areas, not to higher yields or good husbandry.

Some of N. S. Khrushchev's more egregious agricultural notions,

[1] *Cotton in the Soviet Union.* Report of a Technical Study Group, U.S. Department of Agriculture, Washington, 1959, p. 4.

[2] *U.N. Economic Bulletin,* p. 58.   [3] Ibid. p. 60.

[4] Cf. A. N. Malafeyev, *Istoriya Tsenoobrazovaniya v SSSR, 1917–1963* (Moscow, 1964), pp. 266, 270, 290.

[5] L. I. Brezhnev, Report to the C. C. Plenum CPSU, 24 March 1965, *Pravda,* 27 March 1965.

like his obsession with maize, have gained wide publicity. His arbitrary interference with the Central Asian cotton industry is perhaps not so well known. Throughout his term of office he pressed unremittingly for more cotton both in rather stormy confrontations with the cotton growers in Central Asia and at major Party meetings in Moscow, including the Twentieth and Twenty-Third Party Congresses. While keeping up this pressure for increased production, his speeches show little indication that he had studied the technology of his subject or given serious thought to the equipment necessary to implement his proposed policies, or to the equally crucial cotton-grain problem in grain-deficient areas. Since 1940, all grain sowings, especially rice (popular with the native peoples of Central Asia for making their pilau), had been falling precipitately owing to the expansion of cotton on irrigated ground.

Sown Areas of Agricultural Crops in Central Asia
(in 000 ha.)

	1940	1950	1953	1958
All grain	3030	2487	2169	2259
Rice	100	65	64	37
Cotton	1244	1442	1599	1878

Source: *Nar. Khoz. S.A. v 1963 g.* (Tashkent, 1964), p. 134.

The use of irrigated land more or less exclusively for cotton, which made the cotton areas dependent on the central distribution agencies for their grain supplies, had never been popular locally. Experience in the First and Second World Wars when these supplies had broken down only strengthened these misgivings.

This was the background to Khrushchev's first cotton 'rally' in Tashkent, the capital of the largest cotton-growing republic of the Soviet Union, where he summoned representatives of the cotton-growing republics to meet him in November 1954.[1] He was in an imperious, hectoring mood and publicly rebuked Yusupov, the First Secretary of the Uzbek C.P., for not sharing his enthusiasm for the 'square cluster' method of cotton cultivation, while summarily dismissing his advice with: 'He is a man with a hot temperament and must be cooled with a cold douche.'[2] Khrushchev reminded

[1] N. S. Khrushchev, *Stroitel'stvo Kommunizma v SSSR i Razvitiye Sel'skogo Khozyaystva* (Moscow, 1962), vol. I, p. 367.   [2] Ibid. p. 378.

his audience that the Central Committee and the Council of Ministers of the USSR called for more cotton from all the cotton-growing republics, cited the respective 'motley' cotton yields for 1953 and 1954, and tried to shame the Uzbeks by comparing their performance with that of the 'brother' Tadzhiks who had adopted the 'square cluster' method of cultivation, and headed the cotton yield figures for 1953 and 1954.

After his long rodomontade pressing the merits of the 'square cluster' method of cultivation on the cotton farmers he departed without apparently ensuring that any of the essential conditions for successful 'square cluster' cultivation were available for the next harvest, i.e. additional labour, fertilizer, irrigation, and specially adjusted machinery for sowing, harvesting, and other field operations. The 'square cluster' or check-row planting technique has incidentally been abandoned in the United States where it was tried and American experts do not consider it useful even in Russia and believe it will eventually be abandoned there also. It hinders the even flow of irrigation water and does not permit a dense stand of plants which is generally recommended for the best yields per acre and efficiency in machine harvesting. None the less Yusupov disappeared into political oblivion soon after this clash over 'square cluster' planting with Khrushchev.

Klaus Mehnert, who visited Uzbekistan the following year, saw the disastrous results of Khrushchev's characteristically arbitrary and technically incompetent cotton cultivation policy. 'There were scarcely any machines in the Uzbek cotton fields for the 1955 harvest', he reported, 'because it had not been possible to construct the more precise equipment required for the "square cluster" cultivation method.'[1] So the 1955 Uzbek cotton harvest remained behind that of 1954 although everything possible had been done to replace machines by hand labour.[2] Even in 1957 the cotton harvest was far below that planned originally for 1955.

The situation for the cotton producers worsened in 1958 when, as has been mentioned, the high premia-increments and the special

---

[1] K. Mehnert, *Asien, Moskau und Wir* (Deutsche Verlags-Anstalt, Stuttgart, 1958), pp. 172–5.

[2] 'Square cluster' planting has apparently not yet been generally adopted in Uzbekistan. *Pravda Vostoka* (15 March 1966) announced that planting would be 'square cluster' on 790,000 ha., and cross cultivation on 940,000 ha.

grain counter deliveries were abolished. Cotton plans were not fulfilled and in many cases both yields and production fell between 1958 and 1962. Khrushchev kept up the pressure for higher cotton yields and production but failed to offer 'material incentives' which would spur the cotton growers to greater efforts. His harangue at the Twenty-First Party Congress even suggested that he had a kind of sub-tropical cotton 'monoculture' in mind for Central Asia. 'We now have the possibility', he said, 'to reduce and, in future, with the development of the production of grain in other areas of the country, to dispense with procurements of grain in the Caucasian and Central Asian republics so as to develop at great speed such valuable crops as cotton, tea, citrus fruit, grapes, etc.'[1] *Khlopkovodstvo* (no. 9, 1960), the Soviet organ of cotton cultivation, also had fears on this score: 'As a result of the insufficient development of all non-cotton branches and the one-sided development of farming', it wrote, 'it has acquired the character of a monoculture and the needs of the population are badly satisfied.'

At this time the cotton *sovkhozy* were receiving 20 per cent. less than the cost of production for cotton delivered to the State.[2] The cotton collective farmers, on the other hand, made a profit on their sales of cotton to the Government, but in general the position of the Uzbek *kolkhozy* somewhat worsened and their income actually fell 17 per cent. below that of 1957 in 1960 in spite of a rise in the productivity of labour.[3] The fall was probably due largely to the terms on which ex-MTS machinery and other equipment was acquired in 1958.[4] Moreover, many cotton farmers also produced livestock, and livestock prices at this time were below the cost of production and resulted in a loss for the majority of the *kolkhozniks*. The situation was that the more livestock products they produced, the greater their loss. The profits received from the sale to the Government of 'plant products', i.e. cotton, went to cover losses on livestock in Central Asia and lowered the *kolkhozniks'* labour pay.[5]

Instead of increasing cotton production, Party pressure tactics and

---

[1] *Vneocherednoy XXI S'yezd Kommunisticheskoy Partii Sovetskogo Soyuza*, Stenografichisky Otchet (Moscow, 1959), p. 43.   [2] Malafeyev, op. cit. table, p. 294.

[3] V. Khlebnikov, 'O Dal'neyshem Ukreplenii Ekonomiki Kolkhozov', *Voprosy Ekonomiki*, no. 7 (1962), p. 50.

[4] I am indebted to a private communication from Professor Nove for this reference and other help in this section.   [5] Khlebnikov, op. cit. p. 53.

price policy actually provoked a number of highly ingenious frauds perpetrated by harassed officials, farm chairmen, and others involved in the cotton-production plans. There were numerous cases in the Central Asian republics of 'padding the books', fictitious receipts for non-existent cotton deliveries, gross negligence of cotton stocks and machinery. A major upheaval in the leadership occurred in Tadzhikistan in 1961 when the First Secretary, the Second Secretary, the Chairman and a Deputy Chairman of the Council of Ministers, and ten other leading Party and Government officials including the Public Prosecutor were removed from their posts for grossly inflating the figures for agricultural production in the Republic for a number of years, and ignoring large-scale embezzlement, nepotism and other abuses. Padding the cotton returns, it was stated, had involved numerous false documents.[1] In the light of these revelations one wonders if the Tadzhiks had not hoodwinked Khrushchev in 1954 about their cotton yields which he held up as an example to the Uzbeks.

The general state of corruption in Tadzhikistan was reflected in the person of the Public Prosecutor who was described in the Republican Party organ as 'a fawner and a toady. . . . He not only wages a feeble struggle for the observance of socialist legality but, as has been established, he took a direct part in the padding of the reports on raw cotton procurements in Leninskiy rayon.'[2]

After a crescendo of complaints of poor work in the cotton farms, and large variations in productivity, notably in Turkmenistan and Uzbekistan,[3] Khrushchev at last realized that the Party's goals for cotton could not be achieved without a radical change in cotton price and grain delivery policies. A decree of 15 March 1963 raised the cotton procurement prices for *kolkhozy* by 20 per cent. and for *sovkhoz* deliveries by 12 per cent. as from the 1963 harvest. *Kolkhozy* and *sovkhozy* on newly irrigated land would also be paid an additional price for raw cotton, amounting to 20 per cent. of the usual purchase price for raw cotton. Furthermore, as from 1964, *kolkhozy* were to be exempt from contributing their part to the construction of the water economy which would be carried out according to the

---

[1] *Kommunist Tadzhikistana*, 14 April 1961. Cf. *Central Asian Review*, no. 3 (1964), p. 182, for an excellent article on this subject: 'Crime and Courts in Tadzhikistan.'

[2] *Kommunist Tadzhikistana*, 14 April 1961.   [3] *Pravda*, 6 March 1963.

State capital works plan.[1] The importance attached to this subject in Moscow was further stressed in the order to the Central Committee and the Council of Ministers of the Union republics concerned 'to analyse the question of raising the degree of material interest of *kolkhoz* members in producing cotton'. Lest there should be any underhand dealing with the funds intended for the cotton farmers, they were informed in the plainest terms that 'the supplementary assets derived from increased purchase prices for cotton were to be directed to increase the pay of *kolkhoz* workers'. The new grain deliveries plan also aimed at giving satisfaction to the Central Asian cotton farmers on the score of food supplies, threatened, as they suspected, by the Government's expanding cotton targets. Flour and grain were to be delivered to the cotton *kolkhoz* as payment for the labours of their members based on the ration of '3 centners of grain per ton (10 centners) of cotton delivered to the State and up to 4 centners for Soviet fine fibre deliveries'. These grain deliveries were not to be included within the limits of small retail trade. The incentives given to the cotton farmers soon bore fruit in much higher production between 1963 and 1965. The results were notably good in Uzbekistan which produces two-thirds of the Soviet crop.

In addition to the supplies laid on by the March 1963 decree, as grain-deficient areas, the cotton-growing republics of Central Asia receive planned allocations of grain and flour from the 'Union market fund', the allocations being determined according to conditions in the respective areas.[2] Published information on the operation of this system is too scanty to decide the extent to which it meets the grain requirements. Nevertheless, there is no doubt of the dependence of the Central Asian republics on these allocations, especially in view of the steadily falling percentage of the sown area under grain crops in all the four 'cotton' republics.[3] As one Soviet analyst wrote: 'In the Central Asian republics where, like many countries of South-East Asia, vegetable products predominate in the diet, the consumption of grain products is very high although their own production of grain is insignificant.'[4] The Central Asian

[1] *Pravda*, 28 March 1963.

[2] Yu. V. Lasis, 'Porayonnyy analiz potrebleniya khleboproduktov v SSSR.' Article in *Ekonomicheskoye Rayonirovanye i Narodnoye Khozyaystvo SSSR*, ed. Mysl, in the series: *Voprosy geografii 65* (1964), pp. 80–81.

[3] *Nar. Khoz. SSSR v 1963 g.* and *1964*.   [4] Lasis, op. cit.

grain deficiency is made good mainly by supplies from the 'Virgin Lands' of Kazakhstan which sends 20 per cent. of all its grain exports by rail to Central Asia. Much of this grain remains in Tashkent for further distribution, but grain and flour is also sent on to supply Tadzhikistan and the Turkmen SSR.[1]

Owing to the lack of satisfactory statistics relating to incomes and prices, it is virtually impossible to discuss standards of living on the Central Asian farms (or in other occupations) with any degree of accuracy or certainty. But there are some pointers to the situation in recent years which may be noted in passing. In each of the four Central Asian republics (and Kazakhstan) the majority of the population is engaged in agriculture, i.e. in cotton growing in the former and in grain and livestock production in Kazakhstan. Although all collective farmers have a similar obligation to deliver specified quantities of their produce to the State purchasing organs, those producing foodstuffs have the chance of sharing out the residual among their members for their own consumption after satisfying State obligations. But in the case of farms producing industrial crops, like the Central Asian republics, there is practically no distribution to farm members while a much greater share of their income will be in monetary form.[2] Moreover, there may be great differences between farms on good and poor land owing to the high premiums paid for over-fulfilment of cotton plans. Additional income may be made by cotton farmers from their private plots which in these tropical lands yield very profitable crops of fruit and vegetables. On the other hand, everything is more expensive in the country than in the towns and distribution of supplies is badly organized and essential goods often lacking in rural areas.

With the exception of a few privileged international and American delegations of experts, few foreign observers have been able to penetrate the Central Asian cotton belt beyond the boundaries of towns like Bukhara or Samarkand. The first-hand information about conditions there picked up by Professor René Dumont, a competent observer, who visited some Uzbek and Kazakh farms off the beaten track in 1963–4, is therefore worth recalling. He noted

[1] Danilov, *Ekonomicheskaya Geografiya Transporta SSSR* (Moscow, 1965).
[2] For fuller treatment of this subject, cf. A. Nove and J. A. Newth, *The Soviet Middle East —A Communist Model for Development*, to which I am indebted for guidance here.

that all consumer goods, including potatoes, fruit and vegetables (unless locally produced), cost more than in Tashkent or Moscow. He saw a large number of broken-down tractors and compared their state of repair to that of the machines of 'l'Office du Niger au Mali'. There was a general lack of mechanics on the farms he visited; they evidently preferred to work in the towns offering better supplies and amenities. Even the simplest tools like hammers and items like wire were often unavailable and mechanization on the whole was at a low level. Soviet claims to have overtaken the Californian cotton industry are brushed aside with the comment: 'They would do better in a comparison with their neighbours, Iran and Turkey.'[1] Central Asia was far behind California in cotton yields, technical equipment, labour productivity and organization, and cotton cultivation methods, including lucerne rotation, in his opinion. The irrigation installations he saw also left much to be desired, and salinity had done great damage to cotton. The dominant impression left by this area was of defective work due to excessive haste in fulfilling the imperious demands of the Plan, 'often fixed at a high level in relation to the labour force and equipment'. The future was thus sacrificed to the present and much would have to be redone in a few years. Professor Dumont's conclusion nevertheless was that 'Cotton incontestably represents the finest achievement of Soviet agriculture'.[2] While it would be unfair to generalize from Dumont's individual experience, it would be equally foolish to ignore it.

There are also many indications in Press reports of wide differences in living standards and cultural and other amenities throughout the republics. Thus M. Akramov, writing in *Obshchestvennyye Nauki v Uzbekistane* (no. 6, 1966), the journal of the Uzbek Academy of Sciences, reports as follows: 'Investigations show that in Central Fergana, the Hungry Steppe, and other areas of new cultivation, the complex of living conditions, i.e. level of consumption of food, provision of living accommodation and goods of mass consumption, medical assistance, cultural-educational and communal-service institutions is considerably lower than in the old irrigated, inhabited regions of the republic. This is the basic explanation of the flight and constant shortage of labour forces in the newly cultivated areas.'

[1] R. Dumont, *Sovkhoz, Kolkhoz ou le Problématique Communisme* (Editions du Seuil, Paris, 1964). [2] Ibid. p. 123.

With the removal of Khrushchev from the political scene in October 1964 his successors at the March Plenum 1965 expressed disapproval of his handling of the cotton problem and initiated more realistic cotton–grain policies in Central Asia. Before the Plenum some hard-hitting informative articles in the Central Asian journals showed the tension generated locally by Khrushchev's cotton policies which now, of course, could find relatively free expression. Writing in *Kommunist Uzbekistana* (January 1965) G. Gabriel'yants, the Fergana Party Secretary, gave a deplorable picture of the arbitrary methods and bureaucratic ways in agriculture in an area which had 'produced wonderful masters of fine cotton crops for centuries on the irrigated lands of Fergana'. Contempt had been shown, he said, for the experience of leading farmers and experts and agro-technical methods foisted on them without consideration of local conditions. Cotton cultivations had been injured by ignorant 'formalism', i.e. rigid adherence to high-powered instructions. Perhaps the nub of the unsatisfactory situation in the cotton farms, as depicted by Gabriel'yants, was 'the infringement of the principle of the material interest of the *kolkhoz* and *sovkhoz* workers in increasing production of agricultural products'. These workers being badly paid, said Gabriel'yants, went to work in the towns. To prove his point about the 'direct relation between material base conditions and output', he cited the fall in the cotton yield figures in his area between 1956 and 1961 from 31.6 centners per ha. to 25 centners. Gabriel'yants was optimistic about 're-establishing the former glory of Fergana' as a cotton centre thanks to more enlightened irrigation, cultivation, and payments policies and the effects of 'the long overdue Central Fergana Canal which will finally eliminate the problem of water hunger'. Throughout this article one senses the resentment of an expert with cotton in his blood against the overlordship in cotton affairs of the Russians who have never grown cotton themselves in Russia. Even allowing for an element of local pride and exaggeration in this article it undoubtedly has a substantial element of truth.

Other aspects of the cotton problem were stressed in a revealing article in the Central Asian economic journal *Narodnoye Kkozyaystvo Sredney Azii* (no. 1, 1965). Under the title 'Region of Cotton and the Bread-basket of the Country', a group of scientific collaborators of the Central Asian Scientific Research Institute of the Economics of Agriculture came out strongly for an increase in grain production, 'one of the pressing tasks facing the Central Asian republics, for it must not be forgotten that grain can also be grown on irrigated lands'. This was not to deny, they said, that in the all-Union division of labour Central Asia was and remains the basic supplier of cotton. But grain on irrigated lands was to increase about sevenfold in 1970 compared to 1963 and it was planned to plant about 17 per cent. of irrigated land to rice and related crops. 'It is known', they said, 'that in the past, rice sowings on irrigated lands were squeezed out by cotton.' Now the picture has sharply changed and rice sowings will be greatly expanded. 'Research shows', they concluded, 'that in the foothills zone of the Central Asian republics the most economic-ally profitable cultivation was: 74 per cent. cotton, 18 per cent. grain and beans, 5 per cent. barley with lucerne, 3 per cent. vegetables and melons.' Clearly, while the going was good these local pundits were going to use their influence to ensure an expansion of local food supplies.

Shortly afterwards Sh. Rashidov, the First Secretary of the Uzbek C.P., examined cotton cultivation and its problems in some detail in *Izvestiya* (11 March 1965). For the first time, in 1964, all *oblasts* of the Republic had fulfilled the cotton plan and cotton workers were the great majority of the 11,000 workers in various fields decorated by the Soviet Government, he said. He dwelt on the gaps in mechaniza-tion and the lack of some special machines for cultivation and harvesting operations which were clogging the progress of the cotton industry. 'Tashsel'mash' is the only plant in the country producing cotton-harvesting machinery but its production was too small to satisfy all the requirements of the cotton industry, according to Rashidov. Cotton harvesters, 'kurakouborochny' harvesters (i.e. machines for harvesting cotton bolls not opening after frosts), and cotton pickers were all in short supply. There was still no uni-versal tractor-cultivator. Rashidov's idea of using the Vladimir 'T-28-X' tractor by replacing some of the unsuitable parts in Tash-kent and returning the superfluous items to Vladimir seems rather a desperate expedient.

Mechanization of cotton harvesting is still low in Central Asia. The highest level of machine picking in the 1965 harvest was

P

achieved in Uzbekistan where 25 per cent. of the 3,900,000 tons delivered to the State was picked by machines.[1] At the Republican Party Congress in March 1966, Rashidov gave some useful details about the progress of mechanization in Uzbekistan. 'There are now 96,000 qualified tractor drivers and a whole army of cotton-picking operator-mechanics', he said. 'Machinery has taken over 7 per cent. of what was once heavy manual labour in cotton growing and picking. Last year 910,000 tons of cotton were machine-picked, compared with 63,000 tons in 1959. . . . . But', he added, 'even at the present rate of output, Uzbek collective and State farms are unable to pick all the cotton they grow and without large-scale mechanization it will be impossible to pick the 4,180,000 ton harvest planned for 1970. It is therefore proposed to pick 2,500,000 tons by machine in 1970 instead of asking townspeople and students for help.'[2]

Mechanization varies from district to district and from one operation of the cotton cultivation–harvesting cycle to another. The state of the machines is also crucial and often far from satisfactory according to local Press reports. In Turkmenistan, for example, on the eve of cotton harvesting in 1965, it was reported that more than half of the 2,250 cotton-picking machines 'still await overhaul'.

Mechanization is also delayed and even obstructed by 'anti-machine attitudes' among the cotton workers or 'the opposition of conservative elements to mechanization'[3] about which Party leaders have been complaining for some years in Central Asia. The reason for this opposition was that the peasants believed that they could earn better money by hand-picking and that mechanization threatened their livelihood. It seems that up to a point they were right, at all events in 1964, when it was reported that 'a significant portion of the cotton, even the first machine collection, was received at the price of the second and third sorts which greatly reduced the farmers' interests and held back development of mechanization'.[4] Redundancy must also be linked in the peasant mind with mechaniza-

---

[1] *PV*, 29 November 1965. In the following year, the 4,000,000 ton Uzbek cotton harvest was gathered by 24,000 machines and 1,000,000 hand pickers (Moscow Home Service, 22 October 1966).   [2] *PV*, 4 March 1966.

[3] *Pravda*, 28 April 1964. More recently, an article in *PV*, 15 September 1966, headed 'Who Opposes Defoliation?', discussed anti-mechanization feeling in some farms in Bukhara *oblast*. Examples were given of the prevention of defoliation and the flooding of cotton-fields prepared for machine-picking.   [4] *Pravda*, 19 August 1964.

tion. No complete figures on this point are available but Tass (12 February 1966) reported that 'on average 11,000 peasants are made available for other work per year in Andizhan *oblast* after the introduction of mechanization in cotton cultivation'.

'Cotton is heavily fertilized. Some cultural operations are mechanized but hand-thinning, hand-hoeing, and hand-picking are common. A considerable acreage of cotton is now being checkrowed for cross cultivation. The rows are about 2 feet apart. Although some mechanical cotton pickers are in use, about 85 per cent. of the cotton is hand-harvested. It is somewhat doubtful whether mechanical picking pays in view of the large labour supply and the relatively low wages paid.' Such were the views of the Soviet cotton industry recorded by the USDA exchange delegation which visited the Soviet Union in 1963.[1]

The broad hints from the new leadership in the months after Khrushchev's removal left no doubt that his agricultural policies were in the melting-pot. The situation was clarified for the Central Asian republics as for the rest of the Soviet Union in Brezhnev's major policy speech of March 1965.[2] He publicly recognized the errors of the former cotton policy and promised a new deal to the cotton farmers in regard both to prices and grain supplies. 'Our experience in increasing the production of cotton and sugar-beet', he said, 'conclusively shows how important it is to follow a correct price policy for agricultural products. . . . Many comrades remember that in 1949 the prices for raw cotton were considerably raised and that swiftly led to an increase in its production. Then, in the period 1958–62, the premia-increments were abolished and the counter sales of grain and other goods to cotton-growing collectives were liquidated. The yields and gross production of cotton fell subsequently.' Brezhnev then referred to the increase in cotton yields and production following the 1963 price increases for cotton and the restoration of the counter sales of grain to the cotton *kolkho*ᶻ*y*. He stressed the importance of increasing rice production in Kazakhstan and the Central Asian republics (among other areas) so as to reduce Soviet rice imports which amounted to about one and a half million tons in the last five years while demand was rising.

Brezhnev in fact made no change in the last and wisest phase of

[1] *Soviet Agriculture Today*, p. 18. [2] *Pravda*, 27 March 1965.

Khrushchev's cotton policy, but he strongly confirmed the new Government's intention of paying a fair price for cotton and guaranteeing grain supplies. The next harvest in Central Asia fully justified this line. The total Soviet cotton production in 1965 was the largest ever, 5,700,000 tons[1], an increase of 1,200,000 tons over 1964, of which the Central Asian republics produced 5,200,000 tons. The target set by the Seven Year Plan (1959–65) was thus also fulfilled.

Under Brezhnev's agricultural programme the cotton-growing regions are to receive an additional 500,000 ha. of newly irrigated land in the last half of this decade while the 1970 cotton-production plan has been reduced from the previous (Khrushchev) level of 8 million tons (unginned) to an average of 5.6–6.0 million tons for the period 1966–70. This represents a very modest increase in production over the average output achieved in 1963–6 and should be possible during the remainder of this decade.

Irrigation[2]

The post-war period has seen a great development in irrigation in the Central Asian republics and the construction of some irrigation projects of major importance.[3] Inefficiency and waste and considerable discrepancies between irrigation and the utilized area of irrigated land in many places continued to impair the value of many of these projects. The analysis of Soviet sources on the extent of the irrigated area is hampered by confusion and inconsistency in the terminology used by Soviet sources. Thus land with an irrigation network includes not only land with a suitable irrigation system but also land on which the irrigation system is in disrepair or possibly not tied in with a reliable source of water. The most precise term used is irrigable land receiving water and includes land utilized in agricultural production and properly irrigated. For the rest, Soviet data on irrigation in Central Asia must be accepted for what it is worth, contradictions and other discrepancies being noted as they arise.

---

[1] *Pravda*, 3 February 1966.

[2] The periodical articles on irrigation in the *Central Asian Review* contain much useful information.

[3] Irrigation in the Tsarist period was dealt with in Part I, *The Economic Development of the Eastern Regions under Tsardom*, pp. 37–39.

Central Asia, with its vast expanse of deserts and fertile oases depending on irrigation for cultivation, contains the largest irrigated area in the Soviet Union. Here, as elsewhere in the Soviet Union, there is a considerable discrepancy between the area with an irrigation system and the utilized irrigable land.

Area of Lands with an Irrigation System by Union Republics

(in 000 ha.)

	Area with irrigation system			Utilized irrigable land		
	1960	*1962*	*1964*	*1960*	*1962*	*1964*
USSR	11,442	11,755	11,952	9,302	9,410	9,677
Uzbek SSR	3,040	3,160	3,181	2,694	2,721	2,790
Kazakh SSR	1,867	1,872	1,819	1,343	1,265	1,253
Kirgiz SSR	1,159	1,146	1,126	929	949	873
Tadzhik SSR	429	476	465	427	449	458
Turkmen SSR	774	781	871	496	480	535

Source: *Nar. Khoz. SSSR v 1963*, p. 306; *1964*, p. 347.

It will only be possible here to outline the impressive scope of this work and how it is being tackled, to give some examples of irrigation projects in the different Central Asian republics, and to indicate the nature of the problems confronting the Soviet Government in this field. The plans for the irrigation of 3 million additional hectares of agricultural land in 1966–70 announced by Brezhnev in his March 1965 speech, though considerably reduced from the even more ambitious targets of the previous régime, present a formidable challenge. On present form they will scarcely be achieved on schedule. The total capital investment, volume of construction and installation work in irrigation and water economy are now planned to be almost three times as great in the years 1964–70 as in the previous seven year period. In all these measures the four Central Asian republics and Kazakhstan are major participants, because about 63 per cent. of all the Soviet irrigated land is situated there.[1]

Much important irrigation work is being carried out throughout Central Asia to expand the irrigable area and also to try and regulate the flow of the chief sources of water supply, the Amu Dar'ya and

[1] S. S. Kabysh, 'The Permanent Crisis in Soviet Agriculture', *Studies of the Soviet Union*, vol. III, no. 4, p. 179.

Syr Dar'ya rivers, so as to make some of the areas irrigated by them less vulnerable to the vagaries of nature such as seasonal flooding and unpredictable changes in the river beds. Only a broad outline of this maze of construction can be attempted here, a more detailed survey would far exceed the limits of this book.

The largest irrigated area in the Central Asian republics is in the Uzbek SSR where the cultivated area under irrigation was reported to be 12,500,000 acres in 1965.[1] One of the more notable Uzbek irrigation schemes is the old Tsarist Golodnaya Step' or Hungry Steppe project dating back to the '80s of the last century. These lands have been developed with fluctuating effort and success by the Soviets, since Lenin showed interest in a decree signed by himself in May 1918 allocating 50 million roubles for irrigation work in the Hungry Steppe so as to secure increased supplies of cotton for the Russian cotton textile industry.[2] The development of this steppe was long an inter-republican matter involving Uzbekistan, Tadzhikistan, and Kazakhstan as the steppe traversed the boundaries of the three republics. The Kazakh part of the area was transferred to Uzbekistan in January 1963[3] by a decree of the Kazakh Supreme Soviet in order to unite Kazakhstan's cotton-fields (amounting to 107,000 ha. and including the famous 'Pakhta-Aral' farm) with the adjoining large cotton-growing area of Uzbekistan in the irrigated area of the Golodnaya Step'. Other areas handed over at the same time were parts of the Kzyl-Orda and Chimkent *oblasts* in the Kyzylkum Desert which had been used for a number of years by Uzbek stock-breeders. The total territory transferred amounted to 40,000 sq. km.[4] The official explanation of the transfer was that when the Central Asian republics were formed frontiers were drawn solely on the basis of national features and without consideration of economic problems. Thus the Golodnaya Step' was divided between Uzbekistan, Tadzhikistan, and Kazakhstan. But this division was not a success, apparently, cultivation of the steppe as a whole being impeded by lack of co-ordination between the numerous

---

[1] According to a hand-out of the Institute of Water Economy and Hydraulics (Tashkent, 1965).

[2] *Ob Osvoyenii Golodnoy Stepi*, Gosizdat YzSSR (Tashkent, 1956), pp. 9–26.

[3] *Kaz. Pravda*, 29 January 1963.

[4] G. A. Taskin, 'Kazakhstan: Changes in Administrative Status and the National Composition, of the Population', Bulletin, *Institute for the Study of the USSR* (Munich, February 1964).

construction organizations in three separate republics.[1] Since Kazakhstan ceded this territory to Uzbekistan and the Syr Dar'ya *oblast* was formed with its centre at Gulistan, these difficulties have, it is reported, been overcome.

Khrushchev visited the Hungry Steppe several times and focused attention on the need to develop it more intensively. As a result a special decree was passed in 1956 'on irrigation and cultivation of the virgin lands of the Hungry Steppe',[2] on incentives for settlers and other workers coming there, and on housing, communications, and other necessary amenities. The target for the full development of the steppe is 800,000 ha. There is certainly a good way to go before this is achieved and the area is still being developed.[3] Some 200,000 ha. were irrigated and planted in the decade (1956–66)[4] and 102,000 tons of cotton harvested in 1966.[5] A further 150,000 tons is the target for 1966–70. To facilitate development plans a railway was built from the Syr Dar'ya station to Dzhizak on the Tashkent railway, and from Zhetybay to the big Chardara Reservoir fed by the Syr Dar'ya River.

Soviet sources claim that the Hungry Steppe is becoming a 'new cultural oasis' with urban settlements, schools, hospitals, orchards, and motor roads, thanks to the 1,650 km. of irrigation channels which now traverse the area. 'Into the Hungry Steppe, nightingales have been imported from European woods', according to Tass (5 August 1965). 'Wells fed by polyethylene water pipelines have caused minia- ture oases to spring up.' Unfortunately, when the plain facts of irrigation in this steppe and traveller's tales of the drab, dusty towns are more closely examined, little remains of this romantic fantasy.

The Southern Canal constructed in the early years of the Seven Year Plan is the main irrigation system in the Hungry Steppe. It is 136 km. long and of great economic importance. Construction work on farm buildings, irrigation, and drainage has been impeded by a high labour turnover, planning mistakes, and sub-standard work.[6] Salination is also a major problem, 80–90 per cent. of the lands scheduled for irrigation being saline. Under these conditions it will

[1] *Nar. Khoz. S.A.*, no. 11 (1964), p. 66.
[2] *Ob Osvoyenii Golodnoy Stepi*, Gosizdat UzUSSR (Tashkent, 1956), p. 9.
[3] *Osvoyenie Golodnoy Stepi* (Moscow, 1963), p. 22.
[4] *Partiynaya Zhizn'*, no. 10 (1966).   [5] *PV*, 24 December 1966.
[6] 'Irrigation Progress since 1960', *Central Asian Review*, vol. XI, no. 2, p. 139.

take many years to bring 800,000 ha. into cultivation as planned, with a cotton crop of more than 1,500,000 tons.

These large-scale operations are handled by the Main Golodnaya Step' Construction Organization[1] which comprises forty building enterprises and a number of new *sovkhozes* and should ensure that transport facilities, settlements, and all technical irrigation measures are provided before reclamation actually starts. Two advanced methods of irrigation introduced into the Golodnaya Step' under its auspices are raised concrete gutters and underground water pressure pipes. Nevertheless, it appears that no effective means of draining the steppe have yet been found.

The Amu–Bukhara and the Karshi canals are two other major irrigation works in Uzbekistan which promise a solution to long-felt needs in the water economy of the areas concerned. The 200 km. long Amu–Bukhara Canal, begun in 1963, after rejection of an alternative 700 km. gravity flow Kelif–Bukhara Canal, is up to 30 km. wide and 6–26 m. deep. It started to supply the Bukhara *oblast* and the Zeravshan Valley with more reliable, badly needed additional irrigation in 1965. It is filled by a vast diversion canal from the Amu Dar'ya which crosses the Zeravshan River through a 150 m. long reinforced concrete pipeline laid on the river-bed. This mechanical irrigation canal is intended not only to increase the irrigated land for the traditional cotton and karakul sheep-breeding industries but also to supply the new Uzbek gas and oil industry and the important new petro-chemical plant at Navoi—all of which suffer from lack of water. The area which will benefit by the canal waters covers 100,000 ha. and includes the towns of Bukhara and Kagan.[2] Plentiful supplies of cheap electricity from the Navoi power station now make it possible to supply the large pumping stations of the canal, and eventually power is also expected from the Nurek HES.

Work on the big Karshi steppe irrigation canal started in 1964 and it is scheduled to have 200,000 ha. of virgin land ready for cultivation by 1970. A main canal about 175 km. long will be built with a barrage on the Amu Dar'ya at Kizyl-Ayak, six pumping stations to raise the water by a total of 150 m., and southern, central, and northern drainage canals to prevent the soil becoming

[1] *Glavgolodnostepstroy.* Cf. *Osvoyenie Golodnoy Stepi,* p. 10.
[2] *Ekon. i Zhizn',* no. 9 (1965), p. 18.

waterlogged. The future Karshi development programme is extremely ambitious and if fulfilled would yield about 2 million tons of cotton (including fine staple) or more than the Fergana Valley at the present time, as well as grapes and tropical crops.

In the Karakalpak ASSR, where rice has been sown for centuries and is of great local interest, irrigation construction work is now mainly concentrated on developing a large rice-growing area in the lower reaches of the Amu Dar'ya. After a big decline in planting up to 1960, the situation improved in the following years when efforts were made to create a 'rice base' in Karakalpakiya with a production of 60,000 tons annually.[1] *Pravda's* correspondent (3 August 1965) nevertheless expressed concern about the slow progress of irrigation and reclamation work in this area on which fulfilment of the rice plans largely depends. 'Rice had to be sown on badly prepared fields last year and it was no better this year. . . . The bad condition of the irrigation network and lack of capital planning had the result that the Karakalpak State farms lost about 5,000 ha. of sowings. Not a centner of rice was received from this ground. Large expanses of fertile land were marsh-ridden. In this area the Party organizations care little for the cultural demands of virgin land workers. Even the most essential household goods are lacking in the shops. There is a shortage of skilled workers and mechanics in the *sovkhozy*.' It is unlikely that rice production will go ahead, as planned, unless the conditions described by *Pravda* quickly improve.

Two major projects under consideration for some time have the aim of controlling the flooding and flow of water of the lower reaches of the Amu Dar'ya River which unregulated has such disastrous effects on the agriculture of the delta and of south Khorezm. These projects are the Tyuya-Muyun hydraulic complex (in the upper part of the Amu Dar'ya delta) with a dam vital for increasing irrigation in south Khorezm and the dam on the Amu Dar'ya near Takhiatash to ensure the flow of water during the dry season and enable hundreds of hectares to be planted with rice. Between them, the Takhiatash and Tyuya-Muyun hydraulic system will irrigate more than 2,200,000 ha. when completed.[2] But

---

[1] *Uzbekskaya SSR*, p. 453.

[2] E. A. Akramov, 'Perspevtivy Razvitiya Irrigatsii v Uzbekistane', *Ob Nauki Uzbekistana*, no. 10 (1965), p. 6.

satisfactory progress on this canal construction largely depends on supplies of pipes from the 'lagging' concrete industry.

According to many articles in Soviet journals, a serious threat lies over the Aral Sea into which both the great irrigation rivers, the Amu Dar'ya and Syr Dar'ya, empty their waters. Forty per cent. of Central Asian irrigation depends on these two chief water arteries, so that the question of the rational distribution and utilization of their waters and the search for other irrigation sources is said to be acutely urgent.[1] Apprehension is expressed that the future lowering of the flow of these rivers will lead to a lowering of the Aral Sea level and in the not distant future 'to its complete disappearance'. Experts at the Tashkent Scientific Conference on the complex utilization of land and water resources of the Central Asian republics and south Kazakhstan (1962) stated that with full utilization of the Amu Dar'ya and Syr Dar'ya river waters, the Aral Sea may cease to exist about the year 2000.[2] An important local fishing industry is based on the Aral Sea and the reduction of the spawning grounds following the lowering of the Aral Sea level by 120 cm. has also caused anxiety among the fishing organizations.[3]

In spite of extensive water economy work many irrigation systems are still not finished according to schedule in Uzbekistan. They are inadequately supplied with hydro-technical installations, and work in covering horizontal and vertical drainage was only beginning in 1963, according to an official Uzbek handbook.[4] In the irrigation network 50 per cent. of the water is lost through evaporation. Lands suitable for irrigated agriculture in the desert zone of Uzbekistan and still awaiting development are estimated at 4,000,000 ha.[5] The high percentage of salinated soil before and after irrigation is a serious problem. The enormity of the task of desalination is shown by the fact that the planned irrigation of 2,300,000 ha. in Uzbekistan (1964–80) is estimated to involve the extraction of 60,000,000 tons of salt annually from the soil. Of 56,300 ha. of new lands, 50,300 ha. fell out of agricultural use through salination in 1963.[6] The harm done by salination of the upper soil layer meant that over a period of four years (1958–62), cotton harvests on land belonging to the

---

[1] Akramov, op. cit. p. 10.   [2] Ibid.   [3] *Kaz. Pravda*, 18 January 1966.
[4] *Uzbekskaya SSR* (Gosizdat, Tashkent, 1963), p. 214.
[5] Akramov, op. cit. p. 6.   [6] Ibid. pp. 7–8.

Gulistan Production Board (of the Hungry Steppe) fell by 38 per cent. and yields by 54 per cent., due to salination, in spite of the fact that the areas sown to cotton increased 30 per cent. over the same period.[1]

Turkmenistan has been the scene of two great schemes to bring water to the dread, waterless Kara-Kum Desert. This desert occupies nine-tenths of the Republic but it can be rendered fertile with irrigation. The first, the Main Turkmen Canal, was a very complicated project which included irrigation of adjacent areas, creation of afforestation belts, the construction of electric power stations, and the construction of a road along the course of the canal. It was to traverse north-west Turkmenistan from the Amu Dar'ya through the Sarykamysh depression and the ancient bed of the west Uzboy to the Caspian Sea, a total length of 1,100 km. After a great deal of publicity following the early stages of the work on this canal (1951–3), it disappeared into oblivion after Stalin's death. It was soon evident that it had been dropped for various technical reasons in favour of an alternative canal, the Kara-Kum Trunk Canal, to irrigate the south-east part of the Kara-Kum Desert.

The Kara-Kum Canal was also a massive constructional operation, 1,500 km. long, involving 'a number of serious problems which had never arisen formerly in the world execution of irrigation systems'.[2] It is navigable for small craft for about 400 km. from the Amu Dar'ya and it is eventually hoped to make it navigable along its entire length. Some of the sand-hills encountered by the workers in the course of building the canal 'were as high as a ten storey house',[3] and these were only some of the trials and hazards to be faced in excavating and equipping the canal-bed in the Kara-Kum Desert. The canal was built in three sections: (1) Amu Dar'ya–Murgab (1954–8); (2) Murgab–Tedzhen, mainly built in 1960; (3) Khauzkhan–Ashkhabad (1961–2) (820 km. long). In the canal zone about 150,000 ha. of new lands are being developed and more than 400,000 tons of cotton have been added to the Turkmen stocks since it was built. An army of different nationalities has worked on this 'grandiose construction . . . of the friendship of the peoples of

---

[1] S. S. Kabysh, 'The Permanent Crisis in Soviet Agriculture (The Irrigation Problem)', *Studies on the Soviet Union* (Munich, 1964), vol. 3, no. 4, p. 181.

[2] *Pravda*, 9 March 1965.   [3] Ibid.

the country: Turkmen, Russians, Uzbeks, Armenians, Georgians, Kazakhs, and many more'.[1]

It was decided in 1965 to extend the Kara-Kum Canal another 500 km. from Ashkhabad to the Caspian Sea, the work to be completed in 1980. This will brings its waters through the oil and gas areas of south-west Turkmenistan which suffer acutely from lack of fresh water.[2] It is estimated that some 500,000 ha. of virgin lands could also be developed in this area which is specially suitable for the production of sub-tropical crops. Indeed, the further economic development of west Turkmenistan, including oil and gas prospecting, may be said to hinge largely on a successful solution of the water supply. Even when the Kara-Kum Canal eventually reaches the Caspian, many areas of the Republic will still lack water. Research has shown that there are big deposits of underground fresh water beneath the sand-hills of the Kara-Kum, and work is being done on the possibilities of utilizing these water deposits. It is reported that excellent drinking water is now being supplied to the Nebit Dag oilfields and other areas of west Turkmenia from underground sources.

The need for a scientific study of irrigation work is constantly stressed in Soviet publications. Turkmenistan was criticized by *Kommunist* (no. 2, 1966) for the lack of well-qualified cadres in hydro-technical and reclamation scientific institutes though they are regarded as essential if the large investments in the water economy are to produce effective results. The Turkmen Scientific Research Institute has 140 workers but only six with the degree of Candidate of Sciences and not one Doctor of Science.

The irrigated area of Kazakhstan ranks second in extent among the Central Asian republics. It now has more than 1,100,000 ha. of irrigated arable land, mostly sown to rice (not cotton as in the southern republics), fruit, vegetables, and other agricultural produce. Reporting on the agricultural situation to the Kazakh Supreme Soviet in December 1965, the Chairman of the Council of Ministers, Beysebayev, stated that the grain yield on irrigated land in the Republic as a whole did not exceed 13–15 quintals to the hectare though the more efficient farms in the southern *oblasts* obtained 40–50 quintals per ha. The reasons for this state of affairs,

[1] *Pravda*, 9 March 1965. [2] Ibid. 3 April 1966.

he alleged, were gross disregard of good farming practice, use of low-yield seed, insufficient use of mineral fertilizer, and lack of attention to moisture-retaining and irrigation measures. In 1965 irrigation was so poorly organized on many collective and State farms in Kazakhstan that about 251,000 ha. of irrigable land was not watered once though there was no shortage of water, according to Chairman Beysebayev.

The state of semi-chaos prevailing in Kazakh irrigated agriculture in 1963 does not seem to have improved much since. The then First Secretary of the Kazakh C.P., I. Yu. Yusupov, in a speech to the Central Committee of the K.C.P., painted a deplorable picture of negligence and incompetence on the irrigated farms. 'Out of 1,280,000 ha. irrigated prepared land in the current year', he said, '280,000 ha. had not been cultivated. . . . Owing to the careless attitude to the use of irrigated land about 30 per cent. of the water is lost. . . . The wrong crops are sown. The level of mechanization is low, resulting in a high percentage of physical labour.'[1] His successor, A. A. Kunayev, also complained of the failure to utilize the irrigated lands of Kazakhstan properly or to increase their crop yields, in reporting to the Kazakh Central Committee in January 1966.

More than 80 per cent. of all the irrigated land of Kazakhstan is in the southern *oblasts* of Dzhambul, Kzyl-Orda, and Alma-Ata, which are specially suited for growing sugar-beet, cotton, rice, vegetables, and fruit. It is intended to make Kazakhstan one of the chief rice-growing areas of the Soviet Union and much has recently been done to prepare irrigated land for rice-growing in the Kzyl-Orda and Alma-Ata *oblasts*. About 42,000 ha. were sown to rice there in 1965, and 3,900,000 poods of rice were delivered to the State. A Union Rice-Growing Research Institute has been established in Chimkent to plan rice growing in Central Asia, which reflects the Soviet Government's interest in this crop after decades of neglect.

Central Kazakhstan is an area of expanding industry, but local shortage of water, especially acute in the mining–metallurgical centres of Karaganda and Temir Tau, is an obstacle to industrial development. The 490 km. long Irtysh–Karaganda Canal is being constructed to cope with this shortage, as well as to serve irrigation

[1] *KP*, 3 November 1963.

purposes. It is planned to flow from Yermak on the Irtysh to Karaganda and to supply the industrial districts of Ekibastuz (coal mines), Maykain, Boshchekul', Karaganda, and Temir Tau. A further extension 500 km. south to the copper mines of Dzhezkazgan is apparently under consideration. Work on the canal has been slow. It was planned originally to complete it in 1965 but early in 1966 it had only reached Ekibastuz, some 60 km. from its starting-point at Yermak. Progress on this canal was revealed to be very unsatisfactory by the First Kazakh Party Secretary Kunayev at the Twenty-Third Party Congress in March 1966. 'Construction of the 500 km. Irtysh–Karaganda Canal is being carried out in only a comparatively small section. During four years only 15 per cent. of the funds allocated have been employed. The slow progress made will have an adverse effect on development in the Temir Tau, Pavlodar, and Ekibastuz industrial areas. If Irtysh water does not reach Temir Tau in the next few years it will be impossible to put a single new plant into operation at the Karaganda metallurgical works', he said.[1] Plans have been prepared for the construction of the Karaganda–Temir water supply system which will provide piped drinking water for the local inhabitants. The head of the system will be the last section of the Irtysh–Karaganda Canal. Farther west, the first stage of the Karatamar Reservoir on the Tobol River, which will absorb large quantities of additional water from the spring floods, has been constructed (1965). It is intended to supply the important Sokolovka-Sarbay combine and the town of Rudnyy with water from this reservoir.

In the next five year period (1966–70) capital investment in irrigation in Kazakhstan is planned to increase by 200 per cent. more than in the preceding five years and the area of irrigated land to increase by 400,000 ha.

From the extremely frank criticism in Soviet sources of the progress of irrigation in the Central Asian republics and Kazakhstan, it seems fair to conclude that while many constructions like the Kara-Kum Canal are boldly imaginative in design and involve herculean labour in execution, the level of actual building, finishing, and maintenance work is almost incredibly low. As a result there is enormous wastage of water and materials throughout Central Asia.

[1] *KP*, 1 April 1966.

Only 40 per cent. of the water supply system has been constructed by professional engineers while the technically defective irrigation installations supply the fields, it has been estimated, with not more than an average of 27 per cent. of the quantity of the water intended for them, the rest being lost in badly constructed channels.[1]

The development of the Vakhsh River in Tadzhikistan for electrification has been discussed in an earlier section. There are also important irrigation schemes now being developed on the basis of this cheap electric power.[2] Almost half of the Nurek Reservoir, which will hold 10.5 milliard cm. of water, will be used for irrigation of over a million hectares of new land in Tadzhikistan, Turkmenistan, and Uzbekistan. It is planned to irrigate about 400,000 ha. in Tadzhikistan alone. In south Tadzhikistan the main construction work started in 1962 on a big scheme for the irrigation of 57,600 ha. of new land in the Yavan and Obi-Kiik valleys, drawing water from the Vakhsh River. This entails damming the Vakhsh at the village of Boynazy (where it will supply the local power station). From there water will flow into the Yavan Valley through an 8 km. tunnel under the Karatau range and on to the Obi-Kiik Valley through another tunnel under the Kok-Tau range. More than 5 km. of the Karatau tunnel had been completed in 1966 according to the Russian wireless. Moscow metro builders are working on this tunnel. As a result of this irrigation scheme the area is expected to produce large additional quantities of fine-staple cotton as well as fruit and other agricultural produce. The Press reports on the scheme indicate that there have been great difficulties in constructing the tunnels and that progress so far has been unsatisfactory. Speaking at the USSR Supreme Soviet in December 1965, for example, the Chairman of the Tadzhik Council of Ministers, A. Kakharov, said that owing to mistakes in the designs worked out by the 'Giprovodkhoz' Institute of the USSR Ministry of land reclamation and water economy, cultivation of 41,000 ha. of land in the Yavano–Obi–Kiik valleys had to be postponed for two years.[3]

Muddle, wastage, and inefficiency on a huge scale in irrigation has cost the Soviet State dear financially. 'Although annually large

[1] Kabysh, op. cit. p. 180.
[2] 'Irrigation: Progress since 1960', *Central Asian Review*, vol. II, no. 2 (1963), pp. 151–3.
[3] *Izvestiya*, 10 December 1965.

funds are invested in renewing and extending the actual systems, their provision with hydro-electric installations and equipment remains at a low level. As a result the cost of irrigating a hectare of land not only has not diminished but on the contrary is growing. According to the level of return on capital investment, water economy ranks among the most backward branches. ... In recent years much varied machinery has been received but nevertheless the great volume of earthworks are done by hand as formerly and complex mechanization is not yet widespread', reported a writer in the official organ of the Uzbek State Planning Commission.[1]

Finally a revealing analysis of Central Asian irrigation problems and their causes by the Deputy Director of the Central Asian Scientific Research Institute of Hydraulic Problems and Hydro-Technology must be the last word on this subject:

As a result of the poor standards of preparatory calculations, hydro-technical installations for irrigation and land-improvement systems frequently burst under the flow of water, and the locks and water control equipment in many cases work badly. Added to this, research on the correct application of the new irrigation techniques was never completed, there are no effective machines for removing silt and weeds from irrigation and drainage channels, and there are no successful herbicides available. ...

Construction has continued in this region [Hungry Steppe] for more than seven years, and about 1,000 kilometres of drainage channels have been completed, yet they still show the very real gaps in basic solutions of new, complex tasks in hydro-economic construction. ...

These serious defects in planning were aggravated by a lack of any clear technology of construction or of any rules for the exploitation of the technically complicated systems, and it becomes clear why the pace of reclamation is not keeping up with plans, the reclaimed lands partly revert to non-agricultural, and considerable losses are inflicted on the national economy. ...

Inattention towards the advantages to be gained from scientific research is clearly shown in the solution of the acute problem of 'deygish' [land scouring] in areas of Khorezm and the Karakalpak ASSR. The river here falls on a specific part of its bank and is rapidly devouring it. Hundreds of hectares of crops, small villages, important irrigation systems constructed with great difficulty are perishing. ...[2]

---

[1] A. Ulanov, *Ekon. i Zhizn'*, no. 12 (1965), p. 69.
[2] A. Rochinsky, Deputy Director of the Central Asian Scientific Research Institute of

The 'Virgin Lands' of Kazakhstan

Khrushchev's choice of solution to the endemic Soviet grain problem was the development of the Soviet 'Virgin Lands', nearly two-thirds of which lay in the semi-arid steppe of north Kazakhstan. The alternative solution which he rejected would have been a more intensive development of the older areas of agriculture in European Russia and the Ukraine. In line with the crash programme approved in 1953–4 by the Soviet Government, some 25 million ha. had come under the plough in Kazakhstan alone by 1961.[1] The enormous area covered by these figures can be realized from the fact that the total land area of England is only 13,170,000 ha.

In order to work these lands, a nation-wide campaign was launched to recruit young people from European Russia and elsewhere in the Soviet Union. Khrushchev announced at the Twentieth Party Congress in 1956 that 350,000 young 'patriots' had answered the Party's call to the 'Virgin Lands' of the Soviet Union:[2] 500,000 had arrived in Kazakhstan alone by the end of 1956.[3] The all-Union census of 1959 reported the number of non-Asian elements (primarily Russian and Ukrainian) as over 1,700,000 in the area later known as *Tselinnyy kray*, most of them recent migrants to the new farms, compared to a native Kazakh population of 512,352. It was thus clear that the 'Virgin Lands' were being developed mainly by Slav migrants. The Kazakhs were only 18 per cent. of the total population of the area which even before the new developments was largely inhabited by Russians.

State farms (*sovkhozy*) predominated in the organization of the new Kazakh farm lands, though there were also collective farms. Judged by any standard these State grain farms were huge, with an average of 30,000 to 40,000 ha. of land. Various considerations, ideological as well as economic and geographical, weighed the scales in favour of the State farm. The State farm strengthened the Government's control over agriculture and ensured that a larger proportion

Roy D. Laird, 'Agriculture under Khruschchev', *Survey* (July 1965), p. 110.
N. S. Khrushchev, *Report of the Central Committee*, Twentieth Congress of the CPSU (Soviet News Booklet no. 4, London, 1965), p. 44.
KP, 31 October 1956.

Hydraulic Problems and Hydro-Technology, 'Need for a Scientific Basis to Hydraulic Construction', *Kom. Uzbekistana*, no. 11 (1965), pp. 77–82.

of gross agricultural production reached State channels than would have been possible under a system of collective farms. All the costs of establishing farming units in these sparsely inhabited areas had to be borne by the State and it is a tenet of Soviet agro-ideology that State farms are the most expedient and least expensive form of farming unit for the reclamation of new lands. Though soil and conditions vary throughout this large area, it is mainly a spring wheat region similar in many ways to the great spring wheat belt of the Canadian prairies.

The importance of this new agricultural development in Kazakhstan was reflected by the establishment in December 1960 of the *Tselinnyy kray* ('Virgin Lands' territory) consisting of the five northern *oblasts* of Kazakhstan: Kustanay, north Kazakhstan, Kokchetav, Akmolinsk (later Tselinograd), and Pavlodar. These five *oblasts* formed the area of the greatest activity in ploughing up the virgin and fallow lands and constituted not only the main grain-growing region of Kazakhstan but, together with the adjoining areas of west Siberia in the north, of the USSR in Asia as a whole.[1]

In choosing the 'extensive' rather than the 'intensive' solution of the Soviet grain problem, Khrushchev chose that which was likely to produce the most immediate results. It was also beset by serious pitfalls, i.e. soil erosion, dust-bowls, weed infestation, drought—if correct and carefully adjusted cultivation methods were not followed. In the dry farming, light soil lands of the Kazakh prairie these dangers were always lurking for the careless or misdirected farmer.

The bumper crops of 1956 and 1958 in Kazakhstan were a triumphant success for Khrushchev's 'Virgin Lands' policy, after a near disaster crop in 1955 as a result of drought and bad cultivation. Kazakhstan thus became the second 'bread-basket' of the Soviet Union with a record production of 23,823,000 tons of grain in 1956, the first full year of the 'Virgin Lands' scheme; in 1958, production amounted to 21,991,000 tons.[2] Exhilarated by these successes and ignoring the warnings of agricultural experts about the need to leave

---

[1] 'Kazakhstan', Bulletin, vol. 11, no. 2, p. 34 (February 1964) Institute for the Study of the USSR, Munich. This kray was broken up into the original five constituent *oblasts* in December 1965, over a year after Khrushchev's fall, and may be taken as an implicit criticism of Khrushchev's 'Virgin Lands' policy in Kazakhstan.

[2] Frank A. Durgin, 'The Virgin Lands Programme of 1954–60', *Soviet Studies* (January 1962), p. 255. (Figures from official Soviet sources.)

a much higher percentage of these lands to fallow, Khrushchev kept up the pressure for 'merciless ploughing' and scoffed at the idea of fallow. Foreign experts comparing the similar conditions in the 'Virgin Lands' of Kazakhstan and the Saskatchewan prairies of Canada are of the opinion that at least 40 per cent. of the dry farming area of *Tselinnyy kray* ought to be in fallow every year.[1]

The result of Khrushchev's arbitrary enforcement of his policy was disastrous. A precipitous decline in yields set in after the 1958–9 peak production years. The whole scheme was jeopardized by erosion, by dust storms over large areas, and loss of soil fertility following the failure to apply proper cultivation methods. According to the Chairman of the Kazakh Council of Ministers, dust bowls led to 3 million ha. of plough land being abandoned in Kazakhstan from 1955–62.[2] The experts' prognostications about the inevitable cost and consequences of not leaving a proper percentage of these lands to fallow annually was dramatically borne out by the decline in yields from 1.06 tons per ha. in 1956 to an estimated 0.35 tons per ha. in 1963. The magnitude of the Soviet 'Virgin Lands' failure was also reflected in the large Soviet wheat imports from Canada, Australia, and the United States in 1963–6, because of the essential part now played by Kazakh wheat in Soviet production. Another serious defect in Khrushchev's agricultural policy in Kazakhstan before 1962 was that according to the Soviet economic historian A. N. Malafeyev almost a quarter of all the collective farms produced grain at a loss.[3] As elsewhere in the Soviet Union there was no 'material encouragement' for collective and State farmers to produce grain.

Conditions were so hard and primitive that it was stated in 1960 that 140,000 people including experienced mechanics left the 'Virgin Lands'.[4] In the intervening years there have been many similar reports. For example, a plaintive letter in *Sel'skaya Zhizn'* (15 January 1965) from the Kokchetav *oblast* of Kazakhstan complained about the high turnover of people in the 'Virgin Lands', many drivers leaving after a year or two 'because of the lack of normal living conditions'. The writer's State farm had not got a properly

[1] N. Jasny, *Khrushchev's Crop Policy* (George Outram & Co. Ltd., Glasgow, 1965), p. 37.
[2] *KP*, 21 February 1958; cf. J. W. Cleary, 'The Virgin Lands', *Survey* (June 1965), p. 99.
[3] Malafeyev, op. cit. p. 303.   [4] *KP*, 22 January 1960.

functioning hospital, he said, and the small hospital in the neighbouring farm had to serve five settlements but had no qualified
doctor. Housing and the supply of consumer goods was poor and
there was not a single secondary school working locally.

Reporting on his first visit to the 'Virgin Lands' of Kazakhstan in
1954, Khrushchev himself gave a very sober, dismal account of the
general conditions there and the urgent need to improve the position.[1] Special, more advanced types of ploughs were required, he
said, for the 'Virgin Land' conditions. More fuel was required per
tractor than the statutory norm. Norms did not correspond to the
productive conditions of the work on the virgin land. 'It is necessary
to study certain questions so as to ensure high-quality work.
Organization is bad. Under existing norms of petrol consumption,
tractor drivers are in danger of having part of their wages withheld
for over-consumption of fuel. They therefore spoil the fields by
inferior ploughing. The tractor drivers arrive before the tractors.
There is grumbling at low pay. People arriving in the "Virgin
Lands" are badly looked after. In some State farms even bedding is
lacking. There is a lot of equipment lying around but arrangements
are bad for getting it to its destination. . . . Building, especially of
living accommodation, is in a poor way.' Whatever excuse there may
have been for this state of affairs in the first year of the scheme, there
was none for the fact that conditions took so long to improve.

By an ironic quirk of fate, Khrushchev's last tour in the Soviet
Union before his fall from power was to the 'Virgin Lands' of
Kazakhstan, this brainchild of his which, following the disastrous
harvest of 1963, no doubt contributed to his removal. In a big
speech at Tselinograd he made a characteristically cocky defence
of this project.[2] Stressing its achievements and almost overlooking
its massive failures, he claimed that since 1954 the State had spent
6,700 million roubles opening up the new lands and that since then
the marketable grain produced on them alone had made a profit
for the State of 9,700 million roubles. Over 19 million ha. of new
land had been brought into cultivation in the 'Virgin Lands' kray
in the past ten years, and the biggest and richest agricultural region
in the country had been created in the vast steppe of Kazakhstan

---

[1] N. S. Khrushchev, *Stroitel'stvo Kommunizma v SSSR i Razvitiye Sel'skogo Khozyaystva*
(Moscow, 1962), vol. I, pp. 296–305.   [2] *Pravda*, 15 August 1964.

he stated. He airily dismissed 'the problem of fallow land', and the discussions among the scientists and experts on the merits of growing wheat on bare fallow or winter fallow. 'You know that for long years the William's ley system was advocated in our country. Life and experience have fully demonstrated the unsoundness of this system. I think that in this century the fertility of the soil must be restored by chemical means, by the application of organic and mineral fertilizers. All the arguments to the effect that the soil must rest, that it must be given a holiday, are groundless and contradict the findings of science and experience.'

This negative attitude to fallow was directly responsible for the loss of fertility in large areas of the 'Virgin Lands' and cut across expert opinion on the correct treatment of these soils both inside and outside the Soviet Union. Soon after Khrushchev was removed from power in 1964, the agricultural experts got their way and an effort was made to retrieve the situation by the widespread introduction of fallow. Erosion was another evil that developed in the 'Virgin Lands' owing to Khrushchev's arbitrary objection to fallow and other counter-measures. In 1965 the head of the *Tselinnyy kray* agricultural directorate stated that if erosion were eliminated in his kray, grain production could be increased by 50–70 million poods a year. The area of arable land in the kray affected by wind erosion had increased, he said, from 1,500,000 ha. in 1962 to 5,000,000 ha. in 1965.[1]

Large quantities of agricultural machinery were sent to the 'Virgin Lands' from the outset of the scheme. The reverse side of this mechanization is the poor handling and inefficient use of many of the machines. There have been constant complaints about breakdowns, unsuitable types of machinery, and various defects in the supplies of tractors, combines, and other machines. 'In the "Virgin Lands" in 1964 more than 12,000 tractors did not participate in agricultural work, and more than 22,000 combines.'[2] In the following year 'hundreds of machines were laid up for lack of drivers'.[3] Judging by the numbers of these reports published in the Soviet Press, mechanization still seems to be in a poor way in the 'Virgin Lands'.

A down-to-earth report, in 1965, by the Secretary of the Tselinograd *obkom*[4] admitted that there 'had been some blunders in solving a

[1] *KP*, 27 August 1965. [2] *Pravda*, 16 July 1964.
[3] Ibid. 30 July 1965. [4] Ibid. 13 March 1966.

number of organizational-economic and agro-technical questions in the "Virgin Lands" '.

Now they are being uprooted [he continued] through the efforts of the scientists and production workers, a new system of agriculture corresponding to local conditions and above all suited to the soil is being enforced. Seed cultivation is being improved. If in the first years of the cultivation of the 'Virgin Lands' our State farms sowed more than forty types of wheat, they now sow eight, but they are much more productive. ... The guarantee of success lies in skilful utilization of the land. ... Much remains to be done so as to enforce a new system of agriculture and above all of seed rotation with clean fallows.

Correct seed rotation is only carried out in part of the farms. And until recently the question was discussed whether it was necessary to have clean fallows in a steppe zone. The 'Virgin Lands' workers consider that fallows in areas of drought go far to decide the outcome of the harvest, though some workers of the planning organs are not inclined to agree with this opinion.

Mechanization is also important. In recent years, industry has produced many machines and equipment for these regions. But they do not always answer requirements; either they have little durability for work in heavy soils or insufficient productivity. Moreover, there is not a full choice of machine for the new complex agro-technology. For example, the sowing machines produced at the moment require serious constructive improvement and equipment, for pre-sowing preparation of the stubble fields is not made.

From this analysis it is clear that many of the old problems are still unsolved in the 'Virgin Lands'. The difference, however, between the position now and under Khrushchev is that problems can be squarely faced and discussed without deference to his 'subjectivist' ideas.

Khrushchev's successors have no intention of abandoning the valuable 'Virgin Lands' of Kazakhstan and may indeed have arrived just in time to save them from near destruction through his foibles. This was made clear from the authoritative order of the Prime Minister, A. N. Kosygin, at the Twenty-Third Congress of the CPSU to the Ministry of Agriculture of the USSR, the Councils of Ministers of RSFSR, and the Kazakh SSR, 'to devote special attention to the position in the virgin regions, where the fields are heavily choked with weeds and a considerable area is subject to erosion'.[1] But the mistakes made under Khrushchev's aegis are too many and too deep-seated to be eliminated overnight. The great imaginative drive which inspired the proposal to bring these lands into cultivation was unfortunately not matched by the agronomic foresight required to combat the peculiar soil and climatic conditions of the Kazakh steppes. But in spite of the gigantic mistakes and incompetence which have handicapped the development of these new grain districts, their contribution to the Soviet 'bread-basket' is considerable. By 1970 the output of grain in Kazakhstan is planned to reach 21–22 million tons compared with the annual average output of 14,500,000 during the last five years.[2] Most of this grain will come from the Kustanay (4,000,000 tons), Tselinograd (4,000,000 tons), Kokchetav (2,600,000 tons), north Kazakhstan (2,000,000 tons), and Pavlodar (1,600,000 tons) *oblasts*. In good years in the 'Virgin Lands' Kazakhstan has accounted for about 16 per cent. of the Soviet grain harvest.

There have been great fluctuations in the Kazakh deliveries of grain since the peak years of 1956–8 and they sank to their lowest level in 1965 (largely owing to the vagaries of the weather) as is shown in the following table:[3]

Year	Deliveries in million tons
1956	16.1
1957	4.8
1958	14.8
1959	11.5
1960	10.5
1961	7.5
1962	8.2
1963	4.8
1964	15.4
1965	2.3
1956–60 (total)	57.7
1961–5 (total)	38.2

The annual average grain deliveries during the Seven Year Plan period were, in fact, only 8,600,000 tons.[4]

[1] *Pravda*, 6 April 1966. [2] *KP*, 13 March 1966.
[3] Table compiled by Mr. Keith Bush (Munich) who kindly authorized me to reproduce it.
[4] *Pravda*, 31 March 1966.

The sensible policies of the present Soviet Government in the new lands, involving a healthy use of fallow as well as other more appropriate dry-land farming techniques than were encouraged under Khrushchev's régime, should have a beneficial effect on Kazakh grain production in the long run, even if these measures may be expected, in the short run, somewhat to reduce the grain area and output.[1]

Apart from the original main objective of grain production, the 'Virgin Lands' are also being developed for stock-breeding. During the early years of the scheme, some farms tried to breed cattle of many types but the farms are now specializing in not more than two good types of cattle, as a rule. Specialized milk, fowl, and sheep-breeding farms also exist and the grain farms are being urged to develop meat and milk stock-breeding.[2]

Stock-breeding was part of Khrushchev's 'Virgin Lands' plan though it was largely overshadowed by his talk of grain. 'The potentialities of the kray in production of meat and milk have so far not been sufficiently exploited', he declared in his Tselinograd speech in 1964.[3] 'The Soviet people are confident that in a short time you will plough up a second "Virgin Lands" area and give the State large quantities of meat, milk, wool, mutton, and other agricultural products. Today the trade-mark of the "Virgin Lands" kray is grain. I think you will do all you can to make the trade-mark of the "Virgin Lands" kray not only grain but meat and milk as well.'

Stock-Breeding and Meat Production in Kazakhstan

As has been shown in an earlier chapter Kazakhstan has always been an important centre of livestock production (long before the

	Millions of head					
	1928	*1935*	*1940*	*1954*	*1961*	*1964*
Sheep and goats	19.2	2.6	7.0	18.4	28.7	29.5

Sources: *Nar. Khoz. Kazakhskoy SSR*, 1957; *Nar. Khoz. SSSR*, 1960; *Nar. Khoz. SSSR*, 1964.

[1] *Foreign Agriculture* (Foreign Agricultural Service, U.S. Department of Agriculture), 21 March 1966, p. 5.
[2] *Pravda*, 13 March 1966.   [3] Ibid. 15 August 1964.

'Virgin Lands' scheme was mooted). It took many years to recover from the havoc wrought to its cattle, sheep, and goats by the collectivization tragedy in the '30s. Sheep, which are the largest item in the Kazakh animal population, did not reach pre-collectivization numbers until after 1954, as shown in the above table.

The derisory prices paid by the State for livestock products reinforced the traditional dislike of collectivization and increased the stock-breeders' indifference to the care and production of collectivized stock. As elsewhere in the Soviet Union appeals to increase meat production in Kazakhstan were received without enthusiasm when meat was only produced at a loss (except when produced from private holdings and sold at inflated prices on the collective farm markets).[1] An almost incredible state of mismanagement and corruption in State and collective farms for the previous ten years was revealed by Ismail Yusupov, the Kazakh First Party Secretary to the Plenum of the Central Committee of the Kazakh C.P. in 1963.[2] Owing to 'misappropriation of State property' in Kazakh State and collective farms, he said, '29,000,000 sheep and goats had been unproductively expended', i.e. purloined by cattle thieves. Hundreds of other stock had been illegally shared out at wholesale prices. This situation must have caused great material and financial losses to the State. The folly of the existing livestock products price situation was at last realized by Moscow in 1962. As Khrushchev stated: 'Nobody will increase production of meat if the more they produce the more the farm, collective or State, suffers a loss.'[3] By a decree of the Central Committee of the CPSU and the USSR Council of Ministers (17 May 1962), prices on all kinds of livestock and meat were increased with a view to 'raising the material interest of collective and State farms in increasing production and sale of livestock products'.[4] As a large producer of livestock, Kazakhstan was directly interested in these improved prices.

Kazakhstan now ranks third among the Soviet republics for the supply of meat and wool,[5] producing 658,000 tons of meat in 1964.[6] The drought and the bad harvest caused considerable damage to

[1] Malafeyev, op. cit. p. 298; V. Khlebnikov, *Voprosy Ekonomiki*, no. 7 (1962), p. 53.
[2] *KP*, 19 March 1963.   [3] Malafeyev, op. cit. p. 296.
[4] *Sbornik Zakonov*, no. 8 (1962), Statute 66.   [5] *KP*, 12 March 1966.
[6] *Nar. Khoz. SSSR v 1964 g.*, op. cit. p. 362.

Kazakh livestock. The losses to cattle and pigs have been made good, but early in 1965 sheep were still 8 per cent. below the numbers at the end of 1962.[1] Reporting to the Twenty-Third Party Congress in March 1966 the First Party Secretary, Kunayev, stated that the sheep population was now 30,000,000 and large-horned cattle numbered 7,000,000.[2] The development of sheep-breeding is of paramount importance to the Republic and holdings are scheduled to increase to 40,000,000 or 33.5 per cent. above the 1965 figures in 1970. One-third of the Republic's meat deliveries in 1970 are to be in mutton and the target for 1970 is 1,200,000 tons (liveweight) with a total meat production of 1,739,000 tons.[3]

Further expansion of the Kazakh cattle-breeding industry (for which there are great prospects) largely depends on the extent to which the Republic can establish a stable fodder base, improve breeds, and raise cattle productivity. These are long-term problems even under the improved price and other conditions now prevailing in this industry.

Refrigeration has an ever-increasing part to play in securing the deliveries of the large Kazakh meat supplies to European Russia. Reports in the Soviet Press point to frequent muddles or inadequate refrigeration which hold up or jeopardize the deliveries. Quantities of Kazakh meat, for example, seem to have perished when the railways withheld 400 special wagons from the Semipalatinsk meat combine, and its refrigeration capacity was overloaded with meat in 1965.[4] There are also complaints that meat combines are being constructed too slowly to deal with the local volume of carcasses so that there is always a wasteful gap between the production of meat and the possibilities of processing it within the Republic.[5]

TRANSPORT[6]

Kazakhstan has been the scene of the most active new railway construction in the Central Asian area before and since World

---

[1] *KP*, 4 February 1965.   [2] Ibid. 1 April 1966.
[3] Ibid. 12 March 1966.   [4] *Pravda*, 21 September 1965.
[5] Ibid. 5 August 1965.
[6] In the preparation of this section I have borrowed extensively from an excellent article, 'Recent Road and Rail Transport Developments in Kazakhstan', in *Central Asian Review*, no. 2 (1965).

War II. Between the wars railway construction developed rapidly and by 1939 the Turk–Sib railway ran south from west Siberia to link up with the Central Asian railway system. Another north–south line was built from Petropavlovsk to the Karaganda coal-fields to haul this coal to the Urals (1931) and was extended from Karaganda to Lake Balkhash via Mointy in 1939 and south-west to the copper mines of Dzhezkazgan and Karsakpay in the following year.[1] A very important east–west line was rushed through during the war from Akmolinsk (the present Tselinograd) to the Kartaly junction for the metallurgical centre of Magnitogorsk. This 500 mile line shortened the haul of Karaganda coal to Magnitogorsk by some 300 miles and also relieved the overladen Trans-Siberian of this freight.

Since the war some major constructions have been added to the Kazakh railway system. In the first place an extension of the Magnito-gorsk–Karaganda line running eastwards for nearly 700 miles to the Kuznetsk coal basin was completed in 1953 (with the help of forced labour). This extension, known as the South Siberian, begins at Tselinograd and passes through the industrial centre of Barnaul on its way to the metallurgical, chemical, and steel plants of the Kuzbas. Along this line iron ores of the Kustanay region are dis-patched to the Urals and west Siberia, both of which areas are at present short of ores for their iron and steel industries; coal from Karaganda joins the line at Tselinograd and also goes on to the Urals and into Kuybyshev *oblast* (about 60 per cent. of Karaganda coal leaves Kazakhstan).[2] Only about 30 per cent. of Kazakh iron ore is used in Kazakhstan, the rest mainly goes to the Urals (50 per cent.) and west Siberia (16 per cent.) along the South Siberian railway. Much of west Siberian coal is also carried by this line. There is also some traffic in oil and manganese, iron and steel products going to Tselinograd from west Siberia and Karaganda, timber from west Siberia and grain from the 'Virgin Lands' going east.

The Middle Siberian line was completed in February 1966[3] having been under construction since the early '50s. It runs east from Kustanay through Uritskoye, Peski, and Kokchetav to the last 172 km. stretch Kzyl-Tu–Irtyshshkoye. This line, with its

[1] Tupper, op. cit. p. 420.   [2] *Ekon. Rayony*, op. 571.
[3] Moscow Home Service, 18 February 1966.

links with the Trans-Siberian via Barnaul, when fully operational will considerably reduce the loads on other Siberian lines. It is intended that the whole line will eventually be converted to broad gauge, though it seems that some sectors were still narrow gauge in 1965–6, which must give rise to complex handling problems.

Farther south, the pre-war Karaganda–Mointy line was extended southwards to Chu, a junction on the Turk–Sib between Alma-Ata and Tashkent, in 1953. This 281 mile long extension reduced Tashkent's expensive dependence on coal from the Kuzbas more than 700 miles away by delivering coal from Karaganda.[1] In all, 3,410 km. of new railways were built in Kazakhstan between 1952 and 1962, bringing the total length from 8,400 km. to 11,810 km.[2] Though still inadequate to serve the needs of this vast country, the railways are the chief means of transport in Kazakhstan and carry about 95 per cent. of the total freight.[3]

Under the new Five Year Plan some important railway projects are to be undertaken in Kazakhstan and others which were started under the Seven Year Plan have still to be completed. The Gur'yev–Astrakhan 322 km. line has been under construction since 1964 when a start was made on the earthworks from both ends. It will shorten the distance between Moscow and Gur'yev by 700 km. when finished. Exploitation of another line in this area from Makat on the Kandagach–Gur'yev line to Shevchenko on the eastern shores of the Caspian was rushed through in 1965 to serve the needs of the new Mangyshlak oilfields. In north-east Kazakhstan a second line is now being built from Tselinograd to Pavlodar to cope with the heavy transport of Ekibastuz coal.

By 1970 a line is to be built from Kungrad to the Makat–Gur'yev line to provide a link between the western parts of Central Asia and the north-east; the line from Karaganda to Dzhezkazgan–Karsakpay[4] is to be extended to the Aral Sea, and Makat is to be joined to Aleksandrov Gay across the Ural River. These lines will run through

[1] Tupper, op. cit. p. 434; Danilov, op. cit. pp. 288–92.
[2] *Central Asian Review*, no. 2 (1965), op. cit. p. 173.   [3] Danilov, op. cit. p. 288.
[4] Karsakpay is only a short distance from the Baykonur 'cosmodrome' from which the Soviet space satellites are launched and is of course an area of strict security precautions. This may explain why the Karsakpay–Baykonur railway is marked as built on the map *Atlas SSSR* published in 1954 but has disappeared from the map of communications in the *Atlas SSSR* of 1962. Or was it accidentally or deliberately destroyed in connexion with satellite operations? The position of this little railway remains a mystery.

largely uninhabited desert country and may meet with considerable supply problems. This formidable construction list is of through trunk routes only, and takes no account of many completed and projected branch lines serving particular areas or industries, especially throughout the industrialized north of the Republic.

Apart from the normal requirements of a communications system, the main spur for this rapid and extensive development of railway transport has been provided in Kazakhstan by the need to carry large quantities of bulky products: the Karaganda coal and Kustanay region iron ores, the grain of the 'Virgin Lands', and the ores and concentrates of the Kazakh mineral deposits. The urgent construction of the Gur'yev–Shevchenko line was necessitated by the opening up of the Mangyshlak oilfields; at first it was proposed to supply the fields by sea and take the oil away by pipeline, but the high waxy content of the oil made shipment by pipeline technically very difficult (see pp. 131–2); and until this problem is solved the railway should take as much as possible of the oil. The service is already inadequate, however, and only 20–30 per cent. of the oil is going by rail.[1]

A start has been made on the modernization of the railways in Kazakhstan but this has not developed *pari passu* with their construction. When work on the station buildings and track installations is completed on the Mangyshlak–Gur'yev line, it is intended to be 'the most mechanized line in Kazakhstan'.[2] The stretch of line from the Sokolovka-Sarbay iron ore region is being electrified as far as Magnitogorsk while the new Five Year Plan mentions electrification of 1,000 km. in north Kazakhstan. For the rest, however, it is a case of 40 per cent. manual signalling and 80 per cent. point controls and the fact that there is apparently no prospect of improvement has aroused strong local dissatisfaction.[3] One particular problem is the inconsistency of gauge. Even the recently constructed Middle Siberian line still has a section of narrow gauge waiting for conversion to the standard gauge of the rest of the line.

Central Asia (apart from Kazakhstan) has for long required a good transportation system—originally because of its strategic position as the outpost of the Empire, and then to export its cotton and

[1] *KP*, 13 March 1966.
[2] 'Road and Rail Transport in Kazakhstan', *Central Asian Review*, no. 2 (1965), p. 173.
[3] *KP*, 9 November 1965.

mineral ores, and import the coal, wood, fertilizers, and other commodities that are lacking.

The main trunk-lines of Central Asia, from Moscow via the Trans-Siberian to Kuybyshev, then south via Orenburg to Tashkent, Bukhara, Mary, Ashkhabad, and Krasnovodsk on the Caspian, had all been completed before the Revolution. Since 1917 no railway construction on this scale has taken place in this area. The old line from Samarkand to the Fergana Valley was reinforced with branches to its many valuable new industrial and cotton centres and another line linked Chardzhou on the Amu Dar'ya to Kungrad in the Amu Dar'ya delta south of the Aral Sea.

During the 1966–70 Plan period construction of a line from Karshi to Samarkand is to be resumed and is regarded as essential to the success of the vast development scheme planned for the Karshi and Surkhan-Sherabad steppes. At present most goods are carried by the Samarkand–Kagan–Karshi line, a roundabout method involving relatively high costs. It has now been decided to build a direct line from Samarkand to Karshi which will shorten the 144 km. journey between these points and to continue it to Termez and Dushanbe. This line is to be completed, according to schedule, in 1969.[1] A line was also started in February 1966 from Termez via Kurgan-Tyube to Yavan in southern Tadzhikistan.[2] It will cross the main cotton-growing area of Tadzhikistan and link up with the new chemical combine at Yavan.

The main lacunae in the Central Asian railway system at present are the lack of direct services between Tashkent and Dushanbe (trains at present have to go via Bukhara and Samarkand, but the engineering difficulties of building a direct line over the mountainous country between Tashkent and Dushanbe are enormous); and the lack of direct lines from north Kirgizia (Tash-Kumyr or Kok-Yangak) to the Rybach'ye–Dzhambul line, and from Frunze to Chu.

An analysis of rail imports and exports for Tadzhikistan presents a curious picture because of the dimensions, variety, and the distances involved in this traffic. Nearly one-third of Tadzhik external trade is with regions over 3,000 km. away. The main imports are oil, coal, timber, ferrous metal products, chemical fertilizers, and cement. Over half (56 per cent.) of Tadzhik exports consists of

[1] *PV*, 4 March 1966 and 5 July 1966.   [2] Tass, 16 February 1966.

mineral building materials—mainly gravel and sand. The rest is made of cotton and food products. Timber forms one-sixth of the total imports; 90 per cent. of it originates in east Siberia, involving transport over distances ranging from 4,750 to 7,000 km. Only one-third of Tadzhik ferrous metal imports comes from Kazakhstan and Uzbekistan, the rest is obtained mainly from the Urals (33 per cent.) and the Ukraine (21 per cent.). All mineral fertilizers have to be imported (300,000 tons in 1962) and only one-third of Tadzhikistan's grain needs can be supplied domestically. In 1962, 200,000 tons of grain from Kazakhstan and 175,000 tons of flour from Stavropol', Kuybyshev, and Orenburg districts were imported.[1]

Apart from such bulk imports, many regions of the USSR except the Far East provide commodities for Tadzhik needs—the Central region supplies machinery, the North-West cable, shoes, woollen cloth, the Volga region sends cars, lorries, and cycles, the central Black Earth region agricultural machines, west Siberia coke and chemicals, Transcaucasia lorries, steel tubes, and so on.

As Tadzhikistan is the most remote of the Central Asian republics from the chief sources of supply, the distances involved are longer than elsewhere in this region. Nevertheless, owing to the economic dependence of the other Central Asian republics on imports of timber, grain, metals, and other industrial commodities, the rail freight situation is similar in many respects to that in Tadzhikistan.[2]

A new railway will probably be built under the impetus of the new Five Year Plan in west Turkmenistan. Speaking at the Twenty-Third Party Congress the Turkmen Party Secretary, Ovezov, stressed the necessity of constructing a railway between Nebit-Dag and Cheleken so as to facilitate the development of the oil extraction and gas industries. It would be approximately 150 km. long and with the development of some new motor roads should speed up the transfer of natural gas to the centre of the country.[3] No further details of these proposals are yet available but the situation will probably be clarified in the final draft of the new Plan.

River transport also supplements the Central Asian railways. The only navigable rivers are the Amu Dar'ya from the Aral Sea

[1] U. Kh. Kletsel'man, *Iz. AN Tadzhikskoy SSR*, no. 3 (1965), pp. 23–33.

[2] Danilov, op. cit. p. 287.

[3] *Turk. Iskra*, 3 April 1966.

to Termez, and the Syr Dar'ya from the Aral Sea to Bekabad. Little is carried on the Syr Dar'ya, but the Amu Dar'ya is used a great deal for transport of oil products, cotton, grain, mineral fertilizers, and building materials. The main ports are Termez, Chardzhou, and Takhiatash, and its usefulness is extended by the Kara-Kum Canal which it feeds.

The Caspian is also an important element in Central Asian transport, and Krasnovodsk has the third highest turnover on the Caspian after the ports of Baku and Makhachkala.

Air transport has been widely developed in recent years in Central Asia. Tashkent is an international airport at which planes stop on their way from Moscow to Delhi and Kabul. It also has direct lines to Baku, Tbilisi, Sverdlovsk, Novosibirsk, and Alma-Ata, as well as to the other Central Asian capitals. In view of some of the round-about routes by rail, air travel must be essential for passengers who are pressed for time. It takes 48 hours by rail from Tashkent to Dushanbe but only 2 hours by air.[1]

There are no trunk roads in the western half of Central Asia[2] but the east and south-east of the area is very dependent on roads for communications in mountainous areas where railway construction is difficult or impossible, and in Kirgizia roads are the main means of transport.[3]

The most important trunk-roads are the north–south roads from Tamdy-Bulak to Samarkand and Termez, from Dzhambul to Tashkent–Leninabad–Termez; the section from Tashkent to Termez is known as the Great Uzbek road. The east–west roads run from Alma-Ata to Frunze and Dzhambul in the north of the area, and in the south from Osh to Leninabad, Bekabad, and Samarkand. In the south the Khorog–Dushanbe road is known as the Great Pamir road. The Great Pamir road follows a uniquely high mountain course across passes over 5 km. in height. It is the main means of communication between the Tadzhik capital and the Gorno-Badakhshanskaya autonomous *oblast*. Speaking in the Supreme Soviet of the USSR in December 1965, its delegate urged the Soviet Council of Ministers to expedite the reconstruction of this road.[4]

---

[1] Danilov, op. cit. p. 287.   [2] Ibid.

[3] *Razvitiye Proizvoditel'nykh Sil Kirgizskoy SSR v Perspektive*, op. cit. p. 58.

[4] *Pravda*, 10 December 1965.

A trunk-road was opened between Osh and Khorog in October 1964 and owing to the engineering difficulties involved in crossing the Tyan Shan was celebrated as a national event of some importance in Kirgizia.[1] It is 728 km. long and rises to 4,700 m. above sea level and will be kept open by 1,000 snow clearance workers.[2]

A motor trunk-road was opened between Frunze and Osh in 1965. It traverses Kirgizia from north to south linking two large economic regions formerly separated by inaccessible mountains of the great Tyan Shan range. The total length of this road is 600 km. and it crosses many passes, some over 3,000 m. high. Construction of the road started before the last war under local Kirgiz auspices. It was resumed as an all-Union construction in 1964 and the opening was celebrated as a great national event in November 1965.[3]

In the seven year period (1959–65), the length of metalled roads in Kazakhstan increased by more than 100 per cent. to a total of over 24,000 km., but this network is wholly inadequate for such a vast country and First Party Secretary Kunayev has stated that 'the scale and rate of road construction must be considerably increased'. In the new five year period some 10,000 km. of motor-roads are to be built in Kazakhstan including the following: Dzhambul–Karatau–Zhuantyube; Tselinograd–Kurgal'dzhino.[4]

CAPITAL INVESTMENT AND GROSS INDUSTRIAL OUTPUT

The rate of increase of investment in Kazakhstan since 1950 has been well above the USSR average, and among the highest in the country. This reflects partly the apparently relatively low rate of investment in previous years, and partly the high investments since 1950 in such projects as the 'Virgin Lands' campaign, the iron ore basin of the north-west, and the non-ferrous metals industry. Some industries were not yet showing a full return on the capital invested in 1963: the 'Virgin Lands' campaign has had several bad years, although these are not reflected in gross output; the main

---

[1] *SK*, 17 October 1964.   [2] Tass, 22 October 1964.

[3] 'Podvig v Gorakh', *Sov. Kirgizia*, 11 November 1965.

[4] Russian radio, 11 March 1966 and 13 March 1966.

project of the iron ore basin, the Sokolovka-Sarbay combine, did
not come into full service until the beginning of 1966; a great deal of
prospecting and preparatory work is still being carried out in the
non-ferrous deposit areas; the Karaganda Iron and Steel Works,
under construction since about 1953, will not be completed until
1970. The result is that the increases in investments are not reflected
in similar increases in industrial output, and while in 1958–63

*Aggregate Percentage Growth of Gross Industrial
Production in the USSR and the Soviet Republics*

	1959–65 (planned)	1959–65 (actual)	1966–70 (planned)
USSR	80	84	50
RSFSR	80	75	50
Ukrainian SSR	77	84	50
Belorussian SSR	80	107	70
Uzbek SSR	80	80	60
Kazakh SSR	170	112	70
Georgian SSR	Up to 75	60	60
Azerbaydzhan SSR	90	63	60
Lithuanian SSR	80	124	70
Moldavian SSR	120	111	70
Latvian SSR	Over 60	100	50
Kirgiz SSR	120	103	60
Tadzhik SSR	Over 80	85	80
Armenian SSR	120	96	80
Turkmen SSR	100	51	60
Estonian SSR	80	99	50

Sources: Planned industrial growth, 1959–65—*Pravda*, 14
November 1958. Actual industrial growth, 1959–65—*SSSR v
Tsifrakh v 1965 g.*, p. 55. Planned industrial growth, 1966–70—
Pravda, 20 February 1966.

industrial increases were well above the USSR average, they still
fall well short of the extremely high rate of increase in capital investment over the previous thirteen years.

Farther south, capital investment in the Central Asian republics
from 1950 to 1958, excluding the collectives but including State
farms, increased at about the same rate as that for the USSR as a
whole, although it was considerably slower than in Kazakhstan or

the Siberias. With the Seven Year Plan, however, there was a considerable rise in investment in Central Asia at a time when the growth-rate had decreased elsewhere, with the average annual increase 14.4 per cent. compared to the USSR average increase of 8.6 per cent.

On the other hand the increase in gross industrial output in Central Asia has been considerably lower than the USSR average, falling well short of the increases in capital investment. This was to be expected in an area which had to make a great leap into modern industrialization in the mid-twentieth century and where industrial development problems were much greater than in the more advanced European areas of modern Russia. The situation in Central Asia is also partly due to the high share of investment in State farms, which cover about 29 per cent. of the total area under non-private cultivation. Considerable investment also goes into large-scale irrigation schemes for the basic cotton crop. In spite of the high rate of increase in capital investment in recent years in Central Asia, it is unlikely to be reflected in a comparable increase in industrial production for the present.

It must be added as a postscript to these estimates that the validity of the indicators on which the growth and output figures in the Central Asian republics are based are sharply challenged in Tashkent; they have, of course, long been criticized by foreign and Soviet economists for the distortions they can create, though no suitable alternatives have yet been devised.[1] The main charge against these indicators is that they lead to a great exaggeration of the estimate of any form of production which passes from one enterprise to another for processing, thus resulting in manifold double counting of raw materials and weighting against a country like Uzbekistan which is a main producer of a raw material such as cotton. One Uzbek critic of the present methods of accounting reinforces his arguments by a neat allusion to the Leninist nationalities policy, 'thanks to which they made a gigantic leap forward in their economic development and now stand on a footing not only with the old established regions of the country but with the most advanced western states'. Briefly, the idea here is that as Lenin forecast that the under-developed regions of Russia would catch up with the more developed areas

[1] A. Nove, *The Soviet Economy* (George Allen & Unwin, London, 1965), p. 164.

of the Centre, any statistical method which fails to reflect this advance distorts the present position and cannot be correct.[1]

Growth of Gross Industrial Output

	1913	1940	1962
Uzbek SSR	1	4.7	22.8
RSFSR	1	8.7	50.8
Ukraine	1	7.3	31.9

This record, compiled according to the normal Soviet statistical method, is repudiated in favour of accounting based on net production, which produces a very different rate of growth for Uzbekistan:

Growth of Net Industrial Output

	1913	1937	1962
Uzbek SSR	1	13.5	46.8

Source: *Ekon. i Zhizn'*, no. 9 (1965), pp. 38–39.

The Uzbeks naturally stress the merits of a system which would underline their industrial growth rather than their backwardness compared to other Soviet republics. But there seems little prospect at present that this problem, which is also an all-Union problem, will be solved because of their objections.

Judged by the classical criteria of *per capita* production of steel or electricity generated, the Central Asian republics may be said to be under-industrialized. Looked at in a statistical vacuum, this conclusion underestimates, for example, the great strides which have taken place in the development of electric power capacity, the creation of new natural gas and chemical industries, and the introduction of sophisticated techniques into the non-ferrous industry and its expansion in this area.

Looking into the future, two officials concerned with Central Asian affairs in Gosplan and the USSR Academy of Sciences venture to forecast that as a result of the growth of the fuel, electronics, and engineering industries in Central Asia, the average annual growth of industrial production will exceed Union indices for the

---

[1] V. Trubnikov, 'V Krivom Zerkale Vala', *Ekon. i Zhizn'*, no. 9 (1965), p. 36; K. Papadyuk, 'Kriteriy Vyravnivaniya Urovney Razvitiya Ekonomicheskikh Rayonov Strany', *Ekon. Nauki*, no. 2 (1966), p. 73.

period up to 1970.[1] Central Asia is moving forward from a very low industrial level in 1928, in spite of inefficiency, blunders, and negligence, but scarcely at such a rate yet. As suggested in the foregoing pages, a great deal of the responsibility for these shortcomings rests on the unco-ordinated, often inappropriate planning of Gosstroy and Gosplan and the indifference of local officials to the living conditions of the workers.

[1] G. Narzikulov, Chairman of the Central Asian Commission of the Problem Council of the Academy of Sciences, USSR, and V. Zhmuyda, Head of Sector of the Development of the Regions of Central Asia of SOPSa (Gosplan SSR), 'Srednaya Aziya Cherez Sem'Let', *Nar. Khoz. S.A.*, no. 5 (1964), p. 18.

V

Siberia (East and West)

NATURAL FEATURES AND RESOURCES

The huge land mass of Siberia is divided by the River Yenisey into the great plain of west Siberia, largely covered by marshes and bogs in the north, merging southwards into excellent arable land and never rising more than 600 feet above sea level, and the mountains and plateaux of east Siberia with an average height of 1,500–2,000 feet bounded to the east by the hills and valleys of central Yakutia. North to south, the country is traversed by arctic, tundra, forest, and steppe zones.

Siberia contains some of the mightiest rivers of the Soviet Union. In west Siberia there is the great Ob' River system and farther east the Yenisey, the Angara, and the Lena, while Lake Baykal in east Siberia is the deepest lake in the world and has many remarkable features including rare types of fish not found elsewhere.

In recent years the economic region of west Siberia has comprised, for statistical purposes, only the southern third of the west Siberian plain, while the large Tyumen' *oblast* has been included in the contiguous highly industrialized Urals region. Statistically, however, this division conveys a good picture of the comparatively developed areas of west Siberia. The town of Tyumen' on the Trans-Siberian railway is more closely linked with the Urals economically and is far from the industrialized areas of west Siberia. The rest of the *oblast*, until the big oil and gas discoveries of the 1960s, was almost entirely undeveloped. The southern sector of the west Siberian plain is in an entirely different category. It has industries of considerable importance based on the Kuznetsk coal-fields and its agriculture (particularly grain and dairy products) is among the most successful in the Soviet Union. The new significance of Siberia is reflected in the scientific centre at Novosibirsk which is the headquarters of all the scientific bodies of Siberia and the Far East. It also contains historic cities like Omsk and Tomsk which developed a cultural life of their own before the Revolution. The population density of west Siberia (10 per km.²) is about the same as the Soviet average, and much less sparse than the rest of Siberia and the Far East. In the northern half of the west Siberian plain and throughout east Siberia there are large, uninhabited, virtually undeveloped expanses of taiga, forest, and steppe.

The natural resources of Siberia, traditionally believed to be rich and varied, have been much more precisely investigated in recent years and with very satisfactory results. It is now estimated that Siberia has more than half of Soviet reserves of coal, a base for an enormous development of thermal electric power, huge reserves of oil and natural gas, two-thirds of the hydro-electric power potential, and about half the timber reserves of the Soviet Union. It also contains important deposits of iron ore, manganese, copper, nickel, cobalt, gold, titanium, mica, talc, and many other minerals.[1]

There is a good black earth belt in the southern part of west Siberia which was well cultivated before the Revolution and continues to make a useful contribution to Soviet grain, milk, and butter supplies. There are large areas of meadow and pasture land and fertile farm lands in the foothills of the Altay Mountains. Gradually, new agricultural areas are being extended into the forest and marsh zones. During World War II the importance of the west Siberian farm lands increased considerably because of the need to replace the rich agricultural areas of Russia occupied by the Germans.[2]

The emphasis on the extent of the natural resources of Siberia, especially in Khrushchev's speeches and the text of the Seven Year Plan, must not obscure the continuing importance of the Urals and European Russia in the Soviet economy. According to estimates of the Siberian Department of the USSR Academy of Sciences, European Russia contained 80 per cent. of the Soviet population, 80 per cent. of the industrial output, 75 per cent. of the railway network, 70 per cent. of the grain, and 80 per cent. of the meat and dairy production in 1961.[3] These statistics may be somewhat out

---

[1] Coal and timber reserves calculated from *Ekon. Rayony*, op. cit. pp. 260, 279, 281. For oil cf. *Izvestiya*, 12 June 1965; for natural gas cf. Moscow Home Service, 7 July 1965.

[2] Shabad, op. cit. p. 263.　　[3] *Izvestiya Sibirskogo Otdeleniya AN SSSR*, no. 10 (1961).

of date but they still broadly represent the relationship between the two areas. 'Until labour is attracted there', concluded the Siberian Department, 'the huge resources of the East will not be properly developed.' This is the crux of the matter.[1] Meanwhile there are still considerable natural resources in European Russia even if in some cases they are of declining importance. For example, the Donbas, with 2.8 per cent. of the total estimated USSR coal reserves, could be exploited for hundreds of years more. The Volga–Urals oil region is producing about 70 per cent. of the country's oil but though output is still rising rapidly, some of these fields are now reaching their peak. The energy resources of Russia west of the Urals are estimated to be insufficient for the requirements of this major industrial area in the not too distant future. The three major Soviet centres of iron ore reserves and output are Krivoy Rog, the Kursk region of central Russia, and the Kustanay area of north-west Kazakhstan, the latter being more convenient for the Urals industry than that of Siberia. It may be that with these European resources at hand, 'priority for Siberian development is, for the moment, being given to aluminium, magnesium, titanium, pulp, paper, and polymers. Already there are aluminium plants at Irkutsk and Krasnoyarsk and another is being completed at Pavlodar (in north Kazakhstan), man-made fibres are being manufactured in Barnaul, synthetic rubber in Omsk, and chemical plants have been constructed at Kemerovo and Angarsk.'[2]

Siberia's most important contributions to the USSR economy at present are her non-ferrous metals and minerals, especially copper, nickel, wolfram, cobalt, talc, mica, coal, and agricultural products (timber and grain). It is often asserted that Siberia can produce iron and steel more cheaply than any other region of the USSR. This estimate is based on the huge iron ore deposits at Bakchar' amounting to some 100 milliard tons which could be won opencast and linked to Kuznetsk coal to give west Siberia 20–30 million tons of metal per annum.[3] This hypothesis must, however, be viewed against the cold fact that these iron-ore deposits would take about 10–15 years to develop.

[1] *Dimensions of Soviet Economic Power* (US Government Printing Office, Washington, 1962), p. 198.
[2] 'Siberia Poses Problems of the Age', *SU*, no. 187 (1965), pp. 8–13.
[3] Ibid. cf. Estimate of the Economics Institute of the Siberian Department of the AN SSSR.

In the future oil and natural gas in very large quantities will be added to Siberia's contribution to the Soviet economy. No figures are available to show Siberia's proportional output of metals and minerals. However, published statistics show that it produces 20 per cent. of Soviet timber and at least 17 per cent. of Soviet coal. The comparatively small agricultural belt of the southern part of west Siberia is mainly responsible for Siberia's share of 10 per cent. of all Soviet grain (including 15 per cent. of Soviet wheat), 10 per cent. of its meat and wool, and 8–9 per cent. of its milk and milk products.[1]

Transbaykalia

This area is cut off from the Siberian taiga by a series of mountain ranges in Buryat-Mongolia, falling away to a plateau along the borders of Outer Mongolia and China. The native inhabitants of non-Slav origin are greatly outnumbered by the Russians. But although the Buryats are a decided minority in Buryat-Mongolia (20 per cent. against 75 per cent. Russians), unlike the nomadic natives of the northern regions, they are still strong enough to maintain their national identity, linguistically. Out of a total of 253,000 Buryats, 240,000 have kept their own language as their mother tongue and so have the greater number of the 1,800 Mongolians.[2] The Russians have settled mainly along the railway line from the southern tip of Lake Baykal along the Mongolian and Chinese borders and spread into the plateau of the south Chita *oblast*.

The development of this region has taken a different form from that of the rest of Siberia. It grew rapidly in the first ten years after World War II but since 1956 economic development has been slowing down. This could be a reflection of the former intensive use of forced labour in the gold, copper, tin, tungsten, and molybdenum mines in the region which was abolished after the death of Stalin. There is at present little sign of a future reversal of this trend. Plans for the construction of plants for the production of copper, titanium (from the poly-metallic ores), sulphuric acid, and fertilizers east of Lake Baykal have been mentioned by *Ekonomicheskaya Gazeta* (no. 10, March 1966). Its other suggestion that an iron and steel industry could be built on the basis of a

[1] *Ekon. Rayony*, p. 256.
[2] *Itogi Vsesoyuznoy Perepisi Naseleniya 1959 g. SSSR*, p. 184.

milliard tons of iron ore reserves in the south-east of the area does
not seem practicable since this would mean a transport haul of a
least 1,200 km. to the nearest coking coal deposits; such a plan would
not be economically viable unless a similar plant were built simultaneously on the south Yakut coal-field. If, as *Ekon. Gazeta* claims
'the current Five Year Plan will be a turning-point in the development of the region', it is not yet clear which way it will turn
economically.

These proposals for economic development east of Lake Baykal
gave rise to a heated controversy. A cry of alarm about the pollution
of the lake by industrial effluents was raised in a letter to *Komsomolskaya Pravda* (10 May 1966) signed by a group of eminent
scientists, writers, artists, and painters and supporting the dissent
voiced at the Twenty-Third Party Congress about future plans to
build a vast industrial complex including pulp and paper factories
on the banks of the lake and the Selenga River which flows into it
Apparently those who support the Lake Baykal industrial developments are trying to evade public pressure by assurances that the
purification system for the effluents from these undertakings will
ensure that the lake water is preserved as it is, though the arguments
advanced by the scientists prove the inconsistency of these assurances and their complete distrust of the industrial group. It is not
clear at the time of writing what the outcome of this conflict will be.

POPULATION AND LABOUR PROBLEMS

Apart from the southern half of the west Siberian plain, the
population of the rest of Siberia is extremely sparse. The west

	Population in millions			Per cent. increase	
	1939	*1959*	*1 Jan. 1964*	*1 Jan. 1965*	*1939–59*	*1959–65*
USSR	190.7	208.8	226.2	229.2	9.5	9.8
West Siberia	7.9	10.2	10.8	10.8	29.1	5.9
East Siberia	4.8	6.5	7.08	7.2	35.4	10.8

Source: *Nar. Khoz. SSSR v 1963* and *1964*. Last two columns calculated

Siberian economic region, excluding Tyumen' *oblast* to the north,
has a population density of 10.9 per km.² which is higher than the
USSR average of 10.2 per km.²; when Tyumen' *oblast* is added to
the region the density drops by one-half. The great expanse of
east Siberia is even more sparsely populated and the population of

its most heavily populated *oblast*, Irkutsk, is only 2.5 per km.² the average density per km.² being 1.8.

As is shown in the above table the high rate of increase in the population of both west and east Siberia between 1939 and 1959 was not sustained in the seven year period 1959–65. Moreover there was no increase in the west Siberian population between 1 January 1964 and 1 January 1965. The east Siberian population rose by 1.7 per cent., or about the same rate as the USSR as a whole, during the same year.

In Siberia the exodus from the agricultural areas into the cities is extremely large and this is not surprising in view of the poor living conditions in many of the rural areas. Between 1956 and 1960 the net outflow of rural population in west Siberia was 50 per cent. greater than its natural increase and the rural population has been declining faster than in the RSFSR as a whole, in spite of the Government's interest in developing the region's agriculture.[1] Most of the migrants from the land are young people with technical qualifications who can easily get better-paid jobs in the towns.

The overwhelming majority of the population of Siberia is Russian. Siberia is in all respects a truly Russian land. Even in the 'national districts' where the native population is most numerous and concentrated the Russians outnumber any other race and indeed all the others put together, with the sole exception of the Tuvinians, as is shown in the following table:

National Districts of Siberia (1959)

	Total population (in 000s)	Native peoples per cent.	Russians per cent.
Khanty-Mansi National *Okrug*	123.9	14.5	72.5
Yamal-Nenets National *Okrug*	62.3	33.7	44.6
Gorno-Altay Autonomous *Oblast*	157.2	27.2	69.8
Khakass Autonomous *Oblast*	411.0	11.8	76.5
Taymyr (Dolgano-Nenets) National *Okrug*	33.4	9.0	65.3
Evenki National *Okrug*	10.3	33.9	57.9
Tuva Autonomous *Oblast*	171.9	57.9	40.1

The rest of the population is made up of other non-native inhabitants, for example, Ukrainians, Belorussians, &c.

Source: *Itogi Vsesoyuznoy Perepisi Naseleniya 1959 g.*, pp. 202–5.

[1] *Voprosy Ekonomiki*, no. 5 (1962).

The huge little-known marshy tundra expanse of the Khanty-Mansi National *Okrug* covering an area of 215,500 square miles has suddenly swung into the limelight of Soviet publicity and active economic interest with the discovery of large oil and natural gas deposits in the homelands of two primitive native peoples, the Mansi (Voguls) and the Khanty (Ostyaks). Their main occupations have traditionally been hunting, fur trapping, fishing, and reindeer breeding. Now their remote fishing and hunting grounds in the roadless Ob' basin, where few outsiders penetrated, have been invaded by teams of geologists and oil operatives and all the complicated equipment of a modern oil industry.

According to *Pravda* (11 January 1966) the Leninist nationalities policy is exercising a profoundly transforming influence on the life of the natives of the Khanty-Mansi and Yamal-Nenets national *okrugs*. This must be interpreted in a broad, cultural-economic sense for, owing to the Soviet principles of State ownership, i.e. nationalization of all the natural resources of the country, the rich discoveries of oil and gas in their territory will not bring sudden wealth to the Khanty-Mansi or the Nentsy (Samoyed) as it might in a non-Communist underdeveloped country like Kuwait.

In spite of the Soviet agitation about the preservation of national culture, these little peoples seem in danger of losing their cultural identity. Formerly, books were published in the national languages 'for the children of the taiga and the tundra', i.e. the Khanty, the Evenki, the Nentsy, and the others. But that has 'now passed into history' and the 'Education' publishing firm does not wish to publish books for 'the children of the North' because it is unprofitable to produce small editions.[1]

The population of these two above-mentioned national *okrugs* is estimated to increase by 100–150 per cent. by 1970. This increase aan only be achieved through migration and will mean a still further reduction of the strength of the indigenous peoples in the national composition of the area.

Another perhaps more interesting enclave of non-Slav peoples in the Siberian area are the Tuvinians of the Tuva Autonomous Republic, formed in 1961 from the Tuva Autonomous *Oblast*; the latter was created in 1944 when the former Tuva People's Republic

[1] *Uchitel'skaya Gazeta*, 14 April 1966.

set up in 1921 was incorporated in the Soviet Union. The Tuvinians are a Turkic people and speak an archaic Turkic language related to Kirgiz.[1] According to the 1959 census the total population of the country was 171,928, Tuvinians numbering 97,996, or 57.9 per cent., and Russians (the next largest group) 68,924, or 40.1 per cent. Tuva or Uriankhai, adjoining west Mongolia, was part of the Chinese Empire until 1911. Before Outer Mongolia passed into the Soviet orbit, it claimed Tannu Tuva as part of its state. Nothing is now heard of these claims. Strategically and economically this little country was a useful wartime 'picking' for the Soviet Union.

The Yenisey River rises in Tuva whose capital is Kyzyl, situated on the upper part of the river. The Tuva Valley is said to be one of the richest regions of the USSR in the quantity and variety of its mineral resources. Gold, silver, and large deposits of high-quality asbestos are found throughout the country. But Tuva is predominantly a livestock-raising region and has large herds of horses, cows, yaks, camels, and reindeer. Tuva ranks first in the Soviet Union and high in the world in terms of the numbers of livestock *per caput* of the population.[2] According to S. K. Toka, Deputy of the Tuva ASSR to the Supreme Soviet, big local deposits of rare metals and other ores, as well as coking coal, have been discovered in recent years. But they are being slowly developed and retarded by the inadequate development of modern transport and power and the lack of a construction base. He complained about the urgent need to give attention to motor transport on which, he said, Tuva's punctual exports (to the Soviet Union) of grain and livestock depend.[3] The impression given by this speech (one of the rare references to Tuva in Soviet sources recently) was that a poor view was taken locally of the Soviet planning authorities' negligence in not providing a reasonable basis for the development of Tuvinian natural resources. Apparently the great Sayan–Shushenskaya GES complex, which is 'still on the drawing-boards', is intended to

L. Krader, *Peoples of Central Asia*, Research and Studies in Uralic and Altaic Languages, Project nos. 12 and 62 (Indiana University Press, Bloomington, 1963; Mouton & Co., The Hague, 1963), p. 36.

S. P. Suslov, *Physical Geography of Asiatic Russia*. Translated from the Russian by Noah D. Gershevsky (W. H. Freeman, London, 1961), pp. 275–6; Tamurbek Davletshin, 'The Autonomous Republic of Tuva', *Studies on the Soviet Union*, New Series, vol. V, no. 1, p. 97.   [3] *Pravda*, 12 December 1964.

spread its enterprises over a large area 'including Tuva'.[1] This suggests that Tuva may eventually be drawn more closely into the mainstream of Siberian economic development and the development of its resources accordingly speeded up.

The 'flight of labour', both skilled and unskilled, from the rigorous climate and woeful living conditions in Siberia is not a new problem, though it has become more acute in recent years.[2] There is some reason to link the emergence of this problem with the modification of the Soviet labour laws prohibiting 'unauthorized termination of employment' and enforcing severe penalties for infringement of these regulations. For the first time, in 1951, the respective labour decrees were published in the collected Soviet labour laws without mention of the former penalties for offences against these decrees. The law itself was not repealed until 1956.

The Siberian timber industry, which is of great national importance, supplying about 20 per cent. of Soviet timber (and where working conditions are exceptionally harsh) already, in 1953, was affected by the 'flight of labour'. Sixty-three per cent. of the workers and office employees engaged in it had less than three years' service in 1953 and workers in the basic construction industry also had less than three years' service at this time.[3]

At a conference on the labour problems of Siberia and the Far East in 1960, almost every speaker referred to the high labour turnover in the region.[4] In west Siberia it was 37 per cent. above the USSR average, in east Siberia 78 per cent. in 1960. Five years later (15–18 November 1965), a Scientific Conference on Questions of the Formation of Population and Utilization of Labour Resources in areas of the north of the USSR, held in Magadan, again stressed the gravity of the labour problem and reported that not more than 15–20 per cent. of those arriving in the north settled for a more or less prolonged period. Though there was an acute shortage of labour in the factories and construction sites of western Siberia in

---

[1] P. I. Abroskin, Deputy Chairman of the Council of Ministers of the RSFSR, Chairman of the Russian Federation Committee for the Co-ordination of Scientific Research 'Siberia Poses Problems of the Age', *SU*, no. 187 (1965), p. 8.

[2] There is much useful information on this subject in R. Fakiolas's well-documented article 'Problems of Labour Mobility in the USSR', *Soviet Studies*, vol. 14, no. 1 (1962).

[3] Fakiolas, op. cit. p. 20.

[4] Summary of proceedings in *Voprosy Ekonomiki*, no. 12 (1960).

1964, 94,000 less immigrants arrived to work there than the numbers leaving western Siberia, often for other areas of the country where there was no shortage of labour.[1] The chief causes of this state of affairs were stated by many Soviet sources to be the unfavourable living conditions compared to other parts of the USSR (especially the Ukraine and the north Caucasus) and the failure to equate wages to the much higher cost of living in Siberia. Thus it was estimated that the cost of living in western Siberia was 9 per cent. higher than in the Centre and 20 per cent. higher than in the north Caucasus while the level of wages was only 1 per cent. higher than in the Centre and 11 per cent. higher than in the north Caucasus.[2]

The recruitment and retention of a stable labour force to man the industrial plants, the mines, and forests of Siberia has proved one of the most intractable problems confronting the Soviet Government, yet on its solution largely hangs the success of its Siberian development plans and the elimination of a great deal of unproductive expenditure and industrial dislocation. The fact that at the present time there is a lack of labour throughout the USSR complicates the problem. Jobs are easy to find in western and central European Russia so labour has to be attracted by incentives to the eastern regions. The means hitherto used have obviously not succeeded. According to *Kommunist* (no. 3, 1965), 'from 1939–59 there was no growth in population as a result of migration', while it is estimated that the natural increase of the population will only provide a small fraction of the required labour force. Labour direction and moral persuasion were among the chief methods used to swell the stream of migrants. Between 1956 and 1960 700,000 workers including their families were moved to the east under organized recruitment and social *prizyv* (appeal) and agricultural resettlement', while 'more went independently'; yet during this period the general increase in the Siberian population was 'somewhat lower than its natural increase, that is the number leaving Siberia exceeded the number who moved in', and the destination of those leaving was 'mainly to the southern and western areas of the country where there is no labour shortage. . . . 2.5–2.7 times as

A. Gladyshev, 'Obshchestvennyye Fondy Potrebleniya i Migratsiya Naseleniya', *Planovoye Khozyaystvo*, no. 10 (1966).
Geograficheskaya Seriya, Iz. AN SSSR, no. 2 (1966), p. 145.

many went to Central Asia from the Kuzbas as moved from there t(
the Kuzbas.'[1] The State spends vast sums on organized recruitmen
of manpower, in moving it to work sites and in training. Bu
according to a rough estimate the loss to the USSR national economy
mostly in the Urals, Siberia, and the Far East amounts to 2 milliar(
roubles annually, with an average loss of 30 days' working time pe
worker for moving from one place to another.[2]

Grants, free travel, and subsistence allowances are offered by
Orgnabor, the State recruitment organization, to men from 18 to 5
and women from 18 to 50, to attract them to jobs in the mor(
inhospitable areas of the Soviet Union, mainly in the east and north
For these benefits, recruits sign contracts to work at a particula
place for a specific period—usually a year. The recruit receives hal
the grant when he signs up and the balance when he has been on th
job for two or three months. Many recruits are said to show mor(
interest in taking the benefits than in discharging their obligations
They work at the new job only until they have received the ful
grant, then they move on elsewhere and repeat this process. Check
on this conduct, such as the labour book and internal passpor
system, are nullified by leaving these documents behind and getting
new ones. Since local officials and plant and farm managements ar
anxious to secure labour at any cost, they readily accept storie
concerning the loss of labour documents and issue replacements
according to the Soviet Press.[3]

In order to attract and hold manual and white-collar workers fo
the construction sites in Siberia and the Far North, Soviet legislatio:
provides a number of privileges such as monthly bonuses above th
basic wage, extra leave, and benefits in cases of temporary disability
These privileges are awarded:

1. To compensate for the higher prices of food in certain area
(on average 7–9 per cent. higher in many areas including eas
Siberia and 16–18 per cent. higher in the Far North and the Fa
East).

[1] E. Manevich, 'Vseobshchnost' Truda i Problemy Ratsional'nogo Ispol'zovaniya Roboche
Sily v SSSR', Voprosy Ekonomiki, no. 6 (1965).
[2] Z. A. Sayonchkovskaya and V. I. Perevedentsev, Sovremennaya Migratsiya Naseleniy
Krasnoyarskogo Kraya (Novosibirsk, 1964), p. 87. Quoted in 'Ostverlagerung der Sov
jetischen Wirtschaft', N.Z. Zeitung, 15 February 1966; Voprosy Ekonomiki, p. 26.
[3] Komsomolskaya Pravda, 2 February 1965.

dun Rapids (site of the Bratsk Hydro-electric Power Station)

6. The Bratsk Hydro-electric Power Station (4,500,000 kW.) under construc

2. Because of the different working conditions for the same type of work, for example, in the north more calories have to be eaten and more money spent on clothes, fuel, lighting. A family's budget, taking everything into account, will be 60–70 per cent. higher, it is estimated, in the Far North, and 30–40 per cent. higher in areas comparable to the Far North, than in the more temperate areas of European Russia.[1]

Soviet sources are far from clear about how and where these bonuses operate. Officially the following coefficients were applied to basic wages for people working in the regions mentioned in 1963, but it would appear from various references in the Soviet Press that there have been changes in the coefficients since 1960 which I have not been able to identify precisely.

	Coefficients in 1963
Far North	from 1.4 to 2.0
Areas comparable to the Far North	from 1.3 to 1.6
Southern regions of east Siberia and Far East	from 1.2 to 1.3
South-west Siberia	from 1.1 to 1.15
Mountainous regions (over 1,500 m.), and deserts (Central Asia)	up to 1.40

Source: *Ekonomicheskaya Entsiklopediya: Promyshlennost i Stroitel'stvo* (Moscow, 1964), vol. II, pp. 802–3.

Although wages and salaries may be as much as double normal wages in the central regions of Russia, there is very little opportunity of saving because prices are correspondingly high or higher. In fact, these coefficients have failed in their primary aim of establishing stable working forces in Siberia, the Far East, or other inhospitable areas. This is not surprising because of the many defects in both their computation and administration. In the first place, in many cases they do not cover the wide regional differences in the cost of living, especially the much higher cost of food, clothing, and all domestic requirements, between the Centre and Siberia, the Far East, the Far North (and parts of Central Asia).[2] Indeed, it appears that the

[1] *Ekonomicheskaya Entsiklopediya: Promyshlennost i Stroitel'stvo*, vol. II, p. 803; F. Hayenko, 'Living and Working Conditions at the New Construction Sites', *Siberia and the Soviet Far East, Studies on the Soviet Union* (Institute for the Study of the USSR, Munich, 1965), p. 66.

[2] J. Mil'ner and N. Gvozdev, 'Territorialnoye Planirovaniye Urovnya Zhizni Naseleniya na Novuyu Stupen', *Planovoye Khozyaystvo*, no. 4 (April 1966), p. 48.

S

necessary budgetary information on which to base wage differentials more exactly has not been collected by the Soviet statistical organs, i.e. the basic economic criteria have not been worked out so as to establish differentials corresponding to the enormous differences in real wages and standards of living in different parts of the Soviet Union.[1] Moreover, regional coefficients are not yet fully regional in the proper meaning of the word because, for example, the differentials do not apply at all to workers in the food and light industries except in the northern regions. A higher rate is also often paid for the same work done in town rather than in the country. Thus a baker gets 12 per cent. more if he bakes in town rather than in the village.[2]

The basic decree of 10 February 1960 on differentials, which applied to workers and employees in the Far North or places equated to it, has proved so unsatisfactory that two correspondents in *Sovetskaya Yustitsiya* (3 February 1966) urged that it was time to change the law. 'In our view', they wrote, 'payment of allowances should be on a percentage basis according to salary regardless of the length of time spent continuously in the North but of course not exceeding the three hundred roubles maximum monthly. At present cadres lose their lump sum grant if they are sent away for violating labour discipline, for a crime, or for absenteeism in proportion to the time remaining of their contract. In our view, it should also be returned if they leave at their own wish or by mutual consent.'

But the 'flight of labour' problem goes much deeper than 'differentials' however efficiently computed. Differentials will not compensate for lack of housing, hospitals, or schools, or badly organized supplies. The real trouble is the apparent Soviet 'rule' that construction sites come first, dwellings, consumer goods, and general amenities for the workers very much in the second place. As a result, many Soviet workers in the inclement conditions of Siberia or the Far East still have to live as best they can in tents, badly constructed primitive 'barracks', or even mud huts, while engaged in the early stages of major constructions.[3]

Incredible as is the official neglect of the workers' living conditions

[1] Mil'ner and Gvozdev, op. cit.

[2] R. A. Batkayev and V. I. Markov, *Differentsiatsiya Zarabotnoy Platy v Promyshlennosti SSSR* (Moscow, 1964), p. 187.

[3] F. Hayenko, 'Living and Working Conditions at the New Construction Sites', *Studies on the Soviet Union*, vol. V, no. 1 (1965), p. 69.

in Siberia, the repeated complaints that machinery and equipment are manufactured without consideration of operations in harsh climatic conditions is even more extraordinary. Speaking at the Twenty-Third Party Congress, A. A. Kokarev, First Secretary of the Krasnoyarsk *kraykom*, referred to the 'deep anxiety aroused by the fact that even new machines are constructed partly without taking into account their operation in the North'. 'Surely', he said, 'it was due to irresponsibility in the Ministry of Communications that the new electric locomotive VA-80 produced by the Novocherkassk factory would not work at all in the conditions of the North? During two years the Krasnoyarsk depot received 46 such electric locomotives at a cost of 20 million roubles yet they were all immobilized during the winter.'[1] Numerous complaints about this kind of crass carelessness could be quoted from Soviet sources.

The problems involved in creating tolerable labour conditions in Siberia are admittedly vast and complicated but in more conscientious and competent hands more progress might have been made and at least some of the incredible muddles reported in the Soviet Press avoided. A few of the more glaring examples of the seemingly endemic failure of the planning authorities to live up to their responsibilities to the workers must suffice to illustrate what conditions are actually like.

Workers constructing a timber haulage railway through the taiga in the Irkutsk *oblast* described their working conditions as follows:

We work hard but nobody bothers about us; food is bad in the eating house, summer is ending but we have seen no fresh vegetables; there is no meat, sausages, or cheese in the shop. You have to go more than 100 km. for a haircut. There are only cold meals although hot meals could be sent by bus. The mechanized bakery is out of order for the second year and bread is baked in a primitive stove. An old woman travelled here with two boxes of tomatoes to sell but why cannot our own supply organization do as much? Everything is available in Tayshet. We cannot get our boots repaired. Fulfilment of the plan at any price is the aim.[2]

Another correspondent wrote in *Lit. Gazeta* (21 October 1965):

For ten years now I have been visiting the Tyumen' taiga and the prospectors for natural wealth. Much has changed there. They have

---

[1] *Pravda*, 5 April 1966. [2] Ibid. 22 November 1965.

received hundreds of tracked machines capable of going across any kind of country, new types of drilling rigs, seismic stations. The drillings are serviced by helicopters and a powerful river flotilla. The 'black gold' diggers are constantly getting improved technical equipment. But in their living conditions practically nothing has changed. The State has provided compensations, a bonus on wages, and the local heads have countered that by a system of complete indifference for the human being. That appears to me to be the only possible explanation for the living conditions in the settlements of the Tyumen' taiga.

One of them—Uray—has recently been converted into a town. But in what way exactly it is supposed to be a town is difficult to guess. There is not a single well-built street, not a single building with communal amenities. Between the long rows of barrack-like wooden houses there are potholes and bumps over which the cross country vehicle can hardly make its way. Instead of a water supply, a cistern or a tank and pails. Makeshift drainage. But Uray is supposed to be a planned town!... It is the headquarters for a big oil administration, a drilling office, a prospecting expedition, and dozens of other undertakings.

What is preventing the prospectors and oilmen from being properly fed at the present time? Why is it that the markets and shops in Tyumen', Tobol'sk or Ishim and other towns of the *oblast* have been crammed with vegetables all through the summer, whilst in the taiga you cannot get an ordinary potato for love or money? Who is to blame...? At first I imagined the answer was price. Probably the expense of transporting vegetables by plane. On inquiry I found that this was not so.... Therefore the answer once again is the coefficient of indifference, which prevents the supply people from worrying about how the people are fed.

Young builders working on the outskirts of Krasnoyarsk do not fare any better:

The hostels are badly built. The workers have to dry their overalls in their rooms on the radiators. Bed-linen is rarely changed. The boilers are out of order and consequently there is no hot water. In the evenings, the electric light goes off for some reason or other and the hostels are plunged into darkness.... We cannot read, we cannot cook supper on the electric fire, and there are no buffets or canteens in the quarter. In a word, the heads of the building organizations don't trouble themselves over our everyday needs.

Such was the account given by a young bricklayer living in the Komsomol quarter of Krasnoyarsk and printed in *Trud* (26 June 1962).

For some years there has been a constant flow of such unvarnished accounts of living conditions in Siberia in the Soviet Press and journals. Higher authorities have neither contradicted nor protested about these stories and indeed in many cases have confirmed the more incredible details on investigation, and promised to set things right. But the overall impression left by the Soviet sources is that the impact of the measures to improve living conditions is largely negligible owing to the apathy and incompetence of local bureaucrats. A much greater effort is required to make Siberia a place where workers will find tolerably attractive living conditions so that a stable labour force may be established and the flight from the timber camps, mines, and factories halted.

Even at the great new *Zapsib* works near Novokuznetsk (part of the Third Metallurgical Base) the labour problem is acute. According to *Pravda* (10 May 1966), 'more than five thousand building and assembly workers are now engaged in constructing the *Zapsib*, the giant of Siberian metallurgy. But this number is insufficient to fulfil a very strenuous programme. The working front widens daily but the builders are lacking. At the same time there is no concern about stable working cadres. Last year six thousand men left the site, half of whom gave up the job because living accommodation was not offered to them. Moreover, supplies of the necessary equipment and materials for *Zapsib* are unsatisfactory.' The Omsk Deputy to the Supreme Soviet in December 1965[1] also complained of the labour difficulties in the new petro-chemical industry. 'Omsk', he said, 'will require an additional 17,000 skilled workers and more than 2,000 engineering technical workers for the petro-chemical industry alone by 1970. However, the planning organs do not allocate funds for the construction of housing and children's institutions. The establishment of stable cadres is also linked with the problem of the regulation of workers' wages.'

From L. I. Brezhnev's statement at the Twenty-Third Party Congress[2] it would appear that the Soviet leadership is at least aware of the gravity of this problem: 'In order to develop the economy of Siberia and the Far East more rapidly,' said Brezhnev, 'it is necessary to give effect in the new Five Year Plan to a number of social-economic measures which, in particular, will help to stabilize working

[1] *Pravda*, 10 December 1965.   [2] Ibid. 30 March 1966.

cadres there and attract new forces. This is an important Party and Government matter.' At the time of writing, the nature of these measures has not yet been disclosed and it is impossible to gauge how effective they may be. N. S. Khrushchev at the Twenty-Second Party Congress, it may be recalled, also uttered fine words about creating proper living and cultural conditions in developing regions in order to stimulate migration, but at ground level the results, as has been shown, were negligible.

The final word on the Siberian labour problem may well be left to the scientists of the Siberian branch of the USSR Academy of Sciences who met in March 1966 to discuss the directives for the new Five Year Plan with special reference to Siberia.[1] Speaking of industry, a Corresponding Member of the USSR Academy of Sciences noted that in recent years industrial development in Siberia had lagged behind that of the country as a whole. He listed various reasons for this. In Siberia the industrial base lagged badly owing to the shortage of materials and the inadequate production capacities of the construction and assembly organizations. The man-power situation was bad. Many people moved eastward each year, but staff could not be held to their jobs since the living standards in the eastern regions of the Russian Federation were lower than in other areas of the republic, with bad housing and a low level of the social services, 'according to the results of special investigations'.

FUEL AND POWER

Coal

The Kuzbas coal-field of west Siberia contains nearly four times the reserves of the Donbas. Its output not only supplies the metallurgical and other industries built on the basin but provides a major part of the Urals' consumption of coal while considerable quantities go regularly to Kazakhstan and as far west as Gor'kiy and Kuybyshev on the Volga.[2] Output is 17 per cent. of the total coal production of the USSR, only the Donbas is actually producing more coal.

The east Siberian reserves estimated at four times larger than those of the Kuzbas have as yet not been fully physically prospected and

[1] Cf. *Sovetskaya Rossiya* (8 March 1966) for a report of this meeting headed 'Russian Might will Grow with Siberia'. [2] Danilov, op. cit. pp. 75–78.

only certain small scattered sectors of the enormous field stretching from Noril'sk to Chita are exploited for local heating or electric purposes. The main exception is the Irkutsk basin which will be able to supply the Tayshet iron and steel works when completed and which is already sending some of its output to west Siberia and the Far East as well as completely satisfying the requirements of east Siberia.[1] Its output has not been published in recent years but the east Siberian fields as a whole produced 36.5 million tons of coal in 1962 or 7 per cent. of the Soviet total; quite an appreciable amount of this output would, however, be made up of local workings such as the lignite deposits of the Achinsk–Kansk basin and Transbaykalia, the hard coal deposits of the northern part of the region which are only exploited to any great extent at Noril'sk, and the small hard coal deposits at Bukachacha (in Chita *oblast*).

Oil and Natural Gas

Following the recent spectacular discoveries, the claim has been made that the Tyumen' *oblast* of west Siberia could have about one-third of the total Soviet reserves of both oil[2] and natural gas.[3] A more authoritative statement as far as gas is concerned was given in a specialist journal showing that west and east Siberia have about 140 milliard cubic metres confirmed reserves between them, or 7 per cent. of the USSR total, and 360 milliard cubic metres probable reserves, or 11 per cent. of the USSR total.[4] Both the oil and gas reserves of west Siberia are most unfavourably situated in the marshy inaccessible terrain of the lower Ob' basin where there were hitherto no developed industrial areas, the climate is extremely harsh, and all amenities including roads had to be created from scratch. Transport of oil and gas is feasible only by pipeline (the transport of solid fuels from such regions would be virtually impossible) but the development of these deposits is feasible without the development of the whole region. They have come to light at a moment when coal, long the major element in the Soviet fuel balance, is giving place to oil, and it is important for the Soviet Union to find new sources in view of the increasing demand for oil and the declining importance of some of the older reserves. It is intended that oil

---

[1] Ibid. pp. 75–80.   [2] *Izvestiya*, 12 June 1965.
[3] Moscow Home Service, 7 July 1965.   [4] *Gazovaya Promyshlennost'*, no. 8 (1965).

and natural gas, which provided 22.3 per cent. of Soviet fuel in 1954 and 51.5 per cent. in 1964, will supply 70–72 per cent. in 1970.[1] West Siberia will undoubtedly be called upon to make a substantial contribution to the country's oil supplies in the near future.

So little were these latent oil reserves of Siberia suspected to exist (at least by some foreign experts) that it was possible for a well-known analyst writing in 1960 to state: '. . . there is little evidence that the geography of Soviet Russia's oil potential will be changed in the immediate future by present discoveries in this region'.[2] Russian geologists were, however, firmly of another opinion and the position has now radically changed owing to their skill and tenacity. An oil belt stretching along the middle and lower Ob' has been largely confirmed which, it is estimated, contains one-third of the total USSR oil resources.[3] Production started in 1964 with 200,000 tons and nearly a million tons were produced in 1965; this was to rise to 4–5 million tons in 1966 and the Five Year Plan directives aim at an output of 20–25 million tons by 1970.

In spite of the size of the reserves, west Siberian oil production will not be making a major contribution to Soviet supplies until well into the 1970s owing to the great difficulties of extraction and transport. It is estimated that the west Siberian share of the total Soviet production of oil will only reach 7 per cent. in 1970 with the vast bulk of production (about 70 per cent.) still coming from the Volga–Urals oilfields.

Oil has also been found even more recently in commercial quantities on the upper Lena near the old settlement of Markovo in east Siberia. This was an exciting success for Soviet geologists who persisted in their belief that oil existed in this area though the USSR Ministry of Geological Survey and Conservation of Mineral Resources discontinued oil prospecting in east Siberia in 1957 after 25 years of fruitless searches.[4] Markovo oil wells produce Grade A petroleum which may in time form the base of a new east Siberian oil and chemical industry, but they are located at a great depth and are very expensive to drill. Markovo also contains the largest deposit of wet gas in the Soviet Union. Surveying work is now in

[1] Moscow radio, 12 January 1965.

[2] Jordan A. Hodgkins, *Soviet Power: Energy Resources, Production and Potentials* (Prentice-Hall International, London, 1961), p. 120.

[3] *Izvestiya*, 12 June 1965.   [4] Russian radio, 7 December 1965.

progress for the construction of a Markovo–Irkutsk–Cheremkhovo gas pipeline. Development of both Markovo oil and gas is postponed beyond the current Draft Plan period, probably owing to the geographic and climatic difficulties involved and the need for further preliminary work. However, Markovo oil is used to a certain extent locally and is so pure that it is said that 'truck drivers fill their tanks right from the wells and they run as smoothly as they would on gasoline'.[1]

The Tyumen' oilfields in the remote and inhospitable middle Ob' area would require a high standard of well-co-ordinated planning to make the most efficient use of them with the minimum waste and hardship to those operating the oil wells. This, however, is far from being the situation in the Tyumen' oilfields. The planners have done their best with regard to prospecting, drilling, extraction, and export of the product but they appear to have paid extraordinarily little attention to the 50,000 people working there or to auxiliary services. The poor living conditions and the fact that many of the workers had to live in automobile cabins, dug-outs and even tents in freezing temperatures with no amenities has caused an acute labour problem. Teams of students from Moscow, Leningrad, and Kiev are helping to produce the oil[2] and 'uslovniki', 'trusties', i.e. prisoners 'on parole' from prison sentences for all sorts of crime from murder to theft, are being dispatched to the oilfields to replace the 'free' workers who flee from the harsh conditions of the taiga. If they work 'honestly' they receive the pay for the job and may marry or have their family with them. Every year's work in the oil-fields counts as a year's imprisonment and at the expiration of his sentence the 'uslovnik' receives a passport and all rights as a Soviet citizen.[3]

The construction of river ports, roads, and power stations has been apparently grossly wasteful and inefficient. At Surgut, which is the main centre of the Ob' oil basin, seventy-five wharves have been planned over a length of 30 km. to deal with incoming and outgoing freight, and each of these wharves will require its own approach-roads, storage space, and loading and unloading equipment. One large modern port would replace them all. Surgut has

[1] *Soviet Life* (June 1965), p. 40.   [2] *Leninskaya Smena*, 26 January, 1966.
[3] L. Lagunov, 'Neft i Lyudi', *Novyy Mir*, no. 7 (1966).

53 small power stations, with 36 at Nefteugansk and Uray, and another 24 at Megion; all these stations use imported fuel and still cannot meet local needs, while one power line through from Tyumen' would meet immediate needs, and work could start at once on a GRES (regional power station) at Surgut. There is a total lack of co-ordination in transport construction work. Railway lines are being built, but no planning attention has been directed to the roads which are made over marshy land as though they were in the central regions of the country; sand and stone are carried in (at huge expense) over long distances, making the cost about 700,000 roubles (£250,000) per kilometre—and these roads are not surfaced.

In spite of the rapid growth required in accommodation and other building in Surgut, nothing has been done to arrange for the use of local materials; in fact, matters have reached such a ludicrous stage that sand and gravel are being sent from Semipalatinsk, some 3,000 km. distant, although it is known that both are available in Surgut itself.

Perhaps one of the reasons for the delays and absurdities of planning here is that over seventy planning and scientific research institutes are working on the problems of the development of the Tyumen' oil resources but their work is entirely uncoordinated.[1]

Natural gas was first discovered in 1953 at Berezovo in west Siberia, 100–150 km. upstream from the mouth of the Ob'. Since then a natural gas belt stretching from Berezovo eastwards across the vast Ob' estuary through the main Taz field and extending as far as Dudinka within easy reach of Noril'sk has been prospected and is now being developed.[2] This area contains about a third of the total Soviet reserves of natural gas, estimated at some 21×10^9 cubic metres. Production will be about 4 million cubic metres in 1966 or roughly 3 per cent. of the USSR total.[3] The target for 1970 is between 16 and 26 million cubic metres.[4] Under the new Five Year Plan, it is hoped in the distant future to set up large thermal power stations and chemical industries based on these deposits. But it is still too early to speculate about these industrial projects. According to a description in *Oktyabr'* (no. 10, 1966) the extraction

[1] This account of the state of transport and construction in the Tyumen' oilfields is taken verbatim from an article in *Stroitel'skaya Gazeta*, 20 March 1966.
[2] *Pravda*, 19 July 1965.   [3] Moscow radio, 14 July 1966.   [4] *Pravda*, 20 February 1966

of Tyumen' gas is taking place in 'such incredible irrational disorder that the workers are losing faith in the rationality' of what is going on in the Tyumen' *oblast*. Careless drilling in conditions requiring great precision and the failure of the many organizations concerned with the supply situation to agree among themselves are among the many causes of confusion and waste sharply criticized by *Oktyabr'*.

Oil and Gas Pipelines

Up to the end of 1965 the oil from the new Tyumen' deposits was being transported from Surgut entirely by river to Omsk for refining; in the 170 days of the navigational season 850,000 tons were taken by this route and a similar amount was planned to go by river in 1966.[1]

The first oil pipeline was completed in December 1965 over a distance of 436 km. from Shaim to Tyumen',[2] work having been carried out urgently from both ends. Some oil from this pipe is also sent on westwards by rail from Tyumen' to Ryazan', only about 100 miles from Moscow, for refining.[3] Construction of a second oil pipeline from the Tyumen' deposits has been started at Ust'Balyk which will cross 1,300 km. of marsh and forty-eight rivers on its difficult way to the Omsk refineries. This pipeline was to be completed, according to schedule, about 1967.

A pipeline from the western Urals to Irkutsk was completed at the end of 1964 for the supply of oil from the Volga–Urals fields to Siberia and the Far East and it is now planned to extend this pipe to the Soviet Pacific coast (possibly with Japanese co-operation). In the next five or six years the Tyumen' oilfields should be supplying all the needs of Siberia and the Soviet Far East and subsequently large and increasing quantities of this oil will have to be diverted to the central regions (probably using the present pipeline in a reverse direction from Omsk to the Urals or laying a new line from the lower Ob' westwards to European Russia).[4]

A gas pipeline has been laid from Tazovskoye to supply the mining town of Noril'sk, and another is being laid from Berezovo westwards through Igrim to Serov and Nizhniy Tagil in the northern Urals industrial region; this should be completed by the end of 1967.

---

[1] *Gudok*, 11 February 1966.   [2] *Pravda*, 27 February 1966.
[3] *Gudok*, 11 February 1966.   [4] *Pravda*, 27 February 1966.

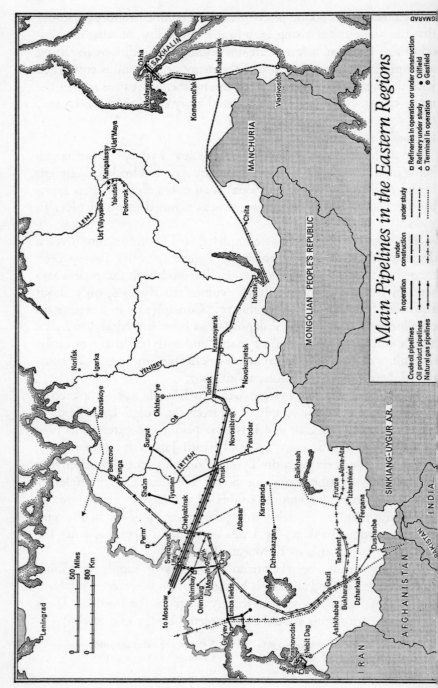

Main Pipelines in the Eastern Regions

It is proposed to link the Berezovo–Nizhniy Tagil line with the Bukhara–Urals pipeline, and continue it to Leningrad and Minsk, but it is not yet known how far the project has been approved or whether it could be completed, as was originally suggested, by 1970.[1] In all, it was reported that some 2,700,000 tons of oil was dispatched from Tyumen' *oblast* for processing in 1966, nearly three times more than in 1965, and the target for 1967 is to exceed 6,000,000 tons.[2]

Oil Refineries

The only oil refinery at present operating in the region is at Omsk, using oil mainly from the Volga–Urals fields. It is still not certain to what extent Tyumen' oil will actually be refined at Omsk or eventually at Angarsk.

A second oil refinery is being constructed at Angarsk in east Siberia which will also be fed by the pipeline coming through from Tuymazy in the western Urals. The whole refinery, together with its plants for lubricants, fuels, and chemicals, stretches for 4 km. along the Angara river bank; oil is already being refined there and it will be operating near capacity with many of its ancillary plants also working by the end of 1966.

Electric Power

Siberia has by far the largest electric power resources and *per caput* output of all the economic regions of the USSR. West Siberia produces 3.4 kWh. and east Siberia 3.9 kWh. against the USSR average of 1.8 kWh.[3] Each of these areas produces more electricity than the whole of Central Asia and Kazakhstan together. This development reflects the Party line on electric power resulting in the spectacular construction of huge power stations in distant regions where the population density is very low but the hydro-electric and thermal potential is high. Soviet sources report some 600 small, integrated electric power stations mostly using local coal or even (inefficiently) natural gas to supply local power requirements, and lately about 150 other small stations have sprung up in the Ob' oilfields. Meanwhile, construction on the massive and expensive Bratsk hydro-electric station (4,700,000 kW.) is still incomplete and running at low power because of the lack of power-consuming

[1] Moscow Home Service, 8 July 1965.   [2] Ibid. 11 December 1966.
[3] *Nar. Khoz. SSSR v 1963 g.*

industries in the area. Khrushchev, speaking at the C.C. Plenum in 1961, wryly commented on this situation at Bratsk. 'We build it quickly', he said, 'but the electric power consumers that the station will require do not yet exist on the spot. The construction of this station will give us the possibility of processing timber here and constructing chemical and aluminium plants. But all that would also have been possible in Uzbekistan and Tadzhikistan. Moreover, the climatic conditions are better there . . . and a cellulose factory based on *kamysh* [a local type of reed] might be built.'[1] The multiple uses of *kamysh* often fired Khrushchev's imagination but it would scarcely be a practical substitute for good Siberian timber in the cellulose–paper industry. These second, rather facile thoughts came ill from Khrushchev whose original enthusiasm was a major factor in initiating the Bratsk scheme in which so much capital and effort had already been sunk.

In fact, the lack of co-ordination between the 'forced pace of construction' planned for the Bratsk GES and the protracted construction of the power-consuming enterprises it was intended to supply, resulted in considerable financial losses. This faulty planning was criticized by *Voprosy Ekonomiki* (no. 8, 1966) on the grounds that 'because there are no large consumers of electric power in the station zone and it is impossible to transmit it to the western regions, the power of Bratsk GES was for a long time only used 25–30 per cent., and after the commissioning of the trunk transmission line to Krasnoyarsk (in 1963) it was only used about 50–60 per cent.'. This situation should, however, be rectified when the Bratsk aluminium plant (which is to consume about 70 per cent. of Bratsk potential) and other industries in the Siberian grid system start working.

The central Siberian power grid stretches from north-east Kazakhstan across industrialized south-west Siberia and into east Siberia while comparatively low-power lines connect it to the Urals system. A super-high-voltage line is projected over 1,500 km. from Siberia to the Urals (and eventually farther west) to cut transmission waste and increase exchange capacity, but its construction has not yet started.

[1] Plenum of the Central Committee of the CPSU, 10–18 January 1961 (Moscow, 1961), p. 531.

At present the central Siberian grid is being supplied by the hydro-electric stations at Novosibirsk and Irkutsk and partly by Bratsk, as well as from thermal stations in east Kazakhstan (Yermak) and in the Kuzbas. The huge Krasnoyarsk hydro-electric station (capacity 5,000,000 kW.) like Bratsk (4,700,000 kW.) is being constructed far behind schedule; and the plan for a series of thermal power stations based on the vast Chulym coalfields to provide 40,000,000 kW. appears to have been postponed for the present. Only the construction of the Nazarovo (2,000,000 kW.) station is going ahead. Construction of the Ekibastuz stations, of which Yermak was the 'pilot', based on local coal, is making good progress and should soon be providing 15,000,000 or 16,000,000 kW. additional power to the central Siberian grid.

Electric Power Generation (1963)

	million kWh.	kWh. per caput
USSR	412,418	1.8
West Siberia	31,800	3.4
East Siberia	30,466	3.9

Source: *Nar. Khoz. RSFSR v 1963 g. Per caput* generation calculated.

The development of electric power in Siberia under the Soviets has indeed made giant strides. Whatever the planned measures for further development of natural resources and industrialization, it appears that there will be no lack of electric power in Siberia to meet eventual requirements and plenty to spare for transmission to European Russia in due course.

THE THIRD METALLURGICAL BASE

In his speech at the Twentieth Party Congress in 1956 Khrushchev spoke of the need to create a Third Metallurgical Base in the east, which was to produce 15–20 million tons of pig-iron within the next two to three Five Year Plans.[1] This would represent an output of about 20–25 million tons of steel, including the scrap

[1] N. S. Khrushchev, Report of the Central Committee of the CPSU to the Twentieth Congress of the CP, Moscow, 14 February 1956, *Soviet News Booklet*, no. 4, (1956), p. 41.

consumption, and 15–20 million tons of rolled finished products. This plan was extremely over-optimistic since only about half of Khrushchev's targets may be achieved by 1970 and three-quarters by 1975 to 1980, representing 15 per cent. in the 1970s rather than the 20–25 per cent. of total Soviet output in the 1960s as was originally planned in 1956.

It was intended in the first place to start work immediately on three new 'green field' sites at Karaganda (where construction had started under the Fifth Five Year Plan), Novokuznetsk, and Tayshet, taking advantage of locally available fuels and ores, and to carry out the complete reconstruction of a small works at Kuybyshev on the Volga. The Kuybyshev scheme has apparently been completely abandoned. The Tayshet works, after a false start on ground levelling, was still carrying out preparatory work ten years later, while construction of the Karaganda *Kazakhstanskaya Magnitka* and the Novokuznetsk *Zapsib* works is creeping along in an almost incredible atmosphere of muddle and inefficiency.

The Five Year Plan directives for 1970 estimate that by that year Karaganda will be completed, and the first stage of the west Siberian works will start production. By way of comparison a recent 'green field' integrated works in Wales, of comparable size to the West Siberian works, of which I learned from an engineer who visited it, may be mentioned. It reached its first-stage production rate of 2 million tons of steel in just over three years, complete with its blast furnaces and rolling mills. Karaganda's *Kazakhstanskaya Magnitka*, of which construction began before 1958, was actually producing 30 per cent. of its pig-iron capacity, 15 per cent. of its steel capacity, and 40 per cent. of its coke and sintering capacity in 1965.[1] Such an imbalance in production throws a heavy strain on the rail transport of the region, but pales in comparison with the *Zapsib* saga. The situation now achieved after about six years is that two giant blast furnaces are making pig-iron based on local coal but owing to the failure to develop any of the ore bases near by, iron ore has to be brought in from the Urals and Kazakhstan. Since there will be no steel-making capacity before 1970, the pig-iron has to go back to the Urals for conversion into steel ingots and slabs and these are returned to the West Siberian works for conversion

[1] *KP*, 22 October 1965.

7. Bratsk workers near the Padun Rapids

8. The construction of the Kara-Kum Canal

into the finished steel sheets. The Karaganda works has not even yet put profitability 'on the agenda' while the price of the finished product at the West Siberian works, according to hints in the Soviet Press, must be something of a world record.[1] The West Siberian works is now cited as a classic example of the fact that industrial enterprises in Siberia usually take two to three times longer than the average to construct.[2] This works, which should produce the cheapest pig-iron in the country, is being constructed more slowly than the Kuznetsk metallurgical combine pre-war. The first blast furnace of that combine was blown in about three years after construction started, but not until seven years after construction began at the West Siberian works, i.e. three years later than planned.

MINERALS AND METALLURGY

One of the possible reasons for the lack of pressure to develop the Third Metallurgical Base has been the renewed prospects for the Urals which already imports large quantities of coal from the Kuzbas and has also been running very low in its own known reserves of iron ore. The opening up of the Kustanay ores at Sokolovka–Sarbay (in north-west Kazakhstan) and modern techniques in opencast mining and ore concentration have meant that full advantage can still be taken of the labour and plant available in the Urals region. Moreover, the ore-fields lie close to the railway leading directly to the Urals; Sokolovka and Sarbay are, in fact, two stations on this line. The output rate of the concentration plants has now reached 26 million tons a year and this is intended to rise in the next few years to 35 million tons.[3] Magnitogorsk, however, is still short of iron ore; the new giant blast furnace blown in last year has been working at half capacity, and there has been considerable criticism of the delays in bringing output at Sokolovka–Sarbay up to its present production level and also of the decisions not to continue its expansion immediately; the rolling mills are short of steel, the steel-makers are short of pig-iron, and if Magnitogorsk is to develop as is at present intended, the trickle of iron ore from the Kursk basin will have to become a flood to keep Magnitogorsk

[1] Ibid.   [2] *Voprosy Ekonomiki*, no. 8 (1966), p. 55.
[3] *Pravda*, 16 February 1966.

T

supplied, though its cost is just double that of the Kazakhstan concentrates, largely because of the expense of transport.[1]

The problem of the iron ore base for the West Siberian works and the future Tayshet works is not yet fully resolved. The only field at present in full operation is the Altay–Sayan basin to the south of Novokuznetsk where about 12 million tons of low-grade, deep-mined ore is produced annually, although with more precise prospecting there seems little doubt that ample reserves could be found for all possible future needs in the region.

Development of an iron ore base has been neglected since the war, first by the concentration on old resources in the rehabilitated European ore mines and more recently by the change of emphasis on economic grounds from deep-mine to opencast ores, resulting in the huge increase in commercial reserves of such areas as Kursk and north-west Kazakhstan, and the consequent neglect of deep-mined ore.

Extravagant claims have been made concerning the iron ore reserves and quality of the Angara–Pit, Lisakovsk, Tagarsk, and Bakchar reserves, and each in turn has been nominated as the future Sokolovka–Sarbay of Siberia. Only the first two, however, are producing small quantities of ore, while the Angara–Ilim basin, with less grandiose pretensions, is being built up first to feed the West Siberian works and later Tayshet; a concentration plant at Zheleznogorsk is now beginning to operate. Nevertheless, *Ekonomicheskaya Gazeta* (25 June 1965) pleaded for the proper development of the Altay–Sayan basin to raise output there to 30 million tons a year in order to save investment and transport costs; the implication was that there would be a famine in ores in the region before any of these fields could be properly developed (in about 15–20 years). Meanwhile, the share of west Siberia in Soviet iron ore output fell from 5.3 per cent. in 1959 to 4.4 per cent. in 1962 and its position among the iron-producing economic regions fell from third to sixth place. East Siberia has been producing a steady 1.5 per cent. of Soviet iron ore output for about ten years.

In the post-war and the Seven Year Plan periods, Siberia's share in the all-Union production of iron ore and in the production of heavy metals fell and in the production of heavy metals it is now

---

[1] *Sovetskaya Rossiya*, 26 February 1966.

lower even than in 1937.[1] According to an analysis in *Voprosy Ekonomiki* (no. 8, 1966) Siberian specialization in rolled metal production is on the wrong lines and does not as a rule correspond to the structure of metal consumption in industry. The Kuznetsk metallurgical combine specializes mainly in production required by the railways and the construction industry. But as Siberian consumption of these lines of production is considerably less than the total output, more than half of the rolled metal produced in western Siberia is exported to the European areas of the USSR, including areas having their own metallurgical base. At the same time, its production of structural metal required for the engineering industry does not satisfy local requirements, and has to be largely imported. This situation produces extremely long and expensive cross-hauls of metal.

The major non-ferrous metals centre in Siberia is at Noril'sk in the Arctic area of Krasnoyarsk kray. Experts estimate that the area will be producing some 60,000 tons of nickel and 120,000 tons of copper annually by 1970. It is also an important source of cobalt production. Noril'sk has a well-developed refining industry in close proximity to these mines, its own coal, and will soon be supplied with local natural gas. Its ore base is being reinforced by the development under the new Draft Plan of the adjacent rich Talnakh copper–nickel mines, where production has already started.[2] It has become an industrial centre within the Arctic Circle. Owing to its geographical position it is ideally situated for testing machines and materials for operation in extreme cold, but judging by the many complaints of unsuitable machinery sent to Siberia, this proving ground has not been properly utilized.

Gold and silver are being mined in four main areas—north of the Angara River, on the Lena–Vitim Rivers near Bodaybo, along the Shilka in the Chita *oblast* and near Abakan, in the Khakass Autonomous *Oblast*.

East Siberia has other important mineral deposits. It is responsible for an important part of Soviet mica production—the most productive deposit in the USSR is at Mama, near Bodaybo, which produces phlogopite mica, and the third most productive mine is at Slyudyanka in the Irkutsk *oblast*. Tin is found in

---

[1] *Voprosy Ekonomiki*, no. 8 (1966), p. 57.　　　　[2] *Ekon. Rayony*, pp. 283–4.

Transbaykalia, with two important deposits in the south of this area at Khokhotuy and Khapcheranga.

Zinc is an important element of the Zmeinogorsk poly-metallic ores. Magnesium and titanium are produced near the mouth of the Angara River and there are recent Soviet reports of a rich find of lead and zinc in the same place.[1] Wolfram is mined south of Irkutsk on the Mongolian border and in the Chita *oblast*. The leading branch of industrial production in this area is mining, yet output, which grew fast in the ten years after the war (probably due to forced labour), has been stagnant since 1956; the production of tin, lead, zinc, and molybdenum has fallen, and several wolfram mines have been closed down. This is not due to exhaustion of reserves or to reduced national demand, but simply to managerial inefficiency all the way up to Gosplan and the former East Siberian Economic Council.[2]

The announcement in the Draft Plan for 1966–70 that a start is to be made in the development of the large Udokan copper deposits must have surprised many (save professional geologists) so little had been previously heard of these deposits. They lie in the inaccessible mountain wilderness of north-east Siberia watered by the River Chara, an area relatively little studied apparently even in the Soviet Union, and some 500 km. north of the main Trans-Siberian railway. The Japanese, who have an ever-increasing demand for copper and virtually no domestic supplies, are reported to have been discussing the possibility of participating in the exploitation of copper reserves 'near Chita' with the Russians, as part of the proposed economic co-operation between the two countries, since at least 1965. The latest information on the progress of this project, at the time of writing, was supplied in a report from Tokyo by Reuter (East–West Trade News, 8 December 1966). Accordingly, the Japanese copper smelters are planning to form a special committee to promote the development of the Udokan copper-mine in co-operation with the Soviet authorities. The Japan Mining Industry Association has stated that this joint development project was proposed by the Soviet side to an official Japanese economic mission which visited the Soviet Union in September 1966, and that it will be carried out under a production-sharing

[1] Moscow Home Service, 21 January 1966.   [2] Russian radio, 20 October 1965.

formula by which the Japanese side will receive Siberian copper equivalent to the sum that Japan will invest in the development project. The copper-mine is alleged to have a large copper belt measuring 7 kilometres long, 5 kilometres wide, and 200 metres thick. The Japanese Mining Association have further stated that it was expected that a specific plan for the development of the mine would be worked out early in 1967 but clearly much remains to be agreed and discussed between Moscow and Tokyo before this scheme can be put into operation.[1]

The main mineral shortage for years in Siberia was bauxite, the most economical and convenient alumina-bearing ore for aluminium production. The advantage of Siberia's abundant supplies of electricity for the production of aluminium would have been largely undermined if it had been necessary to import all its alumina (as hitherto) and the almost equally expensive practice had continued of converting locally available nephelines from Krasnoyarsk into alumina which had to be supplemented by alumina from the Urals and Kazakhstan.[2] The recent discovery of large deposits of bauxite at Ibdzhibdek in east Siberia, after years of prospecting, will guarantee supplies for the huge Bratsk and Krasnoyarsk aluminium plants working at full capacity and should thus entirely change the position in Siberia of this important industry.[3]

There continues to be a shortage of manganese but according to the USSR Minister of Geology there are hopes that large manganese deposits may be located in the area of Lake Baykal.[4]

Iron and steel are produced at Novokuznetsk (where output is largely devoted to the constructional needs of the new *Zapsib* works[5]) with small works at Novosibirsk, Gur'yev, Krasnoyarsk (producing special steels), and Petrovsk-Zabaykal'skiy. At some time in the future the proposed Tayshet works will contribute metal to the Siberian output, but it is impossible to forecast at the time of writing when that will be.

Aluminium is produced at Novokuznetsk using alumina from the Urals; the huge plant at Shelekhovo, near Irkutsk, started its first stage of production in 1964. At Krasnoyarsk aluminium works three

---

[1] *Comtel Reuter*, 14 March 1966.   [2] *Ekon. Rayony*, pp. 283–4.
[3] *Ogonëk*, no. 34 (1966), p. 2.   [4] Moscow Home Service, 18 March 1966.
[5] See also ch. V, 'The Third Metallurgical Base', pp. 267–9.

shops are now in operation and two more are under construction. Bratsk is planned to be the largest aluminium undertaking in the Soviet Union but there have been many difficulties and delays in the construction of the plant. No certain date can yet be fixed for its coming into operation although by present accounts it should be fully running by 1970.[1] According to Soviet sources, it will use 70 per cent. of the output of the Bratsk hydro-electric power station.

Novosibirsk has one of the two Soviet tin refineries, the other is at Ryazan' in European Russia. It refines the output from the southern areas of the Soviet Far Eastern regions while Novosibirsk treats the output of Yakutia and Siberia itself. Zinc is refined at a large works at Belovo in the Kemerovo *oblast* from local ores.

CHEMICAL INDUSTRIES

The unlimited resources of timber and coal in Siberia could provide all the raw materials required for major chemical industries but there are considerable transport, labour, and marketing problems in the way of the development of the wood-chemical industries. These difficulties do not arise to any extent in the case of the coke-chemical industry. As it is a by-product of the coke industry and depends on the existence of near-by coke-consuming industries like the metallurgical industry, it is largely concentrated in Siberia in the Kuzbas where it has been developed in several plants around Kemerovo. But more than half the Union output of this industry is still produced in the Ukraine, though there has been a gradual shift eastwards to the Urals, Siberia, and the Far East since the war. Apart from the Kuzbas, there are coke-chemical works in Irkutsk, Noril'sk (small), and an electrode works is now under construction at Novosibirsk using anthracites of Listvyanskiy deposits of the Gorlovka basin. This is one of the two new plants provided for by the current plan so as to ensure the supply of electrode thermo-anthracite to the Soviet economy.[2]

There were serious shortcomings in the work of this industry during the Seven Year Plan period, and several Siberian works were

---

[1] *Trud*, 26 July 1966, reported that the first corpus of this Bratsk plant had started operations.
[2] *Koks i Khimiya*, no. 5 (1966).

listed among the defaulters. Thus the West Siberian Metallurgical Works was criticized for failing to put new sets of coke batteries and the tar-distilling shop into operation. Coke production is to be greatly expanded under the 1966–70 Plan and new coke batteries constructed to obtain higher capacities.

The oldest and at present the main chemical centre in Siberia is at Kemerovo (in the Kuzbas); it produces nitrogen fertilizers, the old phenol 'bakelite'-type resins, paints, and more recently polyurethane ('foam-plastic'), and possibly now some of the new ion-exchange resins, on the basis of coke from the Kuznetsk basin.

A Siberian synthetic rubber plant (of which there are only twelve in the USSR), is situated at Omsk.

The wood-chemical industries, for which there is such a huge raw material base in the Siberian forests, were long neglected, but large-scale developments were initiated by the Seven Year Plan and are to be pushed forward by the current Plan. Bratsk and Krasnoyarsk are two main centres of these industries with smaller forest industrial complexes now being organized in other Siberian towns, among which are Chunsk (Irkutsk *oblast*), Yeniseysk, Asino (Tomsk *oblast*). A big timber combine to produce cellulose and paper and operating Swedish and Finnish machinery is under construction at Bratsk. Production of cellulose started in 1965, and an eventual output of one million tons is planned.[1] Tyre cord is also to be made at Bratsk.

The large wood-chemical combine at Krasnoyarsk has been operating some of its many units (including the first Siberian cellulose and paper plant) since the early '60s. It contains a cellulose–paper combine with a hydrolysis paper plant, a tyre plant, an artificial fibre plant, a synthetic rubber plant, and a wood-resin extraction unit. Newsprint and school exercise books are made in the paper-making unit.

The poor quality and scarcity of all paper and the complete lack of many of the finer varieties in the Soviet Union is surprising in a country with such excellent raw material for paper making, but is the direct result of the neglect of the paper industry under the Tsarist and Soviet governments until the most recent times. The *per caput* consumption of paper in the Soviet Union is one of the

---

[1] Moscow radio in Swedish, 17 December 1966.

lowest among the industrialized countries (small and great) in the world.

It is likely that in future the oil and natural gas reserves of the Far North will be used as the basis for a chemical industry there, as *Pravda* (24 June 1964) proposed. This would be practicable, since a chemical plant can operate almost without labour, many successive processes can be carried out in the one plant, and the final products are usually comparatively cheap to transport (for example, fertilizers, synthetic fibres). If the estimated very large output of oil and natural gas in Siberia is to be economically exploited, the only alternative to a big network of long-distance pipelines is the establishment of suitable industries, such as the chemical industry, to consume some of it locally.

The Siberian synthetic rubber plant situated at Omsk, nucleus of an entirely new industry, should be using butane and propylene from the petro-chemical works attached to the Omsk refinery. There is no equipment, however, for processing them and the materials have to come from the Tatar ASSR and even from Azerbaydzhan and are woefully insufficient to operate the factory at full capacity.[1] Omsk also produces synthetic alcohol and carbon black, and a sulphuric acid plant is being installed at the oil refinery. Barnaul has a chemical fibre works, and a synthetic rubber factory is under construction.

Of the chief branches of Siberian industry the chemical industry has developed most rapidly in recent years, but Soviet sources allege that there have been serious errors in planning its development.[2] These are chiefly the excessively long periods taken in the construction of the most important chemical plants, the disproportion between the established processing capacities and the local raw material base and between basic and supply production, and the disparity between the specialization of the chemical industry and the local demand for its production. As a result of the inadequate utilization of local raw materials, common salt, sulphuric acid, liquid chlorine, industrial alcohol, and other raw materials and semi-finished goods have to be imported while a large quantity of the chemical products produced have to be exported to other regions because of restricted local demand.

---

[1] *Ekon. G.*, 17 April 1966, p. 9.   [2] *Voprosy Ekonomiki*, no. 8 (1966), p. 58.

ENGINEERING INDUSTRY

The engineering industry had a tremendous boost in the Kuzbas region during the war, and west Siberia now produces a wide range of products. These include mining and power equipment, tractors, agricultural machinery, electrical and radio equipment; in addition, machine tools and instruments are produced at Novosibirsk and Tomsk, and the production of calculators at Tomsk and oxygen equipment at Omsk is starting. Apart from these last two items, however, there has been little engineering development since the war. Construction of a motor vehicle assembly plant was started in Chita in 1964, but was abandoned soon after when investment funds were cut off by the Economic Council. This may well be restarted if the new Five Year Plan is to have any hope of achieving its object of quadrupling car production in 1970.

The engineering and metal-working industries have the biggest share of Siberia's all-Union industrial specialization. Yet as in the chemical industry, the structure of the specialization of these industries is criticized for not fully satisfying the real requirements of the region. In particular, the productive links between engineering and metallurgy and the chemical and timber industries are alleged to be still poorly developed.[1] An official balance of production and consumption of engineering output in western Siberia showed that it was mainly exported to the European regions of the USSR and only to a small extent eastwards. Thus in 1962, only 18.6 per cent. of the engineering and metal-working output of western Siberia was used locally, 16.6 per cent. was supplied to Kazakhstan, eastern Siberia, and the Far East, and the rest to European Russian and abroad. At the same time, western Siberia produced only 27 per cent. of its own requirements of engineering and metal-working products and eastern Siberia only 25 per cent.

The anomaly in the Siberian engineering situation is that a considerable quantity of different types of machines and equipment for which there is a relatively small demand is produced while Siberian output for its own requirements of such essential items as big steam turbines and power boilers is comparatively small and tower cranes, excavators and bulldozers, and wheeled tractors are

[1] *Voprosy Ekonomiki*, pp. 59–60. All the information given here on the Siberian engineering industry is taken from this article.

not produced at all. The very important Siberian power industry is badly served by the domestic engineering industry. For example, the Siberian share in the all-Union production of electric power in 1963 was 15.1 per cent., but the gross output of the electrical engineering industry was only 7.2 per cent. Machines and equipment for the production, transmission, distribution, and consumption of electric power are mainly imported from European Russia. The need to increase local production of many machines so as to reduce long transport hauls and costs is reinforced by the fact that 'as a rule the same machinery is supplied to the Siberian mining and timber industries' as to areas with entirely different natural conditions. The results of this bureaucratic stupidity are very discouraging to the workers concerned and injurious to the economy.

TIMBER INDUSTRY

Siberia, and especially eastern Siberia, has exceptionally rich and promising timber reserves (as has been described earlier in this work). In all the areas of Siberia the forest cover reaches 35–50 per cent.[1] It is predominantly taiga with coniferous forests of spruce, larch, fir, and pine. The quality of Siberian timber is superior for mechanical and chemical processing to that in the forests of European Russia and the costs of its procurement less.[2] These favourable conditions for the development of the Siberian timber industry have not been properly exploited in the view of some Soviet economists. In the first place, wood is mainly exported as lumber, and timber exports have risen slowly on the whole and are still well below those of the chief producing areas of European Russia.[3] Thus in 1963, 56 per cent. of the wood carried by rail from eastern Siberia was unprocessed sawn logs though the cost of hauling logs is estimated to be about one and a half times more than the procurement costs. Transport of this lumber also requires more rail trucks than cellulose, paper, cardboard, plywood, or other processed timber. In spite of the volume of timber procurement in Siberia, relatively little is processed there. Eastern Siberia having supplied 14.2 per cent. of the industrial timber of all-Union significance in 1962 only

---

[1] Danilov, op. cit. p. 293.
[2] *Voprosy Ekonomiki*, op. cit. pp. 57–58.   [3] *Nar. Khoz. SSSR v 1965 g.*, pp. 208–9.

produced 2.6 per cent. of the cellulose, 3 per cent. of the paper, 2 per cent. of the fibre board, 0.7 per cent. of the cardboard, and 2.2 per cent. of the furniture. It is a sorry reflection on this state of affairs in the great forests of Siberia that the little Mary ASSR produces more of these manufactured products than Siberia.[1]

AGRICULTURE

Agriculture has developed only along the southern belt of Siberia, mainly with grain and tillage crop farming in west Siberia and live-stock in east Siberia.

The southern half of the west Siberian plain has a surface layer of good, black earth; but the northern belt is marshy, and the southern belt too dry. Nevertheless, in the stretch along the railway in the Altay kray a highly fertile belt is producing 10 per cent. of total Soviet grain, including 15 per cent. of the wheat; and because of the good soil, high mechanization, and low labour force, the labour productivity is 50 per cent. above the USSR average.[2] Of its considerable grain exports, 55 per cent. goes to east Siberia and the Far East, and 25 per cent. to the Urals.[3]

As in the 'Virgin Lands' of Kazakhstan, the 1954 decision to sow to crops large areas of western Siberia that were uncultivated before, and not properly prepared for cultivation, led to an immediate rise in output in the first two years and to subsequent disasters. Although no figures of output are published, west Siberia, the 'granary'[4] of the USSR, sold the following quantities of grain to the State between 1949 and 1963:

1949–53 (average)	1954–8 (average)	1960	1962	1963
		(in 000 tons)		
2,198	6,727	6,497	2,935	603

Source: *Nar. Khoz. RSFSR v 1963 g.*, p. 269.

Livestock thrives in west Siberia, and production had been in-creasing until the set-back in 1963–4 caused by the poor grain

[1] *Voprosy Ekonomiki*, p. 58.   [2] *SU*, no. 187 (1965).
[3] Danilov, op. cit. p. 156.
[4] 'Thousands of years ago the world's greatest granaries were the Tigris and Euphrates valleys and the "Minusinsky" ', *SU*, no. 187 (1965).

harvest. Normally, it would be adequate to provide for Siberia's needs if the transportation and refrigeration problems involved in supplying such a large area were solved.

East Siberia, much of which lies within the permafrost area, is far less favourably situated for the development of agriculture than the southern belt of western Siberia. But there has been progress in extending the arable area in recent years (especially in the Chita *oblast*) and enlarging the livestock herds. The sown area is mainly under grain and fodder crops and some 4.5–5 million tons of grain are annually produced, but yields are low compared to Soviet average yields, and the costs of all agricultural products (grain, eggs, milk, and wool) very high. The extensive pastures of Transbaykalia and the Chita *oblast* in particular have long been among the chief cattle-breeding districts of the Soviet Union, and east Siberia accounted for about 6 per cent. of Soviet sheep in 1965.[1] The harsh climate, labour shortage, soil erosion, and transport are all negative factors, hindering more rapid development of the latent agricultural potential of eastern Siberia.

Fur trapping, one of the main reasons for the early Russian penetration into north-east Siberia, is still an important asset of this region and provides the main livelihood of many of the smaller peoples. Owing to the numerical decline of these peoples and the growth of the towns, it is unlikely that fur production is rising, though improvements in hunting methods and a certain amount of re-stocking in areas where some of the fur-bearing animals had been completely exterminated are reported; no figures are, however, published for fur production either in the USSR or in particular areas (but furs appear among the most important items of Soviet exports).[2]

A speaker at the meeting of the Supreme Soviet in December 1965[3] had something to say about the difficulties in the remoter fur-bearing regions. They were trying, he said, to adopt modern economic and technical methods in fur trapping and treatment but there was a very rapid turnover of specialists and workers, most of whom had had very little training. The speaker explained the

[1] *Nar. Khoz. SSSR v 1964, 1965 g.*   [2] *Nar. Khoz. SSSR v 1964 g.*, p. 661.
[3] V. N. Uvachan, representative of the *Evenki National Okrug, Pravda* (10 December 1965).

turnover 'by the weakening of "material stimuli" which have great importance in recruitment for the North and by the irrational system of wages'. He suggested that the industry should be in the hands of a single organization so as to avoid the complications of control from several different bodies. His main point, however, was that prices fixed for furs should be fixed according to the real cost of production in difficult natural circumstances. It would seem that the native fur trappers who were long exploited by the Tsarist régime are still not getting a genuinely fair deal from the Government.

Professional fur hunters in the Tomsk *oblast* dropped from 3,600 in 1958 to 1,770 in 1965 according to *Sovetskaya Torgovlya* (24 March 1966). The numbers fell sharply after the change over to the system of *koopzverpromkhoz* (co-operative wild animal industrial farming); in seven years the numbers were almost halved as the 'central fur co-operative' would not guarantee a minimum wage to the trappers. Conditions, however, vary greatly regionally.

TRANSPORT

The old Trans-Siberian railway, now sometimes referred to as the 'Central Siberian line', received an important adjunct in the new 'South Siberian line' which has branches running far south through Kazakhstan and Central Asia.[1] The Trans-Siberian railway is very heavily laden, carrying 9 per cent. of the total USSR railway freight, and its lines have the highest utilization rate in the Soviet Union. Of its freight, 34 per cent. is dispatched outside the area and a further 15 per cent. is in transit. There is only 15 per cent. inward traffic, the remaining 37 per cent. being to areas within Siberia itself. The main exports are coal and coke from the Kuzbas, oil products from Omsk, ferrous metals, timber, and grain; and its imports, oil from the Urals and the Volga, ores from Kazakhstan and the Urals, metals, and building materials. The stretch between Omsk and Novosibirsk, it is claimed, is the busiest freight line in the world.[2] The low level of mechanization of unloading operations at the railway stations of the Trans-Siberian main line was criticized by one of the deputies to the Supreme Soviet in December 1965.[3]

[1] For details of the South Siberian line see ch. IV, 'Transport', p. 231.
[2] Danilov, op. cit. p. 230.   [3] *Pravda*, 10 December 1965.

Some new lines of considerable local importance were built during the immediate post-war and Seven Year Plan period. In the first place there is the link between the Trans-Siberian railway and the Lena River communications system formed by the 700 km. long Lena line running from Tayshet via Bratsk to Ust'Kut on the Lena. Work on this Tayshet–Ust'Kut railway started in 1938 (as a major concentration camp enterprise); it was discontinued during the war but resumed in 1945, and the line went into operation between 1952 and 1954. The railroad and the Lena River are paralleled by airlines and sections of motor highways. These communications may be regarded as the beginning of a major combined transport route, Tayshet–Ust'-Kut–Kirensk–Vitim–Yakutsk, which would link the Yakut ASSR and the north-eastern part of the Irkutsk *oblast* with the rest of the country.[1] The Tayshet–Ust'-Kut railway has played a vital role in the development of the natural resources of the area through which it passes, notably the rich Angara–Ilim Korshunovo iron ore deposits and the forestry industry of the north-western Baykal region. The forestry industry of the middle Angara Valley with its saw mills, wood hydrolysis, and other developments could not have been expanded as it has been without this railway; the shipments of lumber along the former primitive route being much more expensive and lengthy.[2] Farther to the east, the Bodaybo gold-mines are also linked with the Lena railway through the Vitim–Lena waterway port of Osetrovo.

After eight years of very difficult construction work through mountainous country, the railway connecting Abakan, the capital of the Khakass Autonomous *Oblast*, with Tayshet on the Trans-Siberian railway was open to traffic in December 1965. It runs through an area of eastern Siberia otherwise difficult of access but, owing to the lack of industrial development, may be an expensive luxury for some years. A. A. Kokarev, First Secretary of the Krasnoyarsk kray Party Committee, criticized the Gosplan SSSR and Gosplan RSFSR at the Twenty-Third Party Congress[3] for not co-ordinating transport and economic development plans before constructing this line. He pointed out that new railways in the

[1] A. A. Vorob'yev, 'Problems in the Location of Transportation in the Southern Part of Eastern Siberia', *Soviet Geography* (May 1964), p. 11.

[2] *Voprosy Geografii*, no. 61 (1963).   [3] *Pravda*, 5 April 1966.

Krasnoyarsk kray, like the Abakan–Tayshet and the Achinsk–
Abalakovo lines, required large capital investments, but as their
transport capacity was not being adequately used, the funds invested
in their construction were frozen, at least for the time being. The
planning organs, according to Kokarev, did not heed 'our proposals
for the speedy development of the regions traversed by these lines
or consider the establishment of sufficiently large industrial networks
in the areas served by them'.

A short new line of considerable industrial importance now connects the Noril'sk metallurgical combine with the Talnakh ore
deposit and mining town (twenty miles north of Noril'sk).[1] The
line was commissioned in April 1966.[2]

The public announcement in January 1966[3] that it had been
decided to construct a north Siberian line (*Sevsib*) presages a
constructional effort that may be compared in magnitude to that
of the original Trans-Siberian railway in view of the distances
involved and the difficulties of the terrain crossed by the projected
railway. Construction was apparently to start some time in 1966
according to the scanty information now available, while a great
deal of preliminary surveying work still remains to be done on
various sectors. The *Sevsib* will branch off from the main Trans-
Siberian railway at Tyumen' and will run north-east to Tobol'sk
on the Ishim River reaching Surgut on the Ob' (the centre of the new
west Siberian oilfields) by 1970. From there it will go east to the
confluence of the Angara and Yenisey rivers, circling the northern
end of Lake Baykal and continuing roughly parallel to the Trans-
Siberian railway to its probable terminus at Komsomol'sk, on the
northern spur of the Trans-Siberian line which links it to the Tartary
Strait at Sovetskaya Gavan'. It is now estimated that it may take
some fifteen to twenty years to complete this great 4,350 mile long
railway. The whole line, from the Urals to the Pacific, will pass
through regions where there are vast gas, oil, coal, and ore deposits
which have not yet been opened up, and cross rivers with considerable electric power potential.[4] This is indeed *terra incognita* little
penetrated either by the old pioneers or latter-day travellers,

---

[1] *SU* (Moscow), no. 200 (1966), p. 12.   [2] Moscow Home Service, 2 April 1966.
[3] *Izvestiya*, 28 January 1966.
[4] *Novosti Information Service Bulletin*, no. 3623, (7 March 1966).

and it is seldom mentioned in Soviet literature. It is most difficult terrain for the railway builders who, like their Trans-Siberian forefathers, may suffer heavy casualties in constructing this line.

The decision to open up the Udokan copper-mines in an area totally lacking in rail, road, or air transport has in turn prompted the decision to build a new railway from either Mogocha or Chichatka on the Transbaykalian sector of the Trans-Siberian railway to connect with the mines. Aerial reconnaissance is now being carried out to plot an area of some 4,500 km.[2] beyond the Kalar and Olekma watershed and the Yablonov and Udokan ranges to determine the future trace of the line. It will have to cross high mountains and many turbulent rivers on its way to the Chara Valley where the future Udokan Mining and Concentration Combine will be located. According to preliminary estimates the line will be about 550 km. long.[1]

Further railway construction plans have been discussed for this area which contains many important natural resources which are extremely difficult to develop without proper transport. In order to promote the development of the Markovo oil deposits in the valley of the Lena below Ust'-Kut and the aluminium ores in the Vitim River basin as well as the prospect of establishing a large wood-working complex at the mouth of the Kirenga River, the need has increased for the construction of an alternative northern line to the Lena–Chara railway through Kirensk and Bodaybo.[2] It is believed that the construction of a railway between Ust'-Kut and Kirensk parallel to the navigable Lena River and to local airlines would create favourable conditions for the formation of a Lena–Vitim territorial-production complex similar to the transport situation of the Irkutsk–Cheremkhovo complex. No doubt such ambitious plans would entirely change the face of these primitive regions but their realization would also be extremely costly and certainly far beyond the bounds of possibility in the next few years.

River transport is the most important means of transport in the north of west Siberia and in almost the whole of east Siberia where, apart from the Trans-Siberian in the south, no railways or

[1] *Gudok*, 24 April 1966.
[2] A. A. Vorob'yev, 'Problems in the Location of Transportation in the Southern Part of Eastern Siberia', *Soviet Geography* (May 1964), p. 10.

trunk-roads exist. Steamships can travel almost from the Chinese or Mongolian frontier the whole length of Siberia to the Arctic Ocean down the Ob'–Irtysh, Yenisey, and Lena river basins, using many of their tributaries such as the Nizhnyaya Tunguska, the Pod-kamennaya Tunguska, and the Angara, which are equally navigable and provide an admirable network of lateral transport.

The main drawback to river transport in Siberia is its seasonal character. The Ob' is navigable for only 170 days of the year, and rivers farther east for an even shorter period.[1] Aircraft can only carry passengers and light and valuable loads, and no roads or railways pass through most of the region, so that in such areas as the new oil- and gas-fields in the northern half of west Siberia bulk freight deliveries have to be made in less than half a year to last throughout the whole year. This means underemployment of the river fleet and the tying-up of capital goods that may not be required for months, plus the additional expenses incurred in storage.

The transport problem in the lower Ob' basin is particularly acute at the present time because of the discoveries of oil and gas and the intensive efforts to bring them into production. In the natural gas-fields of the far north the ground is frozen for most of the year. A combination of helicopters and caterpillar tractors can carry out the light work while heavy material is brought up the Ob', the Taz, and the Yenisey from the Arctic Ocean ports in the short navigational season.

In the oil-fields farther south, however, although all the wells are being drilled along the Ob' and as near the river as possible, the marshiness of the ground makes it necessary to carry out all the transport work as well as pipe laying in the seven winter months when the ground is frozen (which incidentally greatly adds to the hardships of the workers on this job). Navigation up the Ob', however, is feasible for about six months of the year and in this period the heavy equipment is brought in (a port is being constructed at Surgut) and the oil sent out (850,000 tons in 1965 and the same amount planned for 1966). The bottleneck lies in the shortage of small river craft.[2]

The expansion of air transport has been vital to the development of all areas of Siberia not directly served by the railways or the

[1] *Gudok*, 1 February 1965.   [2] *Pravda*, 26 September 1965.

U

rivers. It has also been used to a large extent for geographical surveys and preliminary prospecting of mineral resources. It has the advantage over railway construction in the wilds of only needing relatively easily constructed airstrips for landing.

The southern half of Siberia is well served with airports and services; Krasnoyarsk has a non-stop service to Moscow and is the main airport for communications with Yakutia. Irkutsk is the main link with the Far East (Khabarovsk, Sakhalin, Kamchatka) to east and west Siberia, to the Urals, and to Leningrad in the west. Novosibirsk is the main air link with Alma-Ata and Central Asia, while from Omsk regular services go to various centres in Kazakhstan, the southern Urals, Leningrad, and Moscow.[1]

Aircraft have also been requisitioned for the supplies urgently required for the rapid development of the gas-fields of the lower Ob' basin; it appears that large numbers of helicopters delivered passengers, drilling equipment, and stores from the airports of Vorkuta and Noril'sk or from the Ob' estuary ports, the only practicable method of delivery to the gas-fields.

CAPITAL INVESTMENT AND GROSS INDUSTRIAL OUTPUT

A great boost was given to industry in Siberia by the war emergencies and the evacuation of plant from European Russia during the war. Then after the war, in the late '40s, an intensive effort was made by the Soviet Government to re-establish industry in the ravaged European areas with the result that much of the plant and equipment evacuated east during the war was sent back west, and investment funds were too scarce to keep industry going, let alone for expansion.

The situation was changed by the Fifth Five Year Plan (1951–5) under which Siberia's share of the all-Union investment funds began to increase substantially and continued to do so until the Sixth Five Year Plan was abandoned in 1958–9. According to official Soviet sources the rate of growth of capital investment in Siberia during this period was considerably faster than the USSR average rate of growth. Between 1958 and 1964 (during the Seven Year Plan period), however, the rate of growth of capital investment

[1] Danilov, op. cit. p. 47.

in both east and west Siberia, but particularly in west Siberia, slowed down and was slightly below the all-Union average rate of growth. Nevertheless, the proportion of Siberia in the capital investments in the Soviet economy as whole remained virtually unchanged during this period, amounting to 11.6 per cent. in 1956–9 and 11.4 per cent. in 1960–4.[1]

It appears from a Soviet source that the volume of capital investment in Siberia in 1960–4 was actually less than that allotted by the Seven Year Plan. The largest divergences from the control figures for Siberia were alleged to be in the chemical industry, ferrous and non-ferrous metallurgy, wood-working, cellulose-paper, and coal industries which are in fact important branches of present and future Siberian industrial specialization.[2]

These restrictions on the volume of capital construction in Siberia are attributed to the miscalculations of the planning authorities in regard to the costs of construction. They underestimated not only the enormous raw material resources of Siberia but also the low costs of their extraction and processing, especially the economies realized on fuel and power which have great significance in Siberian conditions. This is notably so in some branches of the iron and steel, non-ferrous, and chemical industries, where expenditure on fuel and power may absorb up to 35–60 per cent. of current expenditure on production. As capital investments on fuel and power in these industries make up more than half of their capital investments in actual production, economies in fuel and power are an essential factor in reducing production costs. Though there may be an element of local patriotism in this criticism from the Novosibirsk Academy, the planning authorities do not seem to have given due weight to Siberian conditions and potential in their investment policy.

The considerable rise in investment from 1950 to 1958 did not lead to a comparable increase in 'gross' industrial output; the growth-rate was below the USSR average for the first eight years, and since then has scarcely exceeded it. In a discussion on the future of Siberia and the directives of the new Draft Plan (1966–70), A. G. Agan-begyan of the Academy stated that industrial development in

[1] *Nar. Khoz. SSSR, RSFSR* for relevant years. *Voprosy Ekonomiki*, p. 53.

[2] *Voprosy Ekonomiki*, p. 54.

Siberia in recent years had lagged behind that of the country as a whole for various reasons including inadequate production capacities of the construction and assembly organizations and a shortage of materials.

Gross Industrial Production

	1950	1958	1963	Average annual increase 1950–8	1958–63
USSR	100	249	393	12.1	9.5
West Siberia	100	238	376	11.4	9.8
East Siberia	100	243	409	11.7	10.9

Source: *Nar. Kho₹. RSFSR 1963 g.*
Average annual increase calculated.

The relatively slow rate of industrial growth must in the first place be linked with the many unfinished major schemes of Siberian development in which large amounts of capital are tied up and which, even if more efficiently organized than they have been, would not yet be yielding much return on investment. Such, for example, are the huge Bratsk hydro-electric complex, the great Shelekhovo aluminium plant, and the many new arterial roads and railways all very expensive to construct in Siberian conditions. According to *Voprosy Ekonomiki* (no. 5, 1965), investigation of more than 100 new industrial projects in Siberia and also the results of the completion of about 600 new factories, plants, and mines showed that completion took about ten years, approval of plans was delayed by tedious bureaucratic procrastination, lack of building materials held up construction, and that even after 'commissioning', constructions may take from five to ten years to achieve planned economic levels.[1] The manpower situation also plays its part in inflating construction costs in Siberia, thus making it a less attractive area for investment than the Urals or European Russia.

In spite of the slowing down in the shift of emphasis eastwards in economic planning since the heyday of the late '50s, this shift, as far as Siberia is concerned, will inevitably continue for the following reasons: (a) the gradual running down of some Urals and

---

[1] P. Potemkin, G. Devyatov, and V. Sorokin, 'Ekonomicheskiye Voprosy Sosdaniya i Osvoeniya Novykh Predpriyatii Sibiri', *Voprosy Ekonomiki*, no. 5 (1965).

European-Russian natural resources, for example, oil, iron ore, coal; (b) the over-exploitation of resources and overcrowding in urban districts of central and western Russia; (c) the rich and varied raw material resources in the east and in the first place in Siberia; (d) the strategic need to develop the large vacuum in the east and in the first place Siberia by pushing the industrialized frontiers back there before leap-frogging to the eastern seaboard.[1] This shift has been delayed for various reasons, including the ability to maintain some Urals industry longer than was anticipated only a few years ago by the discoveries of further local reserves of raw materials, by the shortage of capital, and by utilizing and developing existing capital investment elsewhere. Taking these various factors into consideration, construction throughout Siberia today should be regarded as merely laying the foundation-stones of Siberian development, the vast range and promise of which must take many more years to complete.

[1] Danilov, op. cit. p. 115.

VI

The Soviet Far East

DEFINITION

The Soviet Far East forms the farthest outpost of Soviet territory in East Asia. It covers an enormous area of some 6,216,000 sq. km., or 28 per cent. of the whole USSR and is the largest economic region of the country. In the north are Yakutia (about six times the size of France),[1] the Magadan *oblast*, and the Kamchatka Peninsula, all now gradually emerging with their great natural riches from centuries of dormant obscurity. In the south, there are the Amur *oblast*, the Khabarovsk kray, and the Maritime kray (Primor'ye). The region also includes the whole of Sakhalin Island (including Karafuto, the southern part having been ceded by Japan to the Soviet Union in 1945), the Kurile Islands, and the Commander Islands in the Bering Sea off the east coast of Kamchatka. The Sea of Okhotsk itself (some 600,000 sq. miles in extent) is now virtually a Russian sea, being officially regarded by the USSR Government as Soviet territory. These Far Eastern territories give the Soviet Union a mainland coastline of more than 6,000 miles and also tend to increase its sphere of influence in the Pacific. Though the extremely severe climatic conditions are a handicap (even the Vladivostok harbour in the south is blocked by ice for three months of the year and can only be kept open by the use of powerful ice-breakers), strategically and economically, this exit to the open sea is of the greatest national importance.

CHINESE FRONTIER CLAIMS

The exposed geographical position of the Soviet Far East creates peculiar strategic and economic problems for Moscow. In the

[1] The Yakut ASSR is now closely associated with Magadan *oblast* and considered part of the Far East and not of east Siberia as formerly. Cf. V. A. Krotov, 'The Economic Geography of Siberia and the Far East in its Present Stage', translation in *Soviet Geography* (May 1964), p. 57, from *Doklady Instituta Geografii Sibiri i Dal'nego Vostoka*, no. 4 (1963), pp. 33–41.

north-east of the territory, Chukotka is separated only by the narrow Bering Strait (30 miles) from Alaska, once the Russian–American colony which was sold to America in 1867 for a paltry $7,200,000. In the south the Amur River (about 2,000 miles long) and its tributaries, the Argun and Ussuri, separate it from China. Historically, the situation on this frontier has always reflected the temper of Russo-Chinese relations and Russo-Chinese military strength. Once again it is a centre of interest and a possible bone of contention between Russia and China. On more than one occasion since the Sino-Soviet split, the Chinese have listed the Amur River provinces among the territories unjustly taken by Russia from China, notably in Mao Tse-tung's interview with a group of Japanese Socialist Party members in July 1964. A brochure distributed at the Chinese Trade Fair in Mexico (7 December 1963–6 January 1964) even contained a map on which the Soviet Far Eastern provinces were included within China's frontiers. The Aigun Treaty of 1858, which delimited the Amur frontier, also figures among the 'unequal treaties' which, according to the Chinese, Tsarist Russia had 'compelled the government of old China to sign'.[1]

There is no doubt that the Treaty of Aigun was forced on a weak and distracted China and that the Russians acquired the Amur in virtue of Murav'yëv-Amurskiy's military occupation of 1857–8, as was shown in an earlier section of this book. It is not surprising, therefore, that they have chosen other, stronger ground than this 'unequal treaty' argument to defend their position *vis-à-vis* the Chinese. Chinese claims to the Amur lands are turned by the contention that China has never exercised any political or cultural influence among the indigenous Amur tribes 'who are endowed with a distinctive independent culture' uninfluenced by China, and that the area was a sort of political no-man's-land until the arrival of the Russians. The most authoritative contemporary statement of this politically loaded thesis comes from the pen of the distinguished archaeologist, Academician A. P. Okladnikov, and appeared in *Voprosy Istorii* in 1964:

Distracted by the struggle for the conquest of China and Mongolia, the Manchurians completely threw off the northern regions—the Amur and Primor'ye, bordering on Manchuria, which never really belonged to

[1] *People's Daily*, 8 March 1963.

them or to China. This was fully revealed when the Russian pioneers began the conquest of the Amur and penetrated to the shores of the Pacific Ocean. The only thing the Manchurians tried to do was to depopulate the Amur region, remove thence the indigenous population of Dauri and Ducheri. This province thus became a neutral zone.[1] The Manchurian conquerors of China never had vitally important interests here. The population of the Amur and Primor'ye, where they survived, led their former pattern of life and were economically and politically independent of the Manchurian Government. Furthermore, when the Manchurians enslaved China, they systematically carried out their traditional policy of isolating Manchuria and the northern areas from China. This isolation of the north and also the merciless exploitation of its population led to an extreme decline of the economy. So it continued until the appearance on the Amur and Primor'ye of the Russians, finally uniting these provinces to the Russian Government and laying the basis here of civilization.[2]

The Soviet case was also argued by Academician V. M. Khvostov in a vehement quasi-official rejection of all Mao's territorial claims against the Soviet Union, published in *International Life* (no. 10, October 1964). 'From the Far Eastern Soviet frontiers', he wrote, 'the Soviet Army in 1945 by mighty blows routed the best part of the land forces of Japan . . . and thereby accorded the most mighty assistance to the Chinese people, the Communist Party of China, and the Chinese national liberation army in liberating their country.' He also referred to the 'tremendous construction work in the Soviet Far East', and concluded that 'in these circumstances the presentation by the Chinese leaders of territorial claims to the Fatherland of the Soviets is truly monstrous'. According to *Pravda* (2 September 1964) echoing Khrushchev, 'these frontiers have been formed historically and consolidated by life itself'. The Soviet title to the Amur lands (and others claimed by Peking) is thus more pragmatic than legal, while the Chinese argument revolves round the thesis of the usurpation of their frontier rights through 'unequal treaties'.

---

[1] Detailed examination of the rights and wrongs of these complex historico-sociological arguments would lead far beyond the framework of this study and must be left to the experts in the field. It would appear, however, from Mr. Owen Lattimore's interesting examination of the Chinese-Manchu attitude to the Amur frontier area that Academician Okladnikov has completely misrepresented the Manchurian position by identifying a buffer state policy of discouraging colonization ('depopulating') with rejection of sovereignty. Cf. Lattimore, op. cit. pp. 104–16.

[2] A. P. Okladnikov, 'Sovetskiy Dal'niy Vostok v Svete Noveyshikh Dostizhenii Arkheologii', *Voprosy Istorii*, no. 1 (1964), p. 57.

Japan is also a major factor in the formulation of Soviet strategic and economic policy in the Far East. The defeat of imperial Russia in 1904–5 and the protracted occupation of eastern Siberia and the Far East by Japan in 1918–22 have not been forgotten in Moscow. The post-war situation has been complicated by Soviet Russia's seizure of Japanese territory (southern Sakhalin and the Kuriles), causing deep resentment in Japan, difficulties over fishing in the northern Pacific waters, and Soviet suspicions of American influence on Japanese policy *vis-à-vis* the Soviet Union and fears of American bases on Japanese soil. At the same time both sides now recognize that they have much to gain by closer economic relations across the Sea of Japan, and apprehension about Japan is at least for the moment minimized by the hostile noises from Red China.

NATURAL RESOURCES

Nature has endowed the Soviet Far East with a great wealth and range of minerals, but exploitation is obstructed by the inaccessibility and difficulty of the terrain and the harsh, forbidding climate. As a result, geological prospecting has far from covered great areas of rough taiga and tundra, though discoveries of national importance, like the famous Mirnyy diamond mines in 1954, are made from year to year by persistent prospectors. The cost of construction and any form of industrialization is enormously increased by these stern natural conditions. In vast areas of taiga and marsh there is still no form of transport. 'Roadlessness' is general, though a few great arterial roads have literally been cut through the marshes and forests.

In spite of the difficulties, the region has already become in some respects of great, even vital interest economically to the Soviet Union. Its gold, fisheries, furs, and timber are valuable items in Soviet foreign trade. The kimberlite diamond pipes at Mirnyy and Aykhal in Yakutia and the Iul'tin and other tin mines in north-east Chukotka add resources of unique value to the Soviet economy, formerly deficient in these minerals, though exploitation in both cases presents great problems. One-third of the Soviet fish catch and 40 per cent. of fish conserves come from the Far East. Yet apart from a few medium-sized towns like Khabarovsk, Komsomol'sk, and Vladivostok, and the mining settlements like Aldan scattered throughout an uninhabited wilderness, there is little general industrial development, and it is likely to remain highly concentrated in the south.

The reserves for future development of power, timber, and minerals are nevertheless impressive. The Magadan *oblast* and Yakutia between them have one-sixth of the total USSR reserves of timber, but they are largely inaccessible and the main producing areas are not there but in the more accessible Khabarovsk and Primorskiy kray and Sakhalin. In all, the Far Eastern region is estimated to contain more than 15 per cent. of the Soviet timber reserves.[1] Coal deposits are also known to be substantial and estimated at one-third of the total geological USSR reserves in Yakutia and Magadan, with useful and considerably more accessible mines in Khabarovsk kray and Sakhalin, the Amur *oblast*, and Kamchatka. The great hydro-electric power potential of the area, estimated at one-fifth of the USSR potential in Yakutia and Magadan alone, is as yet untapped. Thermal electricity is produced on a purely local and restricted scale.

It was recommended at the Seventeenth Party Congress (1934) that the Far Eastern region should create 'its own firm industrial base' and this was echoed by Molotov in his report to the Eighteenth Party Congress on the Third Five Year Plan in 1939.[2] He called for 'a complex development which should be able from its own resources to supply all its fuel requirements and as far as possible its own requirements in metal and machine-building, cement, timber, and building materials, as well as the products of light industry. . . . The Far Eastern region demands the furthest possible strengthening as a powerful outpost of Soviet power in the East.' This programme was mainly inspired by strategic considerations and the shadow of 'Japanese imperialism' from Manchuria. It was largely immobilized by the outbreak of war. In the pre-war period, the development of the Far Eastern special resources of gold and other minerals and timber resulted in a rate of growth of industrial production and capital construction which exceeded the all-Union indices and average rates of growth in the RSFSR.[3] The important Kolyma

[1] A. B. Margolin, *Problemy Narodnogo Khozyaystva Dal'nego Vostoka*, Iz. AN (Moscow, 1963), p. 30.

[2] V. Molotov, *Report on the Third Five Year Plan of Development of National Economy of the USSR* (Moscow, 1939), p. 33.   [3] Margolin, op. cit. p. 52.

gold-mines had been opened up in the early '30s and were being intensely developed by slave labour. Many locally based light industries were established in towns in the southern provinces like Khabarovsk and Ussuriysk (Voroshilov) but the chief industrial developments in the region were the establishment of *Amurstal'*, the first modern metallurgical plant in the Far East, at Komsomol'sk, and some armaments works. In the immediate post-war period the Far East was relatively neglected owing to the enormous resources required for the restoration of the war-devastated areas and 'because as a result of the national revolution in China and Korea the Far Eastern frontiers became frontiers of friendship with socialist countries'.[1] Accordingly, the percentage of the Far Eastern region in Soviet capital investment fell somewhat compared to the levels reached in the Second and Third Five Year Plans and the rate of growth of industrial production also fell in spite of a considerable growth in the absolute volume of production.

The formidable difficulties in the way of the economic development of parts of the Soviet Far East were later frankly summarized by the Director of the Complex Research Institute at Magadan, Nikolay Shilo:

In developing north-eastern Siberia, we once again face enormously difficult but equally challenging problems:

North-eastern Siberia is a land of severe climatic conditions and great expanses. This explains its uneven economic development. In the first stage of development, isolated industrial oases were set up here and there. Now each has its own definite specialization. What we do is skim off the cream from each—a very wasteful procedure, since it makes for one-sided development. Besides that, we do not extract from nature all that she could give us if we had larger and more productive enterprises. . . . For balanced economic development we must have a broad power base and the necessary auxiliary branches to service the major industries. We need a light industry of our own, since shipping greatly increases the cost of the goods we receive from the central regions. . . . We also need a building industry. Up to now we have been using timber a great deal, but the timber reserves of north-eastern Siberia are limited, and wood alone cannot meet our needs. The problem of building materials is urgent. . . . Maritime shipping is our chief form of transportation, a factor which slows down industrial production and raises costs. . . . Building and

[1] Ibid. p. 54.

maintaining highways and railroads in our latitudes is a very difficult undertaking.[1]

POPULATION AND LABOUR PROBLEMS

The ratio of population to area in this huge territory is exceptionally low. Official statistics reported a total population of only 5.27 millions in the whole Far Eastern region in 1964, or only 2.3 per cent. of the USSR population (in an area occupying nearly 28 per cent. of the Soviet land space). Within the area the population density varies from 9.1 per sq. km. in the Maritime kray to 0.2 in Yakutia and Magadan, the average density being 0.8 per sq. km.[2] The vast empty spaces of the Soviet Far East with its proven and latent natural wealth are in glaring contrast to the teeming millions of adjacent Manchuria and China. The risk of aggression in this area of attraction by the 'Peking expansionists'[3] cannot therefore be overlooked in Moscow.

Although still so thinly and inadequately populated, the Soviet Far East has nevertheless had a large increase in population since the 1926 census. Colonization dating from Tsarist days was then fairly well advanced in the southern areas and the number of settlers was subsequently increased by the introduction of 'forced labour' in the '30s and the Draconian Stalinist restrictions on free movement. In fact, the population actually trebled between 1926 and 1964, though latterly the rate of colonization has been dropping considerably.

Year	Far East population	Increase over previous figure (per cent.)	USSR population*	Increase over previous figure* (per cent.)	Far East population as percentage of USSR population
1926	1,777,932	—	167,000,000		1.1
1939	2,976,000	+67.4	190,678,000	+14.2	1.6
1959	4,834,000†	+62.1	208,827,000	+9.5	2.3
1964	5,278,000†	+9.2	226,253,000	+8.3	2.3

* Estimated for present boundaries.

† Includes south Sakhalin, the Kuriles, and other islands seized post-war from Japan.

Source: *Ekon. Rayony*, op. cit. Percentages calculated.

[1] Nikolay Shilo, 'The Siberian Challenge', *Soviet Life* (June 1965), pp. 33-34.
[2] *Nar. Khoz. RSFSR 1963 g.*, op. cit.   [3] *Pravda*'s label, 4 September 1965.

The distribution of this population is very unequal. It is mostly concentrated in towns and settlements scattered thoughout a very sparsely inhabited countryside. The same movement that has been observed throughout the Soviet Union from the rural areas to the urban has led to a great increase in the urban population of the Soviet Far East and to a notable growth in the size of the towns.[1] The urban population, only 37 per cent. of the total in 1926, had risen to 68 per cent. in 1959.

	Urban population		Rural population		Urban population as percentage of total	
	1939	1959	1939	1959	1939	1959
Far East*	1,384,859	3,265,004	1,590,694	1,569,142	47	68
Primor'ye	452,453	928,303	435,540	452,715	51	67
Khabarovsk kray	415,795	848,300	241,557	294,235	63	74
Amur	288,858	428,824	345,228	288,690	66	72
Kamchatka	35,375	140,515	73,960	80,238	32	64
Sakhalin*	50,175	488,853	49,750	160,552	50	75
Magadan	30,657	190,798	142,331	44,780	18	81
Yakutia	111,548	239,411	302,328	247,932	27	49

* The 1959 figures include south Sakhalin.

Official sources.

Immigrants from European Russia were the element most sought after to man the agricultural and industrial development schemes in the Far East. But the area was in the first place the home of many different indigenous peoples. As a result of immigration and *sliyaniye* (assimilation) of the Far Eastern natives with the Slav elements, over 80 per cent. of the total population is now Slav (Russian, Ukrainian, or Belorussian), compared to about 55 per cent. in 1926. In Yakutia alone, whose indigenous inhabitants 'were

[1] The largest towns (as of 1 January 1965) in the Far East are: Khabarovsk (408,000), Vladivostok (367,000), Komsomol'sk (300,000), Ussuriysk (121,000), Petropavlovsk (134,000), Yuzhno-Sakhalinsk (88,000), Yakutsk (89,000), Magadan (70,000). Nakhoda, the new port being developed east of Vladivostok, has grown phenomenally from a tiny fishing village of 300 in 1926 to 54,000 in 1956 and 100,000 in 1965.

significantly more sophisticated than the other native peoples',[1] the Slav population had risen from 30,315 (10 per cent.) in 1926 to 230,058 in 1959, and now greatly outnumbers the native Yakuts. From being 83 per cent. of the total or 235,929 in 1926, the Yakuts had fallen in 1959 to 46 per cent., or 226,053. Thus, as in Kazakhstan, the titular nationality of the county is no longer numerically in the majority.

In his expert analysis, *Russian Settlement in the North*, Dr. Armstrong states that the native peoples are not employed to any extent in mining or industry in the Far East.[2] They are rather encouraged to exercise their traditional skills in hunting and fishing where, for the most part, they cannot be competently replaced by European immigrants. He admirably summarizes the position of these indigenous peoples under the Soviet as compared to the Tsarist régime, as follows:

If it be granted that the native peoples were rescued from dangers to which they had long been exposed, they were nevertheless threatened by new ones. [These were] the constitutional arrangements which gave the impression, as intended, that the minority peoples had full control of their own affairs [which would be] entirely misleading. . . . It is also true that many of the largest economic undertakings in the territory of the autonomous and national regions—mining trusts, transport agencies and so forth—have in any case been run straight from Moscow and have been quite independent of the local government. . . . In fact, with the enormous influx of Russians during the Soviet period, it would be unreal to expect any genuine autonomy to have survived even if it had existed in the first place. . . . Russian domination in almost all areas does not have to be imposed any more. It has become inevitable. The threat to the national identity of the northern peoples is thus increased. Yet the fiction of their national autonomy is still preserved.[3]

The Soviet collectivization policies hit the many native reindeer-breeding peoples of the Soviet Far East very hard. They were used to wandering at will with their herds over vast areas of taiga and tundra. Under collectivization they were compulsorily settled in reindeer farms for which they had no liking and which were not suited to their traditional herding methods. The situation in the

---

[1] Armstrong, op. cit. p. 63.   [2] Ibid. p. 71.
[3] Ibid. pp. 169–70.

Koryak National *Okrug* of Kamchatka was typical of what happened to the herds of these reindeer peoples during the early collectivization years:

	Reindeer
1926	264,000
1932	173,000
1934	127,000

Source: M. A. Sergeyev, *Khozyaystvo Kamchatskogo Kraya*. Quoted by W. Kolarz, *The Peoples of the Soviet Far East* (George Philip & Son Ltd., London, 1954), p. 71.

The effect of such a fall in stock must have been partial starvation for the reindeer owners or a drift to the Russian industrial settlements in search of work and food, leading to an entirely new and probably uncongenial pattern of life, even in cases where it was possible. In recent years Soviet policy has changed towards these reindeer peoples of the Far North and East and more understanding has been shown for reindeer breeding. Reindeer have also acquired a certain economic significance as food in the mining areas. They provide meat for the gold-miners, the hides are good for clothing, and the antlers are exported to Japan.

As in Siberia, problems of labour and costs also bedevil construction in the Far East. For some years now, construction and mining enterprises have been harassed by the flight of skilled workers and others from their jobs which has resulted in a most uneconomic turnover of manpower. *Sovetskaya Rossiya* (18 November 1961) gave an explicit account of this problem: ' ... since spring the Far East *sovnarkhozes* have been flooding Gosplan RSFSR, the Ministry of Higher and Secondary Specialized Education, and central Institutes with letters ... they all ask for specialists. But as in previous years their wants were far from satisfied. ... As a result many responsible posts were held by people without even secondary specialized education. Consequently, the level of technological leadership is low. The fact that few specialists arrive is one loss ... also many young men settle down badly, some work two to three years and then pack their bags. Every autumn two currents move in opposite directions along the Trans-Siberian railway. Last year, for example, 400 doctors arrived in Primor'ye, and over 300 left. 100 geologists arrived, as many returned ... to transfer a man is not to transplant an apple tree.' *Pravda* (15 November 1964) blamed the high work norms resulting in low wages for the extremely high labour mobility among young construction workers at Gornyy (Solnechnyy), a new satellite mining town of Komsomol'sk-on-the-Amur. Here 400 workers at the construction trust departed and only 354 were recruited in one year. 'Recruitment of workers for Siberia and the Far East', lamented *Trud* (12 November 1964), 'is one of the most intractable problems of the Soviet Government.' Writing in *Ekonomicheskaya Gazeta* (no. 35, 1965), S. Borisov, First Secretary of the Yakut Party Committee, stated that 'thousands of enthusiastic people emigrate to Yakutia each year but few settle satisfactorily in their jobs. This is largely due to poor living conditions, unreliable food supplies, shortage of fresh fruit, vegetables, and potatoes, few crèches and kindergartens.' He recommended that the whole system of recruitment of labour to the inhospitable Arctic regions should be overhauled and special incentives offered skilled labour to induce 'youngsters from training establishments' to settle there.

But increased wage rates alone will not solve this problem. Everything costs more and is in shorter supply in these remote regions than 'at home'. The cost of housing, for example, was estimated to be 2–3 times, wages 1.5–2.5 times, heating 10–20 times, and transport 5–10 times higher in the 'medium latitude regions',[1] while public services like hospitals, crèches, schools, which the workers could not supply themselves, were either lacking or far below local requirements.

In principle, the privileges granted to workers in the Far North should apply to workers in the Far East. But it would appear from several recent references that there have been adjustments in the system, though it has not been possible to trace when these changes took place or exactly how they affect increments. Writing in *Partii-naya Zhizn'* (no. 19, 1965), the First Party Secretary of the Primor-skiy kray, V. Chernyshev, specifically stated: 'We consider the step to liquidate the privileges which used to exist for workers of the Far East to be totally unjustified. They helped to strengthen cadres, the influx of new strength was absolutely vital for the development of the economy.' The Magadan Deputy to the Supreme Soviet

[1] G. A. Zakharov *Osobennosti i Perspektivy Razvitiya Metalloobrabatyvayushchey Promysh-lennosti Magadanskov i Kamchatskoy Oblastey* (Novosibirsk, 1962), p. 5.

also complained about 'the unjustifiable haste in cutting privileges for workers in the Far North'.[1] Nevertheless it is not clear what the situation in Magadan actually is because a correspondent in *Sovetskaya Yustitsiya* (3 February 1966) later complained that 'in Magadan, where allegedly there are all the amenities of a modern town, houses with all conveniences, increments are paid as in places in the wilderness'. If *Sovetskaya Yustitsiya* is not spinning a yarn, things have changed in the former notorious Magadan concentration camp but nobody from the outside world has yet seen the miracle.

'During the last twenty-five years the population of the Khabarovsk kray had doubled. It grew chiefly as a result of the big stream of workers from other krays and *oblasts* of the country', the Khabarovsk delegate told the Supreme Soviet in December 1964. 'However, in recent years, in spite of the great need for labour, growth of population almost ceased owing to the rate of departures. Though annually tens of thousands of people arrive, almost as many leave. We beg the Councils of Ministers of the RSFSR and the USSR to increase the grants for 1965 and the following years for living and communal-domestic construction.'[2]

It would appear from these accounts that the population of the Far Eastern region must have fallen in recent years. But as the population figures on page 296 show this is not the case. One explanation of the anomaly may be that local officials, exasperated by the high rate of departures from an area that urgently needs a much larger population, exaggerate their difficulties in the hope of getting stronger government intervention to deal with the problem, either by improving living conditions for the immigrant workers or even by a partial return to the one-time sanctions against leaving the job without authorization.

Automation is also being canvassed by some Soviet technicians as one solution to the 'expensive' labour problem in the more inhospitable areas of the Far North and Far East. Labour recruitment costs in Magadan and Kamchatka alone were reported to amount to about 100,000,000 roubles annually in the early '6os. Analysing the situation in these two places a member of the Novosibirsk Institute of Economics and Organization of Industrial Production wrote: 'The great prospects for the mining and fishing industries

[1] *Pravda*, 3 October 1965.   [2] *Izvestiya*, 12 December 1964.

depend on reduction of expensive human labour by the extension of automation and mechanization of production.'[1] Both automation and mechanization requiring special equipment in these harsh climatic conditions are also expensive and seem rather a long-term solution to this problem.

AGRICULTURE

Agriculture in the Soviet Far East is greatly handicapped by the monsoon climate, severe winter frosts, and heavy rains during the harvest season.[2] In spite of the Soviet Government's efforts, agricultural production has not kept pace with colonization and is still unable to feed its relatively small population. Massive imports of foodstuffs including grain and meat (amounting to one million tons in 1963[3]) are necessary; the local cultivation of potatoes, soya, and sugar-beet, though still inadequate, has somewhat reduced dependence on outside supplies of these crops. This is definitely a food deficit area.

During his two visits to the Far East in 1954 and 1959, Mr. Khrushchev sharply criticized local agricultural conditions and production, but was probably over-optimistic about its 'land wealth'. Following his visits to the Primor'ye, the Khabarovsk kray, and Sakhalin in 1954, he reported to the Presidium that 'the Far East is a very rich region. The lands are good. The climatic conditions are also favourable for the development of agriculture. But unfortunately the exploitation of these rich land resources is extremely unsatisfactory. . . .'[4] He also learned at first hand of shortages in Komsomol'sk and 'other inhabited places' of meat and milk, fruit and vegetables. Things were apparently not much better during his visit to Vladivostok in 1959, when the shops were suddenly filled with goods lacking before his arrival.[5] 'We are very glad you came', a local woman told him; 'the oftener you come the more goods there will be in the shops ... shoes, cloth, milk, for example.' This Potemkin transformation of the Vladivostok shopping scene came as somewhat of a shock to the First Secretary, who urged the RSFSR

[1] Zakharov, op. cit. pp. 96–101.   [2] Jasny, op. cit. p. 129.   [3] Margolin, op. cit. p. 145.
[4] N. S. Khrushchev, Stroitel'stvo Kommunizma v SSSR i Razvitiye Sel'skogo Khozyaystva (Moscow, 1962), p. 397.   [5] Pravda, 8 October 1959.

Council of Ministers to give more attention to questions of supply in the Far East.

Khrushchev maintained that the Primor'ye could supply the population with abundance of potatoes, vegetables, and milk products. The local Party Secretary was harshly criticized for the poor agricultural results and the failure to develop maize, 'a very promising crop for fodder and the rapid development of livestock in Primor'ye.... The Far East could, if properly run, feed its own population with almost all kinds of agricultural products (except grain) without importing them from the central *oblasts* of the country', concluded Khrushchev. 'Both in Khabarovsk and the Primor'ye the agricultural population is small. We must follow the line of *sovkhozes* and high mechanization.'[1] Having pronounced these typically vague and optimistic views, Mr. Khrushchev departed for Moscow. The increased mechanization of Far Eastern agriculture (unfortunately largely with unsuitable equipment) which followed his visit may have been inspired by his comments but otherwise there was no noticeable change in the agricultural position.

Official statistics show the Far Eastern region to be the most highly mechanized agricultural area of the RSFSR for ploughland and grain crops. The total sown area in the Far East between 1958 and 1963 steadily increased, but the area under grain crops actually fell from 1,142,000 ha. in 1958 to 1,065,000 ha. in 1963 and to 1,016,000 ha. in 1964.[2]

	Area of pasture for 15 h.p. tractor		Sown area of grain for one combine	
	(in hectares)			
	1958	1963	1958	1963
RSFSR	134	95	231	250
Far Eastern region	71	51	161	116
Primorskiy kray	79	54	153	127
Khabarovsk kray	45	33	119	78
Amur *oblast*	85	65	171	115
Sakhalin *oblast*	25	14	54	—

Source: *Nar. Khoz. RSFSR v 1963 g.*, p. 336.

Of the Far Eastern grain crop 67 per cent. was produced in the Amur *oblast* in 1963, 25 per cent. in the Primorskiy kray and the

[1] Khrushchev, op. cit. pp. 404–5.   [2] *Nar. Khoz. RSFSR v 1963 g.*; ibid. *v 1964.*

remaining 8 per cent. scattered in small areas of the Khabarovsk kray, Sakhalin, and farther north where some grain cultivation is now possible.[1] The results were particularly disappointing in the Amur region which, with its Zeya-Bureya 'granary', was planned to become the 'bread-basket' of the Far East. It had received more tractors and combine harvesters per hectare than any other area of the Soviet Union, which involved a large capital investment. As yields were far from satisfactory, a brake had to be put on this mechanization in the Amur *oblast*. Moreover, there has been a steady reduction amounting to 20 per cent. of the acreage devoted to grain in this *oblast* between 1958 (the peak year) and 1964, when there was a further reduction.[2] Compared to the RSFSR average, the agricultural yields are generally low in the Far East. The grain yield per hectare is the lowest in the country. According to official statistics this is the highest agricultural cost area in the Soviet Union.

Agricultural Yields in the RSFSR and the Far East
(in 1963)

	RSFSR	Far East
Potatoes (quintals per ha.)	82	64
Vegetables (quintals per ha.)	108	70
Meat (quintals per 100 ha. pasture)	24.8	21.1
Milk (quintals per 100 ha. pasture)	157	149

Source: *Nar. Khoz. RSFSR v 1963 g.*

The livestock position in the Far East is also unpromising, and owing to inadequate fodder supplies and badly organized stock-farming it has even deteriorated in recent years. Milk and meat yields are poor,[3] while the *per caput* livestock production is below that of the Soviet average. The region has 2 million cattle and pigs, about 1.5 per cent. of the Union total.

The only foods produced in abundance in the area are fish and soya beans. More than a third of the arable land in the Far East is given up to soya beans, a crop which is highly valued for its many uses as human and animal food and in industry. Government

---

[1] *Ekon. Rayony*, p. 320.   [2] *Nar. Khoz. SSSR v 1964 g.*
[3] Margolin, op. cit. pp. 136–8.

procurements rose from 62,000 tons in 1960 to 300,000 tons in 1963 but fell sharply to 118,000 tons in 1964, which resulted in a shortage of raw material for the well-developed bean-processing industries (oils, margarine, and fats). Normally the shortage would be made good by Manchurian soya, but this source may now be cut short by the Sino-Soviet conflict. The poor crop in 1964, according to *Pravda's* Maritime kray correspondent,[1] was caused by failure to suit bean-seed selection and cultivation to the kray's weather conditions, inadequate fertilizer supplies, and unsuitable agricultural machinery.

The Ukrainians, who originally colonized the Khanka plain, started sugar-beet cultivation there about 1920, backed by their experience of the crop in their native Ukraine. The Far Eastern sugar-beet crop increased from 14,000 tons in 1950 to 88,000 tons in 1958, then fell sharply to 42,000 tons in 1963, rising to 84,000 tons in 1964. The yields per hectare also rose and fell sharply during the same period.[2] It may be recalled in this connexion that during Khrushchev's Far Eastern tour, the Primor'ye Party Secretary suggested that the local sugar refinery (at Ussuriysk) should be closed down because it produced only 10 per cent. of the Primor'ye sugar requirements, the rest being imported from the central regions of the country.[3] This official had already succeeded in doing away with the only sugar factory in southern Sakhalin, but Khrushchev indignantly rejected the idea of liquidating the Primor'ye sugar industry, so the Ussuriysk plant, the oldest and largest in the Far East, is still operating. In view of the poor sugar-beet crops in recent years (88,000 tons in 1958, 42,000 tons in 1963)[4] it may well be that Party Secretary Mel'nik was right and that it is unprofitable to try to produce sugar-beet in this area; he was overruled by Khrushchev, whose knowledge of sugar-beet cultivation in Primor'ye conditions can have been only superficial at best. Sugar is now shipped direct to Nakhodka from Cuba for Far Eastern requirements.

The cis-Ussuri plain by Lake Khanka is well suited to rice cultivation. It was successfully grown there by the Koreans until they were deported to Central Asia in the late 1930s. It is still grown

[1] *Pravda*, 13 October 1965. [2] *Nar. Khoz. SSSR v 1964 g.*, p. 312.
[3] Khrushchev, op. cit. p. 400. [4] *Nar. Khoz. SSSR v 1964 g.*

Soya Bean and Rice Imports from China

	1955	1956	1957	1958	1959	1960	1961	1962	1963
Rice									
Amount (000 tons)	292.7	457.6	181.1	452.8	658.4	415.6	2.3	150.2	—
Cost (000 roubles)	37,950	57,857	22,894	54,722	74,316	49,666	286	18,351	—
Price 1 ton (roubles)	126	126	126	121	113	119	124	122	—
Soya Beans									
Amount (000 tons)	483.6	548.5	579.0	478.4	638.9	351.0	10.3	—	—
Cost (000 roubles)	42,747	48,242	49,921	45,097	60,679	32,113	935	—	—
Price 1 ton (roubles)	88	88	86	94	95	91	91	—	—

Sources: *Foreign Trade USSR*, 1955–9, 1961, 1963.

there and about 10,000 ha. were sown to rice in 1963.[1] A big increase is scheduled in the area under rice and production is planned to rise to 140,000 tons by 1970. These increases may be linked with the dramatic fall in the rice imports from China since 1959 (not all of which, of course, were destined for the Far East).

According to present indications the Soviet Far East seems destined to have to rely on imported foodstuffs and especially grain for the foreseeable future. Though imports of food seem to be still coming in from Manchuria, the situation is precarious. A high proportion of the large purchases of grain from Canada and Australia in 1963–4 was shipped (at relatively low transport costs) to Far Eastern ports to supplement the local grain shortages and thus reduce the heavy rail transport costs on grain from western Siberia and north Kazakhstan. According to a statement by the USSR Minister of Agriculture, V. Matskevich, this policy has come to stay. Despite the good harvest, he said, it was sensible in his opinion to buy some grain abroad, for example—in Canada—for the Soviet Far East.[2]

INDUSTRY AND MINING

Soviet sources usually list the industries of the Far East in the following order without stating what yardstick is used:

1. Fishing
2. Timber
3. Engineering and metals
4. Mining
5. Furs
6. Construction

Fisheries

The fishing industry employs 20 per cent. of the workers in the Far East and produces 40 per cent. of total Far Eastern industrial production. One-third of the total fish catch of the Soviet Union originates in the Far East and about 40 per cent. of Soviet canned fish products is also of Far Eastern origin. The value of this catch is considerable especially in the north where the proportion of crab and salmon is high. Productivity of labour is two to three times

[1] *Ekon. Rayony*, p. 320.   [2] Tass in Russian for abroad, 27 December 1966.

higher in this industry than in all others. Transport costs are also high on the deliveries of the fish to European Russia, which is the chief market for this fish.

The fish reserves in the northern waters of the Soviet Far East contain the world's largest stocks of salmon and crab, as well as a great variety of other fish. Kamchatka is the leading producer of crabs in the world. And as a result of modernization of her fishing industry with up-to-date steam trawlers equipped with processing plant, Kamchatka has become the second most important fishing-ground in the Soviet Union after the Caspian Sea. The principal centre of this industry is Bol'sheretsk on the west coast of Kamchatka. The refrigerated trawlers and floating fish combines already operating in these waters are to be increased by a series of refrigerated ship factories being built by the Japanese, the first of which was launched in 1965. Meanwhile, most of this catch has to be processed on land. A severe shortage of labour is reported by Soviet sources in this industry and students are recruited from local education institutions to help out in busy seasons. Some 2,500 of these students regularly work as fishermen on the Amur River and the Okhotsk Sea as the Khabarovsk fisheries are always short of labour during the season and workers have even to be brought from western areas of the USSR at a cost of 205 roubles per head for transport.

Soviet-Japanese fishing interests are closely interlocked in the north-west Pacific waters and in the in-shore fisheries. The Japanese have fished for salmon in the North Pacific for hundreds of years and had built up a very prosperous industry there pre-World War I. The territorial base of the industry was extended by the acquisition of the Kurile island chain in 1875, the annexation of southern Sakhalin in 1905, and the colonization of Hokkaido. The Japanese took advantage of the chaotic conditions during World War I and the 1917 Revolution to extend their fisheries in Russian coastal waters and to organize successful fisheries and canning factories on the Far Eastern mainland of Russia.

They were gradually eased out by the Russians who started to develop the Far Eastern fisheries and canneries themselves in a big way in the First and Second Five Year Plan periods (1928–37). The Soviet victory in 1945 after a few days' fighting with the Japanese in Manchuria brought ruin to the Japanese North Pacific fishing industry. The rich fishing-grounds off the Kurile Islands and southern Sakhalin were lost and Japanese fishermen accustomed to fishing in these waters were severely hit by the twelve mile limit imposed by the Russians. The valuable concessions in the Kamchatkan salmon rivers as well as expensive Japanese fishing equipment and many boats were also lost to Japan. Things began to improve (though the position is still far from satisfactory from the point of view of the Japanese fishing industry) after the signature of the ten year Soviet-Japanese Fishing Agreement in 1956. This agreement fixed a ceiling for Japanese catches in north-west Pacific waters and declared waters north of latitude 45 and west of longitude 170 a restricted area. A Soviet-Japanese conference was to meet annually to discuss fishing quotas and other technical questions.

These fisheries are of the greatest national importance to the Japanese, but they are in a weak bargaining position with the Russians who have command of the Sea of Japan and the Sea of Okhotsk. The Japanese quotas for salmon in the North Pacific waters have suffered a continual decline since 1957. Soviet arrests of thousands of Japanese fishermen and confiscation of their gear for infringing the twelve mile limit (often in areas where traditionally they used to fish) or for fishing in the now restricted areas has aroused great indignation in Japan. There has recently been more leniency in dealing with these cases and many Japanese fishermen under arrest have been sent home. In 1964 a concession was made about the twelve mile limit off Habomai in favour of Japanese crab and tangle fishing and by agreement with the Greater Japan Fishery Association the Soviet Fisheries Association permitted licensed fishing boats to collect the specially prized seaweed growing on Kaigara, at the extreme southern tip of the Kurile Islands.[1] The annual joint fisheries discussions have been frequently bedevilled by conflicting Soviet-Japanese claims to the southern Kuriles. So far the Japanese have stood firm on the territorial question and are unwilling to trade 'territorial rights' for fishery concessions. But the Pacific fisheries remain a strong bargaining counter in the hands of the Russians who no doubt will continue to exploit them so as to induce the Japanese to sign a peace treaty and in one way or another to weaken the American-Japanese Alliance.

[1] *The Times*, 15 July 1963.

Forestry

Astronomical figures are often given for the forested areas of the Soviet Far East. They can mostly be taken as little more than rough estimates, for large parts of the forested areas have never been systematically explored. In fact the forest cover is relatively small, in relation to the size of the area as a whole, because of the extent of the treeless north-eastern tundra regions. Transport and power are lacking to develop many still inaccessible forests. As a result, most of the current output of 18 million cu. m. is produced by the Khabarovsk and Maritime krays, the Amur *oblast*, and Sakhalin. Kamchatka, 'the coniferous peninsula', is planned to double its present production of just over 300,000 cu. m. by 1970 so as to supply the treeless Chukotka tundra and the Commander Islands and to increase its exports of timber. A large new wood combine is being set up, the *Srednekamchatka*, and mechanized off-shore loading is being organized at the mouth of the Kamchatka River to facilitate transport of lumber.

The Soviet Union greatly expanded its timber industry by the acquisition of southern Sakhalin (Karafuto) from the Japanese in 1945. The Japanese had developed a modern wood-processing industry there before World War II with saw-mills and large cellulose and paper factories. In 1939 Karafuto produced more than half of the pulpwood of Japan, or 476,457 tons.[1] The industry is now being more actively developed by the Soviets with an eye to Pacific markets, in the first place in Japan and Australia. It far outstrips the very limited development of these industries on the Far Eastern mainland where there is only one hydrolysis plant and a small cardboard factory in Khabarovsk kray and a few small plants in Primor'ye.

Amursk, a new town which has grown up in the taiga between Khabarovsk and Komsomol'sk since 1958, is to be the site of the first wood-chemical complex on the Far Eastern mainland, under the current Five Year Plan; it is planned, when finished, to be one of the biggest in the world and will have automatic equipment for supplying coal and water to the works. It will produce cardboard and viscose, fodder yeast and ethylene spirit, fibre-board and artificial protein.

[1] Robert E. Ward, *The Issue of Sakhalin in Russo-Japanese Relations* (Ann Arbor, The University of Michigan Press, 1957), p. 89.

It is symptomatic of the general neglect of the timber potential and the inefficiency and wastage with which the timber industry is riddled that the Far East should not have developed its own wood-chemical industry many years ago. According to the devastating statistics produced in a close study of the timber industry of the Far East by A. B. Margolin,[1] the under-exploitation of the timber resources is stated to be enormous. Timber deliveries in 1960, for example, formed only some 0.2–0.3 per cent. of the timber stocks in the worked forests of the Far East. In the mechanical processing of timber there was about 75 per cent. wood waste. Waste was particularly high in sawn logs, furniture, plywood, and other special products. But for the most part the wood industry was confined to work in the saw-mills. Large-scale development of cellulose, cardboard, and fibre-board, and the establishment of hydrolysis plants and the dry distillation of wood and other such sophisticated treatments of timber would require considerable capital outlay. But the policy of the central planning authorites has hitherto been rather in the direction of sending undressed timber thousands of miles west in spite of the heavy transport costs.[2] This policy seems now to be changing as interest in exports of Far Eastern timber to Pacific markets increases in Moscow.

Furs

Some of the most valuable Soviet furs on the international markets come from the Far East, which supplies about one-third of all Soviet fur production. Kamchatka contributes sable (which has been exterminated over a large area elsewhere), ermine, squirrel and 'sea otter' in considerable quantities to the national fur stocks. In the remote Commander Islands off the east coast of Kamchatka, Polar fox, fur seal, and sea beaver are abundant, and mink, which formerly did not exist on the islands, has now been successfully bred there and in Sakhalin. The hunting of fur-bearing animals is organized by the State, which provides hunters with the necessary equipment and supplies. When the hunting season is over the furs are delivered to the State bases, and payment is made according to results. The best Russian furs are sold to foreign customers at the Leningrad, London,

[1] Margolin, op. cit. pp. 107–17.
[2] *L'Extrême-Orient Soviétique. Caractéristiques économiques et Perspectives de développement*, La Documentation française, Paris, 30 September 1966, pp. 19–21.

and other fur fairs. The finer furs are seldom available in Soviet retail shops and only the most exalted ladies of the Soviet Union, like the top ballerinas or wives of Soviet Ministers, possess mink or ermine coats.

Minerals and Mining

The veil of secrecy which surrounds Soviet production of non-ferrous minerals, gold, and diamonds prevents any exact estimate being made of some of the most valuable resources of the Soviet Far Eastern region, for example, gold, diamonds, tin, copper, mica.

Experts regard Soviet gold production as second only to that of South Africa. By far the largest producing areas in the Far East are known to be the Magadan *oblast*, the Yakut ASSR, and to a much smaller degree Kamchatka, where the first gold-field was opened up near Petropavlovsk-Kamchatka in 1964. The latest estimate of the US Bureau of Mines for total Soviet gold production in 1963 was 5,100,000 oz.[1] Ninety-five per cent. of this production is estimated to come from the eastern regions and 60–65 per cent. of all mined gold from Magadan and Yakut sources. The Urals, which were long the main gold-producing area, are now estimated to produce only about 5 per cent. of Soviet gold. All Soviet gold is sent to the central gold refinery at Novosibirsk for refining. A gold extraction works is under construction at Nizhniy Kuranakh in the Aldan gold-mining area in south Yakutia and will treat up to 100,000 cu. m. of ore a year. The gold-mining industry's administrative centre is at Ust'-Nera in eastern Yakutia.

A good deal of systematic prospecting has been carried out in the Far East before and since the last war, yet large expanses of this area are still 'white spots' on the Soviet geological map. In spite of the great difficulties of climate and transport, mineral production in Yakutia, where the temperature in winter may fall below −50° C to −70° C, is reported to be going ahead though there have been complaints that more could be done. Thus the annual output of minerals (in proportion to the prospected Yakut reserves) was reported by S. Borisov, himself a Yakut and then First Secretary of the Yakut ASSR, to be just over 1 per cent. for tin, 2 per cent. for mica, and about 5 per cent. for gold.[2] The rate at which the wealth

---

[1] *The Times*, 19 November 1965.   [2] *Ekon. G.*, no. 35, 1956.

of the Republic is being exploited is still too slow', complained
Borisov.[1] Under Yakut conditions large capital investments would
be required for specialized equipment, construction, and transport
if production were to increase greatly. Yet the volume of Yakut
investment has already given rise to controversy, according to
Borisov. 'It is considered unprofitable in some quarters', he stated,
'to sink capital in a sparsely populated region.' His personal opinion,
however, was that any investment in the republic would give good
returns. 'Yakutia's gold is likewise among the country's cheapest',
he stated. 'Yet in 1958 a maximum cost price was fixed for gold-
mining and no gold deposits or reefs are taken over by industry
unless the gold content is high enough to ensure the planned cost
price. All other gold-mines remain untapped.' This is an interesting
comment on the Soviet attitude to its gold reserves.

The main gold-mining areas of the north-east are in the Kolyma–
Indigirka and Chukotsk areas of Magadan *oblast*, and at Aldan in the
south of Yakutia. The great Kolyma gold-fields were discovered
in 1931. They were first worked in appalling conditions by concentration camp labour under the notorious NKVD (later MVD)
organization, Dal'stroy. Dal'stroy was in charge of a vast complex
of mining and construction enterprises throughout the Soviet Far
East and was not finally disbanded until some years after Stalin's
death, in 1956. Magadan *oblast* retained about 80 per cent. of Dal'-
stroy's gold-mining enterprises, the rest went to the Yakut ASSR.
Until quite recently all kinds of euphemisms were used in Soviet
literature to cover up the horror of Dal'stroy's gold-mining operations in Kolyma. 'The mine workers were of all sorts,' we are told
in one publication, 'some lovers of adventure, some just profiteers.
Discipline was at first very bad.'[2] These so-called 'lovers of adventure' are now admitted to have been the 'thousands of falsely
accused and unjustly convicted communists' and others exiled to the
inhuman conditions of the Kolyma gold-fields, 'where we grew so
thin that our bones stuck out but that damned gold had to be
extracted. "No gold, no bread" ran the camp order. . . . The yesterday of Kolyma is a sore which we have reopened so that every man

---

[1] S. Z. Borisov was released from his duties as First Secretary and Member of the Bureau of
the Yakut Party Committee in October 1965. It may be he lost his job because he spoke
too frankly about economic affairs in Yakutia.

[2] *Zolotaya Kolyma* (1963), pp. 61–62.

and woman may know this creeping disease, so that it is never again permitted to poison the country.'[1] This description of the horrors of Stalin's Kolyma was published in *Soviet Life* and sharply contrasts with the usual Soviet secretiveness, even now, about these places. The Kolyma gold-fields are now worked by free labour and mechanization of mining operations is constantly increasing, 'whereas in 1938–9, the Dal'stroy leadership directed its energies not towards complex mechanization but to raising productivity by muscular work'.[2]

Magadan

The Aldan gold-fields, discovered in the early '20s, are second in importance only to the Kolyma–Indigirka group of mines and include some of the main placer mines in the Soviet Union. Before the 'gold-rush' the area was wild and uninhabited. Now the Aldan *rayon* has some 80,000 inhabitants and the town of Aldan (530 km. south of Yakutsk), the headquarters of the Yakut Gold-Mining Trust, is an important centre. It has an Advanced Mining Institute and other educational institutions. The Gold-Mining Trust runs its own dairy cattle and chicken farms to ensure some supplies for the mining workers. Supplies also come from the Trans-Siberian railway, with which Aldan is connected by road, and from Yakutsk, with which there are both river and road connexions. The Aldan gold industry is mainly run and manned by Russians and other immigrants from European Russia. Like the Kolyma industry it was operated by forced labour during the life-span of Dal'stroy.

In Magadan *oblast* and Yakutia labour turnover is a big problem now that workers can freely leave their jobs if conditions prove unsatisfactory. The Magadan Deputy to the Supreme Soviet bitterly complained of the 'flight of cadres and in the first place of mining specialists, geologists, agricultural and also skilled workers', caused, he said, by the 'unjustifiable haste in cutting privileges for workers of the Far North, permitted in 1960'.[3] 'The State Committee on Labour and Wages', he went on, 'obviously is badly acquainted with the geography of our country and its special features. In fact this approach to the question has caused no little material damage to our government. We would recommend the directors of our State Committee to come to us and study our remote region and not

---

[1] *Soviet Life* (June 1965), p. 20.   [2] *Zolotaya Kolyma*, p. 88.
[3] *Pravda*, 3 October 1965.

define its conditions in Moscow. We request that the reconsidera-
tion of the questions of privileges for workers of the Far North be
speeded up.' This question of inducements to attract and keep
workers in the Far East and the Far North is constantly discussed
in the Soviet Press and in works dealing with the mining industry.
All agree about the seriousness of the problem but no effective action
has yet been taken. Probably Khrushchev hit the nail on the head
when he said during his visit to Vladivostok in 1959 that it was not
increased wages but better living conditions that would keep
workers in these regions.[1]

Chukotka, the extreme north-eastern boundary of the Soviet
Union, is one of the newest, most bleak, and yet promising Soviet
mining areas. Its natural riches are hidden in the tundra wilderness
where blizzards and exceptionally cold temperatures are formidable
obstacles to development. But valuable deposits of gold and tin, lead
and mercury have been found in spite of these hazards, and Soviet
geologists believe there is oil and gas there also. Where there was not
a town or a house forty years ago there are now the towns of Anadyr', Bilibino, Iul'tin, and Pevek and the often 'snow-blanketed
airport of Anadyr' '. The gold is produced by the Chaun-Chukotsk
mining enterprise from the Ichuveyem river valley about 700 km.
south-west of the little port of Pevek on Chaun Bay. Chita was long
the sole producer of tin in the Soviet Union and tin, one of the few
minerals in short supply in the USSR, had to be imported in considerable quantities. The discovery of tin in both Chukotka
(at Iul'tin and Val'kumey near Pevek) and Yakutia (at Ese-Khaya,
and Deputatskiy in the wild, little known lands between the Yana
and the Indigirka) was therefore of great if long-term national
importance to the Soviet economy. Exploitation in these places
involved enormous difficulties of supply, transport, and labour, and
correspondingly high costs of production. It is typical of the complicated problems obstructing the working of these deposits that before
the Iul'tin mine could produce tin (in 1959) a port had to be built
at Egvekinot, due south of the Gulf of Anadyr', to get supplies in
and the tin out.[2] Iul'tin was built as the first automated undertaking
in the Far East. It may perhaps be regarded as the prototype of the
automation solution to the endemic labour problem in the Far North

[1] Ibid. 8 October 1959.   [2] Armstrong, op. cit. pp. 133–4.

(East).[1] It was estimated that Yakutia produced 21 per cent. of Soviet tin in 1957.[2] No later estimates of production have been noted though it must have risen considerably meanwhile.

Two new tin-producing areas in the south are also important. First, the large new tin area in and around Gornyy (formerly Solnechnyy) in the Khabarovsk kray, where production started in 1963. Here the metal content is reported to be high and conditions for transport, supplies, and labour much better than in the northern areas. Nevertheless, Gornyy tin concentrate has to be sent for smelting thousands of kilometres west to Ryazan' pending the construction of a smelter at Gornyy planned for completion in 1966–70. The oldest tin-mines in the Soviet Far East are in the Sikhote Alin area of the Primor'ye north of Vladivostok. After the war, mines and concentrators were opened at Kavalerovo, Khrustal'nyy, Vysokogorsk, and Krasnorechenskiy. Khrustal'nyy produces 'almost the cheapest tin in the country', and now has a highly automated, modern plant.[3] The Khrustal'nyy tin mining–concentrating combine has become an experimental centre and is reported to have introduced new operational methods in the mines to improve labour productivity and lower costs. It is to be expanded in 1966–70. Lead and zinc of high quality are also found in the coastal regions of the Sikhote Alin, often associated with silver. The main groups of deposits are located near the Tetyukhe River and the Great and Little Sinancha rivers. The Tetyukhe deposits were worked by a British concession from 1924 to the early '30s. They can be shipped by a narrow-gauge railway twenty miles long to the docks at the mouth of the Tetyukhe. There are at least three concentration plants but no post-war production figures are available.[4]

The discovery of a kimberlite pipe in the dense, 'untrodden' Yakut taiga in 1954 was a wonderful stroke of luck for the young Soviet geologist, Yuri Khabardin. This was the diamond source that scientists and geologists had long sought for in vain (it had been preceded by the discovery of alluvial diamonds in the Vilyuy basin in 1949). 'Khabardin noticed a fox hole and a fresh pile of unusual blue earth alongside it. This was kimberlite. A very ordinary way

[1] *Problemy Razvitiya Proizvoditel'nykh Sil Magadanskoy Oblasti*, pp. 68–80.
[2] *The American Metal Market*, 21 January 1961.   [3] *Izvestiya*, 21 June 1964
[4] E Thiel, *The Soviet Far East*, translated by A. and R. M. Wookwoud (Methuen, London, 1957) p. 191.

to make such an extraordinary discovery.' It turned out to be one of the richest diamond deposits in the world, comparable to the South African diamond mines, and was named 'Mir' or peace. A new town, Mirnyy, has gradually grown up round the diamond deposits with dressing mills and some 25,000 inhabitants in 1965.[1] These mills only work in summer because the intense winter frosts penetrate the walls of the mill and everything freezes, including water. The Academy of Sciences apparently at one time overestimated the importance of artificial diamonds and did not devote proper attention to the peculiar construction problems created by the ferocious Mirnyy weather. A new mill is now being built with aluminium-panelled walls separated by special insulation material which, it is reported, cannot be penetrated even by the sharpest Yakut frosts. From the Mirnyy mills the diamonds go to Moscow and become the responsibility of the Ministry of Finance. Diamonds weighing more than 20 carats are distinguished by name. The largest so far found at Mirnyy, the Oktyabrskiy, weighs 69.4 carats, according to a recent Soviet report.[2] A richer pipe than Mirnyy is now being worked at Aykhal north of Mirnyy and geologists anticipate the discovery of still richer deposits, farther north on the Olenyok River. It is symbolic of the changing conditions of life among the Yakuts that the credit for discovering 'still another new kimberlite pipe with high diamond content' is given to a young Yakut Komsomol geologist, the son of a Yakut collective farm reindeer breeder of the Altankhanov tundra and a recent graduate of Yakutsk State University.[3] A group of young Soviet architects from all over the Soviet Union, including one Yakut, have been given their head to build a fantastic new town at Aykhal. It is to have a blue plastic roof to protect it from the Arctic chill. 'An artificial microclimate will be maintained in the town regardless of the temperature outside', and it will accommodate 8,000 people. How far this ambitious plan will be realized, nobody can yet say.

The diamond industry is reported to have more than paid for itself in the last seven years,[4] despite the fact that large and even unique undertakings involving heavy capital expediture had to be set up in this formerly uninhabited roadless region. The only

---

[1] Much of this information is taken from *Soviet Life*, 'Diamond Town', p. 30.
[2] Ibid. p. 30.   [3] *Pravda*, 4 May 1966.   [4] *Ekon. G.*, no. 36 (1965).

Diamond Institute in the Soviet Union is in Mirnyy. Soviet diamond production is now believed to cover most Soviet needs and to leave a surplus for export. The Yakut kimberlite pipes are estimated in various foreign trade journals to produce about 90 per cent. of Soviet diamond output amounting to 3–6 million carats annually. Exports are marketed abroad by the International Diamond Syndicate. Though Soviet Russia stopped trading with South Africa a few years ago, Soviet diamonds are still reaching this organization, it is believed, through an intermediary.

Extraction of gold, tin, wolfram, mercury, diamonds, and mica in the Far East is to be greatly increased in the Five Year Plan period 1966–70. The specific mention of these commodities in the text of the Plan directives reflects the national importance attached to them by the Soviet Government.

Metallurgy

The question of the creation of a metallurgical base somewhere east of Lake Baykal has been inconclusively discussed for years by Soviet party leaders and technical experts. No iron is produced in the Far East at present. Lack of precise knowledge of conveniently located reserves of iron in this area was long an obstacle to a decision, while the heavy costs of metallurgical construction and production in the Far East were weighed (often unfavourably) against the high costs of importing metal from European Russia and Siberia. A typical analysis of the relative costs of construction and production in the Far East and European Russia, for example, showed that capital investment in the construction of twenty engineering works in the Soviet Far East was 18 million roubles or 30 per cent. above the cost of construction in European Russia; expenditure on one rouble of commercial production in the engineering industry and metal-working industry was stated to be 20 per cent. higher than in European Russia and on many types of machines and manufactured articles 30–35 per cent. higher.[1]

A detailed examination of the problems involved in developing ferrous metallurgy in the regions east of Lake Baykal by the Academy of Sciences of the USSR and several other technical research bodies criticized the disproportion between the production and growing

[1] *Voprosy Ekonomiki*, no. 10 (1965).

demand for metals and machines in the Far East and recommended that the long hauls involved in bringing metals and machines from European Russia to the Far East should be terminated by the local manufacture of metallurgical products. These bodies also agreed on 'the possibility and economic expediency of planning the creation of three new large metallurgical plants in the regions east of Lake Baykal'.[1] Chul'man in Yakutia was selected as the first choice for the new plant because it was in close proximity to the large coking coal deposits of the south Yakut basin and the Aldan iron ore deposits. These rather specious recommendations on this complicated problem were made in 1960, but so far without implementation.

Meanwhile more precise prospecting of the Far Eastern iron ore reserves has revealed that the iron ore deposits of the Amur basin are much larger than was hitherto suspected. The most important mines at Malyy Khingan (west of Khabarovsk) and near Selemd-zhinsk at the confluence of the Zeya and the Selemdzha (the Garinskiy ore-field) are estimated to have large exploitable reserves of high-quality ores which would support a considerable iron and steel industry, if coking coal were also easily available. The cost of importing Sakhalin coal makes it uneconomic to use for this purpose and the more convenient local deposits so far prospected are apparently not suitable for coking.

It is interesting in this connexion to recall that two Soviet scientists discussing the prospects of the Sino-Soviet Amur projects in 1961 stressed their importance for the development of an Amur iron and steel industry: 'Its geological coal reserves are estimated at 200,000 million tons, 40,000 million being in Soviet territory and 160,000 million in China. Sizeable deposits of iron ores (the Berezovskoye, Garsk, and Kimkan deposits in Soviet territory; the Nun'tsyan, Ichun, Tunkhua, and other deposits in China) have been discovered as well. Coupled with the stocks of coking coals this creates the essential prerequisites for the development of the iron and steel industry.'[2] Whatever its merits nothing will be done about this joint scheme until Sino-Soviet relations return to normal.

The need for the creation of a powerful base of heavy metallurgy with a full production cycle and the further extension of *Amurstal*

[1] I. P. Bardin, *Problemy Razvitiya Chernoy Metallurgii v Rayonakh Vostochneye Ozera Baykala* (Moscow, 1960). [2] *Ekon. G.*, 14 August 1961.

into a combine with a fully integrated metallurgical cycle was urged on the Government by the Far Eastern delegate to the Supreme Soviet in December 1964.[1] A policy decision has at last been taken by the Central Committee of the CPSU, at least in principle. The draft directives for the 1966–70 Plan require that 'designing-prospecting work for the creation in the Far East of a new metallurgical base of the country should be carried out'. It must not be expected that even now construction of this base will follow overnight. Much preparatory work still remains to be done. And on the analogy of the third metallurgical base (Karaganda–West Siberian–Tayshet) production should not be expected to start until about 10–15 years after actual construction of the base gets going. For the moment, the situation will be partly eased when the first Far Eastern blast furnace now under construction at the *Amurstal'* steel works is completed.

FUEL AND POWER

The Soviet Far East has large reserves of both bituminous (stone) and brown coal. Geological reserves in Yakutia and Magadan are estimated at 2,500 milliard tons, or one-third of USSR total reserves; there is a high proportion of coking coal in the prospected areas of south Yakutia centred on the large Chul'man mines, but less is known of the quality elsewhere. The main producing area at present is the Raychikhinsk basin (lignite and not suitable for coking) on the borders of the Amur *oblast* and the Khabarovsk kray, with an annual output of 10 million tons, or nearly half the total of 22 million tons of coal produced by the Far Eastern region. The unworked deposits in this area are enormous. North-east of Raychikhinsk is the Upper Bureya basin, the chief production centre for high-quality stone coal (not coking) and directly connected with Izvestkovyy on the Trans-Siberian railway. The Primor'ye is supplied from the old Suchan mines discovered in 1888 and then used mainly for the Russian Navy. This is excellent coking coal. Very large deposits of brown coal are also found in the neighbourhood of Suchan at Artem in the Primor'ye kray and there are other minor deposits scattered throughout the area.

[1] *Izvestiya*, 12 December 1964.

The island of Sakhalin produces both lignite and hard coal amounting to about 4.5 million tons annually and planned to rise to 6 million tons in 1970. The hard coals are of good quality and are exported to Kamchatka, Magadan, up the Amur, and to Japan (but are among the most costly to produce in the Soviet Union). The Far Eastern coal reserves seem adequate for any foreseeable future local requirements. Production represents 4.5 per cent. of the all-Union total. In view of the reserves this quantity could be considerably increased.)

As a result of serious mistakes in planning, 1 million tons of coal are annually imported by Primor'ye, the local Party Secretary told the Twenty-Third Party Congress in March 1966. The imported coal, he said, was more than twice as dear as that produced in the kray and of poorer quality. Coal production should be raised in the new Plan to 12 million tons in 1970 if the needs of industry and domestic consumption were to be satisfied. But the target actually set by Gosplan and the Ministry of the Coal Industry of the USSR only required a negligible increase in coal extraction, according to the Party Secretary, who took a poor view generally of Gosplan decisions for his kray and was no doubt hoping by his intervention to have them revised in the final draft of the Plan.

Oil

Until a few years ago, the only oil wells known to exist in the Far Eastern region were on the north-east coast of Sakhalin Island.[1] Even intensive exploration by the Japanese while the southern half of the island was in their hands failed to reveal any oil there. However, in recent years petroleum deposits have also been geologically confirmed in Yakutia. Sakhalin oil is of the greatest importance to the Far Eastern economy though production is still far short of local requirements. Present production is estimated at about 2 million tons per annum and is planned to rise to 3.5 million tons in 1970 as a result of extraction from new wells. The oil is piped from the main producing area of Okha on the east coast to the petroleum port of Moskal'vo on the west coast of the island and through the Tartary Strait to the refineries at Vladivostok, Khabarovsk, and Komsomol'sk. A second string is now being built to the Sakhalin pipeline.

[1] Fuller technical details of Sakhalin oil deposits and extraction are given in Professor Thiel's *The Soviet Far East*, pp. 178–82.

Sakhalin oil (crude) is also regularly shipped to Japan, but it only represents about 10 per cent. of the total Soviet exports of oil to Japan, the bulk of which comes from the Soviet Black Sea ports. Sakhalin oil is of high quality and suitable for conversion into various products which would also probably find a market in Japan when the proposed refinery is built on the island. Exports to Japan are hampered by the freezing up of the ports during the long winter.

The petroleum potential of Yakutia is estimated in Soviet sources, somewhat vaguely, at 'many milliards of tons'.[1] The main oilfields are at Kangalassy (north of the town of Yakutsk) and at Ust'-Maya at the confluence of the Aldan and Maya rivers south-east of Yakutsk. The development of these oil-fields is not mentioned in the current Draft Plan for 1966–70 and owing to the difficult geographical and climatic conditions of the areas in which they are located will probably be postponed till some later period when the transport position, at least, may be expected to improve.[2] Should the political situation between the Soviet Union and China deteriorate further, development of Yakut oil might be pushed forward to help build up Soviet oil reserves.

Natural Gas

Natural gas is also produced at the Okha oil deposits. It is not yet refined in Sakhalin. A refinery is to be built at Okha to supply Yuzhno-Sakhalinsk and other towns on the island and a new petrochemical industry for the production of fertilizers. It is also proposed to build a gas pipeline from Okha to Komsomol'sk within two years.[3] The gas deposits of the Lena–Vilyuy area of central Yakutia contain enormous quantities of gas, estimated at five or six trillions of cubic metres.[4] Hitherto these gas-fields have not been commercially exploited and only small amounts were used for local consumption. Now, under the provisions of the Draft Plan for 1966–70, they are to be developed. Cost has hitherto been a limiting factor on development owing to the remoteness from industrial centres or organized transport of the deposits. According to a Gosplan report of 1965, the transmission of Yakut gas to the industrial districts of the Far

---

[1] *Ekon. G.*, no. 35 (1965).
[2] *Petroleum Press Service*, vol. XXXIII, no. 4 (April 1966), p. 131.
[3] *Pravda*, 3 June 1965.   [4] *Ekon G.*, no. 35 (1965).

Natural Gas Fields and Pipelines

Gas Fields
★ Large ▲ Medium • Other

Gas Pipelines
—— Working
– – – Under construction
········· Projected

Reproduced from GAZOVAYA PROMYSHLENNOST, January, 1965

East and east Siberia is 'extremely difficult technically and economically inadvisable' and in many cases is dearer than coal in the Far East.[1]
Nevertheless, development is now planned and a pipeline is being
constructed from the major gas concentration at Ust'Vilyuyskoye
300 km. north of Yakutsk to Yakutsk and Pokrovsk. It will be the
first pipeline in the Soviet Union to run through a permafrost region
and was scheduled for operation in 1966.

Electric Power

The Soviet Far East has a huge latent potential for electric power
development which is far in excess of the present industrial–domestic
requirements. In Yakutia and Magadan *oblast*, traversed by the great
Lena, Yana, and Kolyma rivers, the potential is estimated at 70
million kW. of hydro-power, or one-fifth of the USSR potential.
Farther south the Amur, the largest river of the Far Eastern region
(2,690 miles from the Onon source to the delta), awaits development
though economic and climatic conditions are more favourable than
in the north. Here the difficulties are directly due not to nature but
to politics.

The Joint Sino-Soviet Research and Development Project agreed
in 1956 promised great things for the exploitation of hydro-electric
power and the development of industry and natural resources in the
Amur basin. In the early days of this scheme both Soviet and Chinese
scientists referred enthusiastically to its far-reaching possibilities.
Soviet Academician V. Nemchinov emphasized the value of joint
Sino-Soviet exploitation of the considerable iron deposits discovered
on the Soviet side of the frontier and the coal resources on the
Chinese side, while the leader of the Chinese expedition referred to
the great significance of the proposed linking of the Amur to the
Yellow Sea by way of the Sungari and Liao-Ho rivers.[2] A Sino-
Soviet agreement on shipping and waterway maintenance along the
Amur River was signed at a conference in Harbin in 1959 and arrangements were to be made for the regulation of the trade between the
two countries. But nothing seems to have been published about these
arrangements if, in fact, they ever materialized.

Details of the impressive hydro-electric projects envisaged by the
Joint Expedition were published the following year in the *Journal*

[1] *Voprosy Razmeshcheniya Proizvodstva v SSSR*, p. 260.   [2] Tass, 19 March 1957.

of the USSR Academy of Sciences.[1] It was proposed that two hydro-electric stations should be built on the Argun River with a total capacity of 190,000 kW. and five stations on the upper reaches of the Amur River with an aggregate capacity of between 5 and 6 million kW. It was pointed out that the setting up of a single Soviet-Chinese power system in the Amur River basin would make possible the exchange of power between the two countries. If such schemes had actually materialized they would undoubtedly have had a far-reaching effect on the development of the whole north Manchurian–Amur region. But in such a sensitive frontier area, even the soundest economic plans in the last resort depend for fruition on the state of political relations between the Soviet Union and China. It is therefore not surprising that since the Sino-Soviet conflict erupted in the 1960s, nothing more has been heard about the progress of this joint Amur project. A good deal of fundamental research and prospecting of resources seems to have been done but nothing more solid achieved before the project was quietly suspended in 1961–2. The development of the huge reserves of hydro-electric power of the Amur and its tributaries 'is only possible with the general complex solutions of the development and distribution of productive forces in the southern part of the Far East and North-East China', according to a Soviet comment.[2] Large-scale development of Amur hydro-power must therefore await the healing of the Sino-Soviet breach.

The spring floods which have long been so disastrous to crops and animals and even human life in the upper Amur basin are now to be curbed by the construction of a hydro-electric power station on the Zeya River, a powerful, turbulent tributary of the Amur. The scheme was originally proposed by Academician Nemchinov[3] and was approved by the Twenty-Third Party Congress and explicitly mentioned in the Draft Plan (1966–70). Work is now in progress on this station (1,200,000 kW. capacity) and experienced workers from Bratsk, Irkutsk, and other hydro-power sites have moved there. Construction is expected to take about three years to

[1] Tass, 9 April 1960.

[2] V. A. Shvarev (ed.), *Dal'niy Vostok za 40 Let Sovetskoy vlasti* (Iz. AN SSSR, Komsomol'sk, 1958) p. 34.

[3] *Planirovanie i ekonomiko-matematicheskie metody* (Moscow, 1964). Essays on the seventieth anniversary of V. S. Nemchinov.

complete.[1] It is intended to provide cheap power for the industries of the Soviet Far East from the Zeya hydro-power station and it is expected that when the threat of flooding is removed agriculture and some local industries may expand.

A beginning has also been made with the development of hydro-power in Yakutia. The site selected is in the depths of northern taiga–tundra country on the River Vilyuy rapids at Chernyshevskiy where a workers' settlement of 10,000 people has sprung up in formerly uninhabited country. Construction of this *Vilyuyges* is extremely complicated and difficult.[2] It is to be built 30 metres under the river-bed so as to ensure an even temperature in permafrost country with ferocious winters and up to 70° of frost. *Vilyuyges* was scheduled to go on load in 1966 with a capacity, when completed, of 316,000 kW. Its power is destined for the great diamond-mining areas of Mirnyy, Aykhal, and even Udachnaya in the Arctic Circle.[3] Further development of the new city of Mirnyy, the centre of the Yakut diamond mining industry, is being held up for lack of electric power so the completion of the Vilyuy station is extremely important, though fraught with great difficulties.

A hydro-electric station is also planned at Debin on the upper Kolyma to start generation in 1972. It will be linked with the Arka-gala GRES (State Regional Electric Station) and the Magadan TETs to form a single Kolyma grid.

Thermal power stations have also been set up on an *ad hoc* basis in other mining areas of the Far Eastern region. There are thermal stations at Chul'man and Yakutsk which are reported to be too large and now working below capacity. On the other hand Magadan is short of power and costs of the local station are high (it is operated on expensive Sakhalin coal). Other medium-sized thermal power stations exist at Raychikhinsk, Vladivostok, Artem, and Ussuriysk, while others are under construction at Yuzhno-Sakhalinsk (due to start operating at the end of 1965 and to reach full capacity in 1970) and in Bikin (Khabarovsk kray), based on the recently discovered local coal deposits.

Speaking to the Twenty-Third Party Congress, the Primorskiy delegate and First Secretary of the Primorskiy kray, V. E. Cherny-

[1] V. Kolykhalov, 'Rozhdaetsya Zeyskaya GES', *Dal'niy Vostok*, no. 3 (1966).
[2] *Pravda*, 2 November 1966.　　　　[3] Ibid. 21 May and 26 May 1965.

shev, made it clear that in his opinion the planned measures for the development of hydro-power in his kray from the point of view of regulating flooding, agriculture (including irrigation for the expansion of rice cultivation), and economic development were quite inadequate. He urged the construction of a Primor'ye GRES and a Vladivostok thermal electric station and expansion of the Artem and Suchan GRES. But Gosplan has not yet as far as is known pronounced on these proposals.

The first 'geo-thermal' power station in the Soviet Union based on the underground hot springs is being constructed in Kamchatka and was due to go on load at the end of 1965.[1] This experiment should prove a boon to a region otherwise deficient in fuel resources but requiring a considerable quantity of electric power for its development.

LOCAL INDUSTRY[2]

The major industries of this region, i.e. fisheries, timber, mining, have already been discussed. In many remoter areas these are the only industrial occupations because of the lack of small local industries and the heavy concentration of manufacturing industry in the southern districts of the Khabarovsk and Primorskiy krays. Though many new industries of local importance have been established in the Soviet period, and include a wide range of commodities, large quantities of consumer goods, especially clothing and food, are still imported (at heavy cost by rail) from other parts of the Soviet Union and from China.

There is an old-established building materials industry producing bricks, cement, and other materials. The Far East produced 1,692,000 tons of cement in 1963, or 4.5 per cent. of the RSFSR total. Costs of production of building materials are very high, ferro-concrete, for example, being eleven times above the USSR average. It may be because of costs (restricting sales) that brick production was barely higher in 1965 than in 1940 in spite of the large increase in the urban population. In general the subsidiary industries do not provide adequate support for the main industries of fisheries, mining, and forestry; ship repair and port facilities, food and clothing production

[1] Ibid. 20 February 1965.   [2] For details of local industries see Appendix I.

are all below local requirements. The First Secretary of the Primor-skiy kray admitted at the Twenty-Third Party Congress that the development of the shore installations was considerably behind the growth of the commercial fleet and that the construction of ports, refrigeration capacity, and the completion of the refrigeration and transport fleet was proceeding slowly.[1]

It is clear from the following table that output of the light

Selected Items of Industrial Production in the Far East (compared to the whole RSFSR)[2]

1963

	Far East	Main producing areas in the Far East	Far East as percentage of the RSFSR
Population (1 January 1964)	5,278,000	—	4.2
Product			
Paper (tons)	212,000	Sakhalin, Khabarovsk	9.1
Cement (tons)	1,700,000	(various)	4.5
Window glass (sq. metres)	5,088,000	Amur, Magadan	5.3
Cotton textiles[3] (sq. metres)	9,200,000	Khabarovsk	0.2
Knitwear (articles)	1,609,000	Amur, Khabarovsk	0.5
Furniture (roubles)	36,042,000	Primor'ye, Khabarovsk	3.8
Boots and shoes (pairs)	1,253,000	(various)	4.8
Radio sets	57,600		1.9
Sugar, granulated (tons)	47,600	Primor'ye	2.7
Meat (tons)	56,400	Primor'ye, Amur	1.9
Butter (tons)	9,073	Amur, Yakutia	2.2
Vegetable oils (tons)	48,144	Primor'ye, Khabarovsk	5.3
Conserves (conventional cans)[4]	245,000,000	Primor'ye, Kamchatka, Sakhalin	8.5
Confectionery (tons)	65,000	Primor'ye, Khabarovsk, Amur	5.3
Export of industrial timber (million cu. metres)	16,5		6.7

Source: *Nar. Khoz. RSFSR v 1963 g.* (percentages partly calculated).

[1] *Pravda*, 1 April 1966.
[2] Excluding areas in the Arctic Circle and equated to it, in the Far Eastern region.
[3] No woollen, silk, or linen textiles are produced in the Far East.
[4] Mainly fish conserves which are largely exported from the region.

industries in the Soviet Far East is inadequate for the needs of the population and only in a few cases (like paper) contributes to the resources of the RSFSR.

TRANSPORT

The main trunk-line connecting the Soviet Far East with central Russia, the Amur railway, was completed in 1916. This spur of the Trans-Siberian railway branched off from the Transbaykal line at Kuenga and followed an irregular arc to Khabarovsk 'through a forbidding, unpopulated wilderness of mountains, forests, boglands and marshy plains all beyond artillery range of the Amur's Manchurian bank'.[1] The great advantage of this second line to Vladivostok was that it ran entirely through Russian territory while the older southern track to Vladivostok through Harbin traversed foreign Chinese territory and was thus always a security risk for Moscow. Under favourable political circumstances, the Chinese eastern route through Manchuria has the advantage of being 600 miles shorter than the Amur line and much traffic between the Soviet Union and Vladivostok passes that way.

In the Soviet period no construction of parallel importance has been undertaken, but several additions of some local significance have been built: (1) the line from Khabarovsk to Sovetskaya Gavan' through Komsomol'sk; (2) the line from Bureya to the Raychikhinsk coal-fields and several branches leading to the coast from the main line in the southern part of Primorskiy kray. A new line also runs directly from Ussuriysk to the North Korean frontier without passing through Chinese territory. The Soviet claim that the railway network in the Far Eastern region has been trebled seems to be largely based on the acquisition of the Japanese-built line running up the centre of south Sakhalin. Now, twenty years later, this line is being extended to reach the oil- and coal-fields in the north of the island.

As yet there are no railways in either Yakutia or Magadan *oblast*, though recently many voices have been raised urging the need for a railway. Mirnyy, for example, is 1,200 miles from the nearest railway station and the nearest landing stage on the Lena is 185 miles away.

[1] Tupper, op. cit. p. 424.

'The development of the natural resources of Yakutia and the whole of the north-east region of the USSR is also being held up by the absence of a railway', complained S. Borisov, the First Secretary of the Yakut Obkom.[1] He urged the speedy construction of the Bam–Chul'man railway[2] and its eventual extension as far as the town of Tommot (on the south Yakutian main road from Bol'shoy Never to Yakutsk). 'The only motor road linking south Yakutia with the railway is in bad condition', he added. 'Supposing no railway were built, the cost of repairing the road would be almost as high as would have been the cost of building the railway.' The proposed route from Bam, a small station on the Trans-Siberian railway, to the Chul'man coal-fields, would presumably run parallel to the Bol'shoy Never (a station to the east of Bam on the Trans-Siberian railway) to Chul'man main road. In his zeal for local interests, the Yakut First Secretary may well have exaggerated the costs of road versus railway building. In these areas of permafrost and taiga, costs of construction can be formidable, as the Tsarist Russian Government responsible for the construction of the Amur railway, farther south, learnt to its cost. The need for a second Far Eastern railway has also been strongly stressed by V. Kozhevnikov, Chairman of the State Committee for Railway Construction. 'The existing Trans-Siberian railway may very soon become a bottle-neck', he said, 'therefore it is already necessary to work out constructional projects for the North Siberian main line.'[3]

These proposals seem to be partly a revival of the mysterious Baykal–Amur railway, a scheme which aroused lively interest when it was first mooted in the late '30s. The progress of this grandiose project still remains unknown. Construction largely by forced labour started in 1938. The line was planned to run from Tayshet on the Trans-Siberian through wild, partly uninhabited forest areas of eastern Siberia and to cross the gold-fields in the north Amur region to a terminal at Komsomol'sk some 2,200 miles away. The first section of the railway was completed, from Tayshet to Ust'-Kut on the Lena via Bratsk. Farther east nothing is known with any

[1] *Ekon. G.*, no. 35 (1965).

[2] This proposal actually echoed a recommendation made by a Conference on the Industrial Development of East Siberia of the USSR Academy of Sciences held in Irkutsk in 1958 (*Pravda*, 17 January 1959).

[3] *Planovoye Khozyaystvo*, no. 6 (1965).

certainty about its route, but it is generally believed to have been dropped. The difficulties of constructing such a railway would be immense and the cost, estimated in 1941 at approximately $250,000,000, is, in the opinion of some Western experts, prohibitive.[1] Others believe that 'it is a railway of the future and that following its track a belt of settlement will slowly appear'.[2] This view is probably right. Neither cost nor physical difficulties have ever deterred the Russians (who are indomitable railway builders on a grand scale) from embarking on a scheme of this kind, once they decide it is really necessary for economic or strategic reasons. It is all a question of priorities at a particular time. The announcement in January 1966 that the Soviet Government had decided to build the North Siberian railway, which will serve the whole north-eastern region extending from east Siberia through Yakutia, is no doubt the answer to this problem.[3]

Communications between the Primor'ye and Sakhalin should be greatly improved by the train ferry which is being organized between the ports of Vanino, north-east of Sovetskaya Gavan', and Khol'msk on the east coast of Sakhalin Island. Ships of an ice-breaker type will be used on this route in order to ensure all-season services which are now prevented by ice farther north on the Amur route, and to ease trans-loading. Vanino is being built up to be the largest port on the Soviet Pacific coast and thus in time it may eclipse the other new port of Nakhodka, which is also being modernized and expanded to cope with coastal trade. If this rail ferry is to function smoothly, the state of affairs on the Sakhalin railway will have to be greatly improved. A check on the situation on this line reported in *Gudok* (12 August 1966) showed that 'over 6,000 tank cars had accumulated in Yuzhno-Sakhalinsk. They cannot all be dealt with in the available sidings area. . . . It is amazing that the management of the railroad and the Far Eastern service do not give proper attention to these problems', declared *Gudok*.

Access to the Pacific from the Soviet mainland should be facilitated by the projected 14 km. long canal from the Amur to Tabo Bay on the Tartar Straits. According to the Director of the Far East Geographical Institute, one of its sponsors, it would enable

[1] Tupper, op. cit. p. 424.   [2] Thiel, op. cit. pp. 223–4.
[3] This line is discussed in the section on 'Siberia', p. 283.

ocean-going ships to go up the Amur as far as Komsomol'sk and would shorten transportation time from Khabarovsk to Sakhalin and Japan by a month and a half.[1]

The main imports by rail into the Far Eastern region from the west are: mineral oil products, grain, salt (for the fishing industry), machinery, industrial equipment, and consumer goods including food and textiles from China.[2] As the *Amurstal'* works does not yet have its own blast furnaces, pig-iron has been normally imported from Manchuria, and in spite of the Sino-Soviet conflict, still seemed to be coming through in 1965–6. It is not mentioned among Soviet imports by rail from Manchuria but appears among the Chinese exports in the Soviet foreign trade statistics and is therefore probably imported by sea. Exports from the Far East by rail are mainly large quantities of fish products, non-ferrous metal concentrates, cement, and ferrous scrap. Within the region the main items transported by rail are coal, wood products, minerals, construction and oil freight. Incoming considerably exceeds outgoing freight in the traffic with Siberia and European Russia owing to the need for so many manufactures and consumer goods.

In an area in which such large expanses of the country are roadless, the few arterial highways already in existence are of vital importance. During Dal'stroy's twenty-five years of police domination, 7,000 km. of road were built by forced labourers in conditions of terrible hardship in Magadan and east Yakutia. The major construction was the Magadan trunk-road running north-east through the Kolyma and Indigirka mining areas, then south via the Aldan gold-fields to Bol'shoy Never on the Trans-Siberian railway. This good modern road has made the former nightmare journey through roadless, perilous country relatively short and safe. Farther north a road is also to be built from Pevek in Chutkotka via Bilibino to Zelennyy Mys to link the gold-mines' centre with these ports. In the south the road system is much better developed. An important highway from Sokol'chi in Primor'ye follows the railway to Nakhodka, Vladivostok, and Khabarovsk into east Siberia. The nodal point of Ust'-Nera on the Magadan–Yakutsk road is now being connected with Khandyga on the Aldan River by a new road.

River transportation is extremely important in this north-eastern

[1] Moscow radio, 2 November 1965.   [2] Danilov, op. cit.

area of the Far East where roads are few and railways non-existent. It is also much used in the south mainly on the Amur and its tributaries. Navigation along the Amur is by large and small steamers; goods are usually transported by barge. There is also an Amur naval force with its base at Khabarovsk consisting of river gun-boats for frontier patrol. The Amur delta is too shallow to allow sea-going ships to sail far inland past the mouth. Freight has to be transhipped to smaller craft at Nikolayevsk. This situation will be eased when the proposed Amur Canal is built. At the present time there is a rail ferry over the Amur River between the towns of Komsomol'sk and Pivan, and in the near future a rail bridge is to be built to replace the ferry, so that it will be possible for traffic to continue throughout the winter months.

The extreme difficulty of transport in the north and north-east may be exemplified by the tortuous course of supplies between Yakutsk and the tin-mining region of Ese-Khaya. As the two places are separated by the impassable Verkhoyansk range, supplies travel down the Lena to the Arctic, then across the Laptev sea coast and up the Yana, a journey of well over 2,000 km. (complicated by the harsh climate and the seasonal closure of the route). The distance as the crow flies is only 400 km. Tin concentrates sent from the Ese-Khaya mining plants take a year to reach the smelter at Novosibirsk.[1] River transport in these areas is frequently criticized in Soviet sources for inefficiency and particularly for the waste involved in one-way loads. 'On the Lena, for example, river vessels with a total loading capacity of about a million tons are sent empty to port Osetrovo—the terminus of the Tayshet–Lena railway', wrote one of these critics.[2] 'Unfortunately, nothing has yet been done by Gosplan and the Ministry of the River Fleet of the RSFSR to stop or at least reduce one-way river transport. On the contrary this form of transport has been sanctioned: the point is that the cost price of transportation includes all expenses connected with the return trip of the empty vessels, but even if the cost price reckoned in this way were increased half as much again it would be almost 70 per cent. lower than the profit rate fixed for Lena shipping. . . . Reasonable rates for transport by Lena vessels have been repeatedly suggested to the appropriate ministers by the Yakut Committee of the CP.

[1] *Ekon. Rayony*, p. 334. [2] *Ekon. G.*, no. 35 (1965).

z

But they have not yet been adopted.' From this controversy it seems that, failing competition, some intervention is badly needed to shake up the State monopoly of the river fleet and produce reasonable transport charges on the Lena.

An amalgamated Far Eastern Shipping Corporation (directorate) now controls all shipping along the Soviet Pacific coast and around the islands. It was formed in 1964 from the Sakhalin, Far Eastern, and Kamchatkan shipping directorates and has subsequently been active in modernizing its fleet, buying new ships, and increasing the volume and range of its operations.[1] The Kamchatkan directorate of the Far Eastern Corporation, which carried no cargo to foreign ports in 1958, was reported in 1965 to be carrying timber to Japan and to have doubled its cargo in this period. It also acquired a fleet of modern ships, including more tankers. Exports of timber from Kamchatka are being stepped up and facilities are being organized at the ports of Petropavlovsk and Ust'Kamchatsk to handle this timber in 1970. All the corporation's ships were to have been converted to oil firing by the end of 1965 according to local plan. This conversion from coal to oil will make it possible to reduce the size of the crews on cargo ships while increasing productivity (according to Soviet sources). It may also be an answer to the labour turnover problem should it extend to the Far Eastern fleet. There are thus many signs of hitherto unwonted economic activity in the Kamchatkan ports and their inclusion in the current programme for expanding Soviet Far Eastern trade.

In order to link up the enormous 'roadless', 'railless' expanses of the Soviet Far East, air transport was introduced early in the '30s and has been constantly improved and expanded since World War II. It is now the most heavily used, popular means of passenger transport. Every settlement of any size has its airstrip.[2] The main route connects Moscow with Vladivostok via Skovorodino, Birobidzhan, Khabarovsk, Ussuriysk (formerly Voroshilov), and other intermediate stations. There are also regular services to Sakhalin and Kamchatka. Air communications are especially important in the Far North and the Far East both for passenger and goods traffic. There are also purely commercial services to and from the Far

[1] *Pravda*, 25 July 1964.
[2] Armstrong, op. cit. p. 140.

Eastern gold-fields, for example. Planes transport tractors, motor vehicles, and spare parts for dredges to the north. In the more remote areas planes are fitted with skis enabling them to land on snow and ice. The centre of this Far Eastern air traffic is Khabarovsk. Far Eastern air schedules have been greatly accelerated in recent years. For example, in 1960 it took eight hours to fly from Irkutsk to Yakutsk, making two stops *en route*. In 1964, a non-stop flight from Irkutsk to Yakutsk took three hours. Turbo-prop aircraft were introduced on the Yakut air services in 1965. Fares on all these routes are relatively low.[1] There are now airports in Chukotka at Uelen and Anadyr' where people who have never seen a train are familiar with planes. A direct line between Anadyr'–Magadan–Krasnoyarsk–Moscow was established in 1964.

SOVIET FAR EASTERN TRADE WITH THE 'PACIFIC RIM'

Until recent years the Far Eastern regions were not actively engaged in Soviet foreign trade apart from the small direct coastal trade with Japan. The idea that this area should participate more widely and directly in Soviet-Pacific trade now seems to be gaining ground in Moscow. 'The Far East is on the shores of the Pacific Ocean, on the basin of which are found the greatest populations numerically in the world and where more than half mankind lives. In view of the broad economic ties being established by the USSR with other countries of the Pacific Ocean, favourable conditions are being set up in the Far East for the development of the export branches of the economy.'[2] This is now the common Soviet publicity line on this subject. But when the situation is assessed more realistically from the point of view of the 'export branches' of the Far Eastern economy, it would seem that the possibilities of expansion of Soviet Far Eastern trade, however desirable politically and econmically, are severely limited by the small scale and range of the region's industrial output. Though this trade has undoubtedly been increasing in recent years, as the following analysis will show, and efforts will continue to be made to cut down the huge costs of freight imported by rail to the Far East from remote areas of the

[1] *Soviet Life* (June 1965), p. 28.   [2] *Ekon. Rayony*, p. 308.

Soviet Union amounting to some 200–250 million roubles annually,[1] it is unlikely to become a major feature of Soviet foreign trade as a whole.

Before 1917 industrial goods were regularly supplied to the Primor'ye and Khabarovsk regions from the United States of America, Germany, and Britain, while food was imported from Manchuria.[2] The region was in much closer contact with foreign countries than subsequently and as far as can be judged from contemporary reports it was much better off for ordinary domestic requirements than when later forced to rely on scarce Soviet supplies.

Soviet foreign trade figures do not distinguish between the coastal trade and trade between the ports in European Russia and Japan, but the breakdown was made in Japanese foreign trade statistics up to 1961. There were, however, Soviet reports that exports from the Far East had risen 50 per cent. from 1963 to 1965 and that the traditional importers like Japan had been joined by Algeria, Cuba, Yugoslavia, Yemen, Ethiopia, and Chile. Cuba imported Far Eastern timber, paper, and cellulose and sent sugar to Nakhodka. No futher details of these new clients' trade with the Soviet Far East have been traced.

The focal point in this coastal trade remains Japan. Her proximity to the Soviet Far Eastern region and the complementary nature of the resources of the two regions give her potentially a decided advantage over other countries in this trade especially since the crisis in Soviet-Chinese relations.[3] The Soviet Union has oil and

---

[1] Margolin, op. cit. p. 11.   [2] *Dal'niy Vostok*, p. 22.

[3] The great volume of Sino-Soviet trade as it developed to its peak before the Sino-Soviet conflict was not with the Far Eastern regions of the Soviet Union and is therefore not directly relevant to this study. Direct trade has been taking place between the border Heilunkiang province of the CPR and the Primorskiy kray of the USSR since 1958. This was confirmed by an Ussuriysk trade official talking on Moscow radio (5 April 1962), who said that the Amur *oblast* co-operative society has had trading relations with the Heilunkiang province of China since 1958 and that trade has increased each year since then. Exports, he said, comprise steel products, farm implements, petrol, medicine, and machinery. 'From China trains arrive regularly at Grodekovo with Chinese furniture, knitwear, dyestuffs, plywood, and light industrial products. Chinese and Soviet representatives meet to exchange samples', he added. The annual negotiations on trade continued at least as late as 1963 when a Chinese delegation arrived in Khabarovsk to discuss the 1963–4 trade agreement. According to a report in *Komsomolskaya Pravda* of February 1967, the Soviet Far Eastern region has received from China knitted goods, bricks, and cement, in exchange for petrol, bicycles, and watches, on a non-foreign-currency or barter exchange basis. 'But recently China began cutting down this trade.' This border trade even at its peak has never been large but was useful for filling local shortages in the adjacent Soviet areas.

natural gas, timber, and minerals of interest to Japan, while the Japanese engineering industries could supply many goods vital to more rapid development of the remote Far Eastern areas of the Soviet Union. Trade with Japan has been increasing since the signature of a Soviet-Japanese Treaty of Commerce and Navigation in 1957 but it still only accounted for 2½ per cent. of Japan's total trade in 1965. The Soviet Government set up an office of *Dalintorg* at Nakhodka in 1964 to deal with Soviet-Japanese coastal trade and empowered it to sign contracts directly with Japanese firms. It signed its first contract with the Japanese Sea Trading Company to send 2,000 tons of herring and other dried fish to Japan early in 1965. This coastal trade formed the larger part of Soviet-Japanese trade up till 1961 as appears from the following table of this trade between the Asian and European ports of the Soviet Union:

Japan's Trade with the USSR

(in millions of dollars)

	Far Eastern ports of the USSR		European ports of the USSR	
	Imports	Exports	Imports	Exports
1956	2.2	0.7	0.7	0.1
1957	10.8	5.7	1.5	3.6
1959	26.9	19.3	12.6	2.6
1960	40.0	42.6	47.0	17.3
1961	58.4	55.0	87.0	10.4

Source: *Trade of Japan 1963-4*, Japanese Ministry of Finance. Quoted in W. S. Hansberger, *Japan and the U.S. in World Trade* (Harper & Row, 1964), p. 212.

Separate statistics of Soviet-Japanese coastal trade are not now published but it is apparent from the Soviet-Japanese trade protocols that it is only a small part of Soviet-Japanese trade as a whole. According to Soviet sources it is, however, steadily increasing. Japanese imports from the USSR in 1965 were valued in Tokyo at £86,500,000, of which minerals (mainly coal but excluding metals) accounted for £8,000,000, oil for £21,500,000 and lumber for £21,000,000; imports from the Soviet Far Eestern region were however, estimated to be worth less than £1,000,000 in the same year. In addition to the main Soviet-Japanese trade agreement for 1966–70, there is a separate agreement covering the coastal trade between the Far Eastern regions of the USSR and Japan. It is envisaged that this trade should rise from £1.8 million in each direction in 1966 to £3.6 million in 1970 and the subject was discussed at the Japanese-Soviet Coastal Trade Joint Conference in Niigata in March 1966 with a view to further expansion. The present agreement is confined to consumer goods and a few locally produced raw materials and provides for a lower volume of trade than the Japanese apparently hoped for with this area, while the Russians may be reluctant to see it grow too rapidly, lest with Japan's exports, mainly of manufactured goods, the trade balance might be greatly in Japan's favour.[1]

For some years the Japanese and the Soviets have engaged in 'promotional' activities in their respective territories to boost this Far Eastern trade. Thus an exhibition of Soviet Far Eastern products was organized in Tokyo in 1964 by *Dalintorg* and was followed up by a Japanese exhibition of consumer goods organized by the 'Japanese Sea Firm' in Khabarovsk and various other activities on the same lines. Apart from the regular items of fish and shellfish, animal skins, marble, granite, horn and bone, some rather exotic articles appear to be exchanged in this trade. Thus the Japanese *Iskra* company purchased antlers amounting to $150,000 in exchange for laboratory utensils, and aqualung divers of the Far Eastern Sea Products directorate were sent fishing for sea urchins in the south Kuriles 'to be made into caviar for export to Japan'.[2]

More important is the fact that the Japanese are building ships for the Soviet Far Eastern fishing fleets, including a series of refrigerated factory ships, and Japanese saw-milling and logging machinery is also of interest to the USSR for the Far Eastern timber industry. Although Sakhalin is located so close to Japanese ports, the actual share of Sakhalin oil in the total Soviet oil exports to Japan is not more than 10 per cent., or about 300,000 tons annually, the rest being shipped from Soviet Black Sea ports.[3] The Soviets seem anxious to get a larger share in this highly competitive market with exports

---

[1] It should be noted that this section does not cover Soviet-Japanese trade as a whole and is confined to the trade between Japan and the Soviet Far Eastern regions.

[2] *Ecotass*, 30 August 1965.   [3] These estimates are derived from official Japanese sources.

of oil from Soviet oil-fields other than Sakhalin, the limited supplies of Sakhalin oil being heavily in demand on the Soviet mainland and transport from Sakhalin to Japan being blocked by ice for many months a year.

These items are, however, trifling compared to the prospects opened up by the proposals for Japanese co-operation in the development of the Soviet Far East and east Siberia. The idea has been given considerable prominence both in Japan and the Soviet Union since probably the largest, most influential Japanese trade mission ever to visit a foreign country arrived in the Soviet Union in August 1962 with the purpose of investigating possibilities of joint industrial development of Siberia and of broadening the bases of Soviet-Japanese trade.[1] After a reconnaissance of Siberian and Urals industries, this unofficial mission was received by Khrushchev in Yalta and though no conclusions were reached, the Russians seemed greatly interested in working out a Siberian development programme with the Japanese on an exchange basis.[2] The subject was discussed again during the visits of Mikoyan and Foreign Trade Minister Patolichev to Japan in 1963. Speaking in Tokyo, Patolichev stressed the value of inter-coastal trade 'not only as a part of trade but also for the development of Siberia'.[3] Two years later Patolichev again returned to this subject during the negotiations in Moscow for a new five year Soviet-Japanese trade agreement in 1965. Having referred to the new basis of Soviet-Japanese trade 'with broader utilization of the international division of labour and of geographical proximity', he said: 'We are successfully developing and opening up the riches of the eastern regions of the Soviet Union. We could co-operate with you in this matter on advantageous conditions, on a firm and long-term basis, that is if you are interested and wish to do so.'[4]

Among the various projects for Soviet-Japanese economic co-operation now under consideration for some years, Japanese participation in an extension of the oil pipeline from Irkutsk (where the pipe from the Volga–Urals oil-fields now ends) to Nakhodka or

---

[1] Toyko in Russian. Summary of World Broadcasts, 10 August 1962.
[2] Soviet News, 24 August 1962. *Japan Times*, 24 August 1962.
[3] Tokyo Television Service, 11 February 1963.
[4] *Vneshnyaya Torgovlya*, no. XI (1965).

some other convenient port on the Gulf of Tartary seems to have had priority. The idea is that Japan should supply the tankers and pipe for this 3,000 mile long pipeline and be paid in Soviet crude oil. Opinion in business circles in Japan is reported to be divided about the wisdom of such a deal or even of any considerable expansion of oil imports from the Soviet Union which might make Japan dependent on Soviet goodwill for supplies and would arouse counter pressures from the American and other big oil companies now supplying Japan's oil needs of some 100 million tons annually.[1] Nevertheless, at the time of writing, discussions are still proceeding on this Soviet-Japanese project and the scope of the proposed economic 'partnership' may even be greatly extended according to the latest reports.

During the first meeting of the Soviet-Japanese Business Co-operation Committee in Tokyo early in 1966, the Japanese were said to have expressed 'the greatest interest in the development of natural gas in Sakhalin and also in the exploitation of copper resources in Siberia'.[2] Access to Sakhalin natural gas in such close proximity to Japan would be a valuable addition to Japan's overseas 'oil empire' which now extends from Indonesia to the Persian Gulf and in the development of which the Japanese are acquiring a new level of technical expertise. This proposal would involve the supply of Japanese equipment and gas pipes which would be paid for by shipping natural gas to Japan at an average rate of 2,000 million cu. m. annually for fifteen to twenty years or roughly twice the current rate of British imports of natural gas from Algeria. Negotiations on this project were to be resumed in 1967 and agreement has still to be reached on a number of points, including the price of the gas.

Japan has to import large quantities of copper for some of her booming industries, so it is not surprising to learn that she is also interested in the development of the rich and still untapped Udokan copper-mines of east Siberia. It is not clear exactly what form Japanese participation would take in this development but it would probably mean the supply of mining equipment and possibly a concentration plant.

The purchase of crude oil from the Tyumen' oil-fields of west Siberia was also discussed with the Japanese at the Tokyo Business

[1] Hansberger, op. cit. p. 218.   [2] Comtel Reuter, 24 March 1966.

Co-operation meeting in 1966, the pipes, equipment, and other machinery for the proposed 7,000 km. long pipeline from the oil-fields to the port of Nakhodka to be supplied in exchange by Japan. The Soviet delegate to this meeting stated that this pipeline would take three to four years to complete and that the Soviet Union would need twenty years to pay for the Japanese equipment with crude oil.[1] Such a major scheme would require very heavy capital investment and the response in Japan has been very cautious.

It should be noted that these 'partnership' proposals for the joint development of Siberia and the Far East have little or nothing in common with former foreign concessions in Russia such as the Lena gold-fields or the Urquhart mining properties in the Altay. Japanese co-operation would be confined as far as known to supplies of machinery, equipment, and technical advice, while control and management of the enterprise remain entirely in Soviet hands. There is no question, apparently, of the import of Japanese labour. In view of the far-reaching scope of these proposals and the many intricate technical-economic and political issues involved it is not surprising that the negotiations have been protracted.

The expanding trade between the Soviet Far Eastern region, Japan, and other Pacific countries is reflected in the position of Nakhodka (fifty miles south of Vladivostok) where the cargo turn-over has increased 140 per cent. since 1959. Ship repair shops and a modern timber-handling centre with up-to-date equipment are being built. A new floating dock arrived in Nakhodka in 1966 and is the first floating dock in the Far East. It will be used for repairing dredging and other vessels.[2] The largest cold store in the Soviet Far East was reported to have been opened in Nakhodka in 1965 with a capacity of 17,000 tons. Nakhodka is to have the first Intourist hotel in the Far East and according to travellers' reports it is badly needed.

As a result of the substantial increase in freight carried between the Soviet mainland and Japan, an agreement was signed in 1965 to regularize shipping sailings on the Nakhodka–Japan route. An earlier agreement in 1958 between the Far Eastern Maritime Shipping Company and the Japan–Nakhodka line regulated freight lines between Nakhodka and Japanese ports, and following another

[1] Ibid.   [2] Moscow Home Service, 2 June 1965.

agreement in 1961 both a Soviet and Japanese line now run services for freight and passengers between Yokohama and Nakhodka.[1]

Trade with Australia is also of growing importance for the Soviet Far Eastern ports, the main export being timber with some Australian grain arriving via the Pacific. A regular service was opened between Australia and Nakhodka in 1964 by a Japanese timber carrier which brought the first shipments of Russian timber (Siberian yellow pine) to Australia under a deal which was expected to reach £1,000,000 by the end of 1965. The Australian businessmen concerned visited the Soviet Union 'on a buying trip' which most unusually included visits to Kamchatka and Khabarovsk to arrange lumber shipments to Australia (but unfortunately no record of their impressions of Kamchatka seems to have been published). Timber is one of the Soviet commodities which could help to reverse the adverse trade balance with Australia owing to the heavy Soviet purchases in 1964–5 of Australian grain and wool. The latter, for the most part, are landed at European Russian and not Far Eastern ports. In fact the Soviet share of the Australian timber imports is insignificant as the following table shows:

Imports of Timber into Australia

(value in $A 000s)

Year	Total softwoods	Total hardwoods	Total from the USSR
1961–2	16,800	5,200	—
1962–3	16,100	6,800	—
1963–4	23,700	7,500	24
1964–5	23,070	12,200	71
1965–6	23,600	7,670	102

Source: *Overseas Trade Bulletins*, 1965–6.

The first Soviet-Australian trade agreement was signed in October 1965.[2] There are no specific commitments to any particular pattern or volume of trade and no lists of goods or quotas. Australia might therefore run the risk of large-scale Soviet imports reaching the country which she would find it hard to control. At the moment, however, owing to big Australian shipments of grain and wool to

[1] *Dal'niy Vostok*, no. 4 (1966), p. 159.   [2] *Pravda*, 15 October 1965.

the Soviet Union, the balance of trade is, and is likely to remain for some time, much in Australia's favour.

FUTURE PROSPECTS

In envisaging the probable course of development of this vast area the exceptional difficulties and high costs of development must be weighed against the value of selected natural resources (in which the region is so rich) and the strategic interest of this Pacific 'bastion'. In line with the present Soviet investment policy, the share of the Far Eastern region for development purposes, as in Siberia, will not be inspired by unrealistic ideological arguments, but will be decided on a down-to-earth basis of reasonable profitability unless there are overriding economic or strategic considerations. A crisis with China, for example, over the Amur frontier might radically change the situation by focusing attention on the need to build up the Far East by massive injections of capital investment. And it is pertinent to recall in this connexion that fear of a Japanese attack from Manchuria shot up investments in this area between 1939 and 1941.

Though the volume of capital investment in the Far East has been considerable since the war, growth of investment and also of gross industrial production from 1950 to 1963 were both below the USSR average, while according to Soviet statistics the average annual increase in industrial production in the Far Eastern region was lower than in east or west Siberia. Hitherto the Far East has not proved an attractive investment area (at least in the short term). The productivity of labour is low, the number of enterprises not fulfilling production plans is high,[1] while many are working at a loss covered by State subsidies amounting to 150 million roubles a year.[2] The Far East has a huge imbalance in its exchanges with other parts of the country owing to its large imports of oil and metals, food, and consumer goods. Investment, at least at the present level if not at a higher level, must be continued to finance capital construction to reduce this deficit and develop the rich resources of the Far East. The disequilibrium in the Far Eastern economy is partly inherent in

[1] *L'Extrême Orient Soviétique*, op. cit. pp. 33–34.
[2] N. I. Nikolayev, 'O perspektivakh razvitiya ekonomiki Dal'nego Vostoka', *Dal'niy Vostok*, no. 6, 1966.

the nature of the terrain and the industrialization of an area thousands of miles from the industrialized bases of supply, but it also arises from some dubious planning decisions, for example, the establishment of *Amurstal'* as an unintegrated steel works before it was assured of its own iron base. Gosplan must also be held responsible for the primitive state of the Far Eastern timber industry, the main product of which was for years unprocessed wood both expensive to transport by rail and uneconomical compared to finished products.

In assessing the future of this region there is a tendency to dwell on the harsh climate, the lack of transport, and the labour problems as obstacles to development while insufficient attention is usually paid to the inefficiency and mismanagement which bedevil the major industries of fishing and timber, and the agriculture, food, and light industries of the southern areas where the climate is relatively mild. The Far Eastern fishing industry, important though it is to the Soviet economy, only accounts for an insignificant share of the north-west Pacific catch, and Soviet fishermen take seven times less fish than Japanese fishermen and five times less than Chinese from the Pacific waters.[1] Soviet sources attribute this position to the poor equipment and organization of the Soviet fishing industry. The high percentage of wood-waste in the Far Eastern timber industry and the failure to develop a wood-chemical industry until the most recent period have already been discussed. Agriculture and the food industry are in such poor shape that the region can only supply 30 per cent. of its meat, 41 per cent. of its milk and dairy products, and 26–27 per cent. of its sugar, while some 300,000 tons of salt are annually imported (mainly for the fishing industry) which might be procured locally with more initiative and effort.[2] These shortages could at least to some extent be reduced by better local organization of agriculture and in particular by closer attention to rural housing and living conditions so as to lessen the flight of the agricultural population from the land.

This is the background to the directives of the new Draft Five Year Plan for the Far Eastern region. It calls rather vaguely for the 'accelerated development of the economic potential of the Far East' but explicit emphasis is laid on the 'further increase in output of gold, tin, wolfram, mercury, diamonds, and mica'. The Solnechnyy mining-concentration plant is to be completed and that at Khrustal'-

[1] Margolin, op. cit. pp. 120–1.   [2] Ibid.

nyy expanded, new deposits of diamonds are to be brought into production in Yakutia, and of wolfram in the Primorskiy kray. The development of these wolfram deposits may partly be a result of the decline in Soviet-Chinese trade in which Chinese wolfram was normally a large item. Other mining enterprises mentioned for the period 1966–70 are the construction of the Deputatskiy tin-mining concentrate combine in Yakutia and the expansion of the Primorskiy mining–chemical combine. Apart from the emphasis on the extraction of valuable minerals, there is a demand for a considerable extension of geological-prospecting work in the hope, presumably, of still further adding to the known mineral riches of the Soviet Far East.)

The fish catch is to be increased to 35 per cent. of the total Soviet catch from all waters. There is no other mention of the food industry in this Plan (nor of agriculture) though the increased fish catch will be for export to other regions of the USSR as there is already plenty of fish available for the local population.

The Plan provides at last for the badly needed development of the Far Eastern timber industry. The first section of a new cellulose–cardboard combine is to be constructed at Komsomol'sk by 1970 and work started on a big new timber–industrial complex. The Far East is to have a new metallurgical base though no details are given apart from the statement that 'designing investigatory work' is to be carried out. It could either be in southern Yakutia, based on Aldan iron ore and Chul'man coal (suitable for coking), or more likely farther east, based on Garinskoye iron ore in the Amur *oblast* and Chul'man (or Bureya) coal, where working conditions would be better./

There is nothing novel or sensational about these measures, and no hint that they have been influenced by events in China. They are in line with the former lop-sided development in favour of the extraction industries and suggest that no decision has yet been taken in Moscow about that 'complex' development of the economic forces of the Far East which some of its more voluble officials demand with little thought for the costs involved or the unsatisfactory economic performance of the region to date.

These strictures on Soviet policies and results in the Soviet Far East must not be taken to imply that the region is standing still pending decisions of wider import for its development. Apart from mining expansion schemes, cities like Komsomol'sk, Khabarovsk, and Ussuriysk are pushing ahead with local industries and civic amenities (though much more remains to be done in the building construction, light, and food industries), while badly needed improvements are taking place in the Pacific ports and new ports (like Ozernovsky in Kamchatka) are being built to facilitate the timber and fishing industries.

The proposed Soviet-Japanese economic co-partnership opens up entirely new possibilities of development of the Soviet Far East and Siberia. Japanese participation in the construction of the Irkutsk and Tyumen'–Far Eastern trunk pipelines, the development of the Udokan copper deposits, or exploitation of the pulp and timber resources of the Far East would surely expedite these major undertakings, not least because masses of heavy machines would be imported from Japan rather than from the much more remote and unpredictable Soviet supply centres in the Urals and European Russia. It is not clear at the time of writing how far Moscow is disposed to encourage trade between the Far Eastern region and Japan, especially in clothing and a wide range of consumer goods now imported at great expense mainly from areas beyond the Urals. If this trade should develop it could have far-reaching effects on living standards and thus prove a stabilizing factor in the high labour turn-over of the region. If this problem could be solved the 'disproportion between the potential of this kray, so rich in power and raw material resources, and the level of its industrial and agricultural development' might gradually be eliminated by the establishment of a settled labour force.[1]

[1] Nikolayev, op. cit.

Conclusion

Economic plans and development in the lands beyond the Urals have now been discussed in some detail. But certain broader aspects of Soviet policy of considerable national and international importance still call for examination to round off this study. In the first place there is the question of the value to the Soviet economy as a whole of the natural resources of Asiatic Russia. Then the nature and extent of the problems affecting development of these resources must be assessed and in the case of the Central Asian republics and Kazakhstan stock taken of local reactions to Soviet policies and planning. Lastly, reference, however brief, is inescapable here to the controversial Soviet claim that 'the Soviet path to socialism', as exemplified in the Soviet Central Asian republics, is the 'model for the under-developed countries' of Asia and Africa. An exhaustive analysis of this complicated question is far beyond the scope of this book, but at least some points in the propaganda claims must be discussed here.

THE ROLE OF ASIATIC RUSSIA IN THE SOVIET ECONOMY

The wealth and diversity of the natural resources of the Central Asian republics, Siberia, and the Far East may be said to be of inestimable potential value to the Soviet economy. An exact assessment of the value of many of these resources is, however, impossible because of the lack of published information about production of some of the most valuable commodities such as gold and diamonds, copper, platinum, and other non-ferrous metals. There is no doubt, however, that these resources, partly unique, partly supplementary to the reserves of minerals, fuel and power, timber, and agricultural raw materials in European Russia, have helped to reinforce and underpin the Soviet obsession with autarky and Soviet ambitions to become the greatest industrial power in the world.

In Central Asia cotton has for years dominated the economic scene and production has been constantly rising under the Soviet régime. It now supplies all Soviet domestic requirements, which are admittedly low in terms of *per caput* consumption, and in recent years cotton stocks have been sufficient for cotton to rank second after grain in Soviet agricultural exports. This domestic source of supply represents a great saving of foreign exchange and makes the Soviet Union virtually independent of foreign cotton in case of war (an advantage which imperial Russia did not have during the American Civil War).

The great copper, lead, zinc, and chrome reserves of Kazakhstan and the rare metals, mercury, and antimony of Kirgizia are the largest in the Soviet Union and make it almost self-sufficient in these metals; they are to be valued accordingly. In spite of the present muddle in the 'Virgin Lands' of Kazakhstan, under more efficient management (and in its good years) this 'second bread-basket of the Soviet Union' makes a very useful contribution to Soviet grain supplies. Kazakhstan possesses one-sixth of the Soviet coal stocks and great iron ore mines in north-west Kazakhstan and notably at Sokolovka–Sarbay. The fuel and power resources of the Central Asian zone are also of increasing all-Union significance because of the growing deficit in fuel and power resources of European Russia, the Urals, and Transcaucasus. The low costs of capital investment and production per unit of power also make the Central Asian power reserves attractive. This area has almost a third of the Soviet reserves of natural gas (as a result of the recent gas strikes in Uzbekistan, in Turkmenistan, and Kazakhstan); one-fifth of the hydro-energy resources (mainly in Tadzhikistan); considerable resources of oil (mainly in Turkmenistan and Kazakhstan, the suspected resources in Tadzhikistan have not yet been proven); and stone-coal including good coking coals in large quantities in Karaganda and Ekibastuz.[1]

Apart from satisfying local requirements to an increasing extent, Central Asian natural gas is being piped to the Urals and will eventually reach central Russia through the longest, if not the largest,

[1] *Voprosy Razmeshcheniya Proizvodstva v SSSR*, op. cit. pp. 43–44.

diameter pipeline in the world. Though this long-distance piping of gas is taking place, there seems to be a consensus of expert opinion that Central Asian gas should for the most part be used in the Central Asian republics, and 'only the surplus in the Urals and the European part of the USSR,'[1] though official policy has so far ignored this view. It has also been proposed eventually to make good the deficit energy balance of the Transcaucasus area by Central Asian gas transmitted by a pipeline under the Caspian Sea. It is estimated that the cheapest electric power in the Soviet Union is produced in Central Asia at a rate of o.10 kopecks per kWh. and that much larger quantities will be produced in future.[2]

The energy-intensive chemical and other industries (including aluminium) should have a considerable future in Tadzhikistan owing to its large hydro-power resources. In Turkmenistan the chemicals of the Kara-Bogaz-Gol are extensive and valuable, and there are good prospects for the new petro-chemical industry in Uzbekistan, if the water problem can be solved. The phosphorous and nitrogenous fertilizer industries in Uzbekistan, Kazakhstan, and Tadzhikistan (where the fertilizer industry is now being established) should eventually be of material importance for the cotton plantations of Central Asia. At the present time they only produce a relatively small amount of the Soviet output of fertilizer but their local importance should not be underestimated.

The young Uzbek engineering industry has had some notable successes. It is now producing 68 per cent. of all the spinning and 100 per cent. of the roving machines made in the Soviet Union. Few of the other Central Asian manufacturing industries have yet attained all-Union importance. They are, however, highly esteemed locally as criteria of economic progress and they provide also an essential means of employment for the large populations of these republics. The lack of iron ore has been an obstacle to the development of heavy metallurgy (at present concentrated in the Bekabad plant in Uzbekistan) and keeps the southern Central Asian republics dependent on long hauls of metal from Kazakhstan and other regions of the Soviet Union. There is a constant clamour to Gosstroy and Gosplan from the republican capitals to establish new industries, in spite of obvious difficulties. One gets the impression

[1] Ibid. p. 228.   [2] Ibid. p. 225.

that having tasted the fruits of industrialization and the prestige attached to it in the industrially oriented Soviet Union, even a backward country like Kirgizia wants to have some of the most sophisticated industries set up on its soil, without always taking proper stock of the costs involved.

The international aspect of the industrial advance in Central Asia is much stressed in Soviet propaganda abroad and is apparently a matter of no little national pride among these peoples. It takes the form of exchanges of economic delegations from the under-developed countries of Asia and Africa, and more concretely appears in the development of economic links and trade with them, though the exact amount of this trade cannot as a rule be computed from the published Soviet foreign trade figures which do not account separately for the share of the individual republics. Occasionally, however, there is a windfall and statistics from official republican archives are published. Thus an exhaustive examination of the 'international connexions of Uzbekistan', published in Tashkent in 1964, gave full details of its foreign trade and of the wide range of countries with which it has economic relations of one kind or another.[1] According to total value, Uzbek exports were stated to rank second in the Soviet Union after those of the RSFSR. This high place has been achieved mainly as a result of the exports of cotton and karakul pelts which head the list. But Uzbek exports also include increasing quantities of machinery and equipment for cotton cultivation and harvesting, irrigation, and the textile and chemical industries. Seventy per cent. of Soviet exports of cotton originate in Uzbekistan and this cotton is supplied to the 'countries of the socialist camp' as well as to 'England, Italy, France, the German Federal Republic, Japan, and other capitalist countries of Europe and Asia'. In all, Uzbekistan claims to be sending its products to 58 countries, i.e. 18 in Europe, 23 in Asia, 10 in Africa, and 7 in the Americas. *Tashtekstil'mash'* has apparently done especially well with its spinning and roving machines and participated in international exhibitions in Austria, Belgium, Japan, India, and other countries.

Uzbeks and other Soviet specialists have been helping Cuba to expand its paddy fields and their experience in cotton growing has

[1] Ch. Abutalipov, *Mezhdunarodnyye Svyazi Uzbekistana* (Tashkent, 1964), p. 38.

been applied to improve cotton production across the Amu Dar'ya frontier in Afghanistan. Several hundred Uzbeks are helping to build the Dzhalalabad Canal on the Kabul River and as a result of the Soviet-Afghan technical agreement of 1964 a group of experts from Uzbekistan are assisting Afghanistan to develop its natural gas and to construct a pipeline to the Soviet Union.

Some seventy Kazakh enterprises 'helped young Afro-Asian countries in 1965' according to another report.[1] The exports to developing countries were vaguely reported to be growing, in the first place to 'socialist countries', with exports of Kazakh grain, tobacco, cotton, non-ferrous metals, and machinery heading the list. Heavy machinery was made by the Alma-Ata plant for the Anshan metallurgical combine in China before the breach in Sino-Soviet relations. It is more interesting to note that Kazakhstan entered into direct economic relations with the Sinkiang-Uygur Autonomous Region of China in 1959 as a result of an agreement between the Kazakh Consumers Co-operative and the Sinkiang Local Trade Directorate.[2] This agreement has no doubt gone by the board since the Sino-Soviet conflict. It is the only case that has come to light of a direct link between two peoples of similar race, i.e. the Kazakhs and the Uygurs, divided by a Soviet-Asian frontier.

Exchanges of goods are also said to be growing between Tadzhikistan and the Asian-African countries, with Afghanistan delivering hides, India jute and tow, packing cloth and footwear, while Tadzhikistan sends cement, slate, and pipeline fittings to India.[3] In a speech in Ashkhabad congratulating the Turkmen people on the fortieth anniversary of their Socialist Republic, Kosygin said that Turkmenistan, thanks to the Socialist system, 'is now in the world market', sending its products to Hungary, Czechoslovakia, Bulgaria, Poland, Yugoslavia, Cuba, India, the United Arab Republic, and Turkey (this may be somewhat of an exaggeration and Kosygin gave no further details of these exports).[4]

North of the Central Asian zone sprawl the vast Siberian-Far Eastern lands, holding 'first place in the world for unexploited wealth' according to Academician Lavrent'yev,[5] as well as proven

[1] *Partiinaya Zhizn' Kazakhstana*, no. 6 (1965).   [2] Neyshtadt, op. cit. pp. 263–4.
[3] *Kom. Tadzhikistana*, 4 October 1964.   [4] *Pravda*, 26 November 1964.
[5] *Sovetskaya Rossiya*, 8 March 1966.

resources of the greatest value. Here are the largest Soviet deposits of such precious metals as gold, diamonds, and tin; nickel, platinum and copper of great value are found at Noril'sk and there are very large untapped copper reserves in the north-east Siberian wilderness of Udokan (which the 1966–70 Draft Plan has now listed for development).[1]

Siberia's fuel and energy reserves are unique in the Soviet Union and the recently discovered west Siberian oil-fields immensely strengthen the Soviet fuel position. The largest source of oil at present is the 'second Baku' (Volga–Urals fields) but as some of these fields were already reaching their peak, the outlook would have been bleak if the lower Ob' basin had not suddenly emerged as a major producing area.[2] Another potentially rich oil area is at Markovo in Irkutsk *oblast*, on the middle Lena, where oil of high quality was recently discovered after thirty years of prospecting. Owing to its remote location, development except for minor local requirements has been postponed and is not mentioned in the current Plan. The largest coal reserves of the USSR are in Asiatic Russia (though the European coal-fields produce more coal). As a result of its large fuel and power resources Siberia is eventually intended to become the centre of the energy-intensive industries of the Soviet Union, to which the large-scale power construction programme initiated by the two giant hydro-electric stations at Bratsk (4.5 million kW.) and Krasnoyarsk (5 million kW.) will materially contribute. These 'giants' of today will be dwarfed when the Sayan hydro-station (5–6 million kW.), based on the water power of the upper Yenisey, comes into service. The Sayan hydro-electric station is to be the nucleus of a great scheme of industrial development including local coal, iron ore, non-ferrous and rare metals, asbestos, and other minerals in an area fairly well populated but hitherto not actively developed, i.e. Tuva, Khakassia, and the eastern Sayans.[3]

The deficit in fuel and electric power in the highly industrialized areas of European Russia and the Urals (not adequately supplied by their own resources) will increase in the near future according to

---

[1] *Gudok*, 24 April 1966; *Pravda*, 20 February 1966.

[2] *Petroleum Press Service*, no. 4 (April 1966).

[3] V. A. Krotov, 'Geographical Aspects and Problems of the Industrialization of Siberia', *Soviet Geography* (November 1964), p. 55.

Soviet sources. Natural gas is therefore being piped there from Central Asia and a new 5,500 km. long pipeline is also being laid to bring Tyumen' oil to and across the Urals which, according to Soviet sources, will be the longest in the world when completed. Moreover, there is a project to transmit Siberian power to both areas by an extra-high voltage, long-distance transmission line (1,100 miles long) to link up the Central Siberian and European–Urals grids so as to make full use of the much cheaper eastern energy and take advantage of the difference in time zones for peak hours.[1] This ambitious project has not yet started but it is thought to be scheduled for the early 1970s.

Siberia has become one of the major industrial regions of the Soviet Union, accounting for one-fourth of the national coal output, more than one-seventh of the power generation, one-fifth of the wood production, and a large amount of steel and non-ferrous metals, machines and equipment, chemicals and various kinds of mineral raw materials, and farm products,[2] while the newly discovered Siberian oil and gas deposits are estimated to contain up to one-third of Soviet reserves. The Siberian engineering industries are growing, but there is still a heavy concentration of engineering plants in European Russia and the Urals. Thus all trunkline coal and electric engines are manufactured in the southern and central areas of the country though the eastern areas account for more than one-third of the Soviet freight turnover.[3] It is also one of the main grain-producing areas of the USSR.

In view of its still enormous undeveloped resources Siberia may be said to be only on the threshold of its economic potential. One gets the impression that the Party is not promoting Siberian investment and development energetically except in regard to essential or unique commodities like coal, oil, gold, copper, or nickel. But even in these sectors there are complaints that much more could be produced if the Government allocated the necessary funds. The relatively low level of extraction compared to proven reserves of industrial raw materials in both east Siberia and Yakutia and other areas of the Far East is often mentioned in Soviet economic sources.

[1] D. Hooson, 'Industrial Growth—Where Next?', *Survey*, no. 57 (October 1965), p. 116.
[2] *Soviet Geography* (November 1964), p. 52.
[2] *Problemy Razmeshcheniya Proizvoditel'nykh Sil* (AN Moscow, 1960), p. 52.

Thus from the prospected reserves of the industrial category in Yakutia less than 1 per cent. of diamonds, 1.3 per cent. of tin, 6 per cent. of gold, and 2.5 per cent. of mica (phlogopite) are reported to be extracted.[1] Funds for the geological investigations which led to the big gas-oil strike in west Siberia were apparently not easily forthcoming from Moscow, though, as Academician Trofimuk commented at a conference of the Siberian Department of the USSR Academy of Sciences in 1966: 'Nobody speaks against geological prospecting in the European part of the country.'[2]

Government policy now clearly tends to favour investment in the western regions where the best returns can be expected on capital, rather than, for example, developing new projects in the labour and capital intensive industries of east and west Siberia where returns on both capital and labour are below the Soviet average. According to the Draft Plan directives: 'The growth of prospected reserves of useful deposits should be ensured chiefly in areas where exploitation is economically most advantageous.' The old Leninist line of priority development of the under-developed areas has gone by the board and is replaced by economic criteria of profitability as the basis of investment policy.[3] As a result there is a marked difference between the treatment of the eastern regions in the two former plans and in the Draft Plan for 1966–70. There is less emphasis on the area and far less urgency in the call for development. The targets are lower and less precise and there is no trace of the euphoric tone which inspired the former Khrushchevian plans. No figures are given corresponding to the 40 per cent. of total Soviet capital investment which the Seven Year Plan allocated to the eastern regions. The share of the regions east of the Urals, i.e. the Siberias, the Far East, the Central Asian republics, and Kazakhstan in the total Soviet production of certain important commodities is nevertheless planned to reach the following levels: coal, 45 per cent.; natural gas, 35 per cent.; oil, 16 per cent.; electric power, 28 per cent.; aluminium, 65 per cent.; copper, 58 per cent.; cellulose, 28 per cent.; cardboard, 31 per cent. The shift towards the east thus continues but less dramatically than envisaged by Khrushchev. Soviet ideologues claim that the industrialization of Siberia is a good example of the systematic

---

[1] *Planovoye Khozyaystvo*, no. 4 (1966), pp. 17–19.   [2] *Sovetskaya Rossiya*, 8 March 1966.
[3] *Dimensions of Soviet Economic Power*, pp. 198–9.

implementation by the Party and Government of the socialist principles directing the location of productive forces.[1] This is a particularly empty claim, for no government in Moscow (whatever its political colour) could have shut its eyes indefinitely to the 'unlocking' of the Siberian treasure-house. Indeed it is arguable that if the door had been open to foreign capital and labour (as it was in America at a similar stage of development in the last century) Siberia and the Far East might have been spared some of their more acute problems and have advanced more rapidly than they have done under the Soviet régime.

PROBLEMS CONFRONTING THE SOVIET GOVERNMENT

If the development of Siberia and the Soviet Far East were in fact regarded as of urgent national importance in Moscow, rather than as a valuable insurance for the future, it is hard to believe that a solution would not by now have been found to the ubiquitous labour problem (mentioned earlier in this work), either by administrative methods or by a radical improvement in living conditions. Policy hangs fire though the problem has been most intensively discussed in the chief Soviet party and economic journals. As long ago as 1960 a group of Novosibirsk scientists analysed the Siberian migration problem and made recommendations for its solution. 'Nobody disputed the conclusions at which the Institute arrived. But likewise nothing was done', reported V. Perevedentsev.[2] He laid the blame on the planning organs that the abnormal labour situation, with thousands of men 'fleeing from the construction sites', continues today as badly as ever, causing enormous losses and hold-ups in Siberian construction and factories. This basic situation is aggravated by the failure to produce machinery, equipment, houses adjusted to the harsh Siberian and Far Eastern conditions. In his comments on the Draft Plan, Academician Lavrent'yev underlined this point: 'Automobiles for the north', he said, 'are turned out without considering the low temperatures. Metal and rubber in heavy frost become as brittle as glass. . . . Much is said about machinery and transport for Siberia but very little is done.'[3] Another member of

[1] Krotov, op. cit. p. 50.   [2] *Lit. Gaz.*, 10 March 1966.
[3] *Sovetskaya Rossiya*, 8 March 1966.

the Siberian Department of the Academy of Sciences, Aganbegyan, added on the same occasion: 'There should be a service of labour. Such an organ existed during Lenin's lifetime.' Far from there being such a service, official Soviet behaviour in regard to labour problems seems not far short of economic lunacy in many respects. All too frequently it reveals a sort of built-in obtuseness to local conditions on the part of Moscow planners and other responsible bureaucrats (many examples of which are given in the sections of this study dealing with Central Asia, Siberia, and the Far East). From their comments on the Draft Plan, it appears that these Siberian scientists who live in the heart of Siberia and study its problems closely, do not think much of the rather loose Draft Plan directives on either the development of Siberian resources or the crucial Siberian population problem. The note of scepticism in Corresponding Member A. G. Aganbegyan's remarks is very near the surface: 'These measures have a very stimulating significance', he said. 'But all the same they are obviously inadequate for regulating the flow of labour to Siberia. It is also necessary to provide advantages in rates of growth of real income, commodity circulation, and the development of a material base of the whole non-productive sector.'[1]

A labour problem of considerable importance but entirely different in character is also emerging in the Central Asian republics.[2] Here the problem is one of surplus rural labour, not a shortage as in Siberia. The problem is caused by the high birth-rate and the large immigration of skilled labour, mostly Russian, to the towns. According to Kurbanov, the Chairman of the Uzbek Council of Ministers: 'In Uzbekistan the question of the labour force is acute. This question is assuming major significance. The Republic disposes of favourable natural conditions and rich raw material resources for widespread construction of light and food industries and the simultaneous solution of the problem of finding employment for all the able-bodied population in social production.'[3] Demands for new industries to solve the problem of surplus labour have been heard in each of the Central Asian republics recently and the

[1] *Sovetskaya Rossiya*, 8 March 1966.

[2] This subject is discussed in detail in an excellent article in the *Central Asian Review*, no. 2 (1966): 'Labour Problems and Employment in Kazakhstan and Central Asia', p. 164.

[3] *PV*, 9 April 1966.

9. The Bazar-Kurgan cotton-delivery station

10. A section of the Big Fergana Canal

11. Karaganda

republican heads of government and other commentators seem really worried about it. It is frequently stressed in this context that 'the general level of employment of the population in industrial production in Central Asia is considerably below the average for the country'.[1] A work published by the Institute of Economics of the Kirgiz Academy of Sciences stresses 'the special acuteness of the problem of occupying labour forces in social production in the Republic which requires higher rates of development of productive forces there, than in the country as a whole'.[2]

In Central Asia the labour problem is basically connected with the need for better organization of training for the surplus population of the farms and the small towns. This problem confronts the Soviet planning authorities not only in Central Asia but throughout the Soviet Union. To date they have signally failed to deal with it effectively. But it acquires a national–political edge in the Central Asian republics because of the influx of Russians to do skilled jobs which are often filled by them owing to the inadequate facilities to train the local people.[3] Distress signals have been sent to Moscow from Tashkent, Frunze, and Dushanbe for help in organizing training courses for indigenous workers and in setting up new industries or more factories to employ local labour.

The problem of underemployed rural masses is, of course, familiar to most developing countries, whether still under colonial rule or newly independent. The anomaly is that it should exist at all in the planned society of the Soviet Union (which so loudly denounces this social problem elsewhere). Moreover, the Soviet Union has no plan to cope with rural unemployment and no central organ with direct responsibility for population-migration problems, as such.[4] Soviet ideological sophistry has prevented Moscow from coming to grips much earlier with this problem, the Marxist–Leninist thesis that 'unemployment has been banished for all time in the USSR . . .', and other euphemisms such as 'labour imbalances' being used to conceal underemployment and surplus labour problems in the Soviet Union. Yet the claim is actually made that the experience

[1] *Nar. Khoz. S.A.*, no. 5 (1964), p. 18.
[2] *Problemy Trudovykh Resursov* (Frunze, 1965), p. 3.
[3] *Seriya Geograficheskaya, Iz. AN SSSR*, no. 4 (1965), p. 45.
[4] *Trud*, 10 March 1966.

of the republics of Central Asia, having not a little in common with the past of contemporary developing countries, could serve as a model for the successful solution of demographic problems.[1]

REACTIONS TO SOVIET ECONOMIC POLICIES

Dissatisfaction with specific policies of Gosplan and Gosstroy is now frequently expressed in the Central Asian republics (and in Siberia). The days are gone when the Central Asian capitals agreed without demur to Moscow's decisions. Though it would still be foolhardy (or worse) explicitly to criticize Moscow's political decisions, government officials and experts in the republican academies and other posts often attack Gosplan and Gosstroy for producing unsatisfactory plans, hint that they do not know their jobs, and openly demand that they should come to the republics and study local problems on the spot. From these criticisms it appears that there is a lack of confidence in many of Moscow's decisions on the location of industry and the organization of economic affairs in the Central Asian republics. The Soviet Press publishes many instances of this kind of criticism. Uzbekistan's openly expressed concern, for example, about the disposal of a large proportion of its natural gas to the central regions of Russia (which has been discussed in detail above) showed considerable anxiety lest it should not get a square deal and be deprived of valuable raw material for its own requirements. The Uzbeks and Tadzhiks are demanding a larger share of the Soviet textile industry and cogently base their demands on their predominance in Soviet raw cotton production and on unimpeachable Leninist principles about the location of industry: 'At the present time, only 10 per cent. of the cotton fibre produced in the Tadzhik SSR is processed there while 80 per cent. of Tadzhik cloth requirements is supplied by textiles from other regions. It would be more rational both from the point of view of reducing transport expenses and improving the utilization of labour to process an ever-increasing quantity of raw materials on the spot and thus to export ready-made textiles.'[2] This Tadzhik exposé of the

---

[1] M. Karakhanov, 'Aktual'nye Problemy Razvitiya Narodonaseleniya Sredney Azii', *Ob. Nauki v Uzbekistane*, no. 2 (1966).

[2] *Iz. AN Tadzhikskoy SSR*, no. 1 (39), p. 8.

cotton problem by an Academy critic has been echoed frequently and even more forcibly in Uzbekistan.

Housing schemes drawn up in Moscow are also subject to frequent attack locally. Among many such examples, the blunt language used by the Chairman of the Tadzhik Supreme Soviet Presidium to show up the defects of Gosstroy's plans for housing in his republic may be quoted:

In the intense heat of Asia [he said] the proposed multi-storied housing for *kolkhozes* and *sovkhozes* is not only inappropriate but may even prove harmful. The type of house proposed to us is suitable only for the temperate zone of Russia. If people in the north have to struggle with the cold, in the south they struggle with the heat. When the houses for Nurek were being planned we requested the appropriate organizations to consider our particular climate. They only laughed at our specialists. But when they actually came to Nurek, they suffered so much from the heat that they were persuaded that metal did heat up to 80° [C] here.

Chairman Kholov's conclusion was that construction plans are by people who do not know and have not studied local conditions 'whereas the people who live under these conditions and understand what they need are deprived of all rights'.[1]

Turkmenistan, probably because it is less industrialized than the other republics, also seems to make fewer complaints about Moscow's economic policies. But the priority given to the construction of the Central Asian–Centre gas pipeline while the local authorities were not authorized by Gosplan to develop the Mary gas deposits and build a short 20–40 km. pipeline aroused considerable bitterness. The local reaction was that 'as a result, these gas wells remain closed and expensive crude oil (mazout) has to be imported from far away for boilers of industrial enterprises and communal purposes'.[2]

It is surprising to note that Kirgizia, which owes its industrial progress entirely to Soviet power, nevertheless has a long list of familiar 'colonial' grievances against Moscow's economic policies. It is an important producer of fine and semi-fine wool and sugar-beet. Yet the primary processing of wool is all done in 'other regions of the country' and there is not a single sugar refinery in Kirgizia. It also has some fine furs but no factory to process them.[3] It is

---

[1] *Izvestiya*, 7 July 1965.   [2] *Pravda*, 10 December 1965.
[3] *Razvitiye Proizvoditel'nykh Sil Kirgizskoy SSR v Perspektive*, p. 37.

dissatisfied with the quantity of cotton textiles manufactured from its cotton (though as a much smaller producer, its case for a larger textile industry is far less strong than that of Uzbeks and Tadzhiks), and with the fact that so much of its agricultural raw material 'is exported outside the boundaries of Kirgizia owing to the lack of capacity of its light industrial enterprises'.[1] According to an analysis of the Kirgiz Academy of Sciences, 'some of the most progressive branches of industry for which there are favourable natural-economic conditions have not received proper development, i.e. the chemical, electric-power, and construction materials industries. The success of communist construction in Kirgizia in the period of the creation of the material-technical bases of communism' hangs on these developments, declared the Academy, no doubt hoping to impress Moscow with a sound ideological argument.[2]

In these demands for more industry, considerations of capital costs never seem to enter into the calculations of their Central Asian sponsors or if they do they do not figure in their public statements. Kazakhstan is significantly absent from the ranks of the suppliants for more industries and factories though Kazakhstan is actually the scene of the greatest industrial development in the Central Asian area. Expansion of industry means more migrants to run these industries but as far as the Kazakhs themselves have a say in these matters, the indications are that they could do with less rather than more of both.

The central authorities seldom react publicly to these recriminations about their decisions on economic affairs in the Central Asian republics so it may be assumed that at least some are as well founded as they seem to be to an outside observer. It is perhaps relevant to note in this connexion that speaking to the Supreme Soviet in December 1965, N. K. Baybakov, Chairman of Gosplan, admitted that 'serious' mistakes had been made by Gosplan in the location of productive forces (there was no specific reference to Central Asia) and he promised that measures would be taken to improve matters 'with the participation of the Union republics'.[3]

An intriguing stage has now been reached in the economic

---

[1] *Razvitiye Proizvoditel'nykh Sil Kirgizskoy SSR v Perspektive*, p. 36.
[2] Ibid. pp. 10–11.
[3] *Pravda*, 10 December 1965.

relations between the Central Asian republics and Moscow. And the situation seems to open up more promising perspectives of changed relations than can be expected in the inevitably more static political relations. Years of industrializing ideology are producing dragons' teeth which could cause considerable embarrassment to the Moscow ideologues of today. If the Uzbeks and Tadzhiks succeeded, for example, in pressing home their pleas for a share of the cotton industry proportional to their raw cotton production the effect could be serious for the large group of highly skilled Russian workers in the heavy concentration of the Soviet cotton textile industry in the 'Russian Manchester', i.e. Moscow and Ivanovo *oblasts*. However, such a shift would probably not be to the advantage of the country as a whole though in this argument the Central Asians are on strong ideological ground. As things are, the cotton-producing republics are a captive, though restless, market for Russian textiles and knitwear, the already high price of these goods being considerably increased by transport costs from European Russia.

If names can serve as a guide, it often seems as if certain Russian technicians and even officials working in Central Asia and thus in a position to view local problems more closely than the armchair bureaucrats and planners in Moscow may be playing the native hand against the Centre with relative finesse and success. There may even be a parallel here to the situation in British India where Englishmen in official posts were often involved on the Indian side of Indian controversies with Westminster, to the discomfiture of the latter.

SOVIET SOCIALISM AS A MODEL FOR THE UNDER-DEVELOPED COUNTRIES

Finally, what is there to the Soviet boast that the Central Asian republics as developed by 'Soviet socialism' are a model for Asia?[1] Speaking in Frunze a few months before his fall, Khrushchev said: 'You live in the very centre of Asia. The Soviet republics of Central

---

[1] This problem is discussed in detail in Oleg Hoeffding, *Soviet State Planning and Forced Industrialization as a Model for Asia* (The Rand Corporation, California, 1958). A useful and more succinct analysis is given in A. Nove, *The Soviet Economy* (London, 1965), p. 319. *The Chinese Model*, edited by Werner Klatt (Hong Kong University Press, 1965), is also useful.

Asia are a beacon to all the peoples of the east showing them how to build life in a new way on a Communist basis.'[1] In order to press home this claim, the Soviet progaganda machine pours forth attractively produced and illustrated literature in many languages starring the achievements in economic development, education, public health, and general social welfare[2] of these republics, working on a 'non-capitalist basis'. The Soviet Government has indeed much to its credit in these fields. But not a word appears in this literature of any controversies or differences of opinion between Moscow and the Central Asian governments or other local bodies, or any of the muddle and lack of co-ordination in planning, so many instances of which have been mentioned earlier in connexion with Soviet construction in different fields. The hand is thus greatly overplayed in this literature. Its target is the developing countries of Asia and Africa, now faced by many of the problems of illiteracy and industrial development which confronted the former Tsarist colony of Turkestan in 1917.

In this propaganda the coercive aspects of the Soviet 'forced industrialization' and the imposition of Marxist social-cultural policies are swept under the carpet. Yet they are integral to any assessment of the Soviet solution of Asian problems. In the first place, as Dr. Oleg Hoeffding points out, any non-Asian country anxious to initiate economic development on Central Asian lines 'must buy the whole Soviet formula', i.e. 'the Soviet system with the totalitarian ingredients which put teeth into planning'. The Soviet planners only functioned as effectively as they did because they had the essential support of the system of property and production relationships established by the Revolution, 'which gave the Soviet State its control over men's lives, property, and economic activity'.[3]

The havoc wrought on the native way of life in Central Asia by the Soviet dictatorship has been described earlier in this work and was notoriously reflected in the destruction of Kazakh livestock and the ruthless reduction of the nomad populations by Soviet collectivization in the '30s. The Asian countries are mainly agricultural, but as Professor Nove aptly points out: 'To follow the Soviet models of

[1] *Pravda*, 17 August 1964.
[2] These policies are fully analysed in Nove, *The Soviet Middle East*.
[3] Hoeffding, op. cit. p. 3.

collectivization, to launch a struggle with the property-owning peasantry, might have fatal results for Asia. . . . The Soviet industrializing ideology in fact tends to strengthen those elements which have contempt for peasants and are all too ready to neglect agriculture.'[1] The Soviet record in agriculture for the past fifty years has been deplorable in regard both to grain production and livestock breeding, in the Central Asian republics and Kazakhstan as throughout the Soviet Union. And the Soviet leaders have shown no understanding of peasant psychology or ability to stimulate peasant effort in the socialized sector of farming. Having evinced so little skill in handling rural problems at home, the Soviets should not be expected to be more successful in devising models for other countries struggling with such problems. In fact, in most of the developing countries where the Soviets are operating aid schemes, as, for example, in India, they have taken little interest in agricultural problems. But in line with their promotion of heavy industry at home they rather push forward large steel mills and other urban prestige projects. This has left the problem of the over-populated countryside virtually untouched as far as they are concerned, though latterly Soviet advisers have shown a more realistic awareness of the agricultural problem.

Large-scale injections of Soviet capital and Russian skills were admittedly the base for the rapid industrialization of Central Asia and its solid progress in education and public health, and it is inconceivable that these countries could have made the progress they have without such aids from the Soviet Union or some other advanced industrial patron. But the Soviet system of government and its Marxist-based cultural revolution aimed at destroying the traditional Islamic basis of Central Asian society was imposed against the bitter opposition of the local Muslim peoples and involved much bloodshed and hardship among them. This cannot be overlooked, however one assesses the two opposing cultures.

The large immigration of Slavs, including thousands of Russian workers and officials, which has constantly increased throughout the Soviet period, is also far from popular in the republics. There may well be a group in these republics (similar to what were known in Ireland as Castle Catholics) who have linked their fortunes with the

[1] Nove, *The Soviet Economy*, p. 321.

Russian 'ascendancy', support their policies, and have submerged their national-religious identity in the Soviet image. That this is far from being general is clear from the sustained attacks in Soviet Central Asian literature on 'Nationalism', an omnibus term used to castigate all phenomena considered incompatible with Marxism–Leninism. The then Secretary of the Kazakh Communist Party, N. Dzhandil'din, in his book, *Communism and the Development of National Relations*, devotes many pages to those benighted citizens (as he regards them) who prefer Kazakh national traditions and national identity to Marxism–Leninism and 'Internationalism'; 'People suffering from national diseases are as a rule politically shortsighted', affirms Dzhandil'din in a disdainful attack on his Kazakh compatriots who lapse into nationalism.[1] In particular, he inveighs against 'narrow national localism' in the form of 'attempts to prevent the development of productive forces or to encourage only those branches whose production will be used within the republic. . . . The development of the riches of any national republic is the business of the entire people.' Patriotic Kazakhs are thus sternly reminded that large-scale developments like the 'Virgin Lands' scheme, which brought an invasion of millions of Slav migrants in its wake, or the many metallurgical industries in which skilled Russians are an essential element in the labour force, have to be tolerated because of their overall contribution to Soviet economic strength. This kind of sermonizing addressed to the largest and industrially most promising country in Central Asia must at least raise doubts about the local popularity of Soviet development schemes, however valuable and inevitable they may be in themselves.

None of these strains and differences of opinion appears in the glossy literature selling the Soviet-Asian 'model' to the east. On the contrary, the atmosphere is permeated by the harmony of the Soviet peoples' 'friendship and brotherhood' and any hint of opposition to Soviet power is represented as treachery to one's own loyal kith and kin. One of the most plausible features of this literature is the massing of comparative statistics of education, health, and social conditions in Central Asia and in neighbouring Muslim lands like Iran, Turkey, or Pakistan, selective statistics which are always immensely favourable to the Soviet Union, though they

[1] *Kommunizm i Razvitiye Natsional'nykh Otnoshenii* (Moscow, 1964).

are not always strictly comparable. Sometimes these statistics are extended to Western countries and are patently absurd, showing, for example, that there were more doctors in the most backward of the Central Asian lands, i.e. the Turkmen SSR (1 per 529 inhabitants) than there are in England or France (1 per 937). Neither the quality of these doctors (many probably 'feldshers' or half-trained people) nor their distribution (which is very important in Central Asian conditions) is mentioned in the statistical comparisons and of course without some definition of standards and distribution, these comparisons are arbitrary and largely meaningless.

One need go no further than the pages of the Soviet Press to see how far the realities of these much-vaunted social services actually fall short of the advertisements. Some examples seem worth quoting as the Soviet Press is not as accessible as Soviet propaganda pamphlets on Central Asian progress in regard to schools, hospitals, and canteens, for example. They also bring life to the mirage of many Soviet statistics.

The following letter from a collective farmer in Tashkent province shows that people can be neglected in the Soviet Union as elsewhere:

Dear Editor,
    We live not far from Tashkent in the Yakshitep kishlak. We came here from remote Kashkadar'ya. Already we have worked the new lands for fifteen years and we get fair crops of cotton and other products. There are enough houses but the other side of life is painful. There is not a school or shops, a club or a good hospital and everyday services are lacking (for repairs, &c.). Although the kishlak is some five kilometres from the *rayon* centre, there is no road.

We have applied many times to the *rayon*, provincial, republican organizations to help us, but no help was given. Urgently, we beg you to help us.

Khikmat Ishkuvvatova
Collective farmer.

The best proof of the authenticity of this letter is that it was printed in *Pravda* (8 July 1965).

In spite of the undoubted Soviet success in expanding education, there are still many complaints about inadequate school buildings, lack of teachers, and poor educational facilities. The following article in *Kommunist Tadzhikistana* (7 July 1964) is typical of many in this area:

The schools do not have sufficient room for the pupils. There has been an increase of 36,000 scholars but there are only 20,000–23,000 places. Hundreds of school buildings require 'capital repairs'. 1,105 primary schools are in Kibitkas (nomads' tents). The Sovkhoz school for 1,000 (Numinabad) is occupied by more than 1,400 pupils. In Ura-Tyubinsk *rayon*, dozens of children cannot go to school as they live in mountain villages, many kilometres from the nearest school, and there are no boarding schools as there should be. The chief cause of the trouble is the inadequate attention given to school construction. Only 25 per cent. of the school building investment plan was taken up.

Schools for which collective farmers are willing to pay are in a sad plight because there are no means of building them. Construction of rural schools is not included in the central supply plan for building materials so there are no bricks or cement.

Failure to enforce general eight-year education and keep children at school until the end of the school course was reported by Usubaliyev, First Secretary of the Kirghiz CP, and by his opposite number, Rashidov, in Tashkent, at their respective Party Congresses early in 1966. Here is Rashidov's account of the state of education in Uzbekistan:

It must, however, be pointed out that the law on universal eight-year education is not being properly enforced in several areas. Appropriate steps are not taken to keep children at school until they have completed their education. Certain local executive committees have not yet begun systematic registration of children of school age. At some schools the plans for providing boarding accommodation have been regularly neglected and some of the existing boarding houses have not given the children normal living and studying conditions. As a result, a number of children do not go to school; the number who do attend is particularly large in Syr Dar'ya and Tashkent *oblasts* and the Karakalpak ASSR. In some areas the number of children who leave school before completing their education remains high. The standard of teaching is low, especially in the native and Russian languages, and in mathematics, physics, and chemistry.[1]

Thus, on the record, the Soviet system which has brought the

[1] *PV*, 4 March 1966.

Central Asian republics to their present stage of social-economic development can only be regarded as 'a model' if there are no illusions about the prevalence of unplanned phenomena such as labour problems, breakdowns in social services, industrial muddle and incompetence in the Soviet planned society, and if the coercion is accepted as a *sine qua non* of the establishment and continuity of that society.

PROSPECTS AND POSSIBILITIES

Recognition of the many shortcomings in the Soviet system must not, however, blind one to the great prospects of economic development which lie in the lands 'beyond the Urals'. Nor should failure to meet planned targets and timetables on many large construction sites in the Siberias and the Central Asian republics raise any serious doubts that the Russians will eventually reach their set objectives which will year by year reinforce the economic strength of the Soviet Union.

In the southern Soviet Asian republics the native peoples may be expected to take an increasingly independent attitude to the plans and directions of Gosplan and Gosstroy. And as the years pass, their influence will probably become increasingly effective in moulding economic policy affecting their own countries, thus eliminating the kind of errors now too frequently made by bureaucrats unfamiliar with the territory.

In the great northern expanses of Siberia and in the deserts and mountains of Central Asia it is impossible to tell what may yet be uncovered by those indefatigable Soviet geologists who recently laid bare the Muruntau gold and the diamonds of the Yakutian tundra. If the Soviet Government can only solve the crucial labour problem, and overcome the huge distances by modern transportation, the Siberias and the Soviet Far East may reach entirely new levels of prosperity in the next half-century. Following the dictates of common sense some of the more inaccessible sites in the Far North will almost certainly be left to nature. With the development of their new industrial centres, the Siberias may even assume international importance as 'world leaders in the production of electric power, fuels, iron and steel, non-ferrous and rare metals, chemicals and wood products'.[1] From the Pacific coast to the Caspian Sea the industrial map of the Soviet Union is in constant flux with new towns like Mirnyy, Navoi, Zolotogorsk filling the blank spaces of yesterday, where diamonds, natural gas, and gold have come to light after centuries of oblivion. Wherever one looks beyond the Urals there is fascinating stimulus for thought and speculation about the future. If the Russians and the Japanese can smooth out their initial problems, the Japanese may soon be co-operating in the development of Asiatic Russia. This novel and basically sensible proposal would have been unthinkable in the conventional Soviet framework of ideas a short time ago. The course of this experiment, which should facilitate some of the most complicated and important development schemes in Siberia and the Far East, will be followed with the greatest interest abroad and may in time produce not only results unpredictable at the time of writing but also completely new techniques of co-operation.

[1] V. A. Krotov, 'Geographical Aspects and Problems of the Industrialization of Siberia' *Soviet Geography* (November 1964), p. 52.

Appendix I

TSARIST SCIENTIFIC EXPLORATION OF ASIATIC RUSSIA

While the advances on many scientific fronts in Soviet Russia today are well publicized, relatively little is generally known about the manifold and fruitful investigations in Asiatic Russia of Tsarist Russian scientists, explorers, and research bodies before the Revolution. Their contribution to the ethnographical, geological, and archaeological investigation of Asiatic Russia has a special relevance here and their efforts will therefore be briefly summarized. Miscellaneous information about the topography and natural resources of Siberia was collected in a haphazard way by the Cossacks in the course of their conquest of Siberia and Turkestan. But these advance guards of Russian occupation were followed up from the time of Peter the Great by organized scientific investigations into the flora and fauna, soil, natural resources, and other unexplored aspects of these lands. Many learned bodies were established to promote this work, sponsored both by the State and wealthy private individuals, including certain Siberian merchants who had made fortunes in gold, furs, timber, and other local products.

The first Siberian scientific expedition was organized under the personal direction of Peter the Great in 1719. His instructions to the leader of the expedition, the Danziger, Daniel Amadeus Messerschmidt, curiously reflect the bent of his interests: 'to search for all kinds of rarities and pharmaceutical substances; grasses, flowers, roots and seeds, and other related items with medicinal properties'. Messerschmidt's expedition covered an immense amount of ground in Siberia, Zabaykalia, and west Siberia, and returned in 1727 with encyclopedic information on the natural history of Siberia (his report still awaits a publisher). The vast area of Asiatic Russia and its sharply diversified physical and climatic conditions has produced a very interesting and variegated flora. This fact lies at the root of the continuing research into the flora of these territories from the time of Peter the Great. Peter was also curious about the North East Passage and the actual limits of the Far Eastern territories of Russia, i.e. whether they were delimited by the sea or part of the American continent. This problem was solved (though after his death) by the Great Northern expedition (1733–43) led by the Dane, Vitus Bering, who sailed through the strait, now bearing his name, between Alaska and Chukotka, accompanied by a large group of scientists.

The 'Academic Expeditions' which subsequently became famous for their penetration of the remoter parts of Asiatic Russia and the collections they formed of botanical, zoological, mineralogical, and other scientific material started in the reign of the Empress Elizabeth (1741–62), the daughter of Peter the Great. The University of Moscow, founded during her reign in 1755, also played its part in fostering scientific investigation of Asiatic Russia. Scientific knowledge of east and west Siberia and the Chinese borderlands was actively pushed forward in the reign of Catherine the Great (1762–96). The Academy equipped an expedition led by the distinguished scientist-explorer Peter S. Pallas to investigate the 'Eastern provinces of the Empire'. Between 1768 and 1774 he travelled along the Volga, the Urals, and the Siberian towns of Tobol'sk and Krasnoyarsk to Irkutsk and the Zabaykal region, as far as Kyakhta on the Mongol–Chinese border. His careful notes of his travels were soon published in St. Petersburg, and he gained international fame for his major works on Russian flora (*Flora Rossica*) and zoology (*Zoographia rosso-asiatica*) based on data collected first-hand during his travels. Both works were translated into French and English. In 1790–2, the 'Medical Kollegia' organized a search for medicinal plants in Zabaykalia, the Yenisey region, and even as far as the Ala-kul' Valley, under an Irkutsk botanist and apothecary called Sivers.

At the end of Catherine the Great's reign, Count Lapérouse's expedition, equipped by the French Government, surveyed the coast of Sakhalin and Kamchatka and left a good description of his work for posterity. He was rewarded for his services to Russian navigation by a monument in Petropavlovsk-Kamchatka (though he had erred in thinking Sakhalin to be a peninsula and the mouth of the Amur impassable for sea-going vessels).

There was a lull in this work in the early years of the nineteenth century. Then in 1829 the Imperial Academy invited the celebrated German natural scientist, A. Humboldt, to lead an expedition to the Urals, west Siberia, and the Altay to investigate gold, platinum, and non-ferrous ore deposits. The results of his research were published in two volumes under the title *Fragments on the Geology and Climatology of Asia* (1831).

Humboldt was followed by another remarkable natural scientist, Academician A. F. Middendorf. He traversed a vast and inhospitable area of east Siberia, the Taymyr Peninsula, and the Far East between 1842 and 1845. The range of his scientific inquiries was also vast and the zoological and botanical, geological and ethnographical collections he assembled were highly valued. He was also the first scientist to investigate the possibilities of agriculture in the Far North and in Yakutia—problems which many years later would also inspire much Soviet research. After his east Siberian expedition, Academician Middendorf travelled in the north Amur region where his ethnographical investigations had considerable political significance on the eve of Russia's forward thrust to the Pacific along the Chinese Amur frontier. From his questioning of the native inhabitants, he convinced himself, according to *Aziatskaya Rossiya* (vol. I, p. 516), that the peoples inhabiting the lower Amur (the Gilyak lands) were not subject to the Chinese and that the Chinese delimited their frontier much farther to the south, according to the Treaty of Nerchinsk, than 'the Russians consider it to be'. Middendorf also drew the attention of the Government to the great importance of the Amur as 'sole convenient passage from Siberia to the Great Ocean'. His report was read by the Emperor Nicholas I in person and it reawakened his interest in the Amur delta problem and the soundness of the prevailing views about its impassability for ocean-going vessels. This was the background to Admiral Nevel'skoy's adventurous expedition which finally proved that Sakhalin was an island and the Amur passable in 1849. Thirty years later the indefatigable Middendorf was still active, now in Central Asia where he was conducting scientific research in the Fergana Valley in 1878; later he penetrated the high Pamirs. He published many works, including his *Journey to the North and East of Siberia* (1861) which is regarded as a classic.

The Russian advance through the Kazakh–Kirgiz steppes at the beginning of the nineteenth century and the conquest of Turkestan in the '60s stimulated scientific research into the flora and fauna and exploration of these areas. As early as 1840–4 Alexander Shrenk, not Leopold Shrenk (known for his pioneer work on the indigenous tribes of the Amur kray) was exploring Semirech'ye and its flora. The sharply diversified physical and climatic conditions of the vast area of Asiatic Russia have produced an exceptionally interesting, variegated flora which has been the object of much brilliant research on the part of Russian botanists since the time of Peter the Great when the St. Petersburg Botanic Garden was established.

The Imperial Russian Geographical Society was founded in 1845 and soon established a fine record for scientific expeditions in west and east

Siberia, the Amur basin, and Turkestan. Its Siberian branch (the forerunner of the present *Akademgorodok* of the all-Union Academy of Sciences in Novosibirsk) was founded in 1851 and soon was extremely active organizing expeditions to the little-known Vilyuy, Vitim, and Turukhansk country of north Siberia. It also organized some very interesting museums, notably in Irkutsk, Minusinsk, and Omsk. It is gratifying to record that the old Ethnographical Museum of the Imperial Geographical Society in Irkutsk (which I visted in 1964) still flourishes under Soviet auspices and the decorative medallions of famous old Russian scholars and explorers adorn the outer walls.

Even before the Amur became legal Russian territory in 1858–60, the St. Petersburg Botanic Garden sent out K. I. Maksimovich to explore 'nature' in the Amur basin. Maksimovich started his investigations at de-Castri Bay on the Pacific and spent three years in the Amur Valley reaching the confluence of the Amur and the Shilka in 1856, and visiting the Sungari basin in 1859–60.

A great deal of interesting scientific research on Siberia and other areas of Asiatic Russia radiated from the first Siberian University which was established at Tomsk in 1880. Many Russian professors of repute worked there and built up important collections of scientific material on Siberian and Central Asian mineralogy, flora and fauna.[1]

Soon after the annexation by Russia of Turkestan, it is interesting to note the fact that it was represented at the Ethnographical Exhibition in Moscow in 1867, the all-Russian Manufacturers' Exhibition in St. Petersburg in 1870, and the all-Russian Poly-technical Exhibition in 1872—a participation which had at least the indirect scientific result of making European and Asiatic Russia better known to each other. The large museum in Omsk housed an impressive ethnological collection relating to the peoples of the Steppe region; Kirgiz, Kazakh, Dungans, and Taranchis (Uygurs) while the archaeological collection made in the nineteenth–early twentieth century and housed in Omsk still maintains its value, according to experts.

Among the most fruitful and arduous expeditions undertaken under the auspices of the Imperial Russian Geographical Society were those of the great P. P. Semënov whose pioneering exploration of the Central Tyan Shan Mountains and mapping of its glacier fields earned him the suffix Tyan Shanskiy. He was followed a decade later by the even more illustrious traveller N. M. Przheval'skiy. Having explored the Ussuri region (1867–9), Przheval'skiy turned his steps towards Central Asia.

---

[1] P. A. Zaychenko, *Tomskiy Gosudarstvennyy Universitet imeni V. V. Kuybysheva* (Tomsk University, Tomsk, 1960).

He did valuable pioneer exploration in Mongolia, Tibet, and the Tyan Shan Mountains (1870–85). During his travels Przheval'skiy studied the climate, flora, and fauna of these regions and made large and valuable botanical and zoological collections; he discovered the wild horse named after him. He died on the shores of Lake Issyk-kul' in a village which now bears his name, Przheval'sk. Today Przheval'sk is easily reached by plane from Alma-Ata or Frunze but when I tried to visit it in 1964, I was balked by Soviet travel restrictions.

Peter Alekseyevich Kropotkin (1842–1921), better known in the West as a leading liberal anarchist theorist, was also a great geographer—in the broadest sense of the word. He travelled widely in then little-known parts of Transbaykalia, the Far East, and Manchuria, investigating the orographical features of continental Asia. Some of his best work was done in the gold-bearing regions of the Vitimsk and Olekminsk country where his prognostications regarding this rich gold-bearing area were later confirmed by the Lena Gold-Fields which financed his expedition.

Among munificent cultivated Siberians must be mentioned Gennadius V. Yudin, a Krasnoyarsk distiller, who, having made a fortune in the liquor business, devoted himself to building up very fine collections of Russian and Siberian ethnological, archaeological, and bibliographical material. His collection of some eighty thousand books shipped from Siberia to Washington eventually formed the nucleus of the Slavic section of the Library of Congress in 1907.

The Geographical Society's activities in Asiatic Russia were greatly intensified in the late nineteenth and early twentieth centuries. It must suffice to mention a few of its more famous expeditions; G. N. Potanin returned from an expedition in the Zaysan and Tarbagatay areas with a unique botanical collection which was housed in Tomsk University Museum; G. Ye. Grum-Grzhimaylo's travels resulted in a comprehensive description of the natural conditions and native peoples of the Amur and provided a fascinating and authoritative introduction to the subject when it was published in 1894.

Scientific exploration and investigation of Asiatic Russia were not confined to the great institutions like the Imperial Academy but were also undertaken by a number of private individuals and smaller bodies like the Imperial Society for Nature Lovers, Imperial Society for Lovers of Natural Science, the Siberian Railway Committee, and also by the then outstanding respective Governor-Generals of Siberia and Turkestan, Count Murav'yëv-Amursky and General K. P. Kaufman. Pioneer work of the greatest importance was carried out by Professor A. P. Fedchenko and his wife from 1868–70 on the fauna of Turkestan. Fedchenko also collected precise geographical data on the east Kyzylkum Desert and the Alai and Za-Alai mountainous country. At the close of the century a detailed investigation of the lakes of Turkestan, Balkhash, Issyk-Kul', and the Aral Sea was made by L. S. Berg (1898) and some years later Turkestan was the subject of a standard work *Turkestanskiy Kray* in the series *Rossiya*, edited by P. P. Semënov-Tyan Shanskiy (1913).

A great deal of attention was paid to mapping and exploring the Arctic coast of Asiatic Russia during this period. The outstanding feat was probably Nordenskiöld's voyage in the *Vega*. He traversed the entire Arctic coast of Siberia and reached Japan, passing through the Bering Strait. He then sailed to Sweden, thus circumnavigating the globe (1878–89). His carefully illustrated account of his travels and particularly of the types and customs of the native people of north Siberia ranks as one of the great travel books of the world. The whole trip was subsidized by a rich Siberian named Sibiryakov.

The Government was also directly involved in the scientific study of Asiatic Russia, mostly for more practical purposes than pure science, for example, mapping and definitions of border areas, charting currents of great Siberian rivers and the still largely unknown Siberian and Far Eastern coastal waters.

The cadastral surveys made of the Kirgiz–Kazakh nomads' lands at the end of the nineteenth century to determine the amount of 'surplus' land available for Russian settlements also brought to light valuable ethnographical and physical data about these peoples and their way of life. Soil science expeditions were busy from 1908 over vast tracts of Siberia determining the forest and arable zones for settlement purposes, under the auspices of the Resettlement Directorate.

In the multi-national Tsarist Empire embracing so many different languages, the work of the Imperial Society of Oriental Studies finally deserves mention. Courses of East Asian languages were held, the life of the Siberian native peoples was studied and efforts were made by these well-meaning learned people to improve their existence in various ways.

It should be clear from this brief survey that the scientific study of the natural features, peoples, and resources of the vast Asian Empire was progressing apace in Tsarist Russia during the last century of its existence. Much still remained to be done, of course, but a tradition of dedicated scientific inquiry and high standards of scholarship were firmly established before the Revolution. In the search for knowledge, the Russians had shown themselves second to none in endurance and tenacity in the most hostile physical conditions and capable of sustained intellectual effort in many fields. This aspect of the Russian psyche is fundamental and would in due course be harnessed with spectacular result to new tasks and goals after the Revolution. It was an invaluable heritage though the debt to Tsarist scholarship and learned institutions is not always fairly acknowledged by the Soviets. Scientific expeditions and exploration work in Asiatic Russia continued steadily and with every-increasing vigour after the Revolution. The work is now more systematic and co-ordinated than hitherto and is more heavily subsidized under the State Plan than was the largely haphazard pre-revolutionary research.

Sources: *Aziatskaya Rossiya*, op. cit; G. F. Wright, *Asiatic Russia*, op. cit.; V. A. Obruchev, *Ot Kyakhty do Kul'dzhi*, AN SSSR, 1940–56 (abridged by Humphrey Higgens in CAR, no. 3, 1966); P. K. Kozlov, *Russkiy puteshestvennik v Tsentral'noy Azii: izbrannyye trudy*, A N Moscow, 1963; P.P. Semënov–Tyan Shanskiy, *Puteshestvie v Tyan Shan v. 1856–57* (Moscow, 1948); articles in the *Bolshaya Sovetskaya Entsiklopediya* and the *Sibirskaya Entsiklopediya;* G. Ye. Grum-Grzhimaylo, *Opisaniye Amurskoy Oblasti*, op. cit.; L.Shrenk, *Ob Inorodtsakh Amurskogo Kraya*, op. cit.

Appendix II

Distribution of Territory, Population, and the most important Natural Resources by Economic Zones and by the large Economic Regions of the USSR as a percentage of the USSR Total[1]

Economic zones and the large component economic regions	Territory	Population	Fuel and power resources of which				Iron ore resources	Timber resources
			Total	Coal	Natural gas	Hydro-resources		
USSR	100	100	100	100	100	100	100	100
Central zone	12.1	27.8	4.6	4.3	3.4	4.6	35.9	12.5
North-west region	7.5	5.4	4.3	4.1	3.3	3.0	2.7	9.6
Central region	2.0	11.6	0.2	0.2	—	1.1	0.1	1.8
Central black earth region	0.9	4.1					33.1	0.2
Cis-Baltic region	0.8	2.9					—	
Belorussian region	0.9	3.8	0.1		0.1	0.5	—	0.9
Southern zone	6.1	32.6	3.4	3.0	25.1	9.9	28.7	2.2
The large economic regions of the Ukraine SSR	2.7	19.9	2.4	2.3	6.7	1.6	28.5	0.9
Moldavian SSR	0.2	1.4						
North Caucasus region	2.4	6.7	0.8	0.7	11.7	3.4	—	0.7
Transcaucasus region	0.8	4.6	0.2	—	6.7	4.9	0.2	0.6

Ural–Volga zone 12.8	17.8	0.9	0.4	20.0	3.4	11.6	12.9
Volga region 1.5	5.1	0.4	0.2	20.0 ⎱	1.9	0.1	0.5
Volga–Vyatka region 1.2	3.8	—	—	20.0 ⎰		0.1	1.8
Urals region 10.1	8.9	0.5	0.2	—	1.5	11.5	10.6
Siberian zone 51.2	10.2	88.9	90.6	18.8	62.4	7.3	72.0
West Siberian region 4.4	4.8	13.3	13.1	8.3	7.2	0.9	5.3
East Siberian region (including Yakutia) 32.9	3.4	73.6	75.8 ⎱	10.5	41.6	5.6	51.2
Far Eastern region 13.9	2.0	2.0	1.7 ⎰		13.6	0.8	15.5
Central Asian zone 17.8	11.6	2.2	1.7	32.7	19.7	16.5	0.4
Kazakhstan region 12.3	4.8	1.3	1.2	11.7	4.4	16.5	0.3
Central Asian region 5.5	6.8	0.9	0.5	21.0	15.3	—	0.1

[1] *Voprosy Razmeshcheniya Proizvodstva v SSSR*, Izdatel'stvo 'Nauka' (Moscow, 1965), p. 37. Statistics based on Soviet statistical handbooks 1960–3, i.e. before Yakutia was transferred to the Far Eastern economic region.

Appendix III

Soviet Cotton and Cotton Textile Production[1]

	Cotton production				Cotton fibre production				Cotton textile production			
	1963		1964		1963		1964		1963		1964	
	000 tons	per cent.	000 tons	per cent.	000 tons	per cent.	000 tons	per cent.	million l. metres	per cent.	million l. metres	per cent.
Uzbekistan	3,689	71	3,671	70	1,011	70	1,232	70	247	3.5	257	3.5
Kazakhstan	63	1	81	1.5	25	2	24	1.5	20	.5	22	.5
Azerbaydzhan	273	5	340	6.5	85	7	105	6	131	2	142	2
Kirgizia	170	3	168	3	46.3	3	59	3	2	—	2	—
Tadzhikistan	540	10.5	546	10.5	152	9	184	10.5	71	1	77	1
Armenia	15	.5	16	.5	8	.5	6	.5	76	1	83	1
Turkmenistan	460	9	463	9	126.4	8.5	152	8.5	22	.5	21	.5
USSR	5,210	100	5,285	100	1,455	100	1,762	100	6,619	100	6,976	100
RSFSR	—	—	—	—	—	—	—	—	5,639	85	5,924	85

[1] In percentages of Soviet output.

Source: *Nar. Khoz. SSSR v 1964 g.*

Soviet Union: Exports and Imports of Cotton in 1963 and 1964

	1963	1964
A. *Cotton fibre* (000 tons)		
USSR exports	321	394
USSR imports	226	145
Net USSR exports	95	249
B. *Cotton textiles* (million metres)[1]		
USSR exports	227	252
USSR imports	83	69
Net USSR exports	144	183

Source: *Vneshnyaya Torgovlya SSSR*, 1963 and 1964.

[1] The foreign trade year-book does not state whether these figures refer to linear or square metres. The relation of 1 linear metre to 1 square metre is 1:0.75 approximately.

Appendix IV

THE SIBERIAN DEPARTMENT OF THE USSR ACADEMY OF SCIENCES[1]

One of the more interesting permanent measures of decentralization instituted by the Twentieth Party Congress was the establishment of a separate department of the USSR Academy of Sciences for Siberia in 1957. This new department brought under one head the affiliates of the Academy already existing in Novosibirsk, Ulan Ude, Irkutsk, Yakutsk, and the Far East (Vladivostok and Petropavlovsk–Kamchatka). For this department, a new academic township known as the *Akademgorodok* (35,000 inhabitants) was built on the banks of the 'Ob' Sea' 20 km. from Novosibirsk. The excellent laboratory and research facilities offered there attracted many distinguished scientists and the experiment has proved a great success. A second *Akademgorodok* is now being built near Irkutsk on a slightly more modest scale with a population target of about 10,000.

Novosibirsk and each affiliate has its own group of institutes. An exception is the Permafrost Institute in Yakutsk, which is not responsible to the local affiliate, but directly to the Siberian Department in Novosibirsk.

Apart from fundamental scientific research in many fields, the Siberian Department was set up in order to apply scientific research to the problems of development of Siberia and the Far East, i.e. studies of the natural resources, the climate, agricultural potential, the economics of industry and transport in the Siberian context. In 1965, eight years after its foundation, the Siberian Academy included some 15 institutes, employing 13 regular members and 43 corresponding members of the USSR Academy of Sciences while between 200 and 300 young scientists were working

[1] George Vvedensky, 'The Siberian Department of the Academy of Sciences of the USSR'; C. Olgin, Summary of the Bulletin of the Siberian Department of the Academy of Sciences of the USSR: Social Science Series 1962–4. From *Siberia and the Soviet Far East, Studies on the Soviet Union*, vol. V, no. 1 (1965); Ye. Lazutkin, 'Work of Scientists-Economists of Siberia and the Far East', *Voprosy Ekonomiki*, no. 3 (1964), pp. 153–7.

there. The Chairman of the Academy and Director of the Institute of Hydrodynamics is Academician M. A. Lavrent'yev. A new university was opened in September 1959 to train young specialists for the higher research work in the institutes of the Academy.

The orientation of the Institute of Economics at Novosibirsk may be taken as typical of the other institutes in their particular fields. It has been dealing mainly with the distribution of industrial production and the prospects of the complex development of different regions together with the problems of labour productivity. It has a laboratory in Vladivostok which works on problems of the general development of the Far East, the economics of ship repairs and agricultural productivity, and a new laboratory in Khabarovsk studies all aspects of the labour problem in the Far East.

Such institutes as that of Mining and Electric Power Transmission, of Hydrodynamics (including research on blasting and excavation by water pressure), and of Geology and Geophysics have obvious local significance in the eastern regions. In 1961 and 1962 the Novosibirsk Institute signed 182 contracts with industrial enterprises for collaboration in research projects (although these contracts are not all necessarily with firms in the eastern regions). Though a great deal of valuable work is done in Siberia and the Far East, the Siberian Department is not confined to the study of practical local problems. The range and quality of research at the Institute of Nuclear Physics, of Theoretical and Applied Mechanics, and of Inorganic Chemistry and Mathematics are on a par with top-ranking institutes in the United States of America, France, or Great Britain and have greatly impressed many visiting foreign scholars.

Publication of the Academy's five journals began in 1959: *Geologiya i geofizika* (Geology and Geophysics), *Zhurnal Strukturnoy khimii* (Journal of Structural Chemistry), *Kinetika i kataliz* (Kinetics and Catalysis), *Sibirskiy matematicheskiy zhurnal* (Siberian Mathematical Journal), *Zhurnal prikladnoy mekhaniki tekhnicheskoy fiziki* (Journal of Applied Mechanics and Technological Physics). The *Izvestiya vostochnykh filialov Akademii Nauk SSSR* (Bulletin of the Eastern Branches of the Academy of Sciences of the USSR) became the *Izvestiya Sibirskogo otdeleniya Akademii Nauk SSSR* (Bulletin of the Siberian Department of the Academy of Sciences of the USSR) in 1959.

M. Jean Cantacuzène, Scientific Attaché at the French Embassy in Moscow for the past three years, visited Novosibirsk Scientific Centre twice recently and reported his impressions in *Le Monde*.[1] It may be

---

[1] M. Jean Cantacuzène, 'A Novosibirsk, chez l'académicien Lavrentiev', *Le Monde*, 8/9 and 10 May 1966, which has kindly authorized this reproduction of M. Cantacuzène's article.

interesting to note the more important of the first-hand impressions picked up during these rather exceptional visits, in view of the barriers in the way of less-privileged travellers (including myself) visiting this Novosibirsk institution. According to M. Cantacuzène, a visit to this new centre in the Siberian woods of conifers and birches merging eventually after some hundreds of kilometres to the north-east into impenetrable taiga must be a fascinating experience. Large spaces are already reserved for vast expansion plans. The *Akademgorodok* is now a regular town comprising, as well as the university, the strikingly new, imposing buildings of the scientific institutes along the big central avenue, shops, cinemas, theatres, a hotel and blocks of flats. The presiding genius of the whole enterprise and Chairman of the Academy, Academician Lavrent'yev, still lives in a comfortable wooden *izba* in the forest—a survival from the 'heroic' pre-development age. In spite of its nominal dependence on the presidium of the Academy of Sciences of the USSR in Moscow, the Siberian Department (to which the *Akademgorodok* belongs) enjoys considerable autonomy, and its budget is directly looked after by the Council of Ministers of the RSFSR and not by the presidium of the Academy of Sciences.

The scientific institute which most impressed this visitor by its site and its size is devoted to nuclear physics, and directed by a forty-year-old physicist, Academician Budker. Most of the research workers at his institute are also young, averaging twenty-five years of age. The basic work of this institute is in the field of controlled thermonuclear reactions. In addition, this institute has built, and uses, collision accelerators (annular accelerators) whose purpose is to make two groups of charged particles moving in opposite directions meet, and thereby to obtain very high interaction energies. 'Our specialists from Orsay, who have had some success in the field of annular accelerators, maintain good contacts with the people of Novosibirsk.'

A complete department of the Institute of Catalysis is using computers, mainly analogue, and is trying to find mathematical models corresponding to chemical reactions. This departure is still quite unusual in chemical research. Another institute researching on unusual lines is the Institute of Kinetics and Combustion, one of whose directors is Academician Voyevodskiy, a brilliant pupil of the Nobel prize winner Nikolay Semënov, who is chiefly a specialist on free radicals, and gladly shows his visitors how these are produced in a flame by moving it near to a paramagnetic electronic resonance machine.

There are 500 research workers at the Institute of Organic Chemistry who study problems of fundamental chemistry as well as problems specially connected with Siberia, including the nature of the active agents of Siberian plants with peculiar curative properties. Original and practical research characterizes the work of the Institute of Hydrodynamics, directed personally by Academician Lavrent'yev. One of his most remarkable inventions, the water cannon, has already attracted international publicity and is used to extract coal in big mines. With a jet of water of 2,000 atmospheres it can shatter a 1-metre thick wall and with 60,000 atmospheres pierce a copper ingot several centimetres thick. An international patent has been taken out by the Soviet Union for this water cannon.

The oldest institute, and that with the largest number of collaborators, is the Institute of Geophysics and Geology. Siberian research in this field has always been interesting, but this institute is now bending its efforts in another direction and at much greater depth, i.e. to the possibility of boring a hole some 15 km. deep in order to penetrate beneath the earth's crust. All the Novosibirsk scientists enjoy the services of a computer centre inspired by Academician Sobolev and it is used in particular by the team working on forecasts of Siberian weather. The reason given by Academician Lavrent'yev why scientists in all fields were quickly drawn to Novosibirsk was that eminent men 'of the first order' were given *carte blanche* to construct institutes to their own design 'with practically unlimited credits'. They were thus assured of ideal working conditions even if their salaries were the same as in Moscow or Leningrad. The realization of this scientists' 'dream' had cost some 200 million roubles. Each institute is directed by an academician or a corresponding member of the Academy with numerous research workers. The different fields of research are closely integrated. Scientific research work is also linked with the training of students at the university who are regarded as future staff members, and during their last two years (of the five-year university course) they work with the Academy's research teams.

A great deal of hard thinking has been going on about the best means of ensuring that the research students in various scientific disciplines are abreast of all modern knowledge and discovery. It is interesting to learn that the consensus of academic opinion in Novosibirsk is that in biology today, for example, 'a complete biologist cannot exist', because this science requires training in physics, chemistry, and natural sciences. The solution to this problem is to have three teams of biologists each specializing in one of the associated sciences as well as biology. Fields of research are carefully chosen which will yield fruitful important results. The scientists work in close co-operation with industry, though they are careful not to allow themselves to be submerged in a flood of small technological problems. A certain number of the young Novosibirsk scientists are destined eventually to enter industry.

The dominating impressions left by this visit were of the intellectual and material wealth of this Siberian centre and the great dedication, freedom of thought and discussion, and unusual possibilities of foreign travel among the *Akademgorodok* scientists.

Appendix V

LOCAL INDUSTRIES OF THE FAR EAST

(excluding those of all-Union significance, also mines (except coal) and
electricity, which are treated separately)

Iron and Steel
Komsomol'sk *Amurstal'* (producing about 800,000 tons of various
products: profiles, rods, flat-rolled steel, etc.). No blast furnaces;
pig iron for steel-making from Manchuria and from west Siberia.

Engineering
Khabarovsk—agricultural machinery, machinery for forestry and wood-
working industries.
Komsomol'sk—general machinery repairs, forest machinery.
Vladivostok—machinery repairs.
Blagoveshchensk—agricultural and mining machinery repairs.
Svobodnyy—railway and motor vehicle repairs.
Yuzhno-Sakhalinsk—locomotive and railway wagon repairs.
Yakutsk—machinery repairs.
Magadan—motor vehicle and mining machinery repairs.
Ussuriysk—engineering.

Shipbuilding and Ship Repair
Vladivostok, Nakhodka, Korsakov, Petropavlovsk-Kamchatka, Kha-
barovsk, Blagoveshchensk, Surazhevka (near Svobodnyy), Yakutsk.
(With the increasing numbers and sizes of ships in the Far East
repair facilities are entirely inadequate.)
Far East Oil Refineries
Khabarovsk, Komsomol'sk.

Chemicals
First timber-chemical combine under construction in Amursk, first
section due to operate in 1966–7.

Timber, Paper and Cellulose Works
Timber: Khabarovsk, Komsomol'sk, Blagoveshchensk, Svobodnyy, Vladivostok, Yakutsk.
Timber, paper, cellulose: Ussuriysk (timber and paper combine), S. Sakhalin (timber and paper/cellulose combines).
Plywood: Vladivostok (one of the largest mills in the USSR).

Tyre Retreading
Khabarovsk (also one each in Primor'ye and Amur province).

Coal Briquetting
Raychikhinsk (Amur province).

Building Materials (excluding Timber and Glass)
Primor'ye—bricks.
Khabarovsk—asphalt, concrete, ferro-concrete.
S.W. Birobidzhan—timber.
Yakutsk—bricks, ferro-concrete.
Spassk-Dal'niy—cement works, ferro-concrete works (under construction).

Can-making
Vladivostok, Petropavlovsk-Kamchatka, Yuzhno-Sakhalinsk.

Light Industry
Khabarovsk—heating equipment, enamelling, clothes.
Komsomol'sk—clothes.
Vladivostok—buttons.
Yuzhno-Sakhalinsk—tannery (sealskins).
Yakutsk—tannery.
Ussuriysk—new boot and shoe factory (largest in Far Eastern region).

Food Industry (except fish)
Khabarovsk—butter, fats, meat, flour.
Belogorsk—processing Amur *oblast* products.
Vladivostok—tea-blending factory, flour mills.
Ussuriysk—sugar, flour, meat combine, margarine, butter/fats.
Yuzhno-Sakhalinsk—meat combine.

Fish Canning and Preserving
Khabarovsk—fish conserves.
Komsomol'sk—fish conserves.
Vladivostok—fish combine (agar.)

Nakhodka—fish combine (under construction).

Ozernovskiy—new port and centre of the fish and (Kamchatka) crab
    industry (under construction).

Yakutsk—fish conserves.

Magadan—fish conserves.

Select Bibliography

This list contains works I have consulted and found useful. It makes no claim to being a complete bibliography. Direct reference is made in the footnotes to the many articles in Soviet newspapers and periodicals which are an essential source of information on Siberia, the Far East, Central Asia, and Kazakhstan.

I. *Newspapers (N) and Periodicals (P)*

The Soviet Metropolitan Press.
Pravda Vostoka (Tashkent). *N.*
Kazakhstanskaya Pravda (Alma-Ata). *N.*
Kommunist Tadzhikistana (Dushanbe). *N.*
Turkmenskaya Iskra (Ashkhabad). *N.*
Sovetskaya Kirgizia (Frunze). *N.*
Angarskie Ogni (organ of the CPSU Irkutsk Sovkhoz-Kolkhoz directorate and *rayon* Soviet of workers' deputies. A few copies picked up locally). *N.*
Central Asian Review CARC (London). *P.*
Dal'niy Vostok (Khabarovsk). *P.*
Economic Bulletin for Europe ECE (Geneva) 1957. *P.*
Ekonomicheskaya Gazeta (Moscow). *N.*
Ekonomicheskiye Nauki (Moscow). *P.*
Ekonomika i Zhizn' (Tashkent). *P.*
Izvestiya Akademii Nauk Tadzhikskoy SSR otdeleniye Obshchestvennykh Nauk (Dushanbe). *P.*
Izvestiya Akademii Nauk Kazakhskoy SSR (seriya istorii, arkheologii i etnografii and seriya filosofii i iskusstva) (Alma-Ata). *P.*
Izvestiya Akademii Nauk Turkmenskoy SSR (seriya obshchestvennykh nauk) (Ashkhabad). *P.*
Kommunist Uzbekistana (Tashkent). *P.*
Literaturnaya Gazeta (Moscow). *N.*
Narodnoye Khozyaystvo Kazakhstana (Alma-Ata). *P.*
Narodnoye Khozyaystvo Sredney Azii (Tashkent), 1964–January 1965. *P.*

Neue Zürcher Zeitung Handelsteil (Zurich). *N.*

Novoye Vremya (Moscow). *P.*

Obshchestvennyye Nauki v Uzbekistane AN (Tashkent). *P.*

Oktyabr' (Moscow). *P.*

Planovoye Khozyaystvo (Moscow). *P.*

Polar Record (Cambridge). *P.*

Polyarnaya Zvezda (Yakutsk). *P.*

Sovetskaya Etnografiya (Moscow). *P.*

Soviet Geography Review and Translation (New York). *P.*

Soviet Studies (Glasgow). *P.*

Studies on the Soviet Union (Munich). *P.*

Soviet Life (published by the Soviet Embassy, Washington), May–June 1965. *P.*

Survey (London). *P.*

Vestnik Ak. Nauk SSSR (Moscow). *P.*

Vneshnyaya Torgovlya (Moscow). *P.*

Voprosy Ekonomiki (Moscow). *P.*

Voprosy Istorii (Moscow). *P.*

Vostochno-Sibirskaya Pravda (organ of the Irkutsk industrial and agricultural *oblast* committees of the CPSU and of the *oblast* industrial and agricultural Soviets of workers' deputies). (Irkutsk. A few copies picked up locally in 1964.) *N.*

II. Extensive use has been made of the Summary of World Broadcasts published by the British Broadcasting Corporation from which all Moscow broadcasts mentioned and much of the Tass Agency information has been quoted.

III. Reference works. Books and pamphlets.

ABUTALIPOV, CH. A., *Mezhdunarodnyye Svyazi Uzbekistana.* Gos. Iz., Uzbekistana, Tashkent 1964.

AMIDON, WILLIAM C., 'The Issue of Sakhalin in Russo-Japanese Relations' from *Five Studies in Japanese Politics.* University of Michigan Press, Michigan 1957.

ARMSTRONG, T., *Russian Settlement in the North.* Cambridge University Press, Cambridge 1965.

AZIATSKAYA ROSSIYA, 3 vols. Izdaniye Pereselencheskogo Upravleniya Glavnogo Upravleniya Zemleustroystva i Zemledeliya. St. Petersburg 1914.

BALZAK, S. S., VASYUTIN, V. F., and FEYGIN, YA. G., *Economic Geography of the USSR*. Translated from the Russian by Chauncy D. Harris. Macmillan, New York 1949.

BARDIN, I. P. (Ed.), *Problemy Razvitiya Chernoy Metallurgii v Rayonakh Vostochneye Ozera Baykala*. Moscow 1960.

BATKAYEV, R. A. and MARKOV, V. I., *Differentsiatsiya Zarabotnoy Platy v Promyshlennosti SSSR*. Iz. 'Ekonomika', Moscow 1964.

BEDRINTSEV, K. N. and DESYATCHIKOV, B. A. *Promyshlennost' Uzbekistana za 40 let*. Iz. Akademii Nauk Uzbekskoy SSR, Tashkent 1957.

BENNIGSEN, A. and QUELQUEJAY, C. *The Evolution of Muslim Nationalities of the USSR and their Linguistic Problems*. Translated from the French by Geoffrey Wheeler. Central Asian Research Centre, London 1961.

BERNSTEIN, S. A., *The Financial and Economic Results of the Working of the Lena Goldfields Co. Ltd*. The Blackfriars Press, London 1930.

BORZUNOV, V. F., *Arkhivnye Materialy po Istorii Stroitel'stva Sibirskoy Zheleznoy Dorogi (1880–1905)*. Istoricheskiy Arkhiv, Iz. AN SSSR, no. 5, 1960, p. 194.

BOYKO-PAVLOV, D. I. and SIDORCHUK, YE. P., *Tak bylo na Dal'nem Vostoke*. Moscow 1964.

CAROE, OLAF, *Soviet Empire*. Macmillan & Co. Ltd., London 1953.

CARR, E. H., *The Bolshevik Revolution, 1917–1923*, 3 vols. Macmillan & Co. Ltd., London 1950–3.

'THE CASE OF CENTRAL ASIA', Regional Economic Policy in the Soviet Union. United Nations Economic Bulletin for Europe, Geneva 1957.

CHAMBERLIN, W. H., *The Russian Revolution*, 2 vols. Macmillan & Co. Ltd., London 1935.

CHAMBRE, HENRI, *L'Aménablement du Territoire en U.R.S.S.* Mouton & Co., Paris 1959.

CHERNOVA, YE. P. and others, *Naseleniye i Trudovyye Resursy Kirgizskoy SSR*. Iz. 'Ilim', Frunze 1965.

CHEVIGNY, HECTOR, *Russian America: The Great Alaskan Adventure 1741–1867*. The Cresset Press, London 1965.

CHOKAY-OGLY, MUSTAFA, *Turkestan pod Vlast'yu Sovetov*. Yash Turkestan, Paris 1935.

CILIGA, A., *Sibérie: Terre de l'Exil et de l'Industrialisation*. Librairie Plon, Paris 1950.

CLEINOW, J., *Neu-Sibirien, Eine Studie zur Aufmarsch der Sowjetmacht in Asien*. Verlag von Reimar Hobbing, Berlin 1928. 426 pp.

——*Roter Imperialismus. Eine Studie über die Verkehrsprobleme der Sowjet Union.* Verlag von Julius Springer, Berlin 1931. 224 pp.

COLLINS, P. MCDONOUGH, *A Voyage down the Amur.* Appleton, New York 1960.

CONOLLY, V., *Soviet Trade from the Pacific to the Levant.* Oxford University Press, London 1935.

COTTON IN THE SOVIET UNION, Foreign Agricultural Service, US Department of Agriculture, Washington, D.C. 1959.

CURZON, G., *Russia in Central Asia.* Longmans, Green, London 1889.

CZAPLICKA, M. A., *Aboriginal Siberia. A Study in Social Anthropology.* Clarendon Press, Oxford 1914.

——*My Siberian Year.* Mills & Boon, London 1916.

DALLIN, DAVID J., *The Rise of Russia in Asia.* Hollis & Carter, London 1950.

DALLIN, DAVID J. and NICOLAEVSKY, BORIS I., *Forced Labour in Soviet Russia.* Yale University Press, Connecticut 1947.

DANILOV, S. K., GALITSKIY, M. I., KORNEYEV, A. I., *Ekonomicheskaya Geografiya Transporta SSSR.* Iz. 'Transport', Moscow 1965.

DAVIDOV, D. A., *Koloni̱zatsiya Man'churii i Severo-Vostochnoy Mongolii.* Vladivostok 1911.

DAVIDOV, I. YA., *Irtysh Potechet na Zapad.* Alma-Ata 1962.

DAVIES, R. W., *The Development of the Soviet Budgetary System.* Cambridge University Press, Cambridge 1958.

DIMENSIONS OF SOVIET ECONOMIC POWER. Hearings before the Joint Economic Committee of the Congress of the United States, Washington, D.C., 10 and 11 Dec. 1962.

DIRECTIVES OF THE SIXTH FIVE YEAR PLAN AND REPORT BY N. A. BULGANIN TO THE 20TH CONGRESS OF THE CPSU. Soviet News Booklet No. 5, London 1956.

DUMONT, RENÉ, *Sovkho̱z, Kolkho̱z ou le Problématique Communisme.* Editions du Seuil, Paris 1964.

DZHANDIL'DIN, N., *Kommuni̱zm i Ra̱zvitiye National'nykh Otnosheniy.* Moscow 1964.

EASTERN PEOPLES, FIRST CONGRESS OF *(see PERVIY S'EZD).*

EBEL, ROBERT E., *The Petroleum Industry of the Soviet Union.* American Petroleum Institute, USA 1961.

EKONOMICHESKAYA ENTSIKLOPEDIYA, *Promyshlennost' i Stroitel'stvo,* 3 vols. Published by Sovetskaya Entsiklopediya, Moscow 1964.

EKONOMICHESKIYE RAYONY SSSR, Iz. 'Ekonomika', Moscow 1965.

EKONOMICHESKIYE SVYAZI I TRANSPORT, *Voprosy Geografii N. 61.* Gos. Iz. Geograficheskoy Literatury, Moscow 1963.

EKONOMIKO-STATISTICHESKIY SPRAVOCHNIK PO VOSTOCH-NOSIBIRSKUMY KRAYU. Izdanie Kraygiza Irkutsk 1932.

FISHER, R. H., *The Russian Fur Trade, 1550–1700.* University of California Publications in History, vol. 31, XI, 1943.

EUDIN, XENIA JOUKOFF and NORTH, ROBERT C., *Soviet Russia and the East. A Documentary Survey.* Stanford University Press. Stanford, California 1957.

FRASER, JOHN FOSTER, *The Real Siberia.* Cassell & Co., London 1962.

FUTURE CROP YIELDS AND FERTILIZATION IN THE SOVIET UNION (an analysis of P. M. Zemsky's *The Development and Speciali-zation of Agriculture according to Natural Economic Regions of the USSR).* US Dept. of Agriculture Economic Research Service 1964.

GALUZO, P. G., *Agrarnye Otnosheniya na Yuge Kazakhstana v 1867–1914 gg.* Iz. 'Nauka', Alma-Ata 1965.

GODOVOY OBZOR MINERAL'NYKH RESURSOV SSSR 1925–1926. Geologicheskiy komitet Soveta narodnykh kommissarov, Leningrad 1927.

GOLDER, F. A., *Russian Expansion on the Pacific 1641–1850.* Arthur H. Clark, Cleveland, Ohio 1914.

GRINTAL', E. F. and NARKELYUN, L. F., *Osobennosti Geologii i orudeneniya Udokanskogo i Dzhezkazganskogo Mestorozhdeniy Medistykh peschanikov.* In V. S. Preobrazhenskiy (Ed.), *Voprosy geografii Zaybaykal'skogo severa.* Iz. 'Nauka', Moscow 1964.

GRISHKOV, I. G., *Elektrifikatsiya Sovetskogo Kirgizstana.* Iz. 'Ilim', Frunze 1965.

GROSHEV, I. I. (Ed.), *Bratskoye Sodruzhestvo Narodov SSSR.* Iz. 'Mysl' ', Moscow 1964.

GRUM-GRZHIMAYLO, G. YE., *Opisaniye Amurskoy Oblasti.* State Ministry of Finance, St. Petersburg 1894.

GUIDE DU GRAND CHEMIN DE FER TRANS-SIBÉRIEN, Ed. by A. I. Dmitriyev-Mamonov and Engineer Zdsiarsky. Translated from the Russian by P. Tacchella. St. Petersburg 1900.

GUSEV, O. K., *V Gorakh Severnogo Pribaykal'ya.* Iz. 'Mysl' ', Moscow 1964.

HANSBERGER, S., *Japan and the U.S. in World Trade.* Published for the Council on Foreign Relations by Harper & Row, 1964.

HAYIT, BAYMIRZA, *Turkestan im XX Jahrhundert.* C. W. Leske Verlag, Darmstadt 1956.

——*Sowjetrussische Orientpolitik am Beispiel Turkestans.* Kiepenhauer und Witsch, Cologne and Berlin 1962.

HODGKINS, T. A., *Soviet Power: Energy Resources, Production and Potentials*. Prentice-Hall International, London 1961.

HOEFFDING, OLEG, *Soviet State Planning and Forced Industrialization as a Model for Asia*. Rand, Santa Monica, California 1958.

HOLDSWORTH, MARY, *Turkestan in the 19th Century*. Central Asian Research Centre, London 1959.

HOOSON, DAVID S. M., *A New Soviet Heartland?* Van Nostrand, New York, London and Toronto 1964.

——*Industrial Growth: Where Next?* Survey, no. 57, October 1965.

HUBBARD, L. E., *The Economics of Soviet Agriculture*. Macmillan & Co. Ltd., London 1939.

HUNTER, HOLLAND, *Soviet Transportation Policy*. Harvard University Press, Cambridge, Mass. 1957.

HUTCHISON, ISOBEL W., *The Aleutian Islands*. Blackie & Son Ltd., London 1942.

INGRAM, D., *The Communist Economic Challenge*. George Allen & Unwin, London 1965.

INSTITUTE OF WATER ECONOMY AND HYDRAULICS OF THE ACADEMY OF SCIENCES OF THE UZBEK SSR. Academy of Sciences, Uz. SSR. Tashkent 1961.

ISUPOV, A. A., *Natsional'nyy Sostav Naseleniya SSSR*. Moscow 1964.

ITOGI VSESOYUZNOY PEREPISI NASELENIYA 1959 G. (SVODNYY TOM). ITOGI VSESOYUZNOY PEREPISI NASELENIYA 1959 G., KAZAKHSKAYA SSR, UZBEKSKAYA SSR. Tsentral'noye Statisticheskoye Upravlenie pri Sovete Ministrov SSSR. Moscow 1962.

ITOGI VYPOLENIYA PERVOGO PYATILETNOGO PLANA RAZVITIYA NARODNOGO KHOZYAYSTVA SSSR. Izdanie Gosplana SSSR. Moscow 1934.

ITOGI VYPOLENIYA VTOROGO PYATILETNOGO PLANA. Moscow 1939.

IZVESTIYA VOSTOCHNO-SIBIRSKAGO OTDELA IMPERATORSKAGO RUSSKAGO GEOGRAFICHESKAGO OBSHCHESTVA, Tom. XXVII, 1896, no. 1. (Devoted to a survey of fifty years of activity of the Russian Geographical Society, 1846–1896.) Irkutsk 1897.

JASNY, NAUM, *Khrushchev's Crop Policy*. George Outram & Co. Ltd., Glasgow 1965.

——*The Socialized Agriculture of the USSR*. Stanford University Press, California 1949.

——*The Soviet Economy during the Plan Era*. Stanford University Press, California 1951.

——*The Soviet Price System*. Stanford University Press, California 1951.

——*The Soviet 1956 Statistical Handbook: A Commentary.* Angus & Robertson (Sydney, London, Wellington and Melbourne), Michigan State University Press, East Lansing 1957.

——*Soviet Industrialization 1928–1950.* The University of Chicago Press, Illinois 1961. 467 pp.

KAPUR, HARISH, *Soviet Russia and Asia 1917–27. A Study of Soviet Policy towards Turkey, Iran and Afghanistan.* Michael Joseph Ltd., (for the Geneva Graduate Institute of International Studies) 1966.

KAZAKHSKAYA SSR. Kazakhskoye Gosudarstvennoye Izdatel'stvo, Alma-Ata 1960.

KENNAN, GEORGE, *Siberia and the Exile System.* Osgood, Inc., London 1891. 2 vols.

KERNER, ROBERT J., *The Urge to the Sea.* University of California Press, Berkeley and Los Angeles 1946.

KHALFIN, N. A., *Russia's Policy in Central Asia 1857–1868.* A condensed version of the original Russian by Hubert Evans. Central Asian Research Centre, London 1964.

KHRUSHCHEV, N. S., *Stroitel'stvo Kommunizma v SSSR i Razvitiye Sel'skogo Khozyaystva.* Gospolitizdat, Moscow 1962.

——*Za Dal'neysheye Uvelicheniye Proizvodstva Khlopka.* Gospolitizdat, Moscow 1955.

KOLARZ, WALTER, *The Peoples of the Soviet Far East.* George Philip & Son Ltd., London 1954.

KOZLOV, I. V. (Ed.), *Srednyaya Aziya Kazakhstan* (Photo album). Moscow 1964.

KOZLOVSKIY, YE., *Krasnaya Armiya v Sredney Azii.* Tashkent 1928.

KRADER, LAWRENCE, *Peoples of Central Asia.* Minton & Co., The Hague 1963. Indiana University Press, Bloomington 1963.

KRAUSSE, A., *Russia in Asia: A Record and a Study. 1558–1899.* London 1900.

KROTOV, V. A., *Irkutskaya Oblast* (2nd enlarged edition). Irkutskoye khizhnoye izdatel'stvo, Irkutsk 1960.

KURBANOV, L. A., *Sovetskaya Turkmeniya.* Moscow 1964.

KUTAF'YEV, S. A., *Kazakhskaya SSR.* Moscow 1953.

LAIRD, ROY D. (Ed.), *Soviet Agricultural and Peasant Affairs.* Constable & Co., London 1964.

LATTIMORE, OWEN, *Manchuria: Cradle of Conflict.* The Macmillan Co., New York 1932.

——*The Mongols of Manchuria.* George Allen & Unwin Ltd., London 1935.

——*Pivot of Asia. Sinkiang and the Inner Asian Frontiers of China and Russia.* Boston 1950.

LAUE, T. H. VON, *Sergei Witte and the Industrialization of Russia.* Columbia University Press, New York 1963.

LAVRISHCHEV, A. N., *Ekonomicheskaya Geografiya SSSR.* Iz. 'Ekonomika', Moscow 1965.

LENIN, V. I., *The Essentials of Lenin,* 2 vols. Lawrence & Wishart, London 1947.

LEVIN, M. G. and POTAPOV, L. P. (Ed.), *Narody Sibiri. Etnograficheskiye Ocherki* (Ethnographic Survey). Iz. AN SSSR, 1956. (English translation *The Peoples of Siberia,* published by the University of Chicago Press, Illinois 1964.)

L'EXTRÊME-ORIENT SOVIÉTIQUE, *Caractéristiques économiques et perspectives de développement. Notes et Etudes Documentaires. September 1966, no. 3322.* La Documentation française, Paris 1966.

LIED, JONAS, *Return to Happiness.* Macmillan & Co. Ltd., London 1943.

LIPSKIY, A. N., *Man'chzhuro-Tungusy Russkoy Chasti Basseyna Amura.* Khabarovsk 1926.

LITTLEPAGE, J. D. and BESS, D., *In Search of Soviet Gold.* Harcourt Brace & Co., New York 1938.

LIVSHITS, R. S., *Razmeshcheniye Promyshlennosti v Dorevolyutsionnoy Rossii.* Izvestiya AN SSSR, Moscow 1955.

LOBANOV-ROSTOVSKY, PRINCE A., *Russia and Asia.* Macmillan & Co., New York 1933.

LORIMER, F., *The Population of the Soviet Union.* League of Nations, Geneva 1946.

LYASHCHENKO, P. I., *Istoriya Narodnogo Khozyaystva SSSR,* vols. I–III. Moscow 1956.

MALAFEYEV, A. N., *Istoriya Tsenoobrazovaniya v SSSR 1917–1963.* Iz. 'Mysl' ', Moscow 1964.

MARGOLIN, A. B., *Problemy Narodnogo Khozyaystva Dal'nego Vostoka.* Iz. AN SSSR, Moscow 1963.

MAVOR, J., *An Economic History of Russia,* 2 vols. J. M. Dent & Sons Ltd., London 1925.

MEHNERT, KLAUS, *Asien, Moskau und Wir* (6th edition). Deutsche Verlags-Anstalt, Stuttgart 1958.

——*Der Sowjetmensch.* Deutsche Verlags-Anstalt, Stuttgart 1958.

MELLOR, R. E. H., *Geography of the USSR.* Macmillan & Co. Ltd. London 1964.

MICHAEL, H. N. (Ed.), *Studies in Siberian Ethnogenesis.* University of Toronto Press, Ontario, 1962.

MOBLEY, LEONARD A., *Cotton in Russia*. National Cotton Council, Memphis, Tennessee 1959.

MORA, SILVESTER, *Kolyma—Gold and Forced Labour in the USSR*. Foundation for Foreign Affairs, Washington, D.C. 1949.

NARODNOYE KHOZYAYSTVO KAZAKHSKOY SSR (1956). Kazakhskoye Gos. Iz., Alma-Ata 1957.

NARODNOYE KHOZYAYSTVO KIRGIZSKOY SSR. Gosstatizdat, Frunze 1957.

NARODNOYE KHOZYAYSTVO RSFSR V 1963 GODU. Iz. 'Statistika', Moscow 1964.

NARODNOYE KHOZYAYSTVO SREDNEY AZII V 1963 GODU. Iz. 'Uzbekistan', Tashkent 1964.

NARODNOYE KHOZYAYSTVO SSSR V 1963 GODU. Iz. 'Statistika', Moscow 1965.

NARODNOYE KHOZYAYSTVO SSSR V 1964 GODU. Iz. 'Statistika', Moscow 1965.

NARODNOYE KHOZYAYSTVO TURKMENSKOY SSR. Gosstatizdat, Ashkhabad 1957.

NASELENIYE I TRUDOVYYE RESURSY KIRGIZSKOY SSR. AN Kirgizskoy SSR (Institut Ekonomiki). Iz. 'Ilim', Frunze 1965.

NEYSHTADT, S. A., *Ekonomicheskoye Razvitiye Kazakhskoy SSR*. Kazakhskoye Gos. Izdatel'stvo, Alma-Ata 1960.

NORTON, HENRY, *The Far Eastern Republic of Siberia*. George Allen & Unwin, London 1923.

NOVE, ALEC, *The Soviet Economy* (revised edition). George Allen & Unwin, London 1965.

NOVE, ALEC and NEWTH, J. A., *The Soviet Middle East. A Communist Model for Development*. George Allen & Unwin, London 1967.

NOVOMEYSKY, M. A., *My Siberian Life*. Max Parrish, London 1956.

NUTTER, G. WARREN, *Growth of Industrial Production in the Soviet Union*. Princeton University Press, New Jersey 1962.

OB OROSHENII I OSVOYENII GOLODNOY STEPI (SBORNIK MATERIALOV). Gos. Iz. Uzbekskoy SSR, Tashkent 1956.

OSVOYENIYE GOLODNOY STEPI. Izdatel'stvo Sel'skokhozyaystvennoy Literatury, Zhurnalov, Plakatov, Moscow 1963.

PAHLEN, COUNT K. K., *Mission to Turkestan (1908–1909)*. Oxford University Press, London 1964.

PANOV, V. A., *K Istorii Narodov Sredney Azii*, vols. I and II. Vladivostok 1916 and 1918.

PARK, ALEXANDER G., *Bolshevism in Turkestan 1917–1927*. Columbia University Press, New York 1957.

PARNILANTI, UNTO, *Beria's Gardens. Ten Years' Captivity in Russia and Siberia.* Hutchinson, London 1959.

PAVLOV, M. I., *Karakumskiy Kanal.* Moscow 1955.

PAVLOVSKIY, E. N. (Chief Editor), *Geografiya Naseleniya v SSSR.* AN SSSR, Geograficheskoye Obshchestvo Soyuza SSR, Moscow 1964.

PERVIY S'EZD NARODOV VOSTOKA, BAKU, 1920 (The First Congress of the Eastern Peoples, Baku), Stenographificheskie Otchety (Stenographic Reports). Petrograd 1920.

PIERCE, RICHARD A., *Russian Central Asia 1867–1917.* University of California Press, California 1960.

PIPES, RICHARD E., *The Formation of the Soviet Union* (revised edition). Harvard University Press, Cambridge, Mass. 1964.

POST, LAURENS VAN DER, *Journey into Russia.* Hogarth Press, London 1964.

PREOBRAZHENSKIY, V. S. (Ed.), *Voprosy Geografii Zabaykal'skogo Severa.* Iz. 'Nauka', Moscow 1964.

PRICE, M. PHILIPS, *Siberia.* Methuen, London 1912.

PROKOPOVICZ, SERGE N., *Histoire Économique de l'U.R.S.S.* Translated by Marcel Body. Au Portulan chez Flammarion, Paris 1952.

POKSHISHEVSKIY, V. V., *Yakutia. Priroda–Lyudi–Khozyaystvo.* Iz. AN SSSR, Moscow 1957.

PROMYSHLENNOST' SSSR. Iz. 'Statisika', Moscow 1964.

PYATILETNIY PLAN NARODNOKHOZYAYSTVENNOGO STROITEL'-STVA SSSR. Moscow 1930.

RAKHIMOV, R. K., *Perspektivy Razvitiya Energeticheskoy Promyshlennosti v Tadzhikskoy SSR i ego vliyaniye na razvitiye proizvodstvennykh sil Respubliki.* From 'Problemy Razmeshcheniya Proizvoditel'nykh Sil'. Gosplanizdat, Moscow 1960.

RAVENEAU, L., *Travaux des Russes dans l'Asie Septentrionale.* Annales de Géographie. Paris, 15 Juillet 1898–15 Novembre 1898.

RAVENSTEIN, E. G., *The Russians on the Amur.* Trübner & Co., London 1861.

RAZVITIYE PROIZVODITEL'NYKH SIL KIRGIZSKOY SSR V PERSPEKTIVE. AN Kirgizskoy SSR (Institut Ekonomiki). Iz. 'Ilim', Frunze 1966.

REPORT OF THE INTERREGIONAL SEMINAR ON THE PRODUCTION OF FERTILIZERS. United Nations, Kiev 1965.

ROZHKOVA, M. K., *Ekonomicheskiye Svyazi Rossii So Sredney Aziey.* Iz. AN SSSR, Moscow 1963.

RUSSKO-KITAYSKIYE OTNOSHENIYA, 1689–1916 AN Moscow 1958.

RYMALOV, V., *La Collaboration Économique de l'U.R.S.S. avec les Pays Sous-Développés*. Editions en Langues Étrangeres, Moscow (undated).

SAFAROV, G., *Kolonial'naya Revolyutsiya: Opyt Turkestana*. Moscow 1921.

SCHILLER, O., *Die Landwirtschaft der Sowjetunion, 1917–1953. Agrarverfassung und Agrarproduktion*, Tübingen 1954.

SCHRENCK, LEOPOLD VON (see SHRENK, L.).

SCHWARTZ, HARRY, *Russia's Soviet Economy* (2nd edition). Prentice-Hall, New York 1954.

SCOTT, JOHN, *Behind the Urals*. Secker & Warburg, London 1942.

SEBES, JOSEPH, S. J., *The Jesuits and the Sino-Soviet Treaty of Nerchinsk (1689)*. Institutum Historicum. S.I., Rome 1961.

SEMYONOV, YU., *The Conquest of Siberia*. Translated by G. W. Dickes. G. Routledge & Sons, London 1944.

SHABAD, T., *Geography of the USSR*. Columbia University Press, New York 1951.

SHERSTOBITOV, V. P., *Novaya Ekonomicheskaya Politika v Kirgizii (1921–1925)*. Iz. 'Ilim', Frunze 1964.

SHIMKIN, DEMITRI B., *Minerals: A Key to Soviet Power*. Harvard University Press, Cambridge, Mass. 1953.

SHRENK, L., *Ob Inorodtsakh Amurskogo Kraya*, 3 vols. Iz. Imperatorskoy Akademii Nauk, St. Petersburg 1883.

——*Reisen und Forschungen im Amur-Lande in Jahren 1854–56*. St. Petersburg 1859–1900.

SHVAREV, V. A. (Ed.), *Dal'niy Vostok za 40 let Sovetskoy Vlasti*. Iz. AN SSSR (Sibirskoye otdelenniye), Komsomol'sk 1958.

SIBIRSKAYA SOVETSKAYA ENTSIKLOPEDIYA, 3 vols. Iz. 'Pravda', Moscow 1929–32.

SLAVIN, S. V. (Ed.), *Promlemy Razvitiya Proizvoditel'nykh Sil Magadanskoy Oblasti*. Iz. AN SSSR, Moscow 1961.

SMOLYAK, A. A., *Certain Questions on the Early History of the Ethnic Groups Inhabiting the Amur Valley and the Maritime Province*. In *Studies in Siberian Ethnogenesis*. University of Toronto Press, Ontario 1962.

SOROK LET UZBEKSKOY SOVETSKOY SOTZIALISTICHESKOY RESPUBLIKI. Ob.' Iz. Ts. K. Kompartii Uzbekistana, Tashkent 1964.

SOVIET AGRICULTURE TODAY, Report of 1963 Agriculture Exchange Delegation. U.S. Department of Agriculture, Washington D.C. Revised 1964.

SSSR V TSYFRAKH V 1963 G., 1964 G. Iz. 'Statistika', Moscow 1965.

SOVIET UZBEKISTAN TODAY, NO. 8. Uzbek Society for Friendship and Cultural Relations with Foreign Countries, Tashkent 1964.

STALIN, J., *Marxism and the National and Colonial Question* (English translation). Lawrence & Wishart, London 1942.

STALIN, J. V., *Politika Sovetskoy Vlasti po Natsional'nomu Voprosu v Rosii.* Sochineniya, vol. 4, Moscow 1947.

STATESMAN'S HANDBOOK FOR RUSSIA. Edited by the Chancery of the Committee of Ministers, 2 vols. Eugen Thiele, St. Petersburg 1896.

STEPANOV, B., *Razvitiye i Razmeshcheniye Proizvoditel'nykh Sil SSSR v Tretey Stalinskoy Pyatiletke.* Leningrad 1939.

STEPANOV, P. N., *Geografiya Promyshlennosti SSSR.* Moscow 1955.

SUMNER, B. H., *Survey of Russian History.* Duckworth, London 1944.

SUSLOV, S. P., *Physical Geography of Asiatic Russia.* University of Leningrad. Translated from the Russian by Noah D. Gershevsky, University of Washington. W. H. Freeman & Co., San Francisco and London 1961.

SWIANIEWICZ, S., *Forced Labour and Economic Development.* An Enquiry into the Experience of Soviet Industrialization. Oxford University Press, London 1965.

TANG, P. S. H., *Russian and Soviet Policy in Manchuria and Outer Mongolia.* Duke University Press, North Carolina 1959.

TEPLINSKIY, L. B., *Sovetsko-Afganskie Otnosheniya 1919–1960.* Moscow 1961.

THIEL, ERIC, *The Soviet Far East.* Translated by Annelie and Ralph M. Rookwood. Methuen, London 1957.

TREADGOLD, DONALD W., *The Great Siberian Migration: Government and Peasant in Resettlement from Emancipation to the First World War.* Princeton University Press, New Jersey 1957.

TROSHEV, N. I., *Planirovaniye Razmeshcheniya Promyshlennosti v SSSR.* Moscow 1960.

TUPPER, HARMON, *To the Great Ocean.* Secker & Warburg, London 1965.

VEDISHCHEV, A. I., *Problemy Razmeshcheniya Proizvoditel'nykh Sil SSSR.* Iz. Ekonomicheskoy Literatury, Moscow 1963.

VERSTRAETE, MAURICE, *Mes Cahiers Russes.* Editions Georges Crès et Cie. Paris 1920.

——*La Russie Industrielle.* Hachette et Cie, Paris 1897.

VNEOCHEREDNOY XXI S'YEZD KOMMUNISTICHESKOY PARTII SOVETSKOGO SOYUZA. Gos. Iz. Politicheskoy Literatury, Moscow 1959.

VOPROSY ISTORII SIBIRI I DAL'NEGO VOSTOKA. Sib. Otd. AN SSSR Novosibirsk 1961.

VOPROSY RAZMESHCHENIYA PROISVODSTVA V SSSR. Iz. 'Nauka' AN SSSR, Gosplan, Moscow 1965.

VOZNESENSKIY, N. A., *The Economy of the USSR during World War II*. Translated from the Russian. Public Affairs Press, Washington, D.C. 1948.

VSESOYUZNAYA PEREPIS' NASELENIYA (1926). Tsentral'noye Statisticheskoye Upravleniye SSSR, Moscow 1928.

VTOROY PYATILETNIY PLAN RAZVITIYA NARODONOGO KHOZY-AYSTVA SSSR (1933–1937), vols. I and II. Izdaniye Gosplana, Moscow 1934.

VYATKIN, M., *Ocherki po Istorii Kazakhskoy SSR*. Leningrad 1941.

WARDELL, JOHN W., *In the Kirghiz Steppes*. The Valley Press, London 1961.

WATSON, FRANCIS, *The Frontiers of China*. Chatto & Windus, London 1966.

WHEELER, GEOFFREY, *The Modern History of Soviet Central Asia*. Asia-Africa Series, Weidenfeld & Nicolson, London 1964.

——*Racial Problems in Soviet Muslim Asia*. Institute of Race Relations, Oxford University Press, London 1960.

WILES, P. J. DE LA F., *The Political Economy of Communism*. Blackwell, Oxford 1962.

WITTE, S. J. COUNT, *Memoires du Comte Witte (1849–1915)*. Translated by François Rousseau. Plon, Paris 1921.

WRIGHT, G. F., *Asiatic Russia*, 2 vols. McClure, Phillips & Co., 1902.

WU, AITCHEN K., *China and the Soviet Union*. Methuen & Co. Ltd., London 1950.

——*Turkestan Tumult*. Methuen & Co. Ltd., London 1940.

YAKOLEV, B., *Kontsentratsionnyye Lageri SSSR*. Institute for the Study of the USSR, Munich 1955.

ZAKHAROV, G. A., *Osobennosti i Perspektivy Razvitiya Metalloobra-batyvayushchey Promyshlennosti Magadanskoy i Kamchatskoy Oblastey*. Sib. Otd. AN SSSR, Novosibirsk 1962.

ZAPISKI PRIAMURSKOGO OTDELA IMPERATORSKOGO OBSH-CHESTVA VOSTOKOVEDENIYA. Khabarovsk 1912.

ZAYCHENKO, P. A., *Tomskiy Gosudarstvennyy Universitet imeni V. V. Kuybysheva*. Tomsk University, Tomsk 1960.

ZOLOTAYA KOLYMA. Iz. AN SSSR, Moscow 1963.

Index